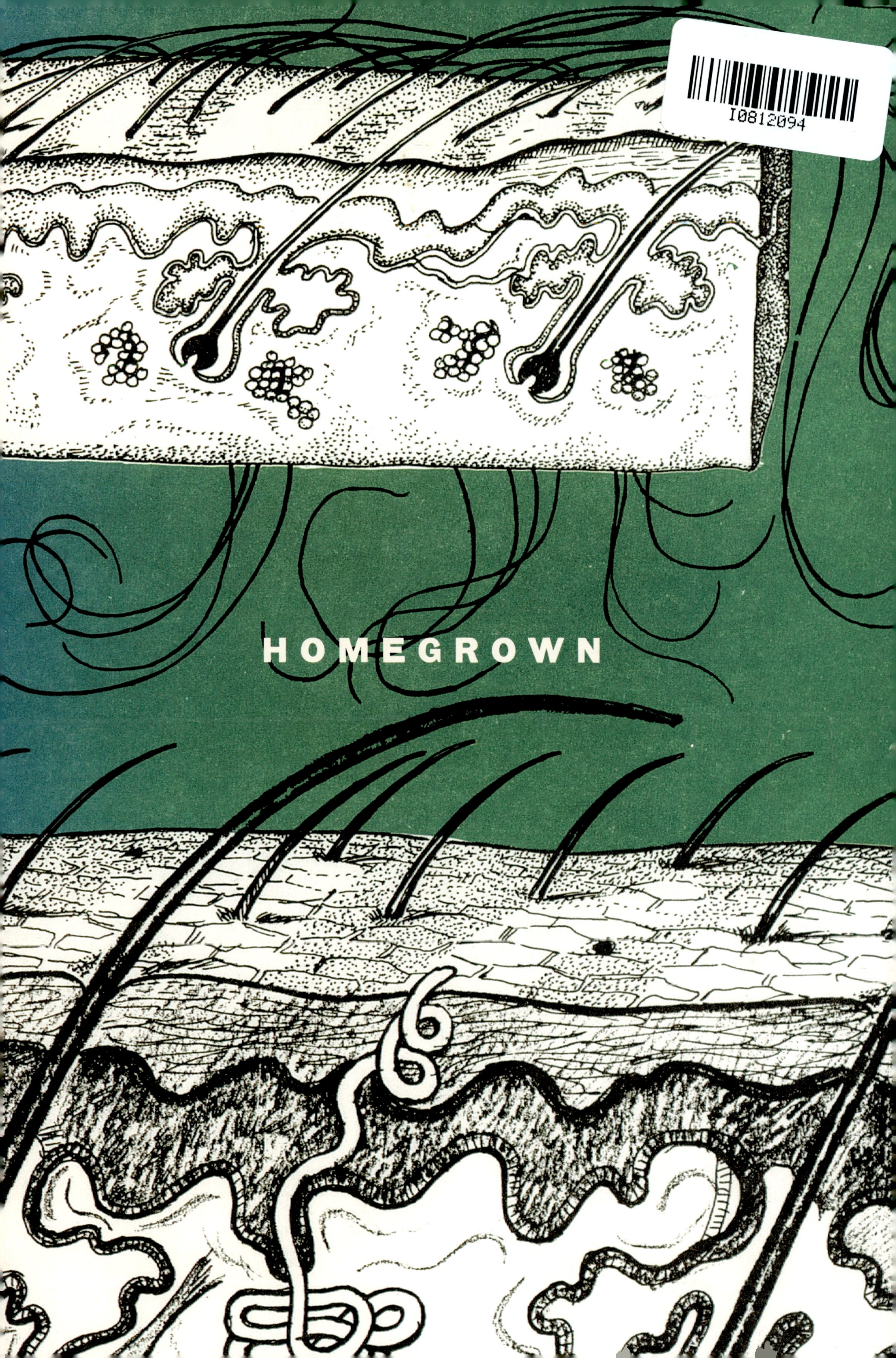
HOMEGROWN

SOUTHWESTERN WRITERS COLLECTION SERIES

The Wittliff Collections at Texas State University

Steven L. Davis, Series Editor

David L. Coleman, Volume Editor

HOMEGROWN

AUSTIN MUSIC POSTERS 1967 TO 1982

The cover image is a detail from the Armadillo World Headquarters grand opening poster by Jim Franklin and the trademark logo used by Armadillo Productions, Inc. d/b/a Armadillo World Headquarters. This image, along with all of the posters from the Armadillo World Headquarters, are used by kind permission of Armadillo Productions, Inc. and Eddie Wilson.

Printed in Malaysia
First edition, 2015
Second printing, 2016

The paper used in this book meets the minimum requirements of ANSI/NISO Z39.48-1992 (R1997) (Permanence of Paper). ♾

Design by Lindsay Starr

Library of Congress Cataloging-in-Publication Data

Homegrown : Austin music posters 1967 to 1982 / edited by Alan Schaefer.
pages cm. — (Southwestern writers collection series)
Includes bibliographical references.
ISBN 978-0-292-76819-2 (cloth)
ISBN 978-0-292-77239-7 (pbk.)
ISBN 978-0-292-77241-0 (ebook)
1. Popular music—Texas—Austin—History and criticism.
2. Posters, American—Texas—Austin—20th century.
I. Schaefer, Alan, editor.
ML3477.8.A97H66 2015
741.6'74—dc23
2014030312

CONTENTS

PREFACE

Austin's musical roots run deep, and one can trace significant developments to the early part of the twentieth century. Yet the emergence of Austin as a center for progressive music and culture accelerated rapidly in the 1960s. As innovative and genre-defying music flourished in Austin during this revolutionary decade, so too did radical lifestyles. The opening of the Vulcan Gas Company in 1967 marked a significant turning point in the history of Austin music, art, and underground culture. One had to travel to New York or the West Coast to find another psychedelic ballroom that regularly hosted avant-garde rock-and-roll acts like the Fugs, Canned Heat, and the Velvet Underground and living legends of the blues like Big Joe Williams and Big Mama Thornton. Following the demise of the Vulcan Gas Company in 1970, the opening of the Armadillo World Headquarters would help Austin establish its status as one of the most vital music scenes in the country. Poster artists visually defined the music and culture of Austin during this pivotal period. Their work not only advertised performances. These posters sold a lifestyle that permeated the city and reflected Austin's transformation from a sleepy university town into a veritable island of underground artistic and cultural activity in the state of Texas.

The Wittliff Collections' assemblage of posters began with the donation of a large collection from Austin music enthusiast Tom Wilmore and has continued to grow with additional donations and purchases. Wilmore moved to Austin in 1972 and quickly began collecting posters. He was a regular patron at the Armadillo World Headquarters, the reopened Ritz Theatre on Sixth Street, and several other holes in the wall around Austin. Wilmore notes that in addition to seeing posters hung on walls, billboards, and telephone poles, he frequently saw stacks of posters sitting in record stores. These posters were available for customers to take home, and Wilmore would often take one for himself and a few extras for friends. While he missed the heyday of psychedelia at the Vulcan Gas Company, Wilmore acquired several posters from a local DJ who decided to relinquish his collection of art from Texas' premier psychedelic ballroom.

Wilmore's donation accounts for a large portion of the collection, but the Wittliff Collections has acquired numerous posters from other notable figures in the Austin music scene, including Jodie Fischer, a longtime assistant to Willie Nelson; Nancy Coplin, a well-respected Austin booking agent and event producer; Joe Nick Patoski, Texas music and popular-culture scholar; Bobby Earl Smith, a founding member and bassist of Freda and the Firedogs; and Houston White, one of the founders of the Vulcan Gas Company. The collection has also been bolstered by acquisitions from several of the artists featured in the book.

Surveying the collection chronologically, one begins with the psychedelia of the Vulcan Gas Company, a body of work that exhibits the influence of San Francisco poster art but clearly stands on its own as a unique and innovative movement that laid the foundation for modern music poster art in Austin. The opening of the Armadillo World Headquarters in 1970 ushered in a new period of poster art, one that focused heavily on the collision between hippie and honky-tonk culture. Eddie Wilson, one of the founders of the Armadillo, refers to the operation not as a club but as a "cultural arts laboratory." Wilson notes that the Armadillo Art Squad, the loose collective of artists who produced posters for the Armadillo, was "the strangest combination of collaboration and competition that I've ever seen." The mid-1970s saw the proliferation of new venues across Austin's quickly expanding music scene. As a result, poster art developed rapidly due to the contributions of a growing body of artists, approaches, and acts to be represented. The emergence of punk brought yet another generation of poster art, one that capped off this fifteen-year period with an explosive and reenergized musical and visual aesthetic.

Bobby Earl Smith explains why Austin artists were such an integral part in promoting the city's music scene:

> Music posters were the way of getting the word out in the most direct and effective way. It was Armadillo style guerrilla marketing. The thing that made the Austin music and poster connection so vital and organic was due to the hanging out, the being together, of the musicians and artists. The poster artists went to the gigs; they knew the band members; we all smoked dope and joked and drank beer together. The artists were at the clubs, the gigs. That is why the artists were able to capture the "who" of an artist or band and the "what" of the music and incorporate it into the designs, the very real art, of the posters. That is why these great old Austin music posters live and breathe the very music they so truly depict.

A history of the city's music scene and a narrative of cultural signs can be viewed in these works. The collection is a testament to Austin artists' mastery of the art form. It is high time to reflect on the contributions that Austin artists have made to music poster art.

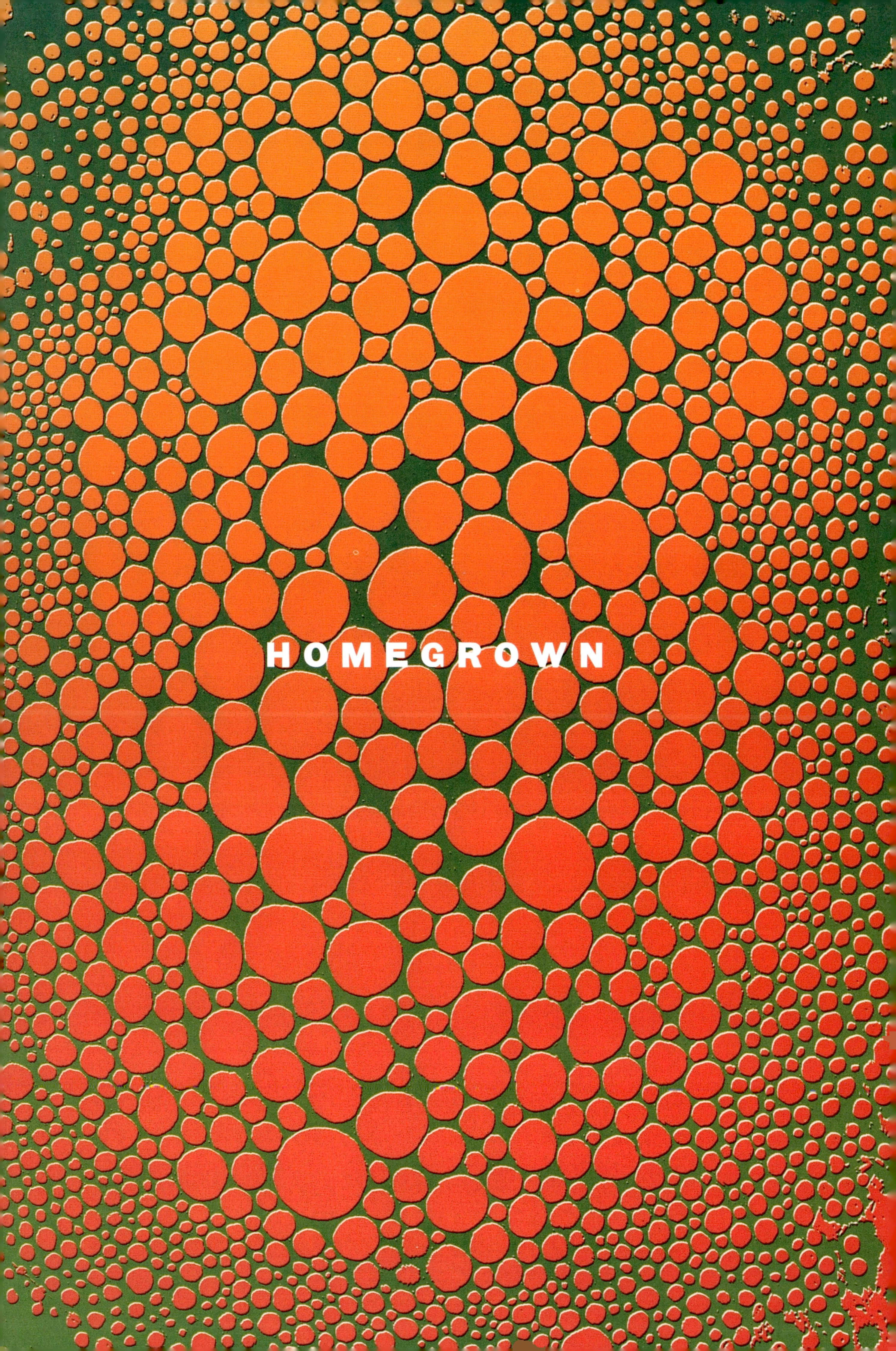
HOMEGROWN

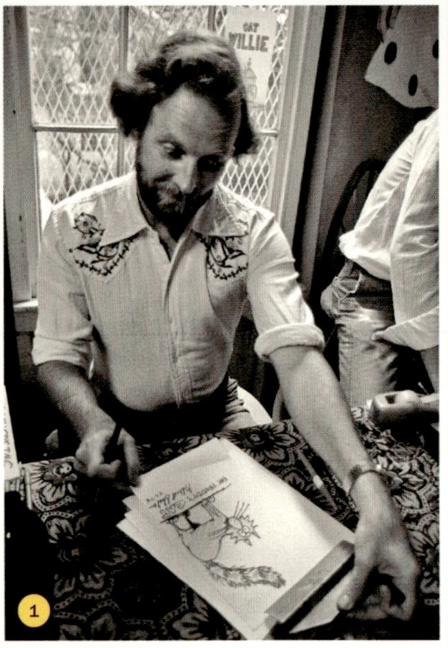

1

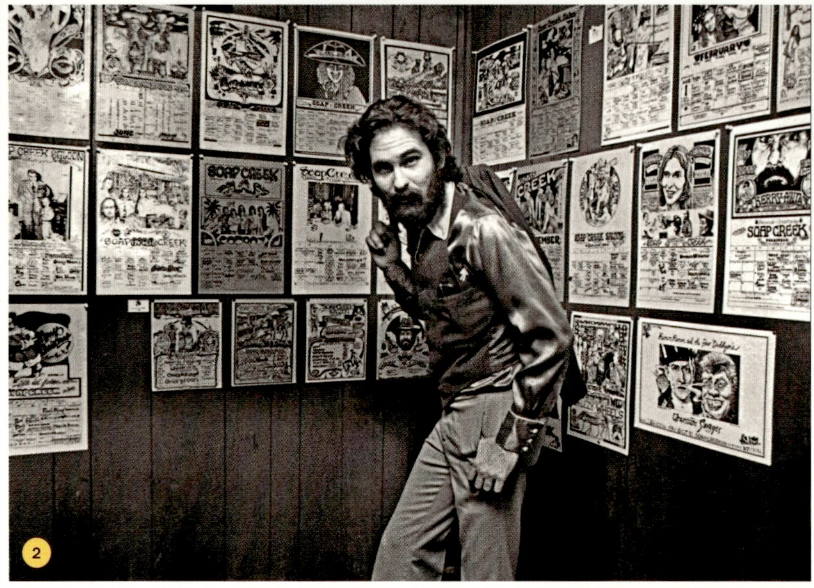

2

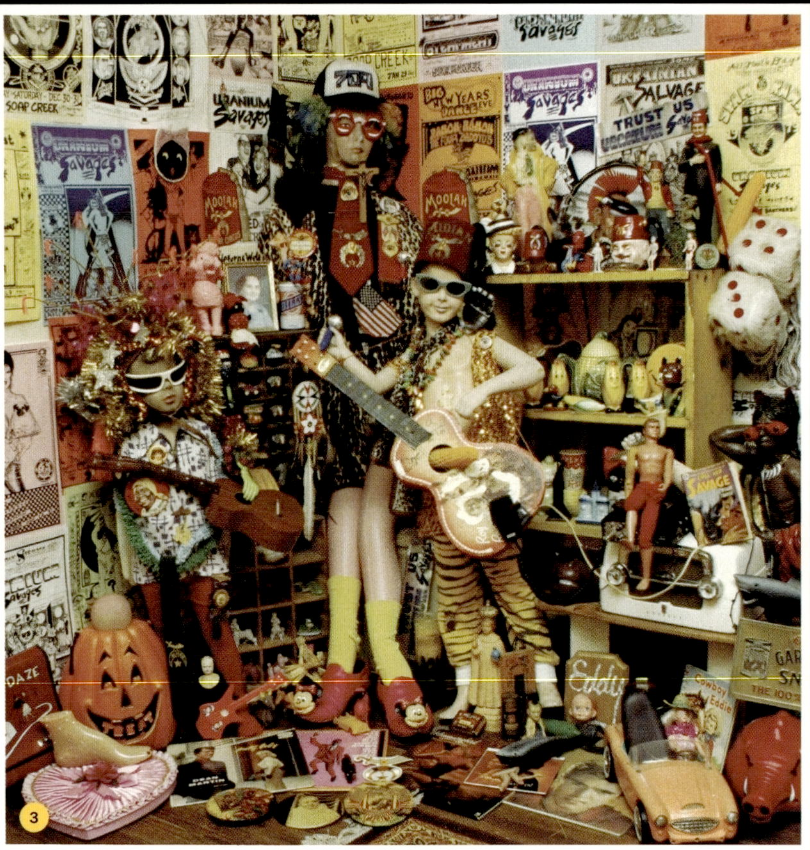

3

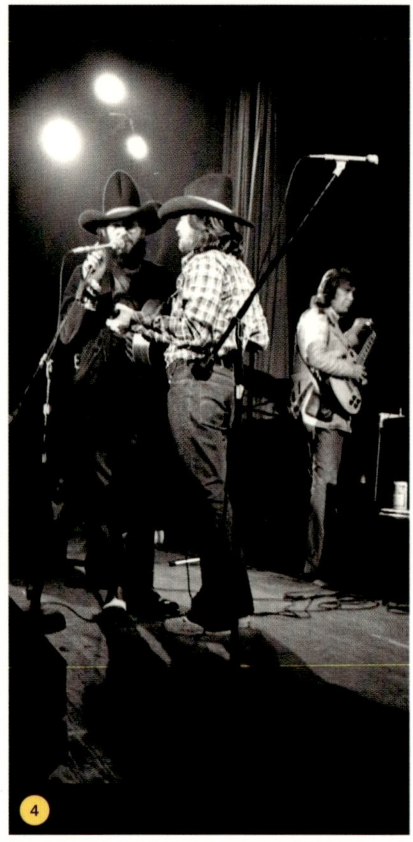

4

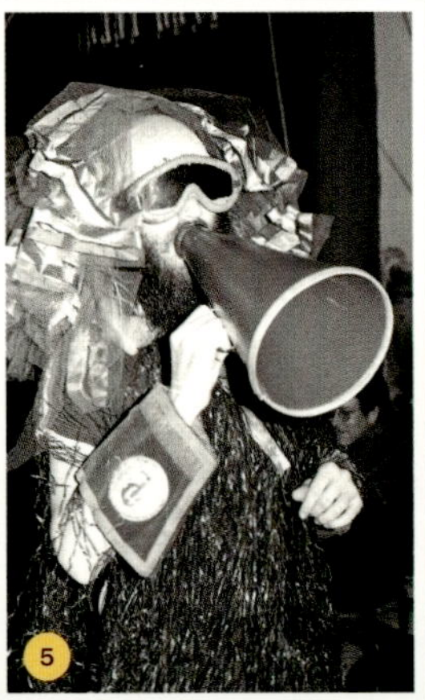

5

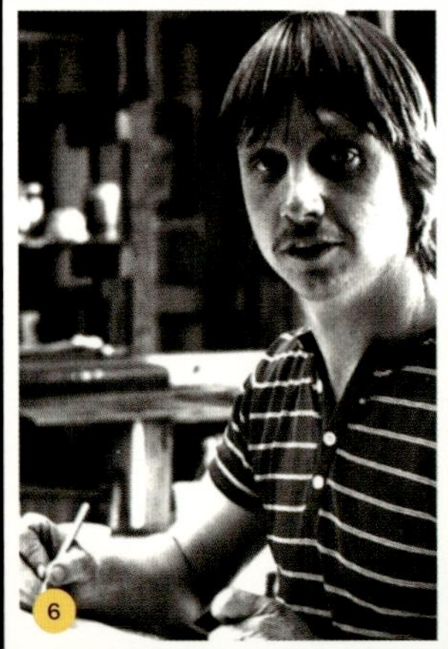

6

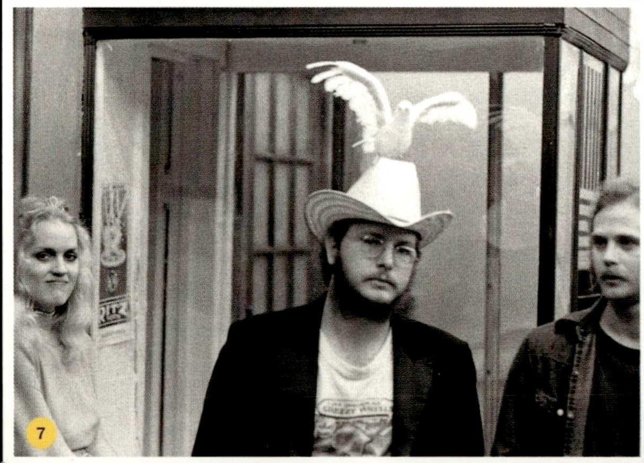

7

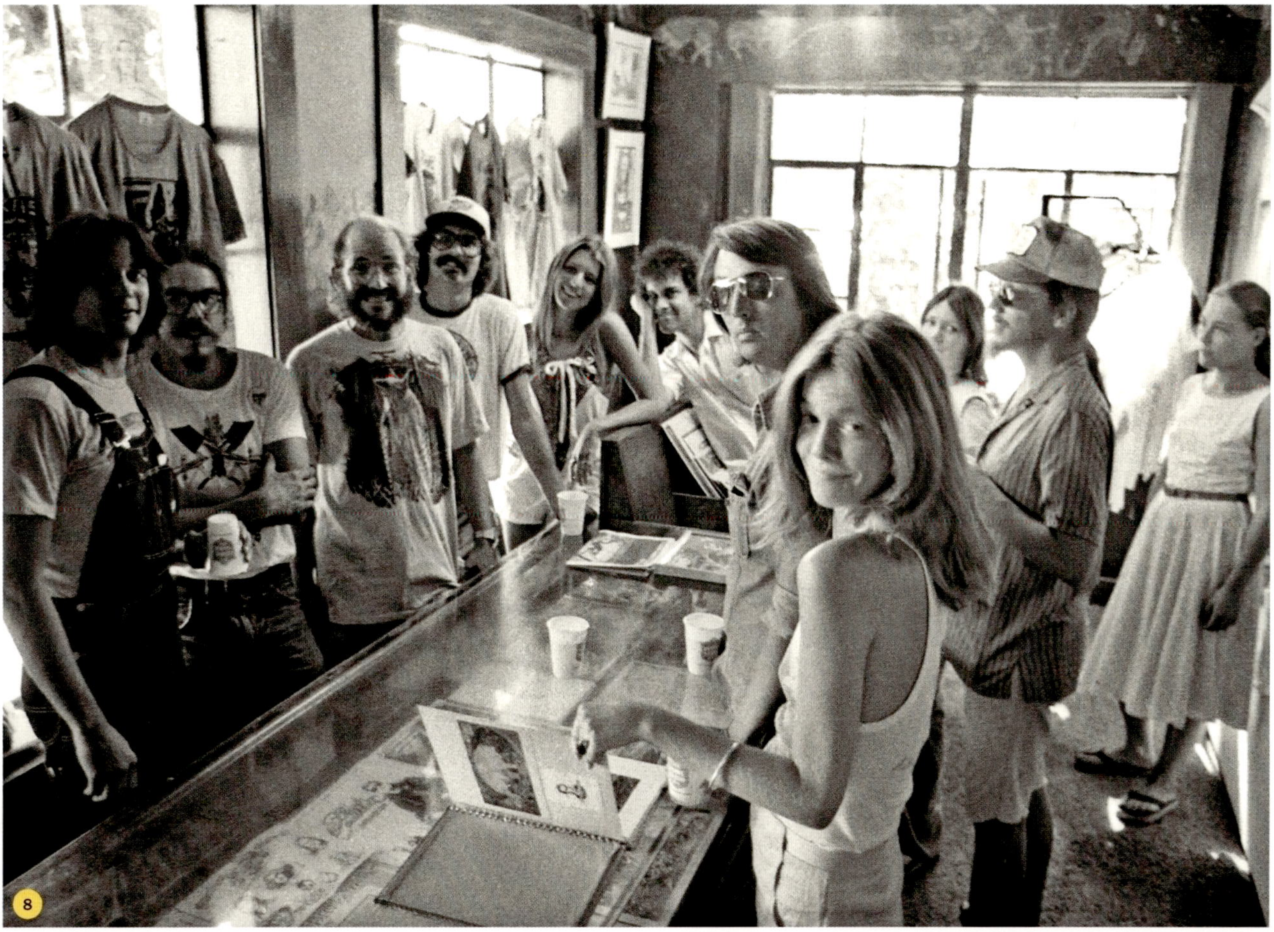

8

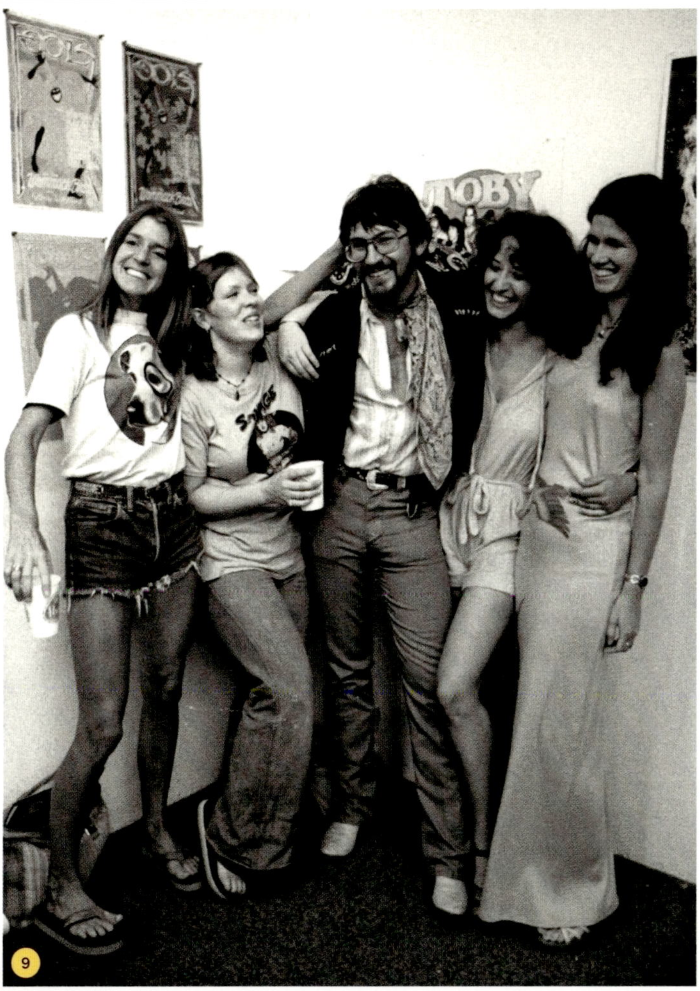

9

1 Gilbert Shelton with a drawing of Fat Freddy's Cat. Photograph by Ken Hoge, August 6, 1978.

2 Kerry Awn surrounded by his work at the Soap Creek Saloon poster show. Photograph by Ken Hoge, December 7, 1977.

3 Randy "Biscuit" Turner's home. Notice the Kerry Awn–designed posters for the Uranium Savages, a group that Biscuit performed with before the Big Boys. Photograph by Ken Hoge, 1979.

4 Jim Franklin, Willie Nelson, and Jody Payne onstage at the Ritz Theatre, 1974. Photograph by Mack Royal.

5 Jim Franklin emceeing at the Ritz Theatre, 1974. Photograph by Mack Royal.

6 Danny Garrett. Date and photographer unknown.

7 Tom Wilmore (center with bird on head), poster collector, in front of the Ritz Theatre, 1974. Photograph by Mack Royal.

8 Joe Bryson, Artly Snuff, Jim Franklin, Kerry Awn, Michelle Arth, Guy Juke, Ramsey Wiggins, Kitten Holloway, Margaret Moser, Sam Jones, and Vanessa Cargo at the Austintatious T-shirt shop, August 3, 1977. Photograph by Ken Hoge.

9 Micael Priest and friends at his Quick Draw show at the Armadillo World Headquarters. Photograph by Ken Hoge, August 1, 1977.

IT ALL STARTED HERE

JOE NICK PATOSKI

The concept of printing words and images on cardboard and attaching it to a wall or pole to advertise was hardly new. The first Anglo colony in Texas would not have been settled if Stephen F. Austin, the Father of Texas and its first real estate speculator, had not posted broadsides all over New Orleans to entice potential colonists to go west and settle the wild frontier known as Texas, then a province of Mexico, beginning in 1821.

> TEXAS!! Emigrants who are desirous of assisting Texas at this important crisis of her affairs may have free passage and equipments by applying at the New York and Philadelphia Hotel on the Old Levee, near the blue stores.

Such posters got results. A sufficient number of arrivals migrated from the east to form communities, a government, and an army that would defeat Santa Anna and gain independence from Mexico, with Texas becoming its own republic before eventually joining the United States.

Postering was just getting started in the town named after Stephen F. The first two businesses in the new town of Austin in 1839 were Bullock's Tavern and Sam Whiting's print shop. A year later, George Bonnell was publishing the *Austin Sentinel* newspaper, while the *Austin Spy*, the town's first political satire publication, produced its first issue, and Joel Miner was printing posters as a business. As the state capital and seat of government, Austin distinguished itself from just about every other community in the southern United States and the frontier territories by claiming more printing presses than churches.

Posters were a most effective way of getting the word out. According to an 1860 edition of the *Austin Gazette*, John L. Buaas, proprietor of the Buaas Saloon, remodeled and expanded his drinking emporium into Buaas Hall and Garden, "the largest, best arranged and neatest of any public room in the City." A broadside printed in 1863 advertised a benefit concert at Buaas's—Austin's first documented music poster.

After the railroad arrived in Austin in 1871, bringing traveling entertainment acts from the outside world never seen before, posters became commonplace around Austin. Posters adorned poles, walls, and fences to advertise coming events. John Reed of San Antonio offered his services as the "original city bill poster" in the 1877 edition of the Austin City Directory, with "liberal terms" to managers, agents, and traveling showmen. A year later, Captain C. F. Millett remodeled a warehouse into the Millett Opera House, Austin's largest entertainment venue. Almost every event staged at the Opera House over the next twenty years was announced with a poster.

For the following ninety years or so, advertisements printed on hard cardboard affixed to telephone poles were the most effective means for announcing coming music acts, circuses, tent revivals, boxing matches, rodeos, and other traveling attractions working rural Texas and cities, including Austin, particularly around African American and Mexican American neighborhoods. During election campaign season, poster boards promoting political candidates joined in the advertising.

By the 1950s, music posters were a common sight around Austin. In early 1955, generic posters advertised the *Louisiana Hayride*, a roadshow featuring cast members from the weekly live radio broadcast from Shreveport but heard throughout Texas. Sandwiched between Archie Campbell and Wilma Burgess was the name Elvis Presley. Six months later, the image of Elvis, Scotty, and Bill topped the billing of stars from the *Louisiana Hayride* at the Sportcenter at 501 Barton Springs Road, above emcee Horace Logan, country star Johnny Horton, Dalton and Lulu-Jo, and others. Domino Records used posters to hype the national success of local rock-and-roll acts Ray Campi and the Slades. The Continental Club, "the club with the purple doors," produced posters with bold block printing to publicize its live music and fine food.

Most music posters were limited to a single image, such as a floating-head likeness of the performer being advertised, or a scale of music notes, and a plain white background.

Somewhere around the mid-1960s, music posters took a whole other direction and took on a whole other kind of meaning. An entirely different type of poster, descended from the hard cardboard style that catered to ghetto/barrio/rural neighborhoods, started appearing in Austin neighborhoods around the campus of the University of Texas. They were aimed at hippies, a new cultural phenomenon growing in numbers around the country. These posters advertised music concerts that appealed to a long-haired, counterculture audience that championed peace, love, and understanding as moral virtues and embraced marijuana and psychedelic drug consumption as pleasurable accompaniments to their concertgoing experience.

Rock posters, or music posters, didn't just advertise. They were considered art, worthy of collecting. Similarly, the people who created the posters were regarded as serious artists whose visuals enhanced listening to music, so promoters encouraged their creativity. The artists responded with brightly colored fluorescent inks and cryptic lettering representative of an LSD trip, if not the entire hippie aesthetic.

Austin was just an outpost, albeit a highly influential one. Ground zero for this new kind of poster was San Francisco, where two venues, the Fillmore Auditorium, run by promoter Bill Graham, and the Avalon Ballroom, overseen by a hippie collective known as the Family Dog, generated more than 450 posters over a five-year span beginning in 1966.

The Family Dog's leader was Chet Helms, a University of Texas graduate who grew up in Austin and would also manage the band Big Brother and the Holding Company, for which he recruited another Texas-ex, Janis Joplin.

Helms learned poster making from the grandfather who raised him, who happened to be a Holy Roller fundamentalist preacher. His uncles printed the handbills, biblical tracts, and posters that spread his granddaddy's word. Spending his summers as a boy working in his uncles' printing shop and observing the effectiveness of posters in evangelical soul saving and collection-plate filling was a life changer. Helms started a bill-posting and canvassing service for his uncles' clients. After he crossed over the cultural divide and leaped the spiritual chasm that has defined America's culture wars ever since, Helms retained the family knowledge and put it to good use in San Francisco.

Posters spread the word of Family Dog events at Golden Gate Park, the Fillmore, and other venues before they settled at the Avalon. Helms recruited Jack Jackson from Austin in 1966 to be art director of the Family Dog's poster division. Jackson rounded up a small group of graphic artists to create posters and handbills. Rick Griffin, Alton Kelley, Victor Moscoso, Stanley Mouse, and Wes Wilson would become known as the San Francisco Five, renowned for their respective styles as free ranging as the new music they were hyping.

Most communities across the United States in 1967 either heard, saw, or read about what was going in San Francisco during the infamous Summer of Love through newspapers, television, or radio. In Austin, the phenomenon was local, courtesy of a music club that opened that October at 316 Congress Avenue, eight blocks from the Texas Capitol.

The Vulcan Gas Company was hardly the only venue presenting rock, blues, folk, and psychedelic music around Austin, the sounds tied to San Francisco and the Summer of Love. But the Vulcan most definitely was the one club in Austin directly linked to San Francisco.

The Vulcan produced music posters like those in San Francisco. "But being in Texas, we decided to make our posters twice as big as the California posters," explained Gilbert Shelton, the Vulcan's first art director. "I think I got a budget of $100 a week to print these posters, which was enough to print about 100 posters." Shelton designed the grand opening poster and about ten others, while assisting in another ten posters he commissioned.

Shelton, a lean, lanky Houston native with a fondness for race cars, had honed his chops as a graphics illustrator for the *Texas Ranger*, the edgy humor magazine at the University of Texas, beginning in 1959. His style was described by editors as being "in the old wild manner," a reference to exaggerated human figures with too-big eyes, too-long legs and arms, and too-floppy feet, informed by the cartoonist Virgil Partch, a.k.a. VIP.

In addition to posters, Shelton started drawing underground comix, as they would become known, including a strip called *Wonder Wart-Hog, the Hog of Steel*, a collaboration with fellow Rangeroo Tony Bell that began in 1962, parodying Superman, and later, *The Fabulous Furry Freak Brothers*, cataloging the lives of three hippie brothers, Phineas, Freewheelin' Franklin, and Fat Freddy, based on real Austin characters.

The response to Shelton's cartoons and his intricate, elaborate psychedelic posters prompted a move from Austin to San Francisco in 1968. Along with artist/cartoonist Jack Jackson (a.k.a. Jaxon), Fred Todd, and Dave Moriaty—all Austin exiles—Shelton cofounded the Rip Off Press. The initial intent was to print posters and do underground comix on the side. But music posters began losing their cachet in San Francisco, and the comic books were flying off the shelves, so Rip Off ultimately dropped printing to focus on publishing.

Inheriting the art director position at the Vulcan was Jim Franklin, an artistically inclined hippie born on Galveston Island and raised inland in La Marque, south of Houston. The title meant Franklin had a space to work in, which also functioned as a crash pad. "I'd sit up all night, draw a poster, and take it to the printer. I never had to pacify anybody. That was really one of the magical things about that time.

"The Vulcan Gas Company was really the first place in Texas of its kind," Franklin said. "It had light shows, music, it was a psychedelic haven. We booked original music, no copy bands, which was the big thing at the time. The Vulcan was why I started doing poster art in the first place. Conqueroo was basically the house band. Shiva's Headband became the second house band. We started booking road shows like Steve Miller, Canned Heat, and Moby Grape, some of the groups that had gotten well-established in San Francisco. It was a pretty exciting time."

Franklin signed his work "JFKLN" and took a realistic approach to posters in general, typically lifelike pen-and-ink crosshatch renderings of strange and unusual objects in the tradition of Magritte or Dali, per his depiction of the heads of country blues legend Mance Lipscomb and Charlie Prichard of the band Conqueroo attached together as Siamese twins, to advertise the Vulcan double bill of the two musical acts. Franklin was simultaneously pursuing a serious art career, exhibiting at Dave Hickey's A Clean, Well-Lighted Place gallery, with Hickey getting him into two shows at the Whitney in New York. But posters interested him more.

Financial constraints at the Vulcan prompted Franklin to switch to handbills with a single-color format that allowed him to break away from the visual trickery of psychedelia and concentrate on pen-and-ink realism. "It communicates more than it just decorates."

Posters became Franklin's oeuvre. "I was making art without having to attend the University of Texas. My art was all over town. We were creating our own world. If you think about it, when a concert is over, if there's no poster there, it's just a memory. But if there's a poster, there's visual proof that something happened that night. So the visual proof was going up all over the state and literally around the country. Johnny Winter told me one time he checked into the Chelsea Hotel in New York and the bathroom was a decoupage of Vulcan and Armadillo posters."

His body of work became defined by his fetish for armadillos, the docile, prehistoric-looking creatures common around Texas and most often seen as highway roadkill (the nocturnal creatures have very poor eyesight and total disregard for automobiles). JFKLN's first poster with an armadillo as the focal point was for a benefit at Wooldridge Park in downtown Austin in 1968 to aid people in the local music scene who had been jailed for possession of drugs. "It was a perfect symbol for the whole notion of underground culture," he said. "The poster depicted an armadillo smoking a joint. It clicked. Everyone picked up on it."

Vulcan posters were prominent in the display window of the music venue that faced Congress Avenue. A few were prominently taped in windows of campus-area stores, with the rest attached to poles and walls around the university to get the word out about an upcoming gig. Cool-looking posters didn't last long; fans quickly removed them to add to their personal collections.

Over the course of the club's two-and-a-half-year run, thirty-six posters, fifty-eight handbills, and two postcards were created by Franklin and Shelton, along with Tony Bell, Jim Harter, Mark Weakley, Don Evans, Robert Rush, John Shelton, Charlie Loving, and Jim Fowler. The club would gain renown for Johnny Winter being discovered opening for Muddy Waters and then signed to the record industry's first six-figure contract, and bands that otherwise would have avoided playing Texas altogether, including the Velvet Underground, the Fugs, and Moby Grape. Unlike the police in San Francisco, Austin police and vice squad capo Harvey Gann harassed and hassled the hippie joint, running off customers and harassing one partner, Don Hyde, to leave Texas. New ownership took over in late 1969 before the club shut down for good the next year.

Franklin continued drawing armadillos for the *Rag* underground newspaper and skewering University of Texas regent Frank Erwin, the bombastic, caricatured face of the fat cats who ran the university. One JFKLN *Rag* centerfold caricatured Erwin's order to clear several street blocks of old oak trees to make way for a basketball arena by depicting Erwin's swarthy, bloated, double-chinned head with a tree growing out of his skull. Franklin titled it "The Frank Erwin National Shrine and Cement Construction Memorial Monument, 1969." Twice, Franklin drew the UT library tower, the tallest building on campus and in the city at the time, once as a pencil pointing skyward with a pencil sharpener hovering overhead, the second time flopped over like a limp penis, bulging veins and all.

Franklin dropped enough bait for Erwin to publicly ask, "What does this armadillo mean?" The question inspired Franklin to run a What Does It Mean? Contest over several subsequent issues of the *Rag*. The *Rag* remained an outlet for Franklin and other artists taking on topical subjects. But something bigger was about to come along.

The San Francisco music and accompanying poster artist scene was entering its postclassic phase, as the Fillmore and Avalon gave way to Winterland. Monterey Pop turned into Altamont, and rebellious rock became a very lucrative commodity.

Meanwhile, the golden era of Austin music was just beginning. And with it, a small community of poster artists was about to get a whole lot bigger.

The catalyst was the building at 525½ Barton Springs Road that once housed the Sportcenter, where a fresh-faced Elvis Presley had performed fifteen years earlier. A former beer lobbyist–turned–band manager was looking for a new home for Shiva's Headband, a psychedelic group that had become the house band at the Vulcan Gas Company when the Conqueroo packed up and headed to San Francisco, before the Vulcan closed.

Eddie Wilson had been taking a leak outside George's, a small beer bar just across Town Lake from downtown Austin one night after the bar's plumbing had fritzed out. Standing between two musicians, John X. Reed and Jimmie Dale Gilmore, he spied the cavernous building across the street and went to investigate. With the help of a clutch of friends, Wilson rented the old building that once housed a National Guard armory and commenced to clean it up and fashion it into a music hall along the lines of the Fillmore and Avalon in San Francisco, run by a loose committee of hippies.

The name of the place, the Armadillo World Headquarters, came easy. Shiva's Headband had released an album on Capitol Records and Jim Franklin designed the cover, depicting a great big crack in the earth between two steep canyon walls that was populated with armadillos, and a great big crack in the sky revealing an even larger herd of armadillos.

For the accompanying poster commissioned by the record company, Franklin painted a lunar landscape with unusual objects emerging from craters—a hammer, a telephone, a human hand, pyramid eyes, an umbrella, a pair of scissors, horn-rimmed glasses, and an open Lone Star beer can. Emerging from the largest crater was the frizzy-haired head of Spencer Perskin, the band's leader. Hovering above Perskin was a cartoon thought balloon that read "Take Me to the Mountains," the name of the album's first single. The poster was blown up into an advertising billboard that hovered briefly over the intersection of Nineteenth and Guadalupe Streets, the gateway to the Drag, the commercial strip across from the University of Texas. "It was my biggest painting ever," Franklin said.

Franklin designed the poster for the Armadillo World Headquarters' opening night on August 7, 1970, advertising a lineup of Shiva's Headband, the Hub City Movers, and Whistler. The poster was an eyeball-straining, four-color depiction of the earth, divided into four equal parts, each with an armadillo attached (real armadillos give birth to four offspring per litter), reflecting the wordplay of "world" and "quarter." The "head" part was already understood. The quartered globe straddled a huge crack in the earth, suggesting the Armadillo World Headquarters had risen from the underground.

For the following three years, Franklin produced many of the Armadillo's finest posters, despite taking extended breaks to paint rocker Leon Russell's swimming pool in Tulsa and tour Europe with bluesman Freddie King. Franklin's painting of Freddie King with an armadillo bursting out of his heart as the performer scrunched his face while hitting a high note hung permanently inside the Armadillo.

Franklin would eventually drift away to run the Ritz Theatre, a former B movie house on Sixth Street downtown, with Bill Livinggood, whose Slow Printing company sold T-shirts designed by Austin poster artists. At both the Ritz and the Armadillo, Franklin favored portraitures for posters advertising concerts by pioneer rockers Jerry Lee Lewis and Bo Diddley, bluesman Bukka White, cosmic cowboy Michael Murphey, and reggae star Jimmy Cliff.

Franklin's absence from the Armadillo was hardly noticed. A new cadre of poster artists had filled the void. Micael Priest, who designed the sad cowboy listening to the jukebox poster for Willie Nelson's first show at the hippie hall, was the most prolific. From 1972 to New Year's Eve 1980, Priest sketched, drew, inked, or painted ninety-nine originals, exceeding Guy Juke's production of sixty-one posters and Jim Franklin's fifty-nine.

And like Jim Franklin and Guy Juke, Priest's work stood out in a crowd. Priest grew up in suburban Fort Worth and exhibited a talented hand early on, working summers for a commercial artist named Don Ivan Punchatz alongside cartoonist Gary Panter, computer animator and illustrator Steve Pietzch, and visual artist Georganne Deen, before enrolling as an art student at the University of Texas in 1969. He transferred to UT Arlington for two years but was called back to Austin in 1972 to design posters for a new advertising firm, Directions Company, which was working with the Armadillo.

Through Directions, Priest would head up the Armadillo Art Squad, assembling a small stable of like-minded artists including Kerry Awn, Ken

Featherston, Sam Yeates, Danny Garrett, Henry Gonzales, Cliff Carter (who was also the Armadillo's house recording engineer), Tommy Beeson, Jose Carlos Campos and John Rogers from San Antonio, and Bill Narum. Artists were paid seventy dollars for each poster they produced. Priest worked fast and knew commercial art. "I knew how to prepare art for reproduction, how to schedule it, and how to handle multiple jobs at the same time." He was also color-blind, an asset in his line of work because black-and-white production was cheaper than color.

Ken Featherston caught Priest's eye when he was shown portraits of Janis Joplin and Jimi Hendrix drawn with "an overactive Bic pen," Priest said. "It leaked so he could smear the ink on paper with his finger. It was on clay stock so it smeared very nicely. Although the likenesses weren't really right on because there was no way to control the proportions, the skin tones and half-tones that were created with this technique were just amazing. They made really, really vivid portraits."

His forte became surrealistic crosshatching, such as portraying a harmonica as the Eiffel Tower for a J. Geils Band show, waterfalls gushing out of the State Capitol Building for the Bluebonnet Mall mural near the UT campus, a cloud-choked celestial scene for a Mighty Clouds of Joy gospel show, and a locomotive engine pulling a train through the sky for Oat Willie's head shop.

Featherston, who came to Austin from Corpus Christi, also worked fast and did double duty as a bouncer. For two and a half years, from January 24, 1973, when he drew his first poster for Rat Creek, a local favorite, until he was shot dead in the Armadillo parking lot by a disgruntled concertgoer who'd been thrown out of the club, Featherston averaged three posters a month, including one for the Marshall Tucker Band that later became the cover for the album *Searching for a Rainbow*.

De White, a classically trained artist from San Angelo, moved to Austin as the guitarist/pianist/steel guitarist for the Doak Snead Band in 1973. White ran into Micael Priest in the Armadillo kitchen, where White was doing prep work for a friend, and showed him a poster he had made for the Snead band. Priest assigned White the bottom half of a poster depicting humorous songster Martin Mull, the opening act for Frank Zappa, whose Priest-designed visage occupied the top half. De White became Guy Juke, whose hand was as identifiable as Franklin's, Priest's, or Featherston's.

Juke integrated cubism and realism into a spare, minimalist style influenced by mainstream Hollywood movie cartoonists Tex Avery and Bob Clampett, and of colleagues Ken Featherston and Jim Franklin. His first stand-alone poster was for the East Texas band Navasota, for which he drew the television icon Mr. Ed, the talking horse, and his sidekick human, Wilbur. Juke became the go-to artist to promote edgier acts, such as the touring bands Talking Heads, Devo, and the Ramones.

After a stretch serving in the army in Vietnam, Danny Garrett landed in Austin, made contact with Jim Franklin, and got a poster gig for an Amazing Rhythm Aces concert when Franklin couldn't meet the deadline. Garrett, who grew up in Lake Jackson, near the Texas coast, was self-taught, raised on the graphic-gore in EC comics drawn by Will Elder, Will Davis, and Wallace Wood. Garrett's early poster works were heavily influenced by art nouveau, riffing off Maxfield Parrish and Alphonse Mucha, both pioneers of the artistic poster. But Garrett's style rapidly evolved, reflecting the influence other poster artists were having on his work.

Sam Yeates arrived in Austin fresh from a coat-and-tie teaching gig at an art school in Dallas, his newly minted bachelor's degree in fine art in drawing and painting from North Texas State University in hand. A native of Morgan Mill in west-central Texas, he intended to enroll in graduate school at the University of Texas but wound up working in the Armadillo kitchen instead.

"We had an art show at the Armadillo of people who worked there—Featherston, Priest, and some other people who weren't necessarily part of the artist group there," Yeates said. Ramsey Wiggins, the house publicist who took over assigning poster art from Micael Priest, saw Yeates's work and asked him to do a poster for a Doak Snead/Greezy Wheels double bill. In spite of his experience, he had a lot to learn. "I had no experience with layouts, printing technology, what had to be done to make things ready for the printer," Yeates said. "I had no idea what a percentage wheel was. A percentage wheel scales up and down. Now, on a computer, you can tell it what you want it to be."

The other Armadillo artists provided cues. "I looked around and saw what these other guys were doing. The first poster was rather derivative. I was learning on the job. All these other people had already been doing art and had established their little niches. The hard thing was coming in and trying to find your own spot amongst all that. Terry Raines, the guy printing the posters, deserves a lot of credit. He was always willing to experiment. But he also had the technical knowledge to experiment. He'd been doing printing for awhile, doing split-fountains, things like that."

Of thirteen posters he produced for the Armadillo, Sam Yeates was proudest of the relatively obscure Ruby Starr/Bob Seger billing, which he interpreted as a Big Top event. "I've always been a fan of circus posters," said Yeates.

> I've always loved the lions and the tigers coming out at you. Sometimes, shows at the Armadillo were circuslike, like the Balcones Fault Full Moon Concerts. I was trying to marry music and the circus together. The tiger had flames wrapped around him. The guitar neck was one of my favorite images that represent rock and roll. It was done in pencil on textured illustration board and shot as a line shot. It was Terry Raines' idea to do a split fountain two ways to give it a glow radiating from the center. It helped give it a circus feel.

Bill Narum arrived with a reputation and pedigree. His paternal grandfather was an artist and illustrator who designed maps for the State of Texas. His father had illustrated the Sears catalog and was president of the Artists Guild in Houston. Bill, who was born in Austin and raised in Houston, had done posters for such storied sixties-era Houston venues as the Love Street Light Circus and Feelgood Machine, Jubilee Hall, the Catacombs, and Liberty Hall. He had a background in commercial design, illustration, and underground comic books and had dreamed up the logo of a running antique radio with cartoon arms and legs that the Houston FM rock station KLOL used for more than thirty years.

Narum knew album covers too, having designed the front of ZZ Top's first album, appropriately titled *ZZ Top's First Album*, and the *Tejas* and *DeGüello* albums. Narum's Armadillo poster output was limited. His ZZ Top posters, the Armadillo debut of bluegrass titan Bill Monroe, and the Holy Modal Rounders were his most memorable works; his greater contributions were advising other artists and being the first to videotape Armadillo concerts for a small rural cable television company called Taylorvision. He was also the official keeper of the live longhorn steer and turkey buzzard that were part of the stage set for ZZ Top's breakout Worldwide Texas Tour.

Other artists drifted in and out, among them Jim Harter, the Lubbock-born Vulcan veteran who executed three ubersurreal posters in the psychedelic tradition; Henry Gonzales, a Corpus Christi–raised Chicano who applied his lowrider style to the Armadillo walls as well as posters; Kerry Awn's mural collaborator Rick Turner; Jose Carlos Campos; Sam Richardson, a tall, affable cartoonist who worked for KTBC Channel 7; and Gary McElhaney, a trained artist and sculptor from Corpus Christi.

Collectively, their poster art reflected the times. LSD had run its course, along with op art that played visual tricks on the eyes. Beer and marijuana were the inebriants of choice, and Austin was the home of ten-dollar pot and dollar six-packs. The Armadillo's shoestring budget mandated posters be legible and easy to comprehend.

"We covered a lot of ground," Micael Priest said. "Juke with his cubist bebop art. Franklin always different every time. Danny Garrett did a lot of fine surface beauty, classical engraving styles and letters. Gary McElhaney did really big, really intricate pencil drawings. Ken Featherston always did pointillistic and crosshatch pen-and-ink, delicate stippling, lots of portraiture and realism."

When Directions Company closed up shop, Priest, Narum, Garrett, Juke, Dale Wilkins, and Butch Hancock started a business called Sheauxnough Studios, which produced posters for the Armadillo, illustrations for the *Austin Sun* biweekly, and contract work for beer companies, concert promoters, T-shirt makers, and commercial accounts. Yeates would be commissioned by Warner Brothers to design an album cover for Rank and File and local band PM Heat. Two younger artists at Sheauxnough, Frank Kozik and Andy Blackwood, would become future standard-bearers for Austin poster art.

The Armadillo was hardly the only venue commissioning posters. George Majewski, who with his wife, Carlyne, ran Soap Creek Saloon, a roadhouse in semirural Westlake Hills, hired Kerry Awn (real last name: Fitzgerald) to design the club's monthly calendars beginning in late 1973. Awn was a Houston native whose brother helped run the *Rag*, to which Awn became a major contributor when he enrolled at the University of Texas. Awn did a Mance Lipscomb poster for the Armadillo at Jim Franklin's request and, ultimately, eleven more posters for the venue. But his freestyle, cartoony creations found a home at Soap Creek.

> Soap Creek was perfect for me. I immediately knew that's where I wanted to be, not the Armadillo," Awn said. "After a couple years, when they built the beer garden, the Armadillo started seeming like a tourist attraction. Soldiers from Fort Hood would come in on the weekends. Straight people were hanging around. Soap Creek was more like a private country club. It was hard to get to. Plus, they sold real alcohol, tequila shots for 40 cents. It was just a lot cooler. Armadillo had all these touring bands come through. All the bands I liked played Soap Creek—Paul Ray, Greezy Wheels, Doug Sahm."

Awn's exaggerated-but-not-quite-caricature depictions of people were impulsive. "I didn't design anything. I didn't plan anything. I'd just start drawing." Awn also created street murals, most notably *Austintacious*, an Austin-centric mural on Twenty-Third Street and collaborative project with Tom Bauman and Rick Turner that depicts the city through a fish-eye lens with founder Stephen F. Austin at the center. The following year Kerry Awn also designed the cover for the Doug Sahm album *Groover's Paradise*.

The Split Rail, a no-cover country-and-roots joint on South Lamar, just south of Town Lake, and the Rome Inn, a campus-area dive on Twenty-Ninth Street, utilized posters as their main promotional vehicles.

The opening of the Texas Opry House less than a mile from the Armadillo in 1974 by Wallace Selman and Bronson Evans was a game changer, mainly because the venue had air-conditioning and mixed drinks, attracting Willie Nelson, Michael Murphey, and numerous other acts that would have otherwise played the Armadillo. Danny Garrett, who also did posters for the Armadillo, became one of the Texas Opry House's go-to guys.

Garrett also designed the logo for Castle Creek, the folk club where Guy Clark, Jerry Jeff Walker, and Jimmy Buffett regularly headlined. He designed posters for the Alliance Wagon Yard, a Willie Nelson–sanctioned country-rock club downtown; and the Texas Opry's successor, the Austin Opry House, which also enlisted the work of Pauline Walsh Jacobson.

Garrett eventually became the house poster artist for Antone's Home of the Blues, an association that stretched over thirty years and four locations. For the first few Antone's shows, the club printed its own primitive posters with just the facts. Clifford Antone decided to upgrade by hiring Garrett. "He said he just wanted me to treat the artists with respect and make the images look like them." Garrett complied, leaning heavily on portraiture and confining experimentation to backgrounds and color separations.

Jack Jackson returned to Austin from San Francisco in the mid-1970s. Jaxon comic strips appearing in the *Austin Sun* weighed in on music trends and Austin's growth, including "Cosmic Cowboy: A Handy Guide for Out-of-Staters" in 1976, "The Rise and Rapid Decline of Austin Tacious" in 1977, and "Great Moments in Austin Music at Houston Prices," parodying Delbert McClinton charging a ten-dollar cover to a club gig. He also did a comix-style single-panel rendering of Sir Doug Sahm and the Texas Tornados for a weekend gig at Soap Creek Saloon in 1976, as well as a multipanel Sir Doug and the Texas Tornados "Hit the Road" promotional poster for ABC Records, supporting the release of the album *Texas Rock for Country Rollers*.

The Armadillo closed on New Year's Eve 1980, done in by soaring real estate prices. Counterculture poster art as the primary means of advertising rock concerts had run its course. Production values had changed. Big colorful posters were no longer the most effective means of promotion. But poster art wasn't dead. It just smelled funny, like photocopies.

While the Armadillo was winding to a close, punk rock was blowing up in Austin around two small venues, Raul's and Duke's Royal Coach Inn (in the same location as the old Vulcan Gas Company), and one large venue, Club Foot. Raul's and Duke's were hardly mainstream showcases, as the Armadillo had become, but rather seat-of-the-pants operations. Bands played for a percentage of whatever was collected at the door, and clubs had no promotional budget.

Posters became more homegrown, and more essential than ever, with bands doing collages and using improved copying technology to produce handbill-sized posters on the cheap. Getting the message out was their primary purpose. Most bands made their own posters, owing to economic necessity, as was the case with Cam King, the guitarist for the Explosives, and myself, Joe Nick Patoski, the manager of Joe "King" Carrasco and the Crowns. Still, a few poster artists managed to stand out.

Jagmo, a.k.a. Nels Jacobson, rose to the forefront of the new wave of poster artists, thanks to working at Club Foot, which actually had a promotional budget. The Chicago native moved to Austin in 1978. Three years later, he was making posters in addition to managing Club Foot. His clean, spare style with vague traces of cubism was mightily influenced by Guy Juke, as was the work of Mike Nott, who drew under the pen name NOXX, and the Art Maggots, an art collective in the spirit of the Armadillo Art Squad, which included Frank Kozik, Andy Blackwood, and Paul Sabal.

Another trailblazer was Randy "Biscuit" Turner, the lead singer of the Big Boys, a popular funk punk band, who dreamed up distinctive designs and stage sets for his band, as well as creative posters.

Frank Kozik, a native of Spain who served in the air force in Austin before he was discharged and embarked on the art path, was entirely self-taught. He soaked up the stylistic quirks of Guy Juke at Sheauxnough Studios and mastered production at Marty Bebout's Bee-Bop Screen Printing, and it showed. One of his most provocative early pieces, a poster of Joseph and Mary barbecuing the baby Jesus on a grill, was banned by the University of Texas, only to have the image blown up on the front page of the *Daily Texan* with an accompanying news story about the ban. Kozik eventually relocated to San Francisco and remained a major presence on the poster art scene, working with bands such as Queens of the Stone Age, Green Day, the White Stripes, Beastie Boys, Neil Young, and Nirvana, recognized for his silkscreen techniques and keen sensibility in contrasting bright colors. He also started a record label and directed music videos. His collected works were published in the book *Man's Ruin*. Kozik eventually shifted into fine art, art toys, and commissions for designs and products.

Jim Franklin continued chasing commercial projects after the close of the Armadillo. An aborted series for Jiffy Franks hot dogs, which claimed to be the first burpless wiener on the market, yielded one poster titled "Hot Dogs and Lily Pads," a waterscape that portrayed dogs on buns floating on lily pads on a tranquil lake, a scene that could have easily been dreamed up by Neon Park, the Los Angeles painter who did covers for the band Little Feat. A second poster visually described a hot dog on the moon next to astronauts and a lunar rover.

In 1981, he tried to continue his Lone Star longneck series of posters of beer bottles in strange places through the auspices of Mort Cooperman, an advertising executive who owned the Lone Star Café in New York. A bottle of beer masqueraded as a windmill tower in an otherwise serene setting of cattle and horses grazing on the plains.

Guy Juke continued working on the cutting edge of poster art after the Armadillo shut down, at one point earning the ultimate backhanded compliment when his artwork, drawn for Raul's punk club in Austin, was blatantly ripped off by the Ramones' management for the album cover for *Pleasant Dreams*.

In the early nineties, Sam Yeates joined Danny Garrett, Jim Franklin, Micael Priest, Bill Narum, De White, and Gary McElhaney in the most unlikely of all post-Armadillo ventures. Origin Systems was an Austin software company founded and co-owned by Richard Garriott, a game designer who also happened to be a big Armadillo World Headquarters fan. Garriott's enthusiasm and financial wherewithal prompted him to hire as many Armadillo artists as he could, treating them like royalty.

Franklin and White didn't last long. "I don't play video games and I failed to read those kinds of comics," White drolly observed. Yeates, Priest, Narum, Garrett, and McElhaney did. "Like every other business back in the boom days, they hired the least amount of people they can and overwork the shit out of them," Garrett said. "I don't care about video games. I don't care about super heroes. I don't care about dragons and spaceships. Yet, when you're working 50 and 60 hours a week, you are dragons and spaceships and you aren't anything else. I went to MicroProse and to Looking Glass Technologies, briefly. Now I'm out of it. I miss it."

"I learned on the job and moved out of the game department into marketing, doing covers for the video games," Yeates said. "I did the cover for Wing Commander." The salad days of Origin ended when the company was bought out by Electronic Arts. The marketing department was downsized and then killed off altogether. Priest managed to hang on through 1997. Yeates went to work for MicroProse doing more video games and dabbled in ad work. Yeates, McElhaney, and Garrett all taught art at Austin Community College. Garrett also taught art in New Zealand for a stretch.

McElhaney's figurative sculptures are easy to find on the University of Texas campus. His bust of Willie Nelson is displayed at the Performing Arts Center, numerous white-stone relief sculptures of a herd of charging longhorn cattle are in the bowels of Darrell K Royal—Texas Memorial Stadium, and his cast-bronze Bevo steers are given to major UT alumni contributors.

Jim Franklin appeared in the 2004 Richard Linklater film *Before Sunset*, in which he played an artist painting a cityscape on the Seine in Paris as the romantic characters played by Ethan Hawke and Julie Delpy pass by on a river barge.

Kerry Awn pursued a career in comedy, earning accolades as the Funniest Comic in Texas at one point, before returning to art. In 2013, he completed an eighty-foot triptych mural, *Paradise of the Violet Crown*, above the produce section of Central Market Westgate in South Austin.

Gilbert Shelton moved to France, where his sketchbooks are published. Although several entities obtained the rights from Shelton to make a Fabulous Furry Freak Brothers film, none has made it to completion.

All of these artists have had their work shown at the South Austin Popular Culture Center, where Henry Gonzales has created an organic shrine to cool Austin people who have passed away.

Chet Helms became a successful art dealer.

The concert may have ended, the music might be over, but the posters remain, telling the story of a time in a place like none other.

COLORFUL TALES & EARLY TECHNIQUES

Postering in Austin

NELS JACOBSON

Only two things that money can't buy
That's true love & homegrown tomatoes
GUY CLARK

Without a doubt, the treasures cultivated by hand in our own backyard are the sweetest and most satisfying. Before the hi-tech revolution, Austin music posters were hand-designed by artists working in the real world with unforgiving tools, and without the aid of design software and digital tricks; yet their makers captured the spirit of the music and the times with humor, vitality, and unbridled imagination. The posterists of Austin chronicled the changing social landscape and graphically redefined Texas for the rest of the country and the world—a world in which, until fairly recently, entertainers and impresarios depended in large part on posters to publicize upcoming performances.

Within that long-standing entertainment-promotion paradigm, whether in nineteenth-century Paris, San Francisco during the Summer of Love, or Austin in the 1960s, '70s, and '80s, gifted artists produced posters that have become emblematic of their eras. In Austin the music venues that reigned supreme in the 1960s and '70s were the Vulcan Gas Company and the Armadillo World Headquarters, and the best of the posters and handbills created for these two clubs, and their counterparts, have come to be considered historically important documents. Many of these paper advertisements are regarded today as works of exceptional quality not unlike the nineteenth-century posters of Chéret, Mucha, and Toulouse-Lautrec and the San Francisco posters of Griffin, Moscoso, and Wilson. The Austin poster artists who produced them—Shelton, Franklin, Priest, Juke, and so many others—shared a love of music and a passion for creating music art. And very often these artists were characters in their own right, no less colorful than the art they were creating.

This is certainly true of Gilbert Shelton, art director for the Vulcan Gas Company, Texas' original counterculture dance hall. The Vulcan logo and the grand opening poster were designed by Shelton, who is best known today as the creator of underground comic-book characters the Fabulous Furry Freak Brothers and Wonder Wart-Hog. He was an editor of the University of Texas student humor magazine, the *Texas Ranger*, in the early 1960s, and he collaborated on posters and other projects with Tony Bell, who also worked there. Shelton credits the sixties San Francisco artists with influencing his poster art and names Bob Fried in particular as an inspiration for his lettering style. Shelton would begin his designs with a pencil sketch in most cases, on drawing board "or whatever else" he could get. Then he would finish with a dip pen and India ink, using white acrylic paint to correct mistakes.

For the final look of each poster Shelton frequently enlisted the help of printer Johnny Mercer, who ran most of the Vulcan posters on his twenty-nine-inch Harris single-color offset press. Shelton would furnish black-and-white board art, and Mercer would shoot a negative and then a reverse negative for the second color run. As Shelton explains: "These two images would then be printed in different colored inks, the two images fitting together perfectly." Mercer was good at the split-fountain technique—running two or more ink colors on the same roller during the same run to achieve a gradual transition from one color to the next. Says Shelton, "Each image would be printed using different colors of ink, mixed together in the inking trough of the press." In this way, Shelton, Bell, and Mercer experimented with the colors—fading one into another. In Mercer's words, "We flew by the seat of our britches." Bell maintained that rather than trying to create art, Austin's early posterists were simply striving for maximum visibility—merely attempting to allow the Vulcan to survive as a venue. Because the Vulcan had trouble covering printing costs, Mercer remembers sometimes being paid with coffee cans full of coins and wadded-up bills. Yet the posters were so popular the printer would find young enthusiasts rooting through his trash in search of misprints and rejects.

At least two of the large-format Vulcan posters were screen-printed rather than printed on Mercer's offset press, though handbills for both designs were still offset-printed. Fellow *Ranger* contributor Roger Baker taught Shelton and quintessential Austin artist Jim Franklin how to screen-print at home using a couple dollars' worth of chemicals from the drugstore. "We would coat the silkscreen in a light-sensitive liquid inside in the relative darkness," explains Shelton, "and when it dried we would tape the transparent image over it, take it outside in the sun for two minutes, and then take it into the bathroom and wash it off with hot water. The coating had become insoluble where the sun had touched it, and the other parts washed away, leaving a silkscreen ready for printing." Franklin's 1968 Big Joe Williams design was printed this way.

Of all the Vulcan posters, Shelton's favorite is the one from late December 1967 for Conqueroo because it approximates the look of the light-show images that would be projected on the wall through glass dishes full of colored oil and water.

Jack Jackson, a.k.a. Jaxon, was a major contributor to the counterculture movement in both Austin and San Francisco. Born in Pandora, Texas, Jaxon had no formal art training, as was the case with Shelton and Bell, but as a kid he sketched endlessly on Big Chief tablets and any other paper surface that was handy. Also a *Ranger* alum, Jaxon authored in 1964, with help from longtime Shelton collaborator Lieuen Adkins, what many regard as the first underground comic, *God Nose*. He would acknowledge this achievement with a sly wink sometimes, as the comic had been printed in the basement of the Texas State Capitol Building. When Jaxon hit California a couple years later, in addition to his affiliation with Rip Off Press, he oversaw the Avalon Ballroom poster operation for the Family Dog. Returning to his home state after

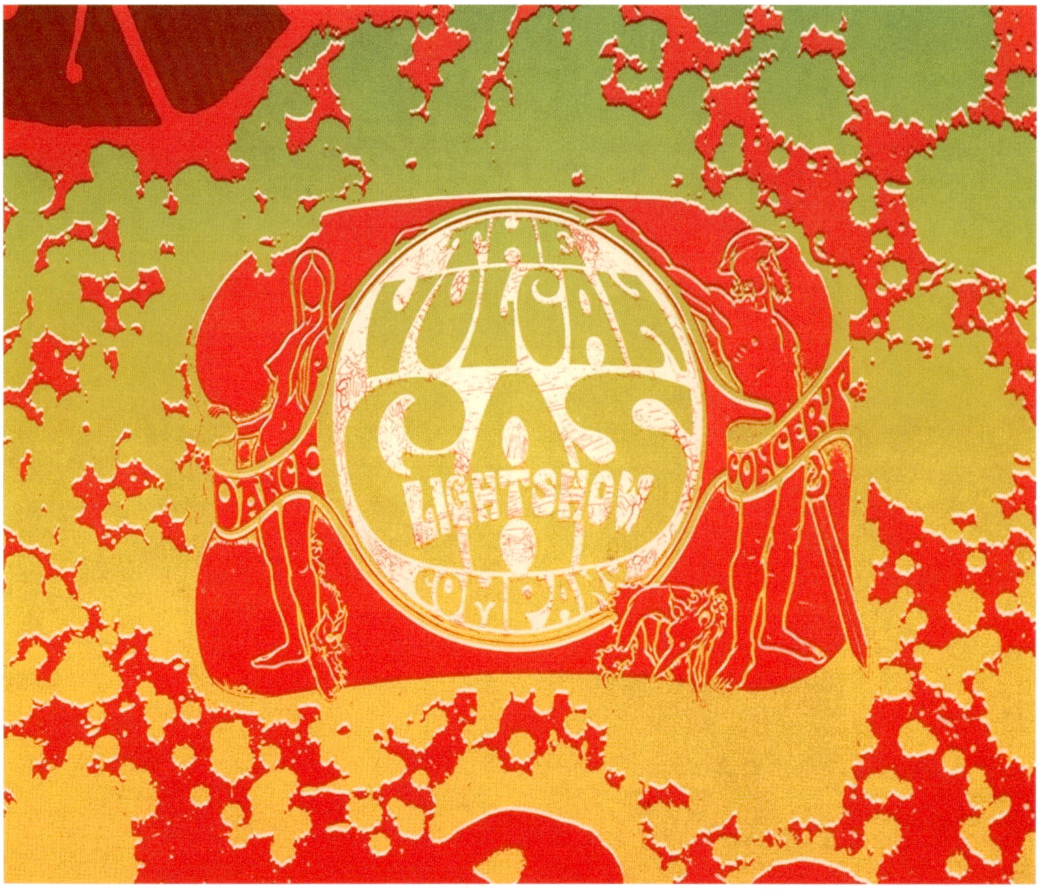

Detail of poster 5, Gilbert Shelton poster.

a few years, Jaxon produced at least one handbill for the Vulcan, followed by a number of well-researched and skillfully rendered comic books about Texas history.

Lubbock-born collagist Jim Harter was exposed to the psychedelic art movement during a San Francisco trip in 1966 while working as a truck driver. Three years later Harter visited the Vulcan during spring break from West Texas State and left Franklin a few poster designs that were complete except for band names and dates. "By this time Gilbert and Tony Bell had left for California," explains Harter. "John Shelton had moved into the Vulcan some time before so basically he and Franklin were doing all the poster work." John Shelton, who was no relation to Gilbert, created a number of Vulcan designs and later designed for the Armadillo an anatomically detailed poster of the underside of its namesake. When Harter returned to Austin after graduation in June, he found Franklin had completed lettering one of the posters Harter left with him. It had been printed as a split-fountain handbill and was plastered all over the windows of the Vulcan, thus launching Harter's tenure as a Vulcan artist. His designs from that period, and later for the 'Dillo, often feature psychedelic-style lettering and a drawing, photo, or collage. He worked in pencil and then with a dip pen and India ink. Harter's lettering was inspired by Wes Wilson in San Francisco, who in turn had been influenced by a 1908 poster by Viennese Secessionist artist Alfred Roller.

Franklin, after brief stints in San Francisco and New York, had been lured to Austin in the mid-1960s by a chance encounter in Galveston with some of the *Ranger* crowd. He had no formal art training but knew as early as grade school that he wanted to be an artist, constantly drawing in notepads and amassing a collection of art prints torn from magazines in the school library. Franklin learned what he knows of commercial techniques from just doing them, and also from an artist friend in Galveston who taught him "to do layouts and to get work ready for camera." Much less inclined to imitate the prevalent San Francisco style than his peers were, Franklin began to evolve a distinctly Texas poster look through his pen-and-ink renderings. Moreover, unlike Bay Area artists who rarely incorporated portraits in their work, Franklin often included images of musicians in his posters, such as the Big Joe Williams design mentioned previously. He drew this portrait from a photo taken by Burton Wilson at the Victory Grill in East Austin. Not one to shy away from reusing a good illustration, Franklin repurposed his Williams portrait for two more handbills in 1969. So that an image could more easily be liberated from one poster design and used with another, Franklin reportedly even discouraged other poster artists from overlapping image with text.

The Vulcan closed its doors for good in mid-1970, but just three months later the new Armadillo World Headquarters would offer artists an inspirational and nurturing environment, a supportive fraternity, and an ongoing mission—and the posters it inspired began to exhibit a piquant, uniquely Texas flavor. The 'Dillo artists, following Franklin's lead, began to appropriate familiar western visual clichés, frequently contorting these traditional symbols into subversive new configurations. Lettering was typically less ornate and "trippy" than the San Francisco look, and production costs were kept to a minimum by forgoing halftones in favor of crosshatching and stippling.

Throughout the body of work produced for the Armadillo can be seen a pervasive playfulness, as in Franklin's Flying Burrito Brothers illustration depicting Wilbur and Orville launching a heavier-than-air craft with humongous burritos for wings. This image first appeared as the centerpiece of a Franklin poster in 1971. Four years later the original horizontal poster design was adapted by fellow Armadillo artist Micael Priest for a vertical poster on which he replaced Franklin's text with more dominant lettering and a crowd of cartoon cowboys whooping it up in celebration of Texas Independence Day.

While Franklin's influence cannot be overstated, several other important artists emerged during the Armadillo years: Kerry Awn, Danny

Garrett, Ken Featherston, Guy Juke, Bill Narum, Sam Yeates, and particularly Priest—the most influential 'Dillo-era poster artist other than Franklin himself. Priest moved to Austin in 1972 to help found its first counterculture advertising agency, Directions Company, which was succeeded by Sheauxnough Studios in 1976. Having worked with commercial illustrator Don Ivan Punchatz since high school, Priest brought to Austin's alternative community a sense of commercial sophistication. His longtime fascination with old-school sign painters, and the knowledge he gleaned from patient observation, old textbooks, and countless sign-painterly conversations, armed Priest with an array of graphic tricks and a formidable facility with typography. His gift for lifelike caricature empowered Priest to fashion a graphic landscape dotted with big-finned Cadillacs and cactuses and populated by cannabis-toking cowboys, long-haired mustang riders, and musicians of every sort.

Priest has said that he hand-drew everything, inking his designs by hand "so they would have the little cricks and grizzles" that people could relate to. In attempting to make his posters as visually interesting as possible, Priest often filled them to the brim with content. This is a trait he shared with Kerry Awn, noting that they sometimes were accused of feeling that for any given poster, "if there was any negative space left it wasn't finished." Awn, when asked how he knew a piece was done, answered, "When there's no more room, I stop." Priest credits Awn with showing him how to use correction fluid for changes by painting right on the art. Prior to that Priest was doing everything on tissue: gluing it down, cutting out the parts he wanted to correct, shooting a photostat, and then inking on the stat. When bookings were confirmed late, Priest remembers working all night and then running the art to the print shop first thing in the morning. Printer Mike Morgan swore that Priest

Detail of plate 81, Jim Franklin & Micael Priest poster.

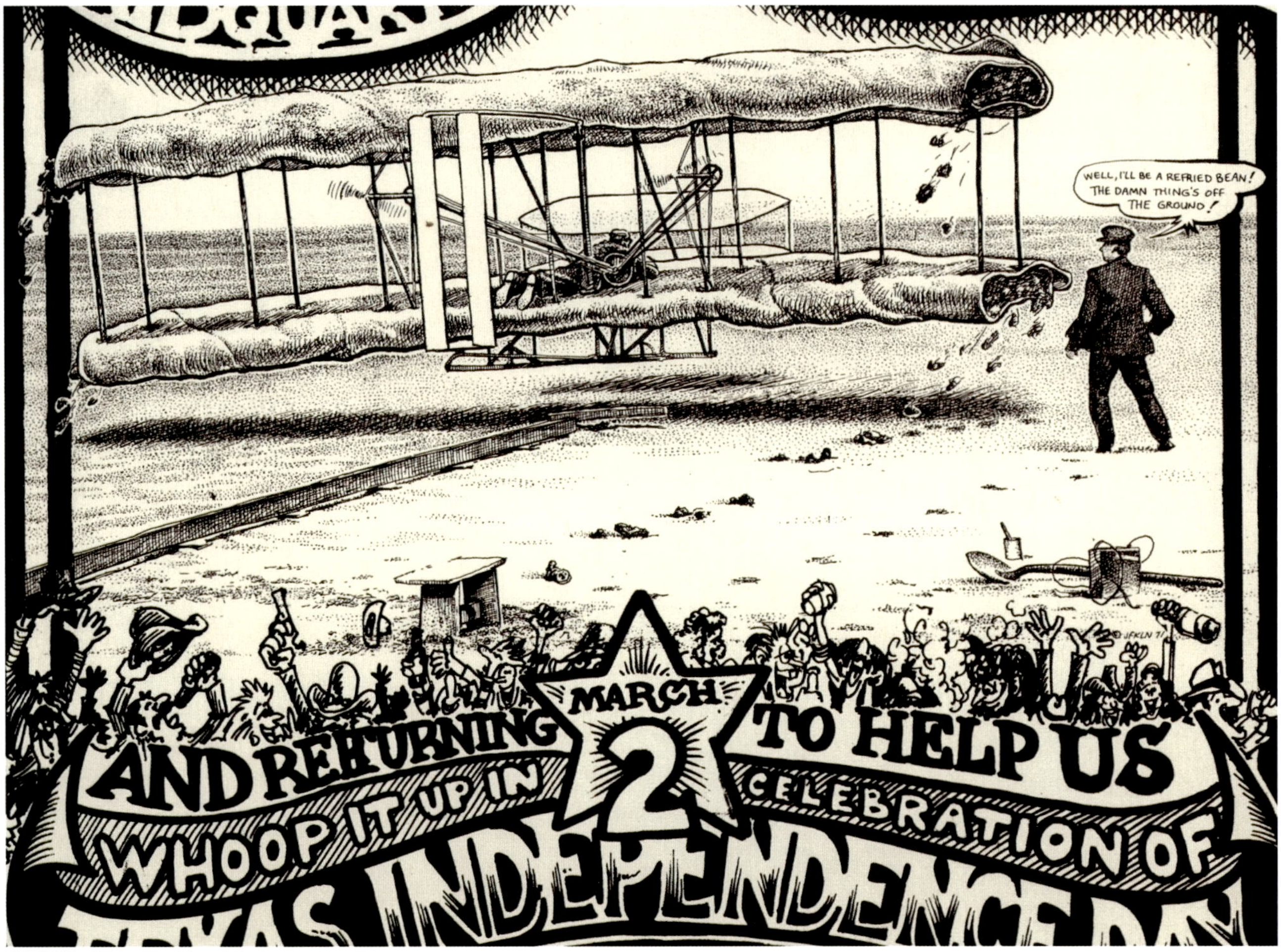

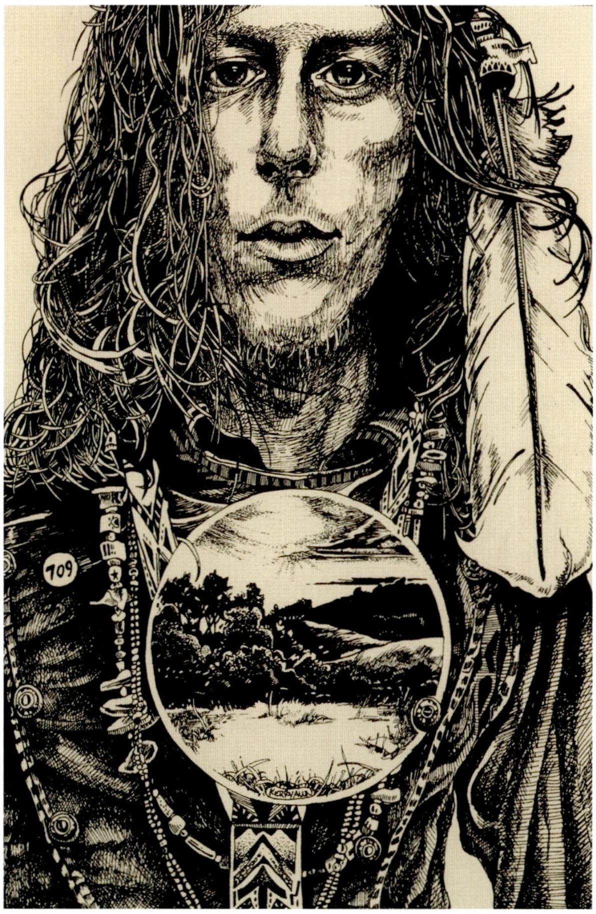

Detail of plate 57, Kerry Awn poster.

would often be adding the finishing touches to a poster design even as the press was printing it.

A cadre of printers, in addition to split-fountain maestro Mercer, supported the Austin poster community with their printing expertise and artistry. Two printers who worked extensively with poster artists in the 1970s were Benny Binford of Calico Printing and the aforementioned Mike Morgan of Express Press. Over the years, however, no Austin printer has been as consistently involved with Texas music graphics as Terry Raines. Fascinated by caves and underground exploration, he originally began printing in the mid-1960s as a means of disseminating information to other caving enthusiasts. A couple years later he was printing Vulcan handbills in the basement of the UT undergraduate library. Raines printed Franklin's initial handbills for Big Joe Williams, as well as most of the other handbills for the Vulcan. He also was responsible for many Armadillo World Headquarters posters. For a time Raines was printing with a Multilith 1350 offset press in a bus that he previously had driven down to Oaxaca, Mexico, to view the total eclipse in 1970. He replaced the Multilith in 1975 with a thirty-five-inch Harris press on which he was able to print two or three different posters at the same time on a single sheet of paper. Raines eventually sold the Harris press to Binford and purchased a succession of precision Heidelberg presses.

One Austin artist who worked particularly closely with printers is Dale Wilkins. After moving to town from Beaumont in 1969 and earning a bachelor of fine arts degree at UT, he worked as a graphic artist at Futura Press and then with Binford and Calico Printing doing layout, graphics, and art. Wilkins has said that his basic poster formula consisted of placing a catchy banner at the top and inserting below that "a drawing of the performer, including some kind of visual twist." He credits Franklin's influence for his appreciation of visual whimsy and pen-and-ink crosshatching. "A rough pencil sketch would start the process," explains Wilkins. "If the sketch proved a good likeness then it would be inked with Rapidograph or Speedball pen in India ink. I liked to use my Paasche VL airbrush for shading or stippling. Then after creating black-and-white art, color plates could be added by hand-cutting Rubylith film overlays for each additional color." Between his output at the print shops and as a freelance artist, Wilkins produced many memorable pieces. Among them is his 1978 J. J. Cale split-fountain poster for the Austin Opry House; Cale liked it so much he asked Wilkins to adapt it for use in the Nashville booking catalog.

Awn, whose given name is Kerry Fitzgerald, moved to Austin in 1970. He was creating posters for the Armadillo within a year and later inaugurated his decades-long series of Soap Creek Saloon calendars and a seemingly boundless bounty of posters for the band he performs with—the Uranium Savages. Growing up in Houston, Awn knew by the fifth grade that he wanted to be an artist; soon he had notebooks full of drawings. He was drawing for local underground newspaper *Space City!* by the time he was fifteen, and he drew his first cover for Austin's underground paper the *Rag* while still in high school. In the early days he would draw on shirt cardboard, using black ink cartridge pens. Later he would work with pen, India ink, and illustration tablets. When he had a poster to do, Awn would first sketch an idea and then flesh it out, inking it in as he went. For lettering, Awn says that he sometimes used sign-painting techniques, and otherwise just did whatever worked. Priest insists that no one was able to work as fast as Awn and that, of all the poster artists, Awn is the only one whose style couldn't be copied: "Nobody is as primitive as Kerry. It's a masterstroke that cannot be lifted. You can't fake it."

Like Awn, Danny Garrett began drawing in Houston. He created his first poster in 1970 for the band Sweet Peter, then moved to Austin and jumped headlong into the Austin poster melee. A profusion of exquisitely crafted posters followed—for the Armadillo, Antone's, Castle Creek, and the Austin Opry House. In his Antone's posters for blues artists he often incorporated a playing card as an embellishment: aces for deceased performers, kings for current stars, jacks for the up-and-coming, and queens for women. The delicacy of Garrett's pen-and-ink illustrations and his tendency toward traditionally realistic representation contrast sharply with the surrealist tendencies found in many of the other Austin posterists. He worked with pen and ink on either cold-press or hot-press illustration board, using crosshatching or stippling to mimic tone, and introducing gesso, a white paint mixture, when necessary to add highlights or make corrections. Sometimes he preferred the effect of black Prismacolor pencil on coquille board because it freed him from pen-and-ink stippling by allowing him to achieve shading gradations with just a line shot for the printer. Garrett worked out lettering on a separate paper and then transferred it to the poster original; he favored heavily serifed nineteenth-century lettering and says he learned a great deal from Priest.

Pauline Walsh Jacobson (previously Fernandez) joined Garrett as an Opry House artist in the mid-1970s. Her day job was as a draftsman/cartographer in those days, so Jacobson used Rapidographs and India ink on poster board for her poster work. She hand-drew everything using outlines, stippling, and crosshatching techniques—rendering the musician's portrait in pencil on drafting vellum placed over a photograph, and then transferring it to the poster board by coating the back with graphite and retracing it onto the poster board. Eventually she began using semitransparent drafting film, which allowed her to render in ink directly on the artwork, thus eliminating the pencil step. For text, because Jacobson was fond of art nouveau and antique lettering, she incorporated styles from old lettering books or would "just make up freeform lettering and 'wrap' it around the musician's portrait."

Ken Featherston was one of the most gifted young artists drawn to the Armadillo. The 1972 Mahavishnu Orchestra poster he did for the venue became just the first of many. Though he worked predominantly with delicate pen-and-ink stippling and crosshatching, Featherston occasionally combined airbrush and pen-and-ink techniques in a single piece. Among his best-known designs is the album cover he created for the Marshall Tucker Band's *Searchin' for a Rainbow* LP and the 1974 poster on which it was based.

Henry Gonzalez grew up in Corpus Christi with Featherston. He moved to Austin in 1973 and was enrolled in the art program at UT for a time. Featherston introduced him around the Armadillo, and Gonzalez readily joined the team, helping out wherever he could. Gonzalez had learned a lot about lettering from his father, who was a sign painter, including the centuries-old technique of pouncing—transferring a design from one surface to another by perforating a sheet of paper while tracing the lines of the design and then forcing chalk or fine charcoal onto a new surface through the pricked holes. To work the dust through the holes, usually a "pounce pad" is used. Gonzalez used a sock filled with chalk for his pounce pad. His poster images—sketches that he wedded with text and other elements by photocopying, cutting, and pasting—often recalled themes from the Mexican Revolution.

De White, better known as Guy Juke, comes from a long line of architects and counts among his progenitors the lavishly mustachioed Stanford White. Juke moved to town in 1973, and before the year was out, he was working with the Armadillo. More than any other Austin poster artist, his work exhibits a strikingly broad cross section of styles and is imbued with wry twists and visual puns that rival Franklin's own. Juke often started with a photo—something unpublished, or one frame of a video—that he drew small at first to get a sense of the whole design. Juke found pen and ink more demanding than pencil or paint and copied the techniques of Franklin and Featherston. Juke says he borrowed lettering ideas from Priest and reciprocated by sharing his knowledge of color with Priest, who calls Juke "the most accomplished and articulate colorist I could possibly imagine." In the late 1970s, Juke began to forgo intricately detailed pen-and-ink illustrations in favor of an angular minimalist style. He painstakingly crafted designs using the fewest lines possible to represent a subject. For Juke, "It's a matter of the rhythm of the lines—how they fall." He's likened his angular style to jazz. People who today marvel at Juke's work from the 1970s and '80s sometimes ask how he did vector graphics back then. His answer: "With a pen and an X-Acto blade."

Bill Narum had studied and produced artwork all his life; both of his parents were artists. Born in Austin and brought up in Houston, Narum acquired his first printing press in the fourth grade, started printing comics the next year, and began producing posters in junior high. During the late 1960s he was active as a poster artist and political cartoonist and served as art director for *Space City!*. Narum returned to Austin in the early 1970s, bringing with him a wealth of experience in commercial art. He produced several posters for the 'Dillo and a series of poster calendars for the Continental Club. But it's likely his most well-known designs are the album covers he created for ZZ Top when he served as house artist for the band.

In 1974 Sam Yeates moved to Austin with a degree in drawing and painting and the intention of pursuing a master of fine arts degree at UT. He was wooed away from academia, however, and into the Armadillo Art Squad. Yeates drew first with pencil and then with a dip pen and India ink, using tracing paper so that he could move things around. For the final drawing, he ordinarily preferred ink, not only because it didn't require a screenshot for the printer and was thus less expensive but also because pencil was less predictable.

The first 'Dillo poster Yeates created was for Greezy Wheels and the Doak Snead Band in 1975, and it triggered a free-for-all of drawing styles among the other artists. Juke recalls that "Yeates did a poster that looked like all the artists had done it." Suddenly all the Armadillo artists began doing posters in styles they hadn't used before. The piece Juke remembers doing at this point was his Asleep at the Wheel poster for June 27–28, 1975, which he describes as "pure Dada, surrealism of the improbable." Priest recalls that, upon seeing Yeates's poster, each artist thought that one "of the other guys had done it and it turned out it wasn't any of us, it was this new guy Sam Yeates that we didn't even know. All he had to say about it was that I just did it in the generic Austin style, and oh god, we all swallowed our tongues, and our eyes bulged out and we thought oh god, we've created a generic style. Oh no."

It was in UT's Fine Arts Department that Rick Turner ran into Awn and fellow artist Tommy "Bee" Bauman, both of whom he later performed with as a member of the Uranium Savages auxiliary unit, the Shrovinovers. They began drawing together and emulating the sixties poster style—doing "a lot of jamming; passing the page around." Eventually Turner found his way to the Armadillo, where one of his more successful efforts was his 1977 poster for Darryl Rhoades and the Hahavishnu Orchestra. It depicts a formation of oversized hamburgers floating past the Texas State Capitol Building, a design he reprised both as an album cover and then a mural at the Bitter End in New York. Turner's most readily identifiable work, however, is what he's done in the punk collage style. One example is his Patti Smith poster incorporating as its main character the Gustave Doré engraving of Nimrod from Dante's *Divine Comedy*, with which he attempted to convey the dark, melancholy tone he heard in Smith's music. Turner enjoyed illustration and crosshatching and worked with a dip pen at first and later a Rapidograph. But then he hit on the idea of making collages out of old engravings: "I thought about how I could get the kind of work I'd like—old engravings, fine pen and ink, my pen work, furious neurotic, hatchings, you know that kind of stuff, but do it fast so I could paste something together. I loved it." For his lettering, Turner approximated the look of a ransom note by forming words out of incompatible individual letters severed from books and magazines—a nod to the mismatched-font style associated with the Sex Pistols and other punk bands, and a way to distinguish his collage work from that of Harter and other collagists.

The punk movement was a rallying point for those who felt betrayed by mainstream rock, which had become predictable by the mid-1970s—even respectable—as had much of the poster art. Punk handbills and posters, on the other hand, reflected the spirit of the new music. The vast majority of them, in keeping with the do-it-yourself punk mandate, were photocopied rather than offset-printed and celebrated unpretentious exuberance, simplicity, and outrageousness. One of the earliest artists on the punk scene was Ric Cruz, whose work ran the gamut from deliberately clumsy and childlike marker-scribblings to masterfully executed illustrations. Born in San Antonio, Cruz began designing posters for punk bands in 1979. Although his elaborate pen-and-ink work reflects the common ground he shared with his Armadillo-era antecedents, the overall look of his posters and handbills, and their oftentimes sci-fi and violent themes, represented a definitive rejection of the 'Dillo hippie/cowboy motif. Cruz did posters and handbills for several venues, but most of his designs were for shows at Raul's. Owners Roy "Raul" Gomez and Joseph Gonzales originally conceived of Raul's as a Tejano nightclub. But given its location across the street from the University of Texas, they soon began booking punk bands—and in so doing, inadvertently unleashed a rampaging stampede of handbills intended to shock and to challenge traditional standards. Typically, for these advertisements an antisophisticated, deliberately primitive look was the goal—something simple, DIY, and exuding childlike crudity.

Mike Nott, who lived next door to Raul's, became closely associated with the art of the punk movement. His work had a measured simplicity to it but ran counter to the trend to be

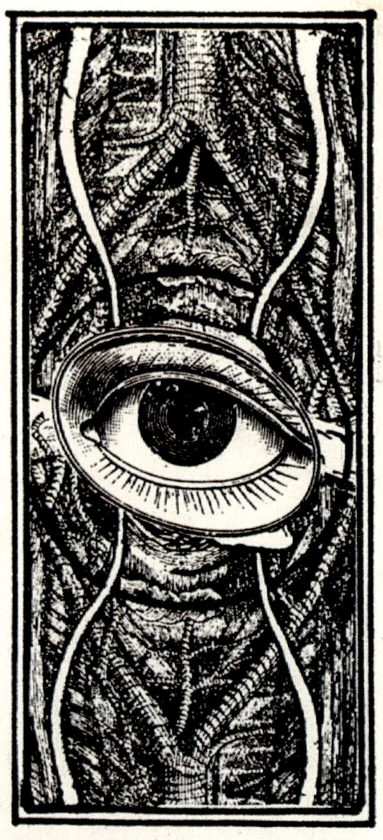

Detail of plate 102, Rick Turner poster.

crude, shocking, and primitive. He had earned a bachelor of fine arts degree as a student in UT's Design Program and strove for a look that was "clean and sharp." Much of his work tended to be meticulously geometric. Using a Rapidograph, T square, X-Acto knife, press type, and Zip-A-Tone, he worked according to a grid system—on an "X" with all of the elements arranged to draw the viewer's eye to the center and then "everything flew out from there." Nott never used preliminary sketches or roughed out anything. For the signature on his work, Nott would tip over the last two letters of his surname to get "NOXX." This is how he signed the logo and other designs he created for Club Foot, the largest Austin venue regularly booking new wave and punk acts in the early 1980s.

Located on Fourth Street behind the Greyhound bus station and dubbed Club Foot by owner John Bird, this nightclub/concert hall hosted local bands and major touring acts. As at Raul's, the music at Club Foot was complemented and promoted by a profusion of posters and handbills, and for three years I was bar manager and promotional director there. Because I had been collecting the work of Franklin, Juke, and all the rest since moving from Chicago to Texas in 1978, I found it especially exhilarating when my duties allowed me to commission posters, and even to experiment with designing some myself. Signing my work with the genial Chicago pejorative "Jagmo," I used markers and X-Acto blades for the simple sketches and collages I attempted first. By the mid-1980s, I was using a Rapidograph to create the crosshatching, stippling, and lettering found in my more mature efforts.

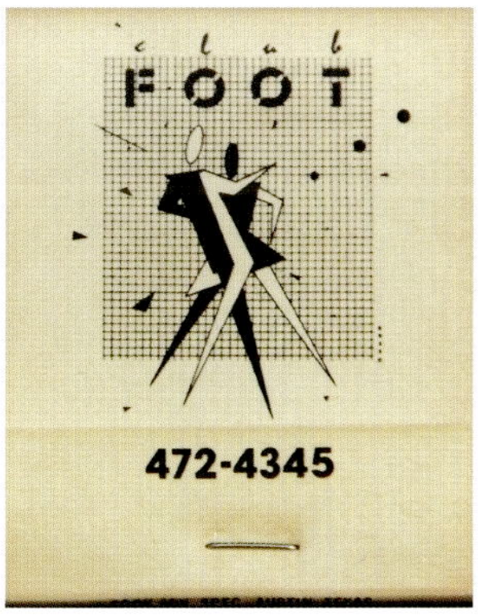

Club Foot matchbook, design by NOXX (Michael Nott).

In Austin as elsewhere, there has always been some overlap between performers and graphic artists. During Juke's first few years in town he was known more for his guitar work with Doak Snead and Butch Hancock than for his graphics; and for years Juke fronted his own band, Blackie White and the Halftones. Franklin performed with the band Ramon Ramon and the Four Daddyos, Awn is a founding member of the Uranium Savages parody band, Yeates is a guitar player, and Shelton occasionally performs on the piano. This musician-graphic artist connection was just as common in the punk and new wave era in part, no doubt, because of the DIY homemade aesthetic. Among performers generating the intermittent punk handbill was guitarist Davy Jones, who played with the Next, the Ideals, and others during Austin's punk heyday. He is best known for his work with Austin "hard-corn" punk band the Hickoids—reputedly named after an offhand remark by Jones about a dumpster-diving homeless guy in a smashed-up cowboy hat: "There's a real hickoid-looking son of a bitch." Two other musician-cum–poster practitioners active during this period were Randy "Biscuit" Turner of the Big Boys and Cam King with the Explosives.

Biscuit moved to Austin in 1970 from his hometown of Gladewater in East Texas. In the late 1970s, after performing around town in various capacities, including a stint as a Shrovinover with Awn's band the Uranium Savages, he helped found and became lead singer for the seminal hard-core punk band Big Boys. Biscuit created untold numbers of handbills for the Big Boys—handbills overflowing with unrelated found images, small drawings, collages, hand lettering, and the mismatched characters of ransom-note typography—all communicating an unmistakable sense of joyous and unfettered craziness. Unfortunately for Steve Hayden, who bought Raul's from Gonzales and Gomez in 1980, a little too much was communicated by one of Biscuit's handbills, and Hayden was arrested. The offending handbill, captioned "Hot and Bothered Men," featured the unexpurgated photo of an oily stud sporting only a cowboy hat and a hard-on.

Cam King was guitarist for the three-piece band the Explosives. Formed in 1979, the Explosives were booked regularly over the next few years by venues like Raul's and the Continental Club as an independent unit and also as Roky Erickson's

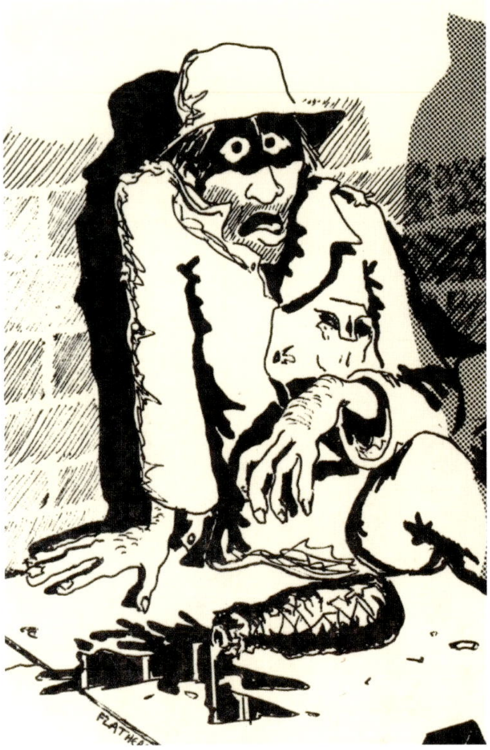

Detail of plate 107, Cam King poster.

backup band. For many of the gigs, King created a poster or handbill, signing his work with the nom de guerre "Flathead." He began with a pencil sketch and then inked in the design with a Sharpie or ballpoint pen. For text, King used press-on letters or worked with clear plastic straightedges to create his own lettering. Although he sometimes had his posters printed using the split-fountain technique, he felt no pressure to cultivate any pretense of uniformity and scrupulously avoided developing a specific style. His work in this way reflected an elemental trait of Austin poster art in general, wherein the character and themes were constantly evolving. While Austin's posterists used novel compositions to faithfully echo the feel of the music and the tenor of the advancing times, the sole constant was change—one technique invariably supplanting another and one graphic look overtaking the next.

From the 1960s to the '80s, by appropriating and adapting first the psychedelic style and symbology of San Francisco, then western themes and surrealist tendencies, and ultimately punk-rock moxie, Austin poster artists shaped our perception of cultural reality. Acknowledging horticultural reality, Guy Clark's popular paean to homegrown tomatoes extols their desirability and pricelessness; it reminds us that store-bought produce pales in comparison to what comes from our own thriving garden. And the realization of how true that is has the power to enrich our lives. Likewise, recognizing the richness in imagery and wit of so many of the posters and handbills produced in Austin can enhance appreciation of our shared heritage and revive those heady days of idealism, experimentation, tolerance, and punk rebellion, if only for a moment. As music drove the poster movement, Austin's artists elevated Texas street art to an unprecedented status and relevance. Through their powerful designs, these posterists spoke to hippies, rednecks, punks, and passersby; they provided a paper-prefiguring of every advertised performance and a dated visual trophy with which to commemorate each event after the fact. Long before computer graphics and digital art, Austin poster artists, wielding only pens, pencils, and X-Acto blades, constructed by hand a sprawling illustrated monument to Austin music and culture. They shared not only a passion for their craft and the joy of creating something clever out of nothing but also the conviction that what they were doing was important; that it made a difference. "The energy was so high at that time," says Harter; "we thought that we were going to transform the world with the posters we were doing, and of course the music. Perhaps we did."

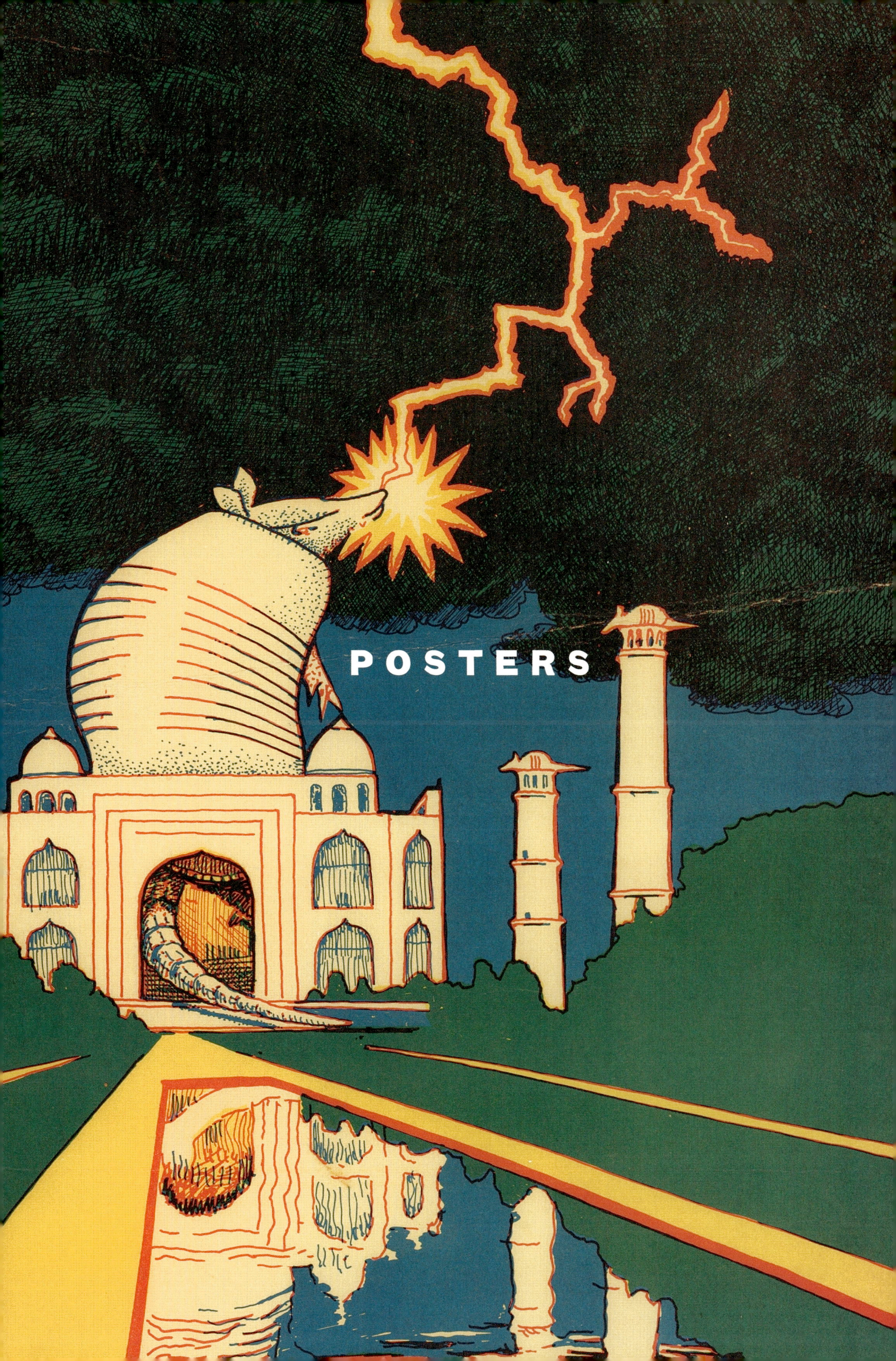

POSTERS

VULCAN GAS COMPANY

The opening of the Vulcan Gas Company in the autumn of 1967 initiated a radical shift in the cultural, musical, and artistic landscape of Austin. By booking rock acts that played original music, not just cover tunes to please the fraternity crowds, the Vulcan opened the door for psychedelic bands, most notably the 13th Floor Elevators. The club also booked the who's who of sixties blues: Mance Lipscomb, Lightnin' Hopkins, Jimmy Reed, Big Mama Thornton, Muddy Waters, and many others. European film screenings rounded out the programming, and an elaborate projection system and light show added to the visual spectacle. Because of the limited opportunities for affordable and effective advertising on radio or in local print publications, the primary means of advertising for this counterculture haven was the poster. Danny Garrett explains the impact that posters had on the psychedelic scene that emerged from the Vulcan: "When the music started, it was so unique, and the community that was interested in it was so concentrated, that the poster was very, very effective." Led first by art director Gilbert Shelton, who would leave Austin for San Francisco in 1968 and become a key figure in the world of underground comix, and then Jim Franklin, the artist who would introduce the armadillo as a symbol of the Austin underground, the Vulcan Gas Company artists laid the groundwork for the music poster in Austin. Along with Shelton and Franklin, artists such as Tony Bell, Jim Harter, and John Shelton became significant figures in this rapidly developing form of art and advertising.

Gilbert Shelton introduced to the Vulcan artists split-fountain inking, a laborious and expensive process that allows for the blending of inks in a fountain that would normally contain just a single color. The results of the process are spectacular, allowing for a neonlike effect of subtly blended colors. Jim Franklin notes that the artists paired opposing colors in order to create "vibrating complementary effects," which are at the core of psychedelic art. The Vulcan artists found a printer, Johnny Mercer, who was willing to work with split-fountain inking. Regarding Johnny Mercer and the split-fountain inking process, Gilbert Shelton says, "It's hard work. He probably didn't make much money on these things, but he got an award for Texas printer of the year!" Jim Franklin notes that the Vulcan account with Mercer was eventually suspended due to unpaid invoices, though Mercer several years later told Franklin that because their art was so remarkable, he regretted the fact that he stopped working with the artists.

Financial difficulties and increasing pressure from local law enforcement threatened the venue, and the Vulcan Gas Company finally closed its doors for good in the spring of 1970, which brought to an end a profoundly innovative era of Austin music poster art. Yet a standard would be set for poster art in Austin, and a new decade would welcome a host of young, ambitious artists inspired by the developments of the Vulcan Gas Company crew.

NEXT SPREAD

Outside the Vulcan Gas Company, winter of 1967. Photograph by Belmer Wright. Photograph courtesy of South Austin Popular Culture Center.

1 Joe Fish
2 Charlie Prichard
3 Shirley Becker
4 Angela Strehli
5 Heddy Lawrie
6 Bob Tom Reed
7 Houston White
8 "Stick" Whipple
9 Doug Brown
10 Unknown
11 Rick Speed
12 Judy Brown
13 Spencer Perskin
14 Susan & Sativa Perskin
15 Carlyne Majewski
16 George Majewski
17 Gary Scanlon
18 Cynthia Holden
19 Bob Brown
20 Kay Shepard
21 Marilyn Guinn
22 Ed Guinn
23 Gilbert Shelton
24 Sammy Ivy
25 Steve Patrochyk
26 Steve Plasky
27 Carolyn Hyde
28 Don Hyde
29 Jerry Green
30 Roger Baker

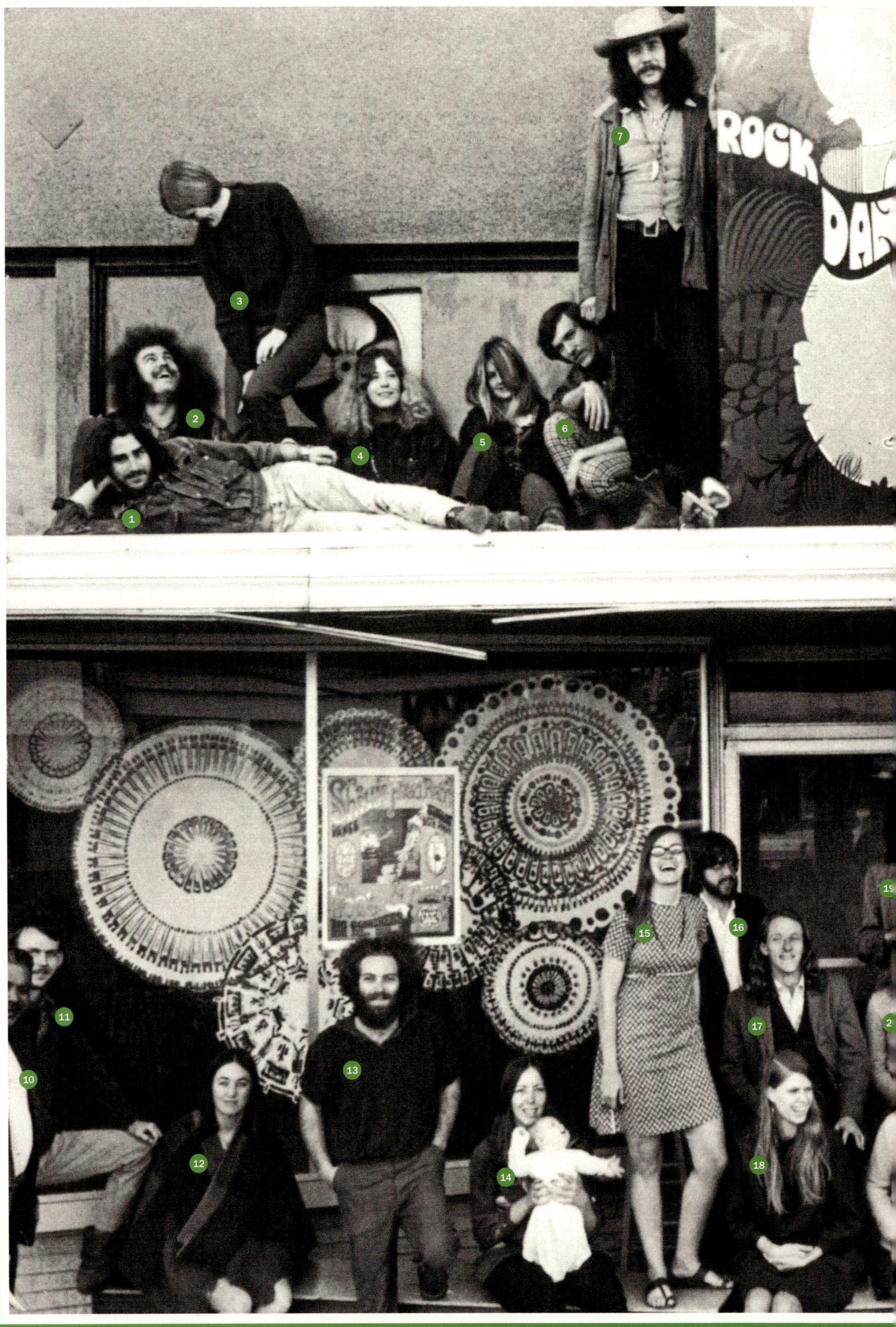
ROCK
1
2
3
4
5
6
7
10
11
12
13
14
15
16
17
18

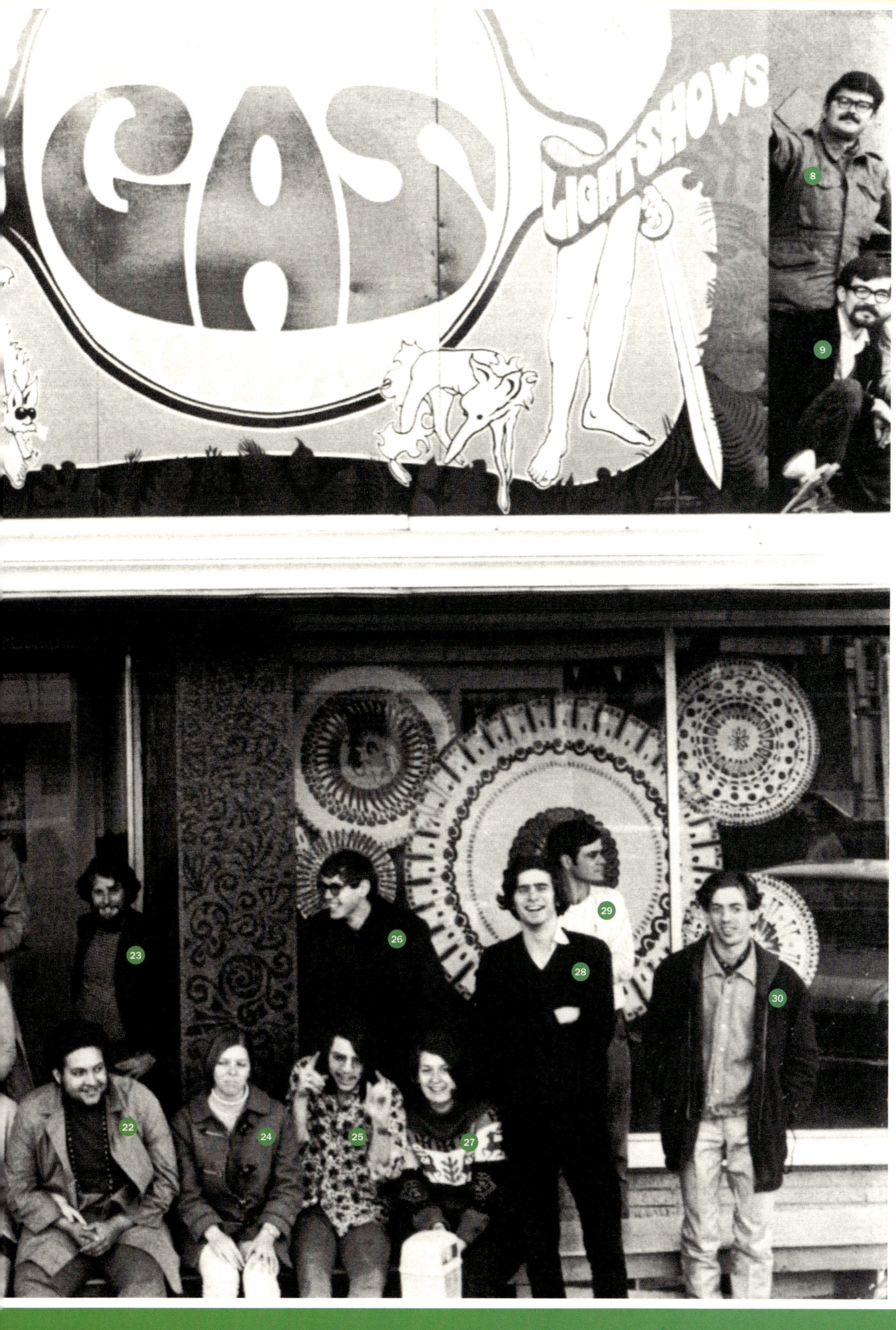
LIGHTSHOWS
8
9
22
23
24
25
26
27
28
29
30

1 GILBERT SHELTON & TONY BELL. Conqueroo & The Swiss Movement. Vulcan Gas Company. November 10 & 11, 1967. 21.75" × 17.5". © Gilbert Shelton & Tony Bell.

This collaboration between Shelton and Bell eschews radical psychedelia in favor of bold lettering that recalls Old West bond certificates and a central image that echoes early twentieth-century erotic photography.

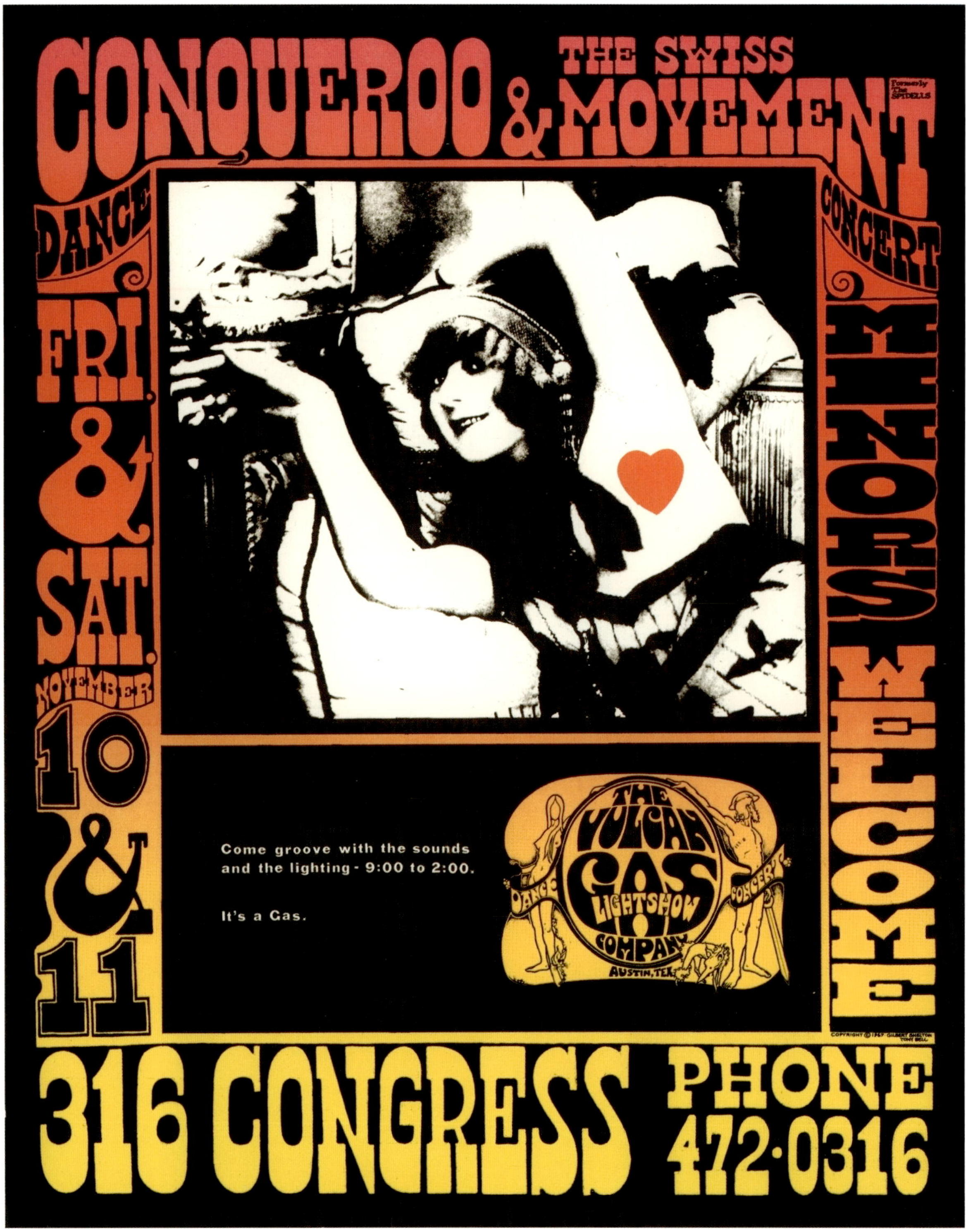

2 GILBERT SHELTON. The Golden Dawn & The Thingies. Vulcan Gas Company. November 24 & 25, 1967. 28.5" × 22.5". © Gilbert Shelton.

Shelton's mind-blown subjects prefigure the characters of his wildly popular comic *The Fabulous Furry Freak Brothers*.

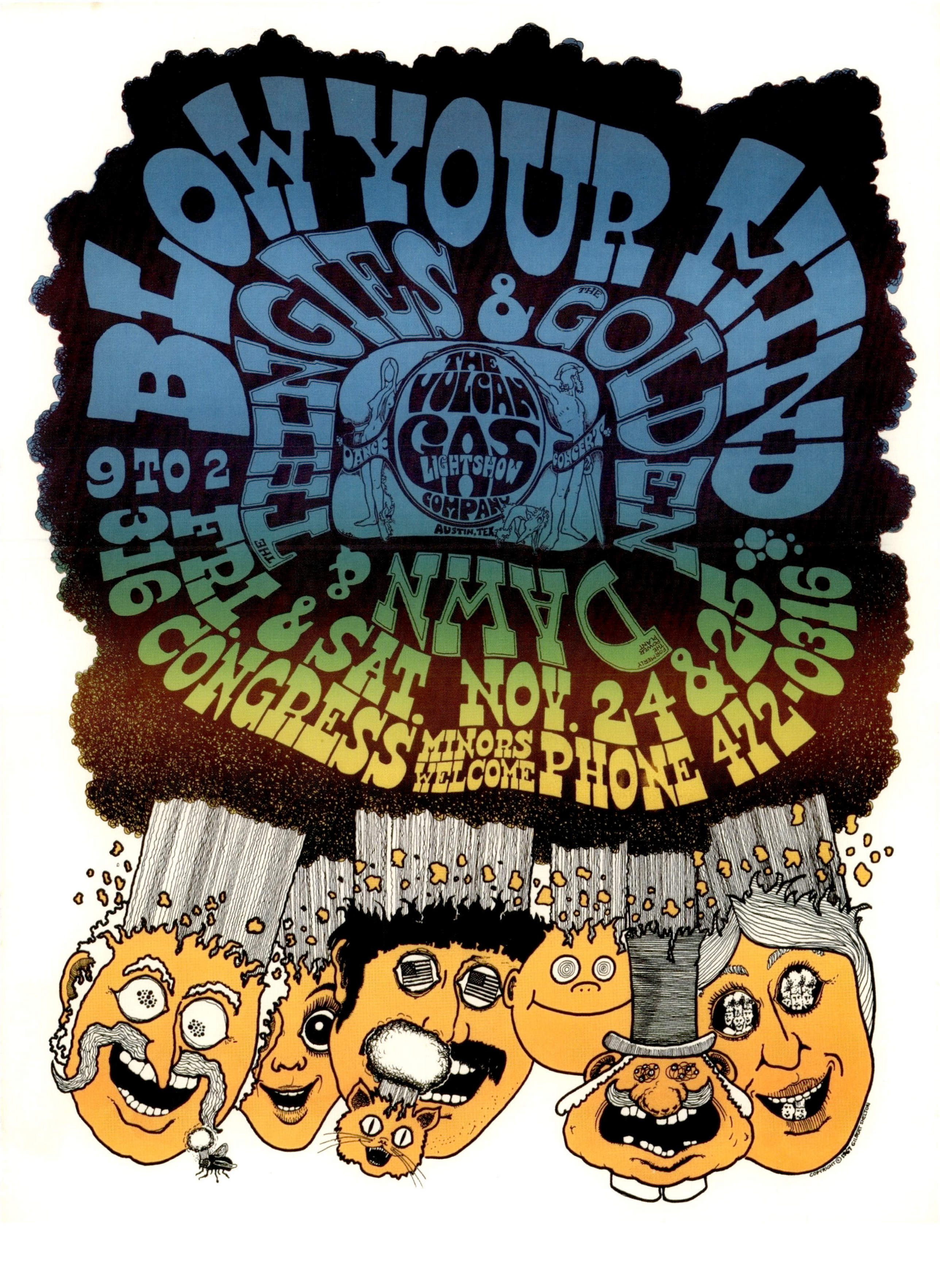

3 TONY BELL. Lightnin' Hopkins & Conqueroo. Vulcan Gas Company. December 1 & 2, 1967. 24" × 20". © Tony Bell.

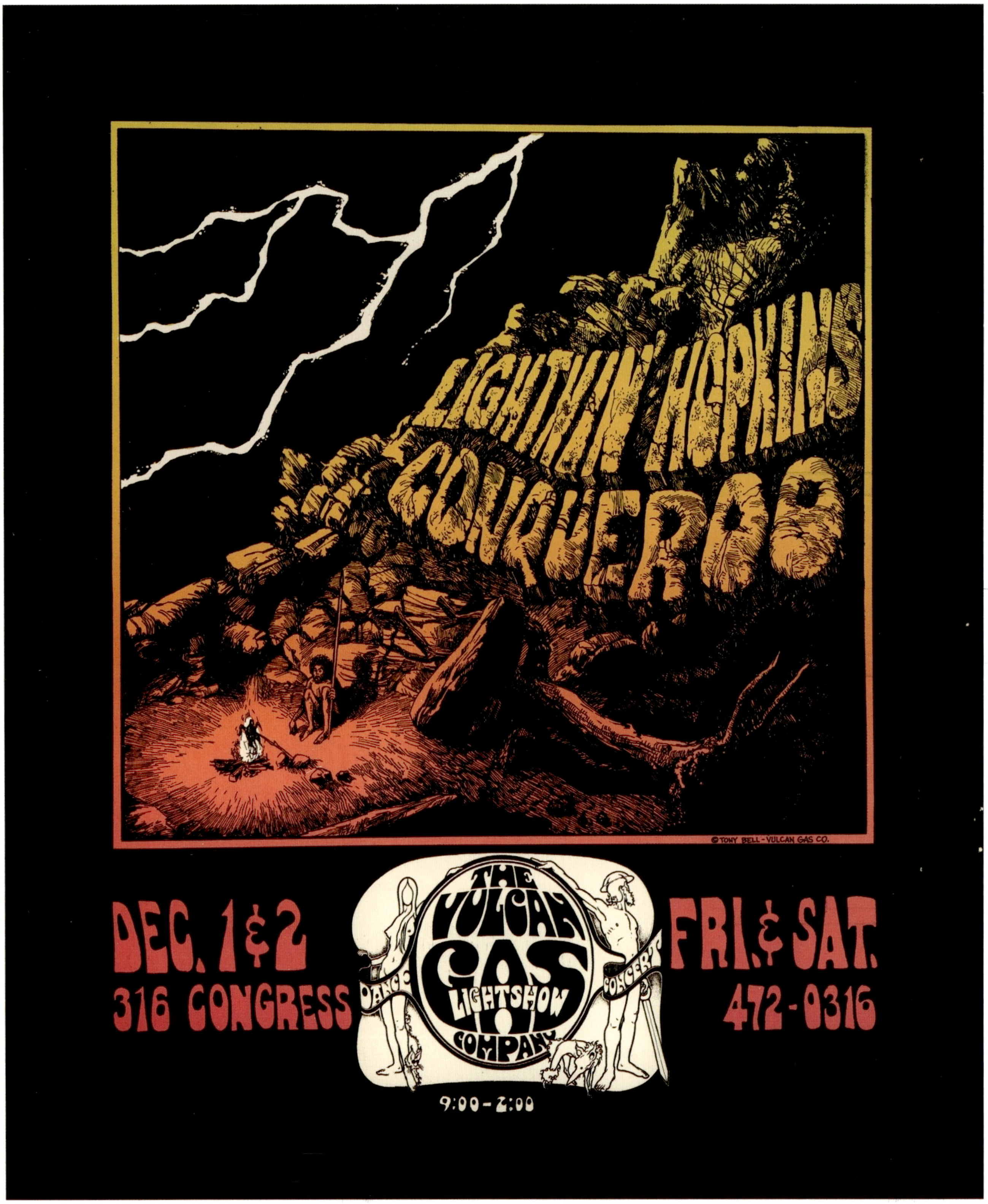

4 GILBERT SHELTON. The 13th Floor Elevators, The Swiss Movement, The South Canadian Overflow, & Shiva's Headband. Vulcan Gas Company. December 8–10, 1967. 28.5" × 22.5". © Gilbert Shelton.

The word "pot" emerges from the maze of brainlike matter in this poster for the 13th Floor Elevators, Austin's premier psychedelic band.

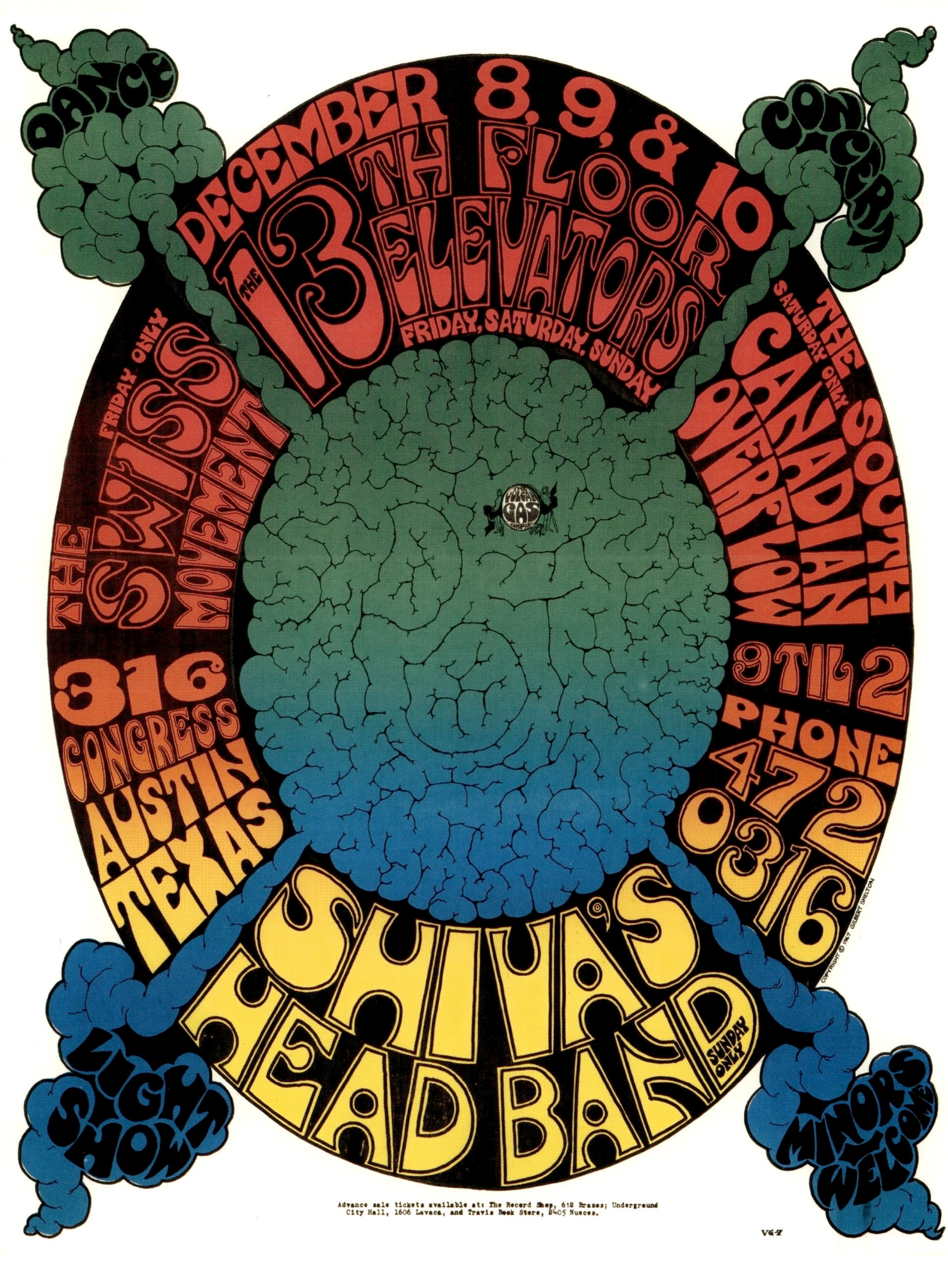

5 GILBERT SHELTON. Conqueroo & The Afro Caravan. December 22 & 23, 1967. Conqueroo & The Golden Dawn. December 29, 1967. Shiva's Headband & The Golden Dawn. December 30, 1967. Shiva's Headband & Conqueroo. December 31, 1967. Vulcan Gas Company. 28" × 21.5". © Gilbert Shelton.

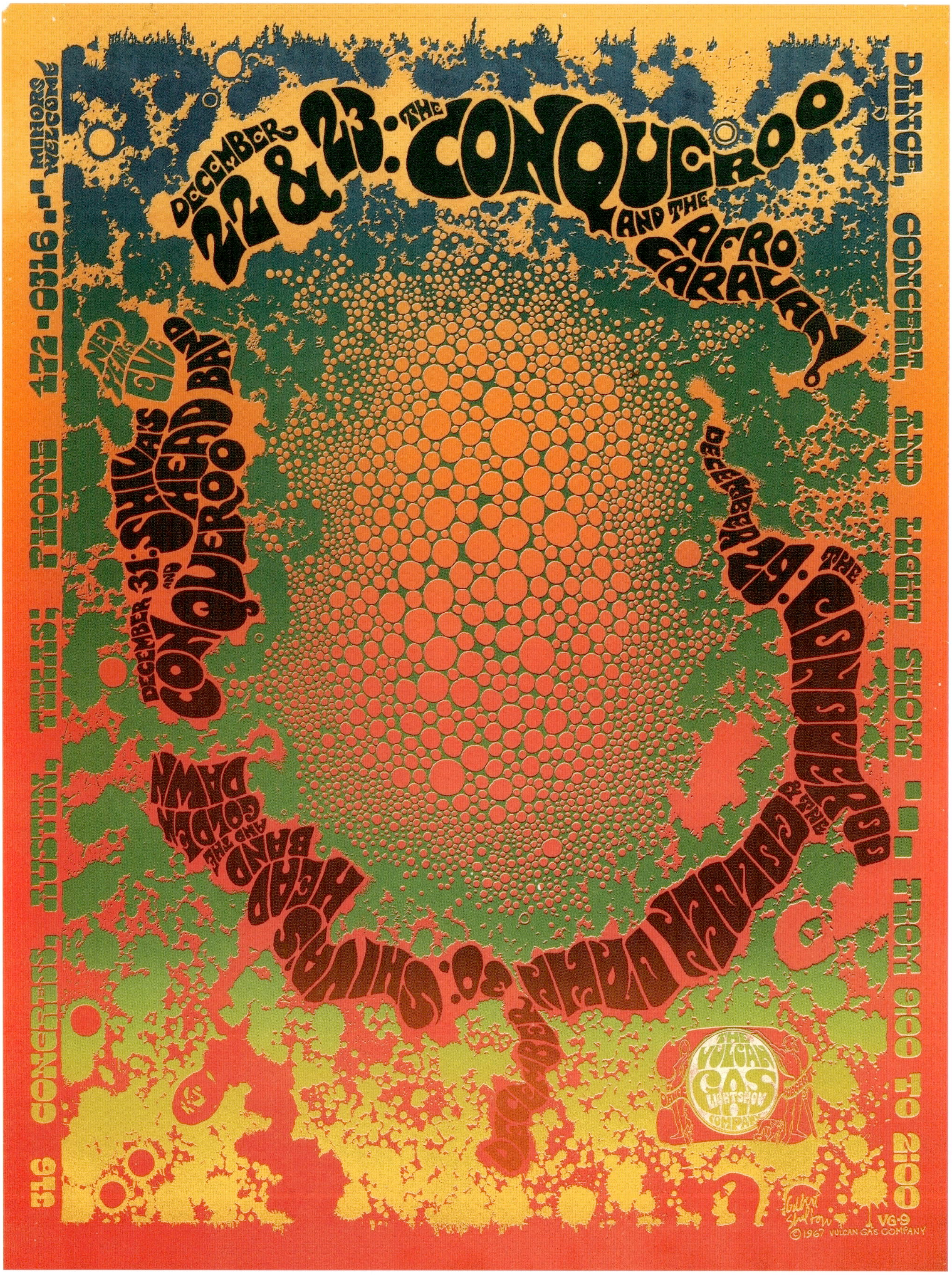

6 GILBERT SHELTON. Shiva's Headband & Rubaiyat. April 12 & 13, 1968. Conqueroo & Sleepy John Estes. April 19 & 20, 1968. Vulcan Gas Company. 27" × 21.5". © Gilbert Shelton.

The poster features a collage with a beheaded James Joyce playing a parlor guitar, Arthur Godfrey's head(s) in the syringe, and Oat Willie, a character invented by Joe Brown and Gilbert Shelton who became the namesake for the famous Austin head shop.

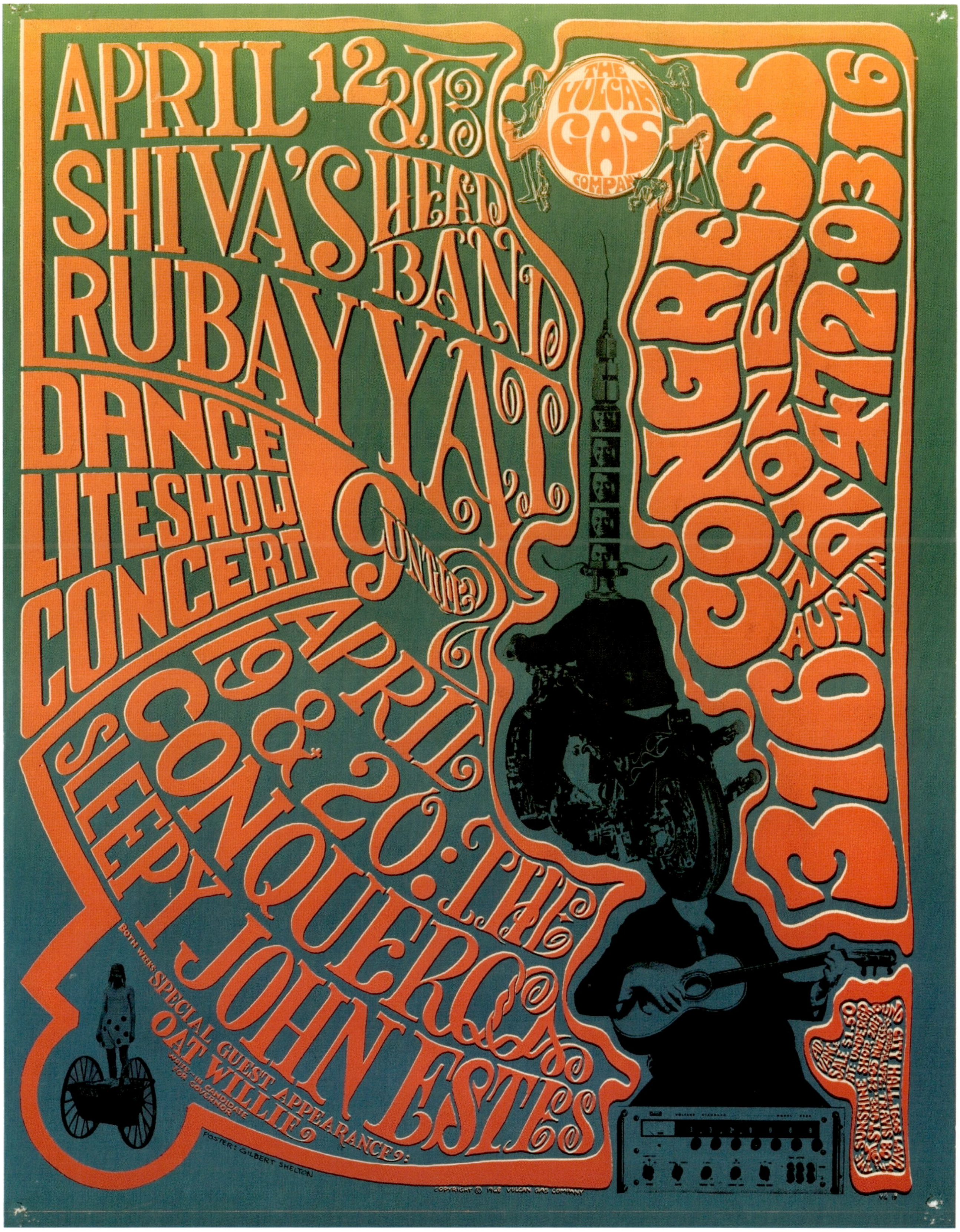

7 GILBERT SHELTON. Conqueroo & Shiva's Headband. May 10, 1968. Canned Heat, Conqueroo, & Shiva's Headband. May 11, 1968. Vulcan Gas Company. 27.5" × 22". © Gilbert Shelton.

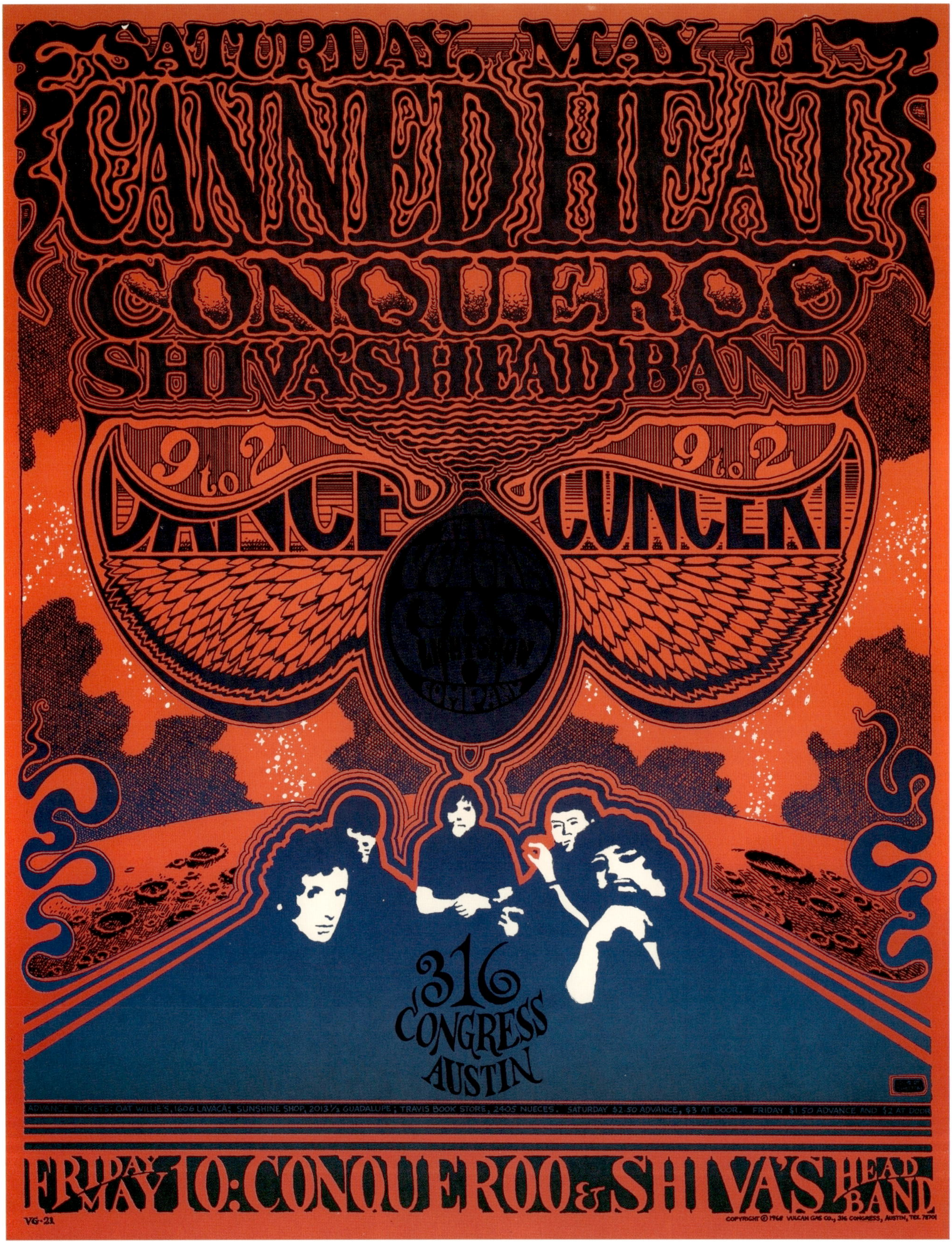

8 GILBERT SHELTON & JIM FRANKLIN. Conqueroo & Bubble Puppy. Vulcan Gas Company. May 31 & June 1, 1968. 7" × 5". © Gilbert Shelton & Jim Franklin.

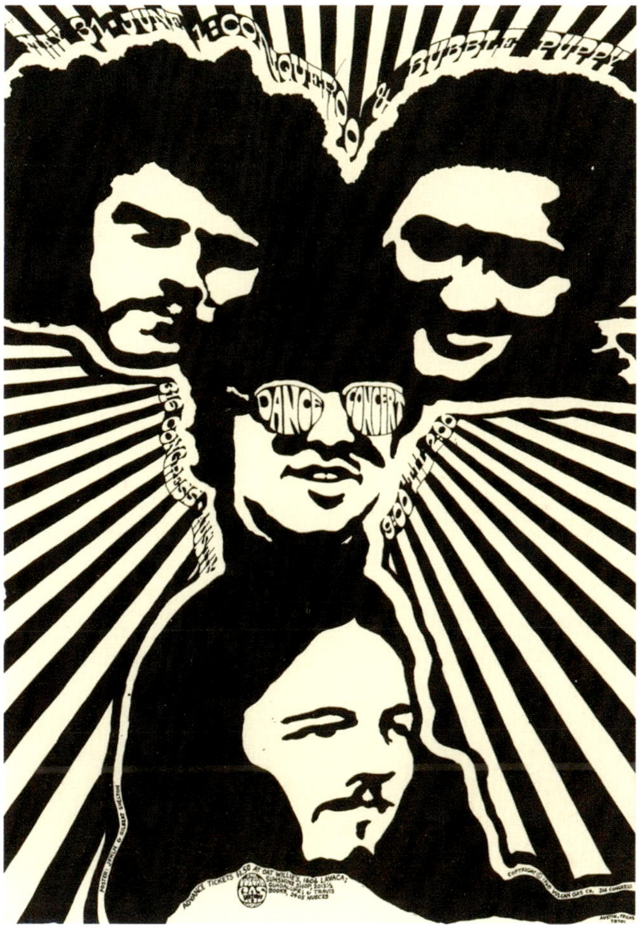

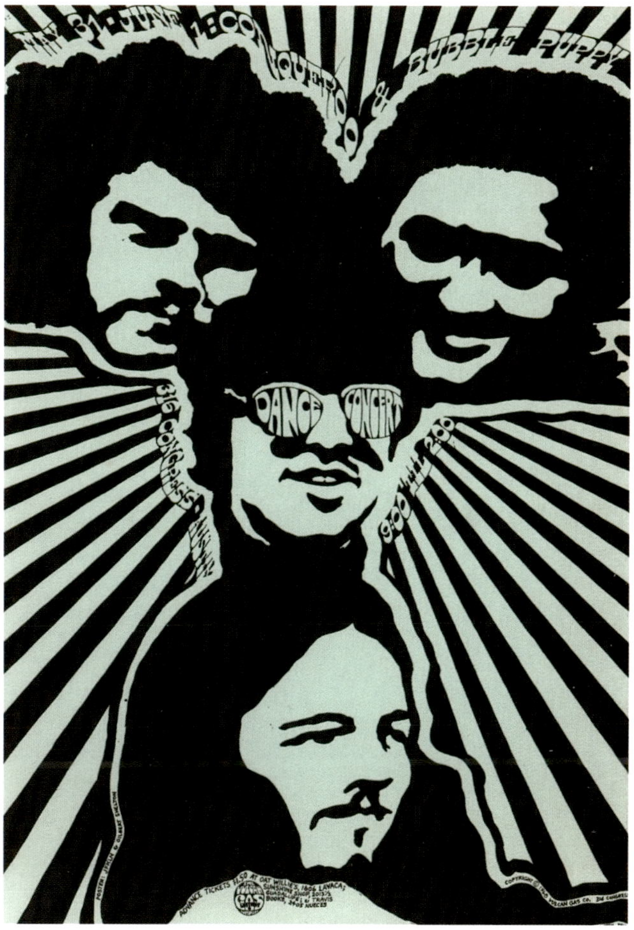

9 JIM FRANKLIN. Shiva's Headband, Conqueroo, & Rubaiyat. February 16 & 17, 1968. Lightnin' Hopkins & Conqueroo. February 26 & 27, 1968. Vulcan Gas Company. 28.25" × 22". © Jim Franklin.

Franklin notes that the hot plate represents Lightnin' Hopkins. Because of segregation in the South, black traveling blues performers often had to bring their own provisions for cooking while on the road.

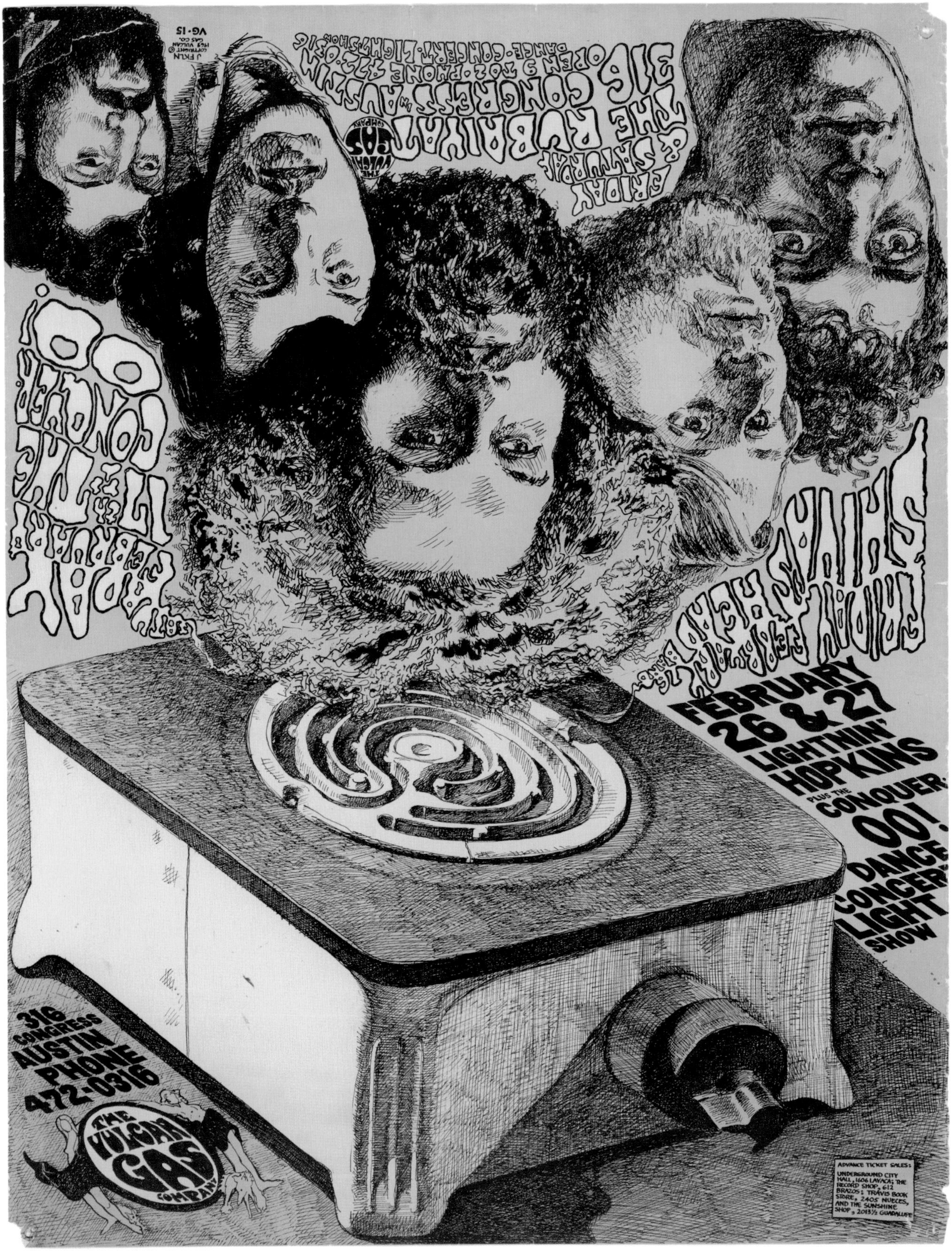

10 JIM FRANKLIN. Shiva's Headband & Bubble Puppy. Vulcan Gas Company. December 6 & 7, 1968. 9.5" × 9". © Jim Franklin.

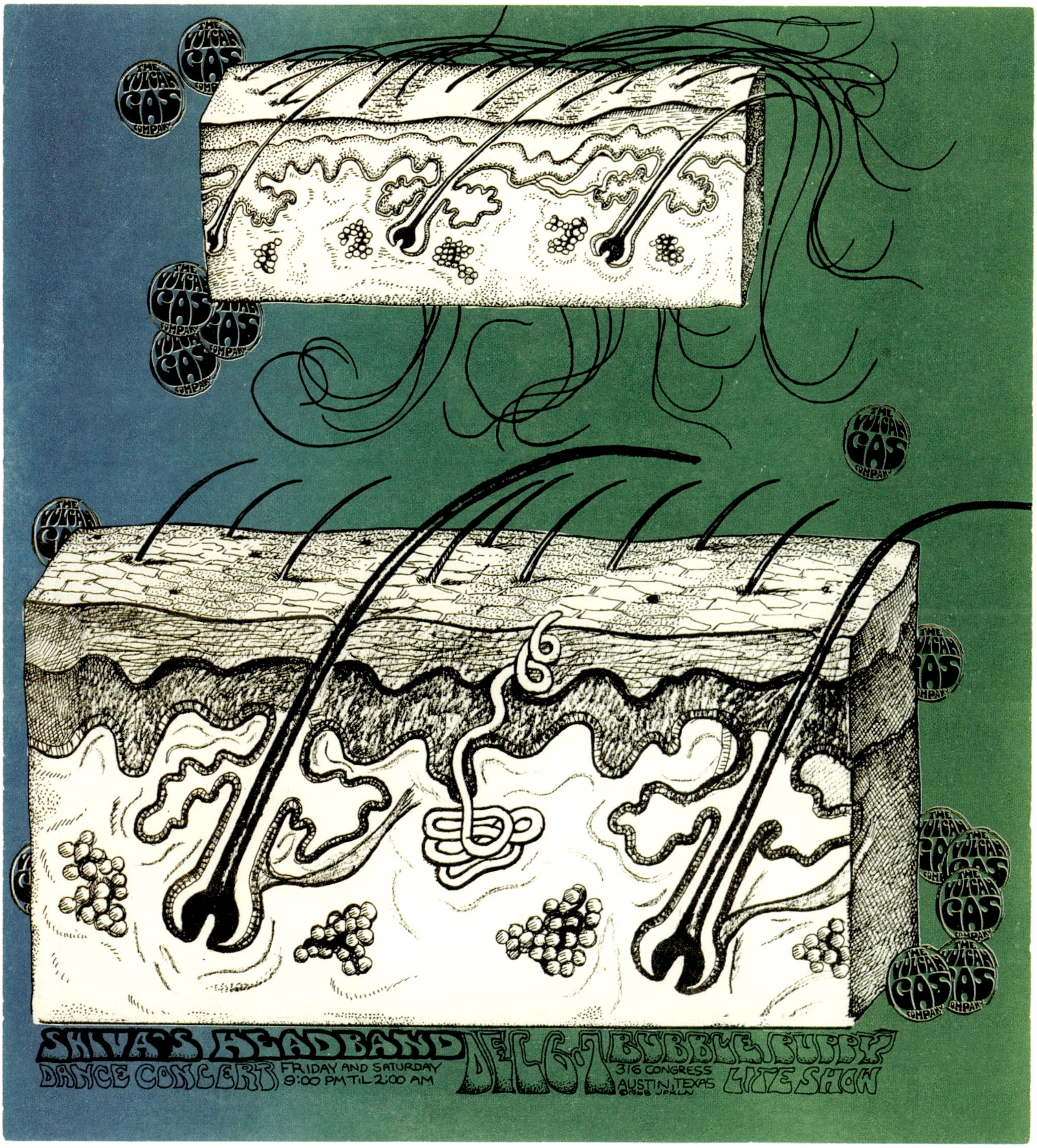

11 JIM FRANKLIN. Ramon, Ramon and the Four Daddyos, Water Brothers, Texas Rangers, & Crowbar. Vulcan Gas Company. October 10 & 11, 1969. 25" × 20".

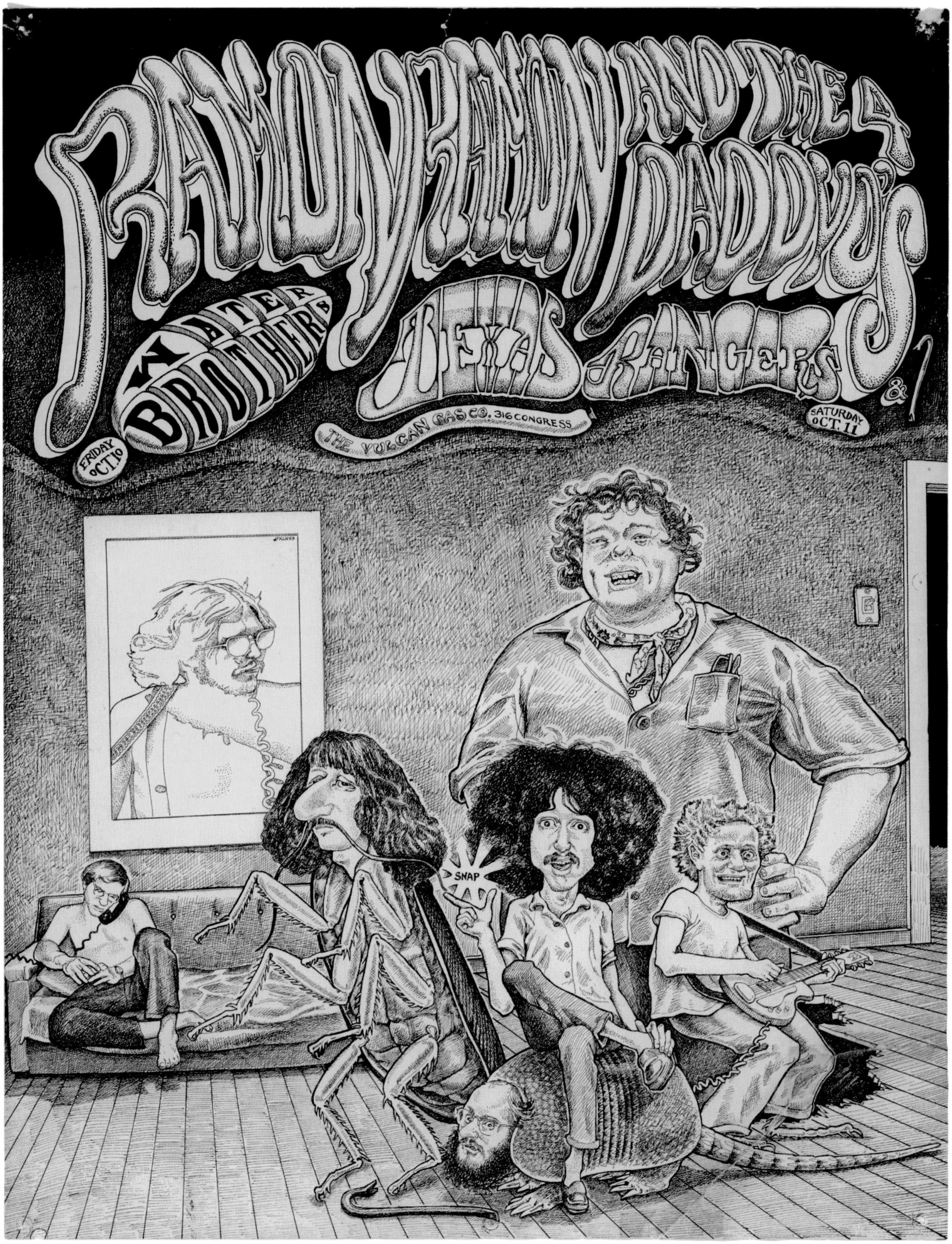

12 JIM FRANKLIN. New Atlantis. August 12, 1969. Ramon, Ramon & Jomo. August 13, 1969. Mother Earth & Shiva's Headband. August 15 & 16, 1969. Vulcan Gas Company. 9" × 6.5". © Jim Franklin.

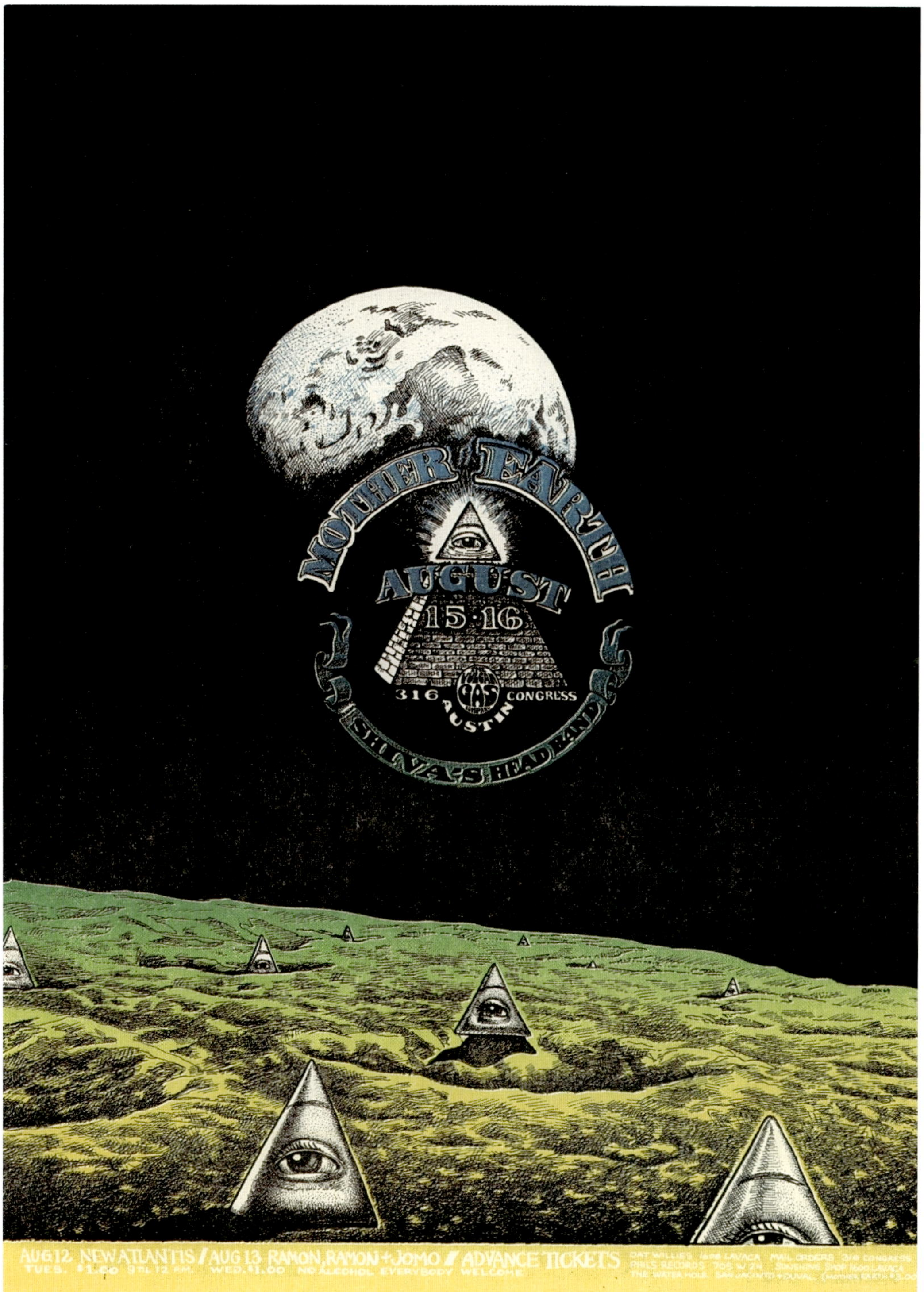

13 JIM FRANKLIN. Fugs & Shiva's Headband. Vulcan Gas Company. February 21 & 22, 1969. 11" × 8.5". © Jim Franklin.

The downtown Austin skyline is seen uprooted by a massive toilet. The poster reflects the cultural upheaval that shook the city in the late 1960s as psychedelic music and lifestyles emerged in a town that was mostly known for legislation and Longhorn football.

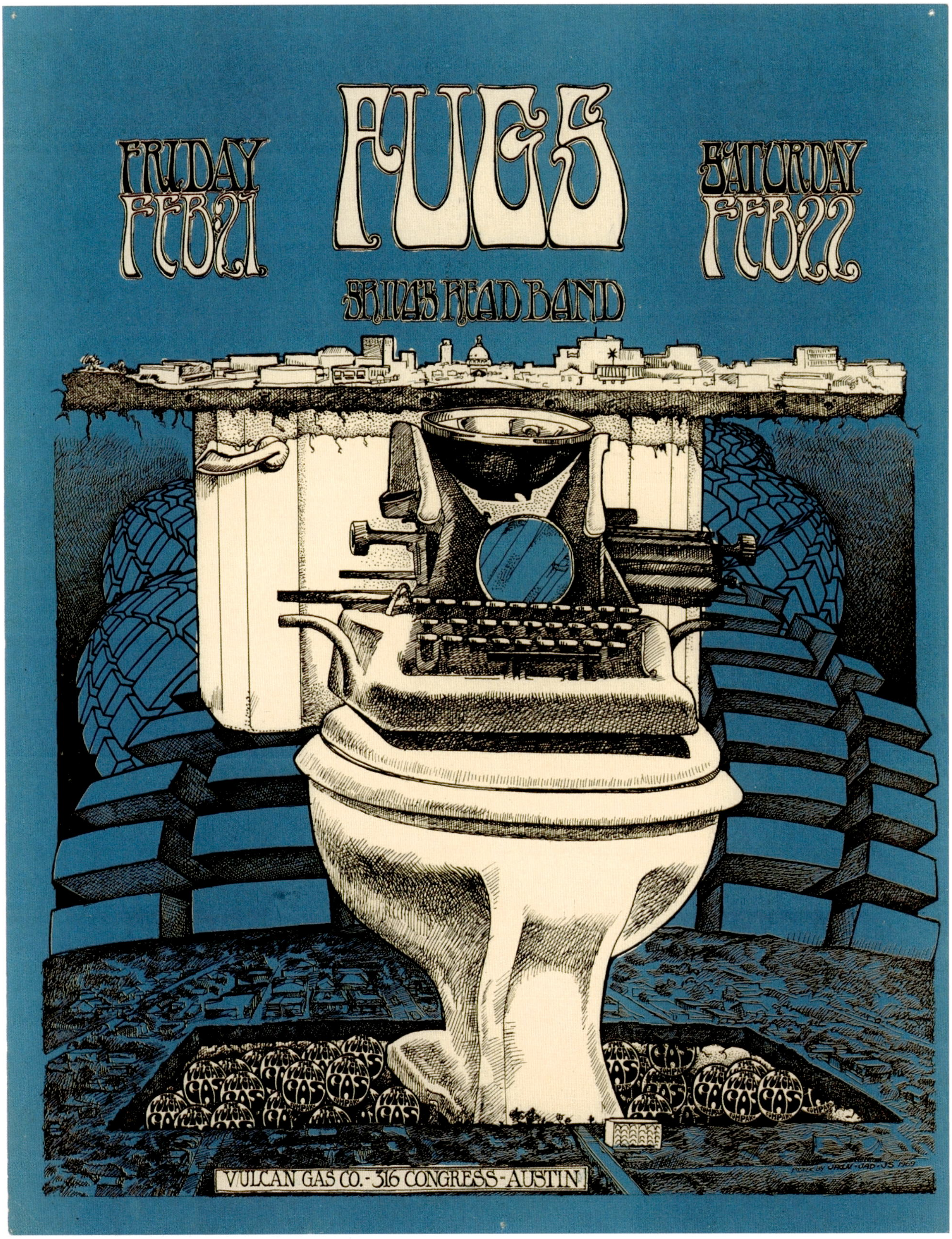

14 JIM FRANKLIN. The Velvet Underground, Ramon, Ramon and the Four Daddyos, Crowbar, & Water Brothers. Vulcan Gas Company. October 23–25, 1969. 10.5" × 8.5". © Jim Franklin.

Franklin recalls a conversation with Lou Reed of the Velvet Underground at a diner following one of the concerts. Reed questioned Franklin's choice of a tomb for the poster's central image, noting that the Velvet Underground was a happy band.

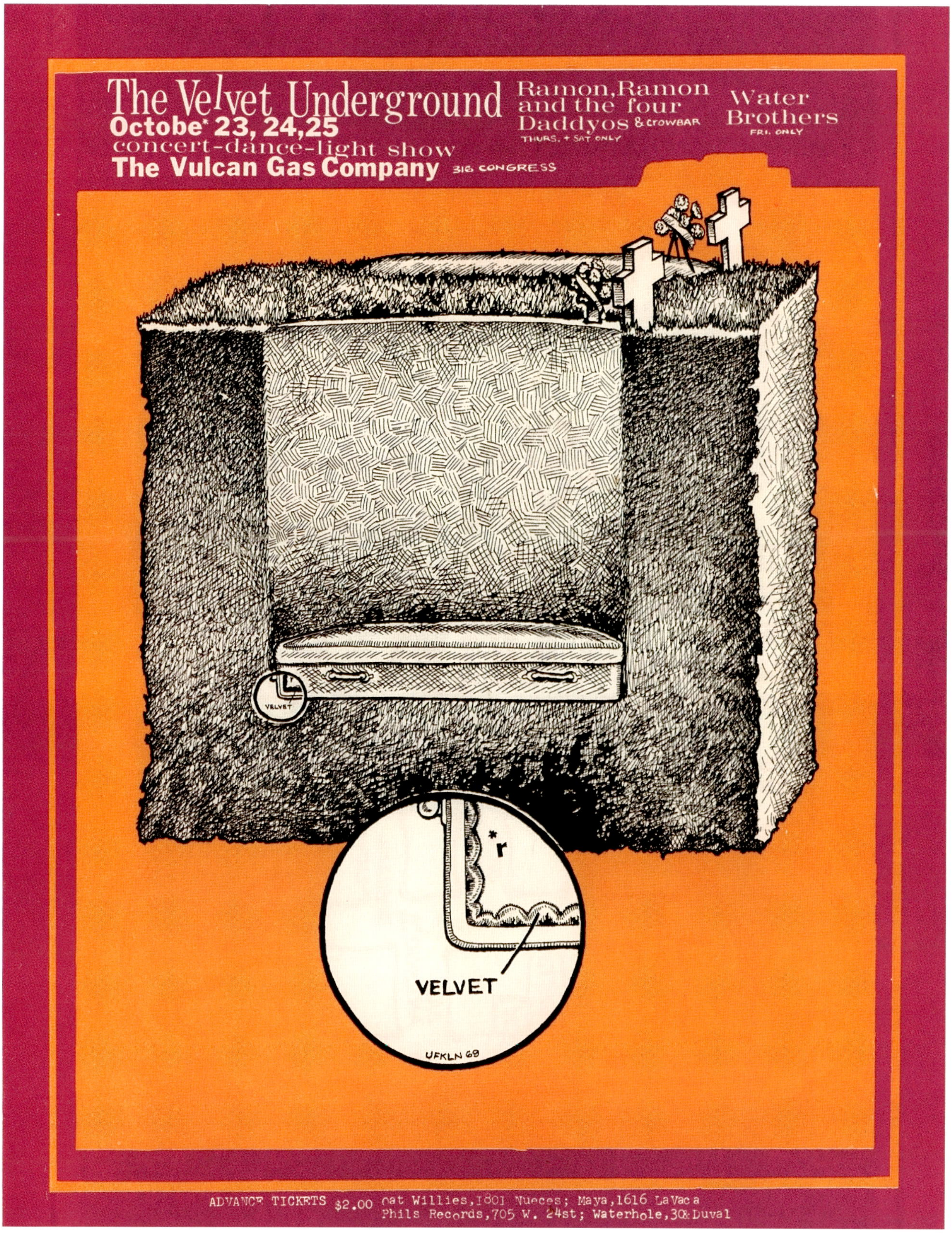

15 JIM HARTER & JIM FRANKLIN. Shiva's Headband & Onion Creek. Vulcan Gas Company. July 4 & 5, 1969. 11" × 8". © Jim Harter & Jim Franklin.

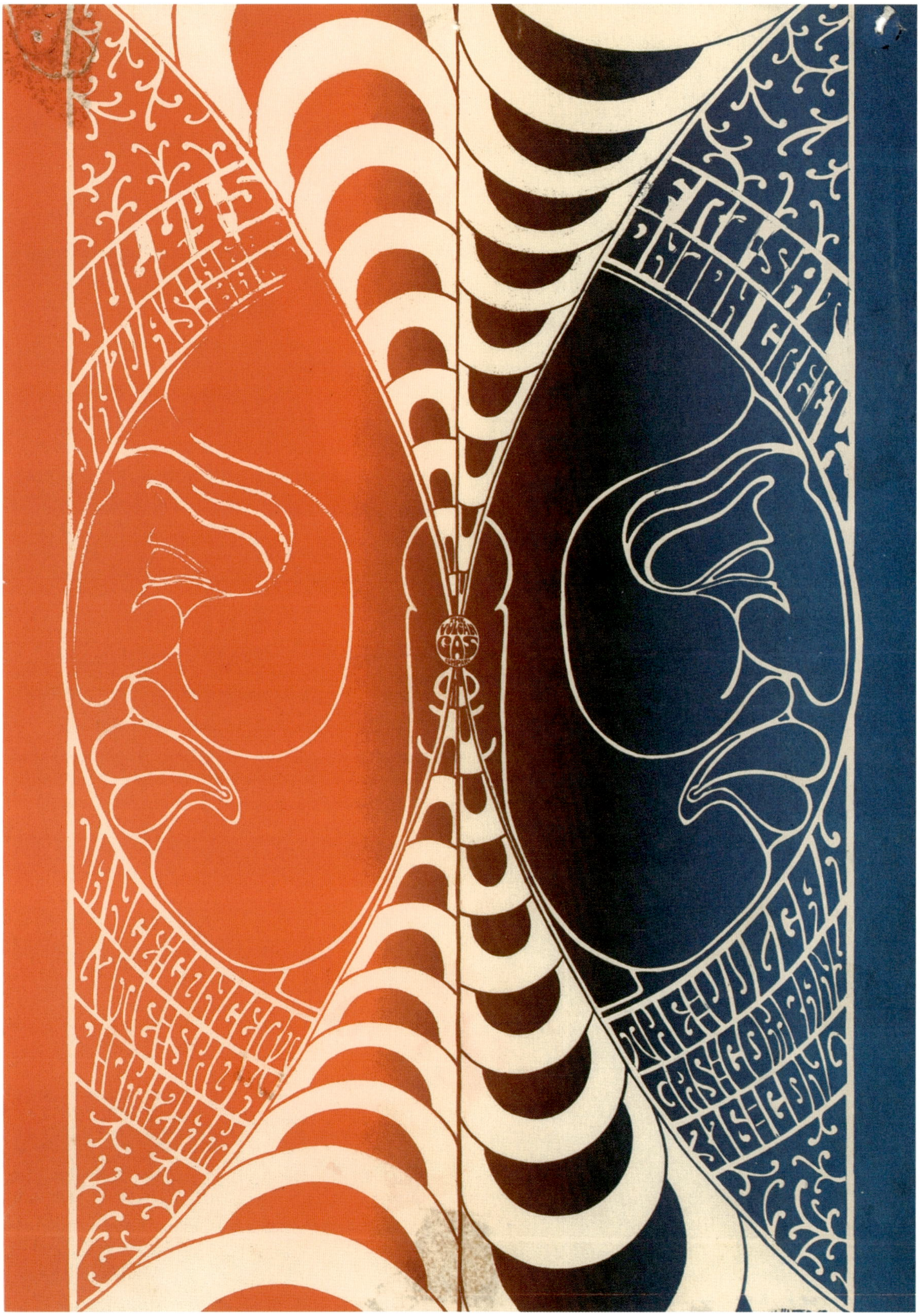

16 JIM HARTER. New Moan Hey, Onion Creek, & Shiva's Headband. Vulcan Gas Company. July 18 & 19, 1969. 11.5" × 8". © Jim Harter.

Harter describes this poster as a work that recalls a monastic procession that is accompanied by nineteenth-century French organ music. These monks, however, are smoking joints (new-mown "hay"). Harter explains that the lettering for his Vulcan posters was inspired by Austrian Jugendstil artist Alfred Roller, a common influence for poster artists of the era.

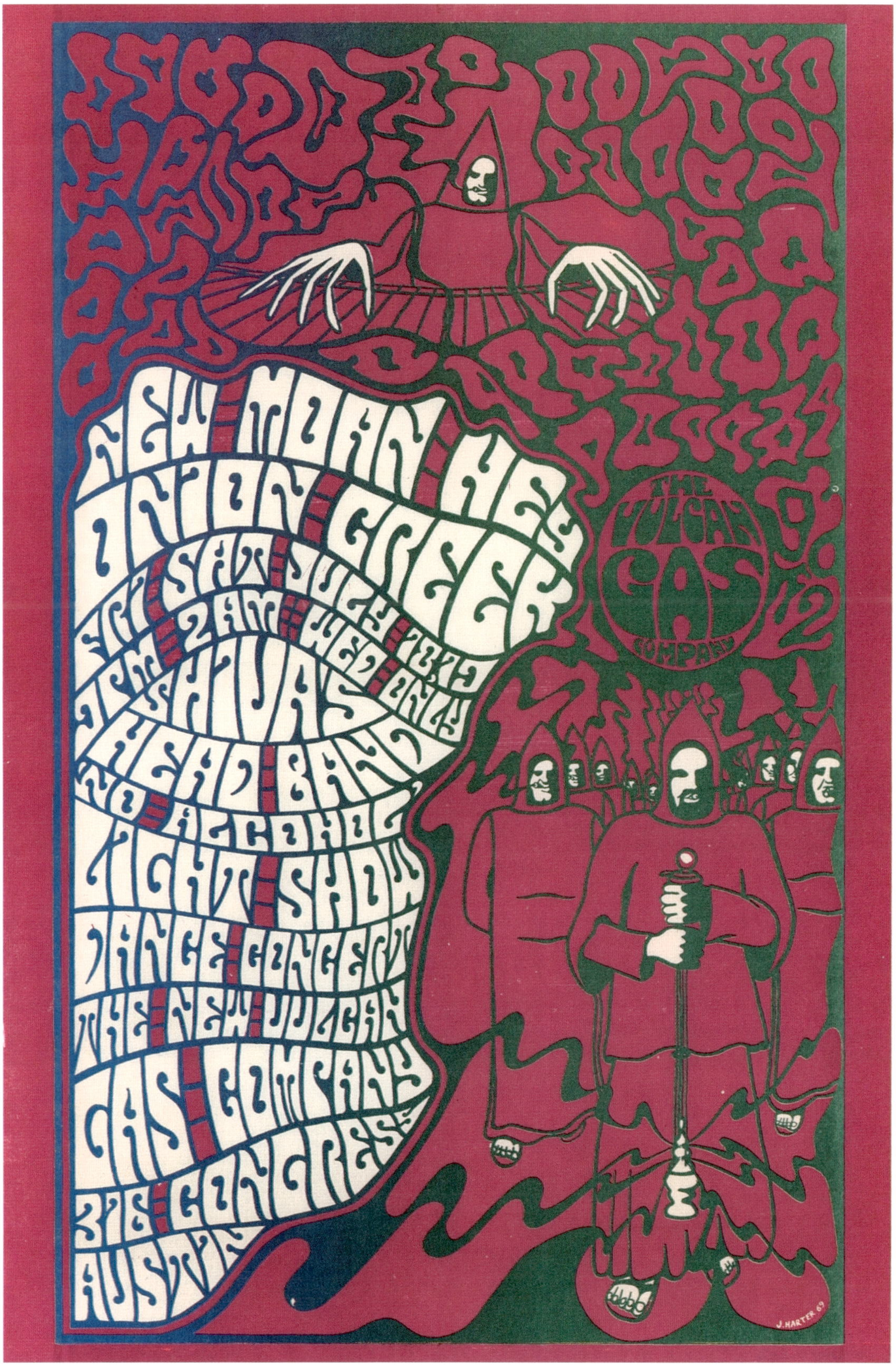

17 JOHN SHELTON. Shiva's Headband & Sunnyland Special. Vulcan Gas Company. April 11 & 12, 1969. 10.75" × 7". © John Shelton.

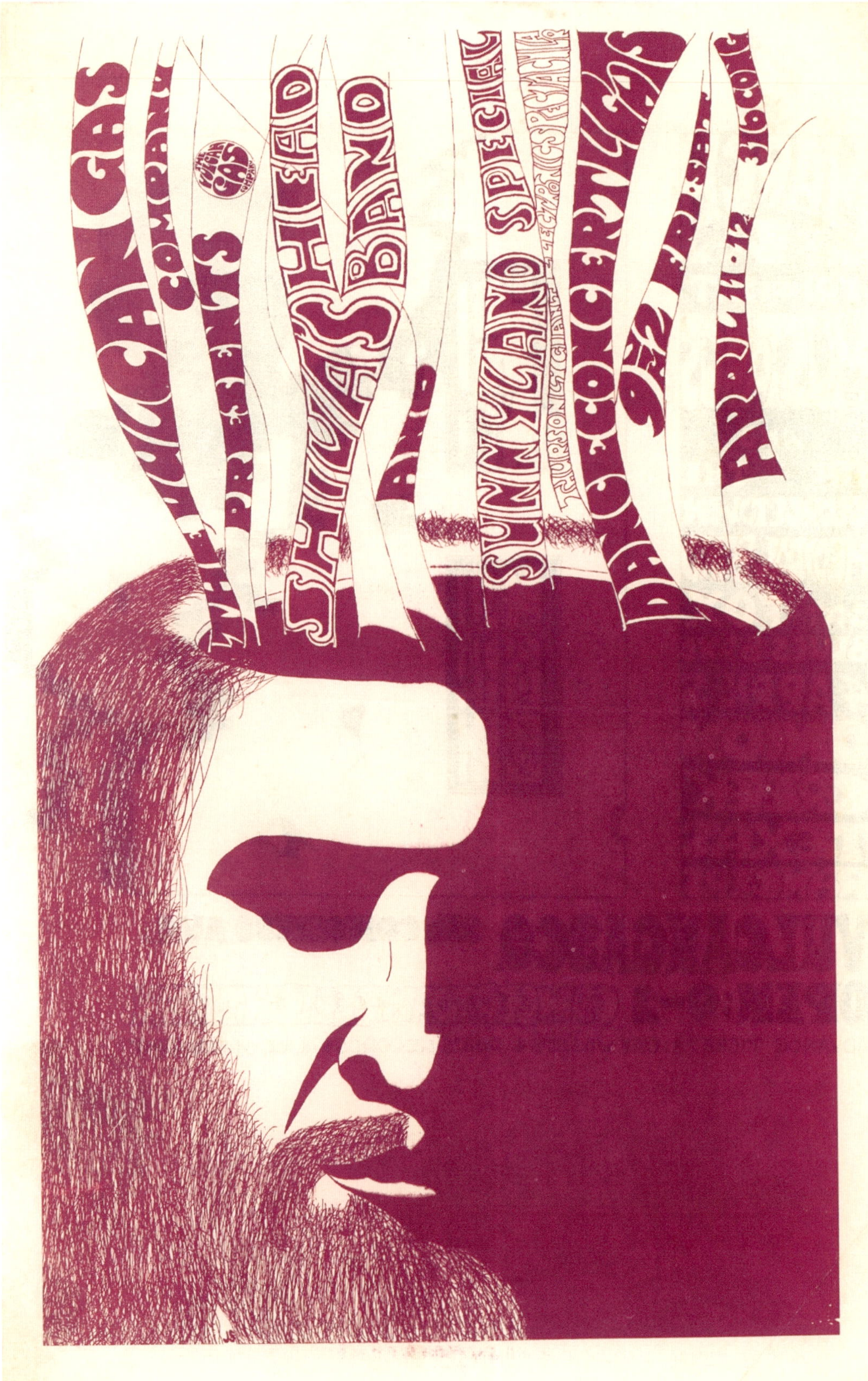

18 JOHN SHELTON. Johnny Winter, African Descent, & Hub City Movers. Vulcan Gas Company. March 10 & 11, 1970. 22" × 14". © John Shelton.

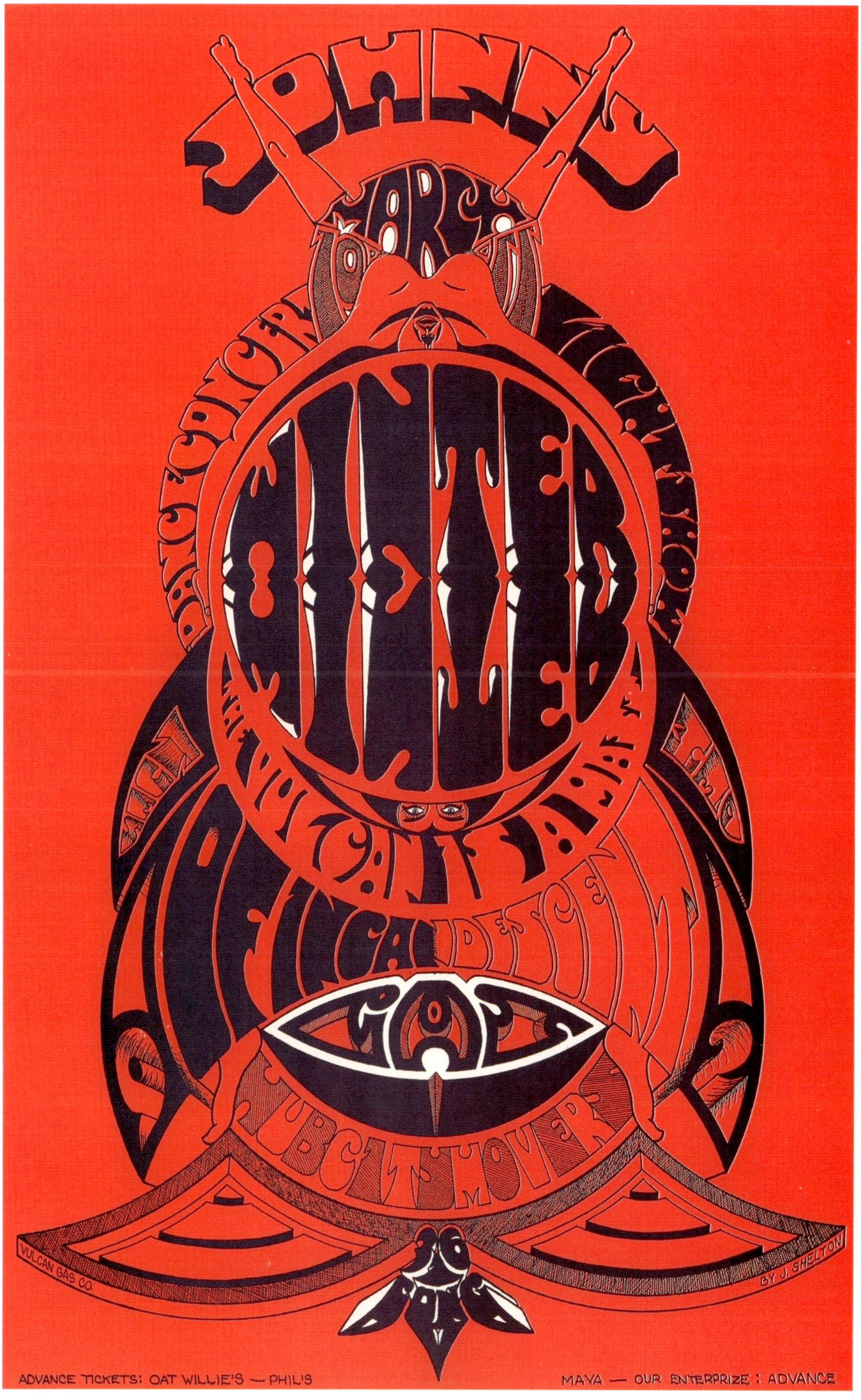

BLUES PORTRAITS

Throughout the 1950s and '60s, blues, rhythm and blues, soul, and gospel performances were often promoted with boxing-style posters. Featuring package bills with an overwhelming list of talent, the posters followed rather predictable but effective design patterns with masterful split-fountain "rainbow" inking and stock publicity photos of the performers.

In January 1968 Jim Franklin featured a portrait of Mance Lipscomb in his poster for the Navasota native's Vulcan Gas Company performance. Lipscomb, whose picking and singing attracted audiences throughout the decade to Kenneth Threadgill's North Lamar outpost for folk and blues music, naturally fell into the progressive booking at the Vulcan Gas Company. With master portraitist and blues aficionado Franklin producing posters for the Vulcan, the proliferation of blues portraits in Austin music posters began.

By the 1970s Austin was a prime destination for the great blues performers. The Armadillo World Headquarters, the Ritz Theatre, and Antone's featured the blues on their stages on any given night. Portraiture was a consistent feature of blues concert posters throughout the decade, culminating in the posters produced by Danny Garrett for Antone's, the club that cemented Austin's reputation as a blues town. Danny Garrett notes that Antone's owner, Clifford Antone, "absolutely prescribed that every poster be a portrait." Antone demanded respectful portraits that were free of exaggeration or comic touches. Garrett explains the process of acquiring source material for portraits: "When we did do portraits, whether it be a bust shot or full figure, we always strived to get something other than publicity stills that their [the musicians'] management would hand out because these were common currency. So that's why we would turn to people like [Austin-based photographer] Burton Wilson, who was extremely helpful and accommodating." Jim Franklin's adaptations of Wilson's photograph of Big Joe Williams are strong examples of this exchange among local visual artists.

19 JIM FRANKLIN. Mance Lipscomb & Conqueroo. Vulcan Gas Company. January 19 & 20, 1968. 28" × 22". © Jim Franklin.

Navasota, Texas, bluesman Mance Lipscomb sits at the bottom of the poster while Charlie Prichard, guitarist for Conqueroo and, according to Franklin, the inspiration for Gilbert Shelton's character Fat Freddy from his underground comic *The Fabulous Furry Freak Brothers*, floats above.

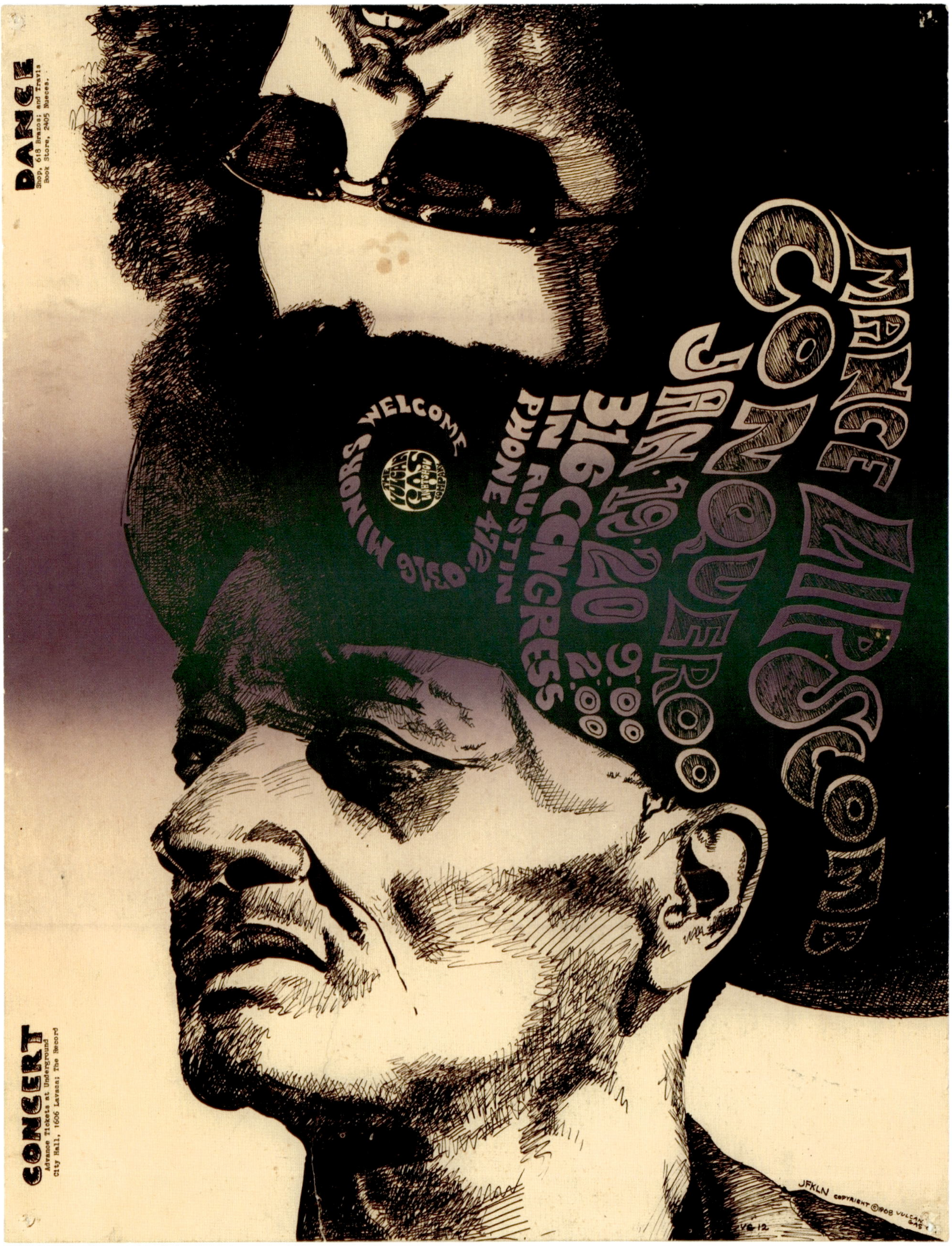

20 UNKNOWN ARTIST. Sun Ra. Armadillo World Headquarters. November 8, 1978. 11" × 8.5".

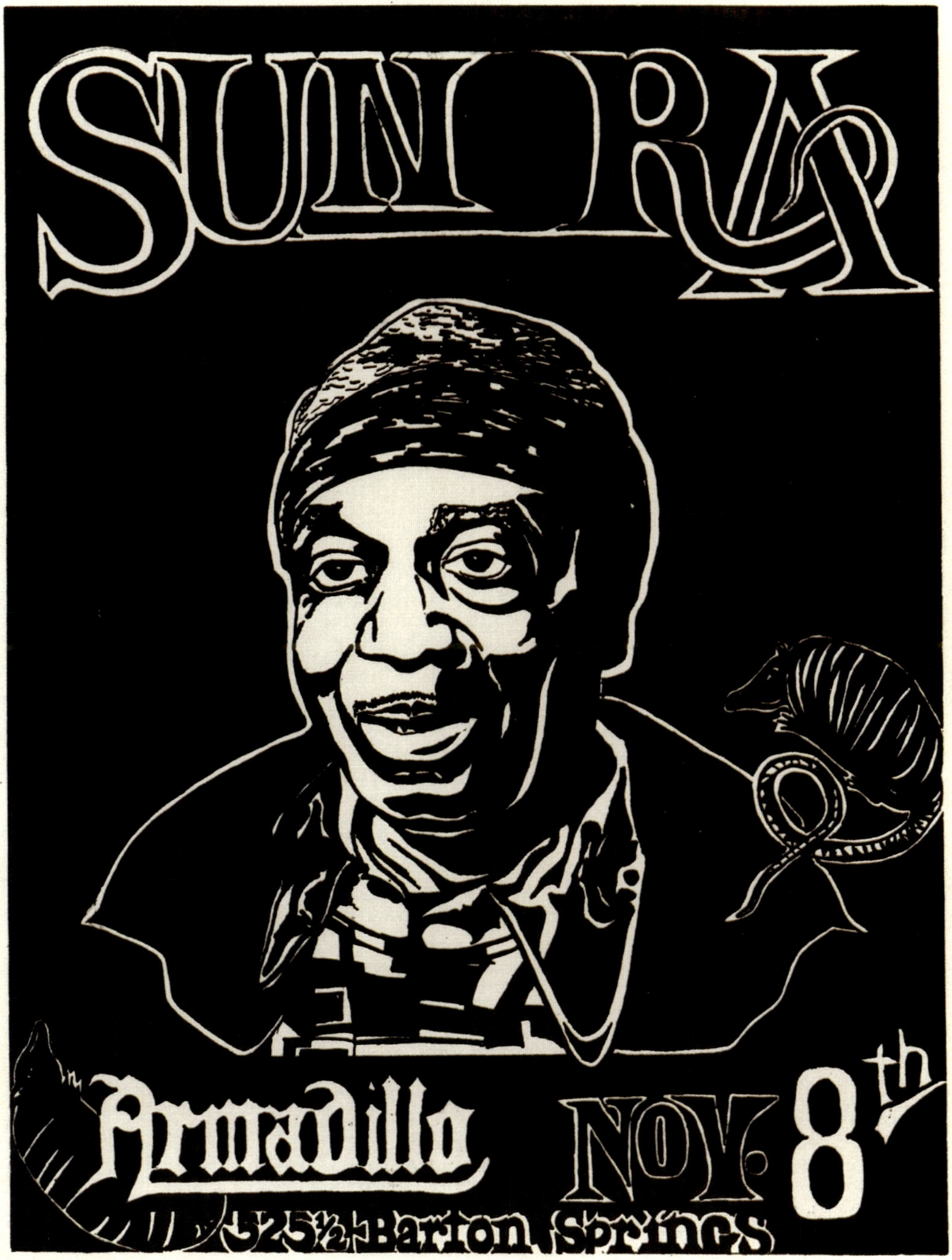

21 JIM FRANKLIN. Big Joe Williams & Sky Blues. Vulcan Gas Company. September 27 & 28, 1968. 9" × 7". © Jim Franklin.

Franklin's portrait of Big Joe Williams and collage on the opposite page are based on a photograph taken by Burton Wilson after a dinner at East Austin's Victory Grill.

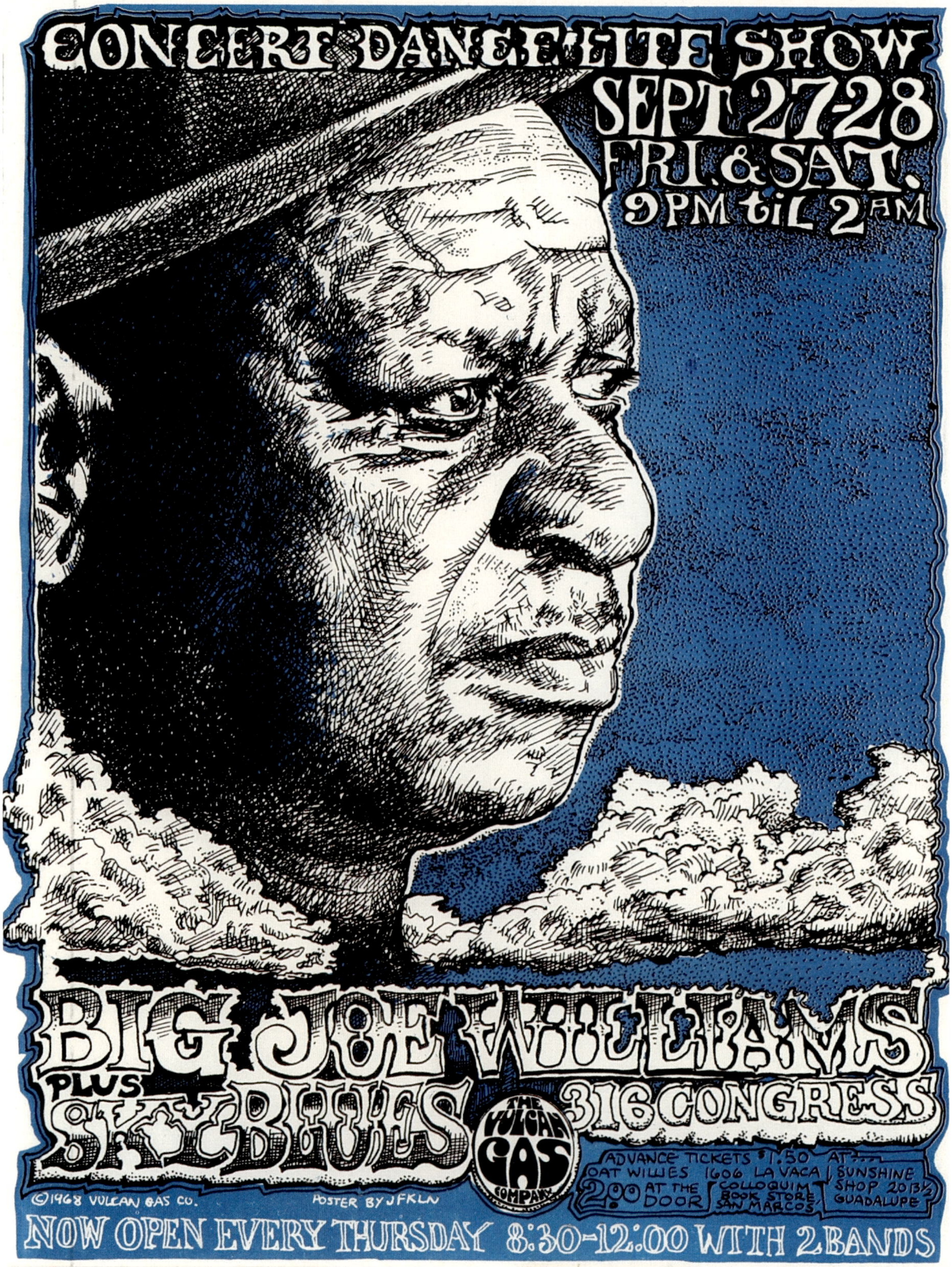

22 JIM FRANKLIN. Big Joe Williams & New Atlantis. Vulcan Gas Company. January 17 & 18, 1969. 9" × 8.75". © Jim Franklin.

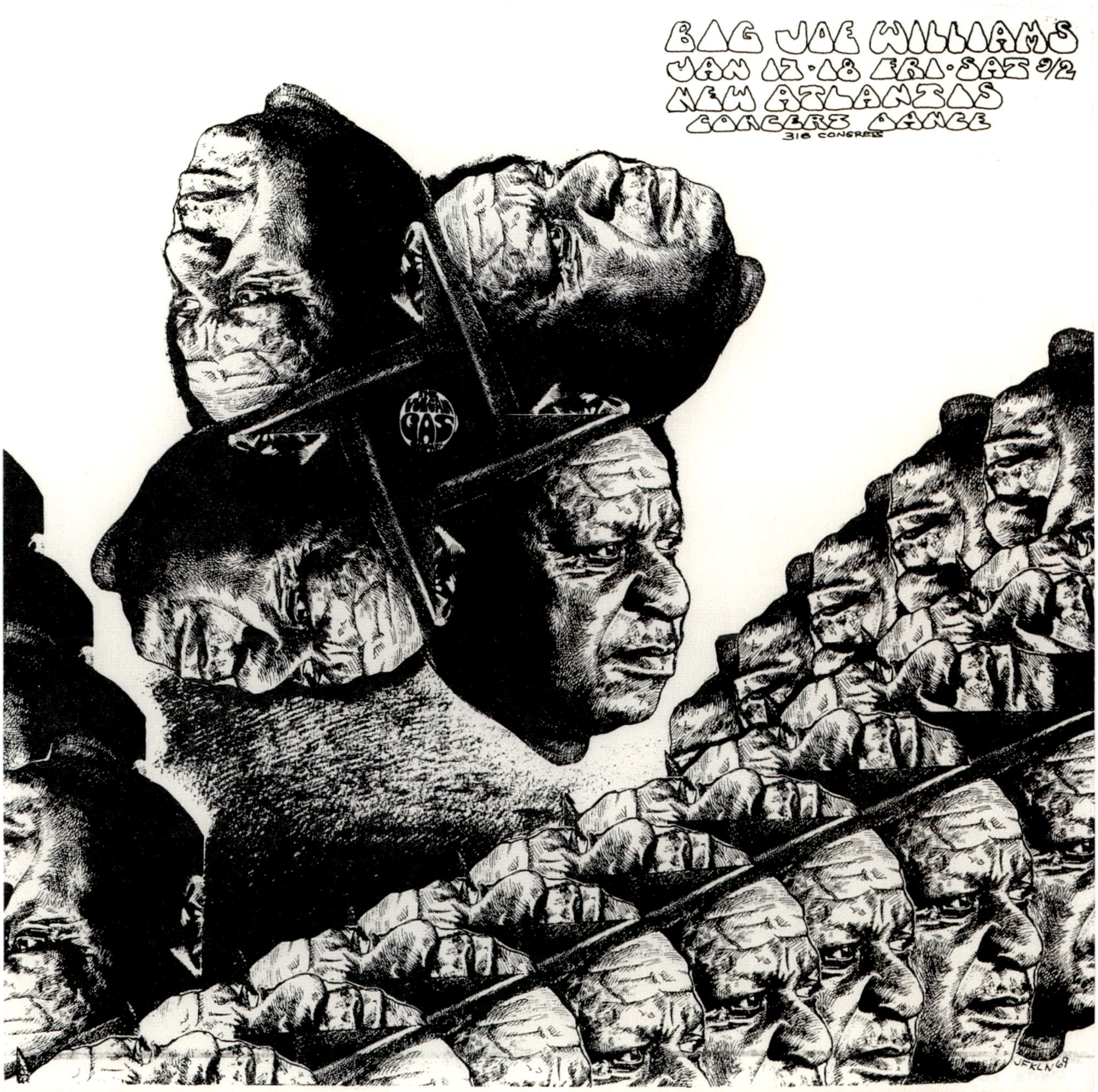

23 JIM FRANKLIN. Freddie King backed by Storm & Wildfire. October 2 & 3, 1970. Mance Lipscomb, Ginger Valley, & Storm. October 9 & 10, 1970. Armadillo World Headquarters. 11" × 17". © Jim Franklin.

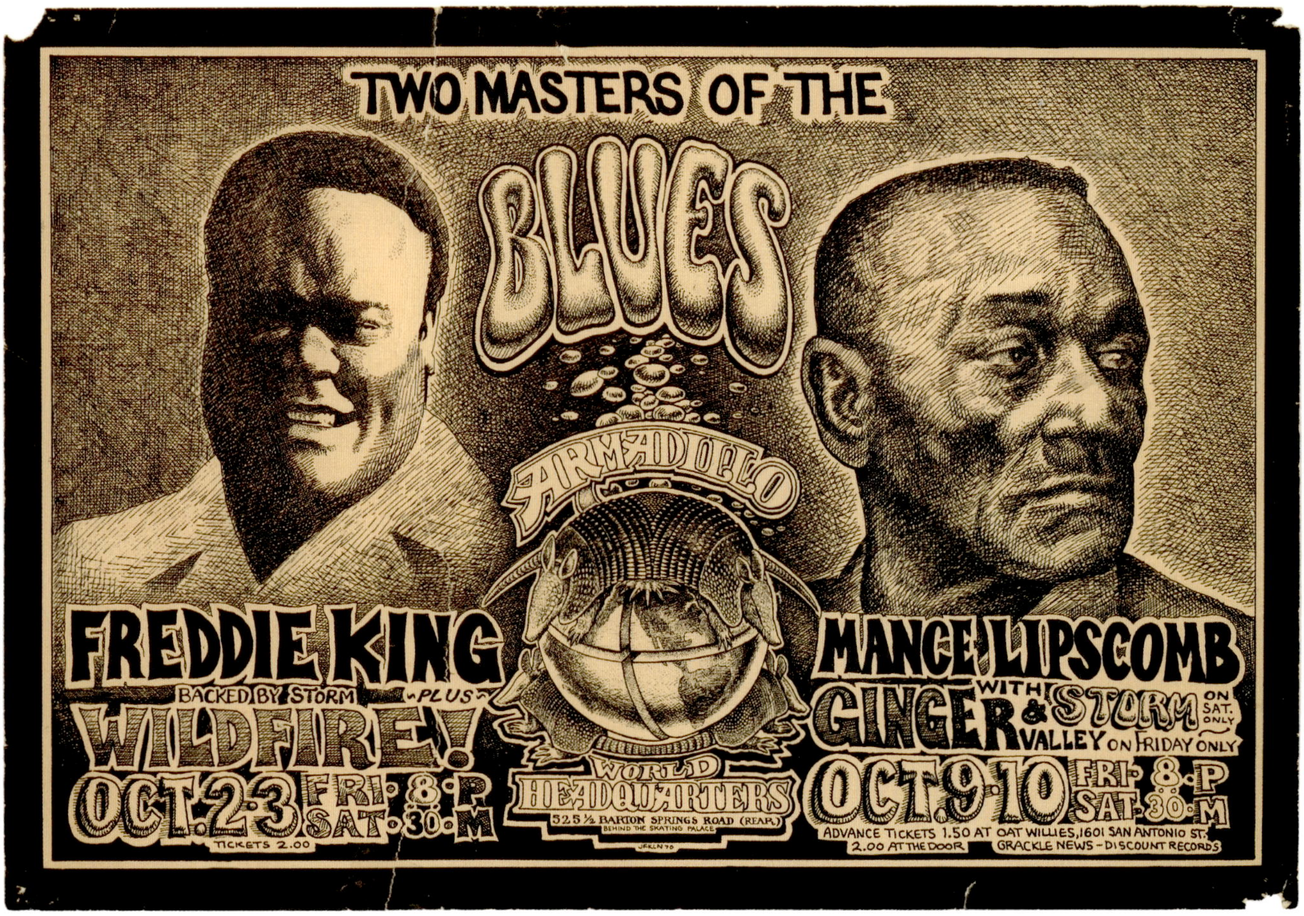

24 JIM FRANKLIN. Sonny Terry & Brownie McGhee. Armadillo World Headquarters. January 16–20, 1973. 11" × 17". © Jim Franklin.

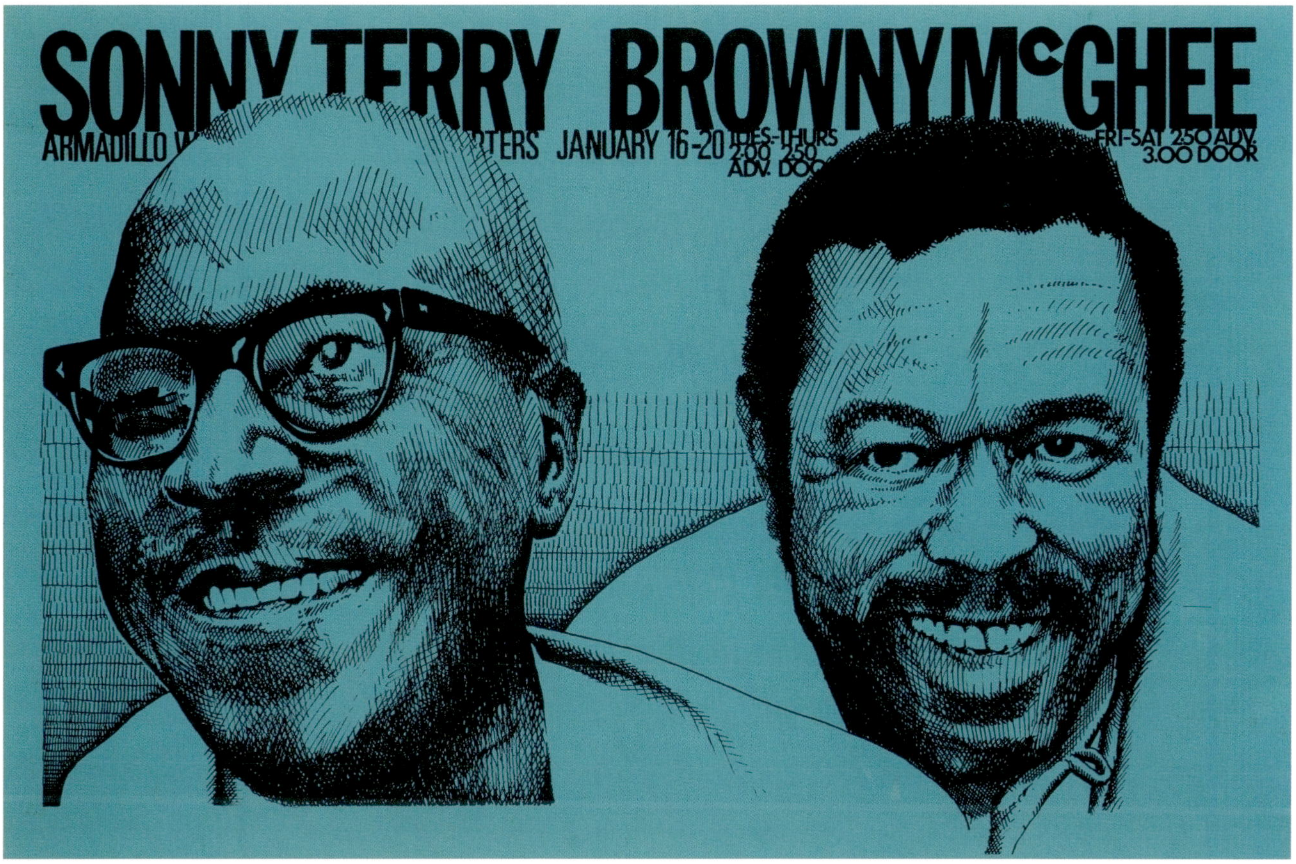

25 MICAEL PRIEST. Freddie King. Armadillo World Headquarters. March 15–17, 1973. 17" × 11". © Micael Priest.

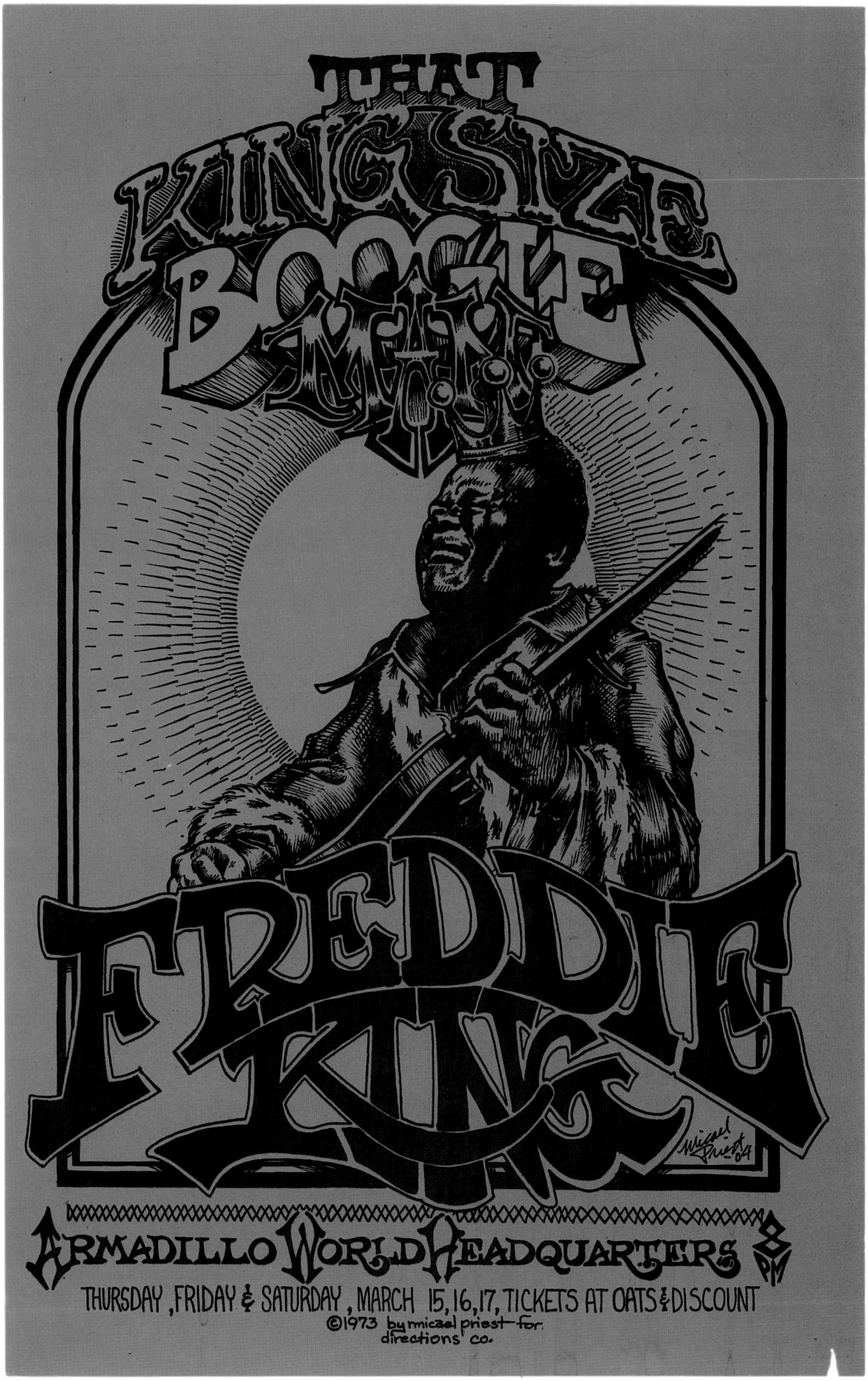

26 SAM YEATES. Freddie King & John Hammond. Armadillo World Headquarters. October 31, 1976. 17.5" × 11.5". © Sam Yeates.

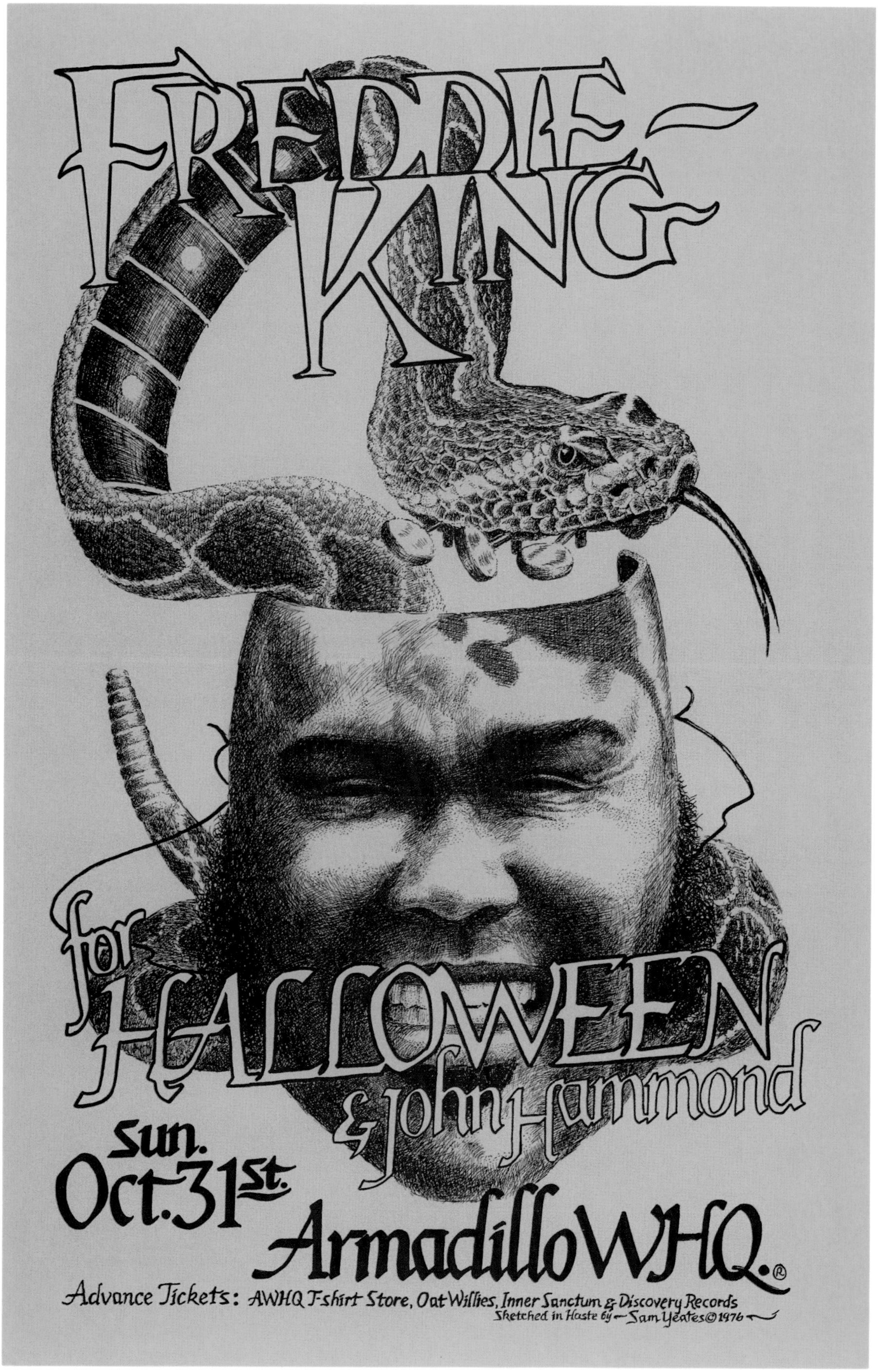

27 MICAEL PRIEST. Mose Allison & Alex Moore. Armadillo World Headquarters. June 15, 1974. 17" × 11". © Micael Priest.

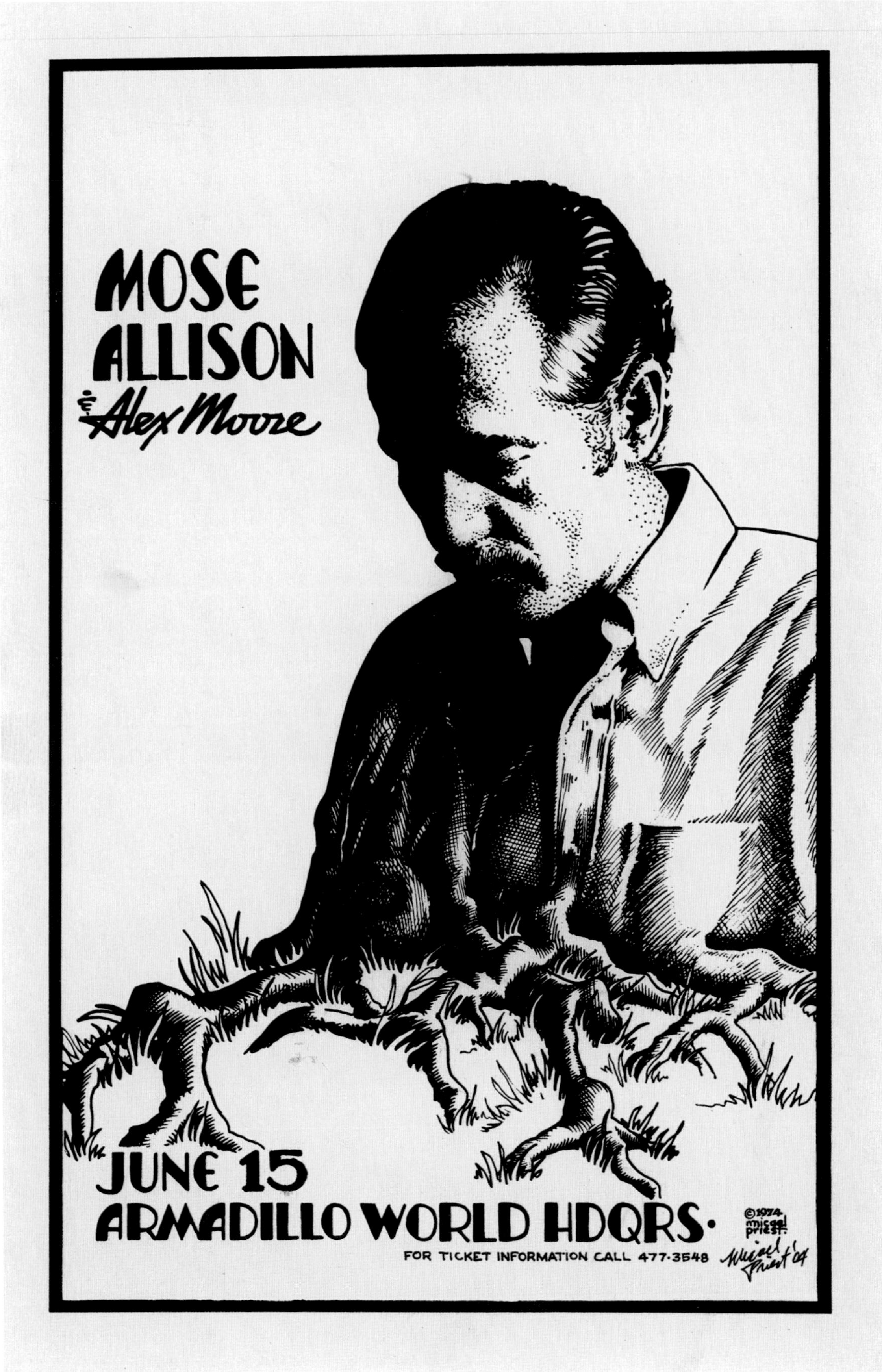

28 JIM FRANKLIN. Count Basie and His Orchestra. Armadillo World Headquarters. January 14, 1980. 13.5" × 11". © Jim Franklin.

Franklin's skill with the airbrush is exemplified in this portrait of Count Basie.

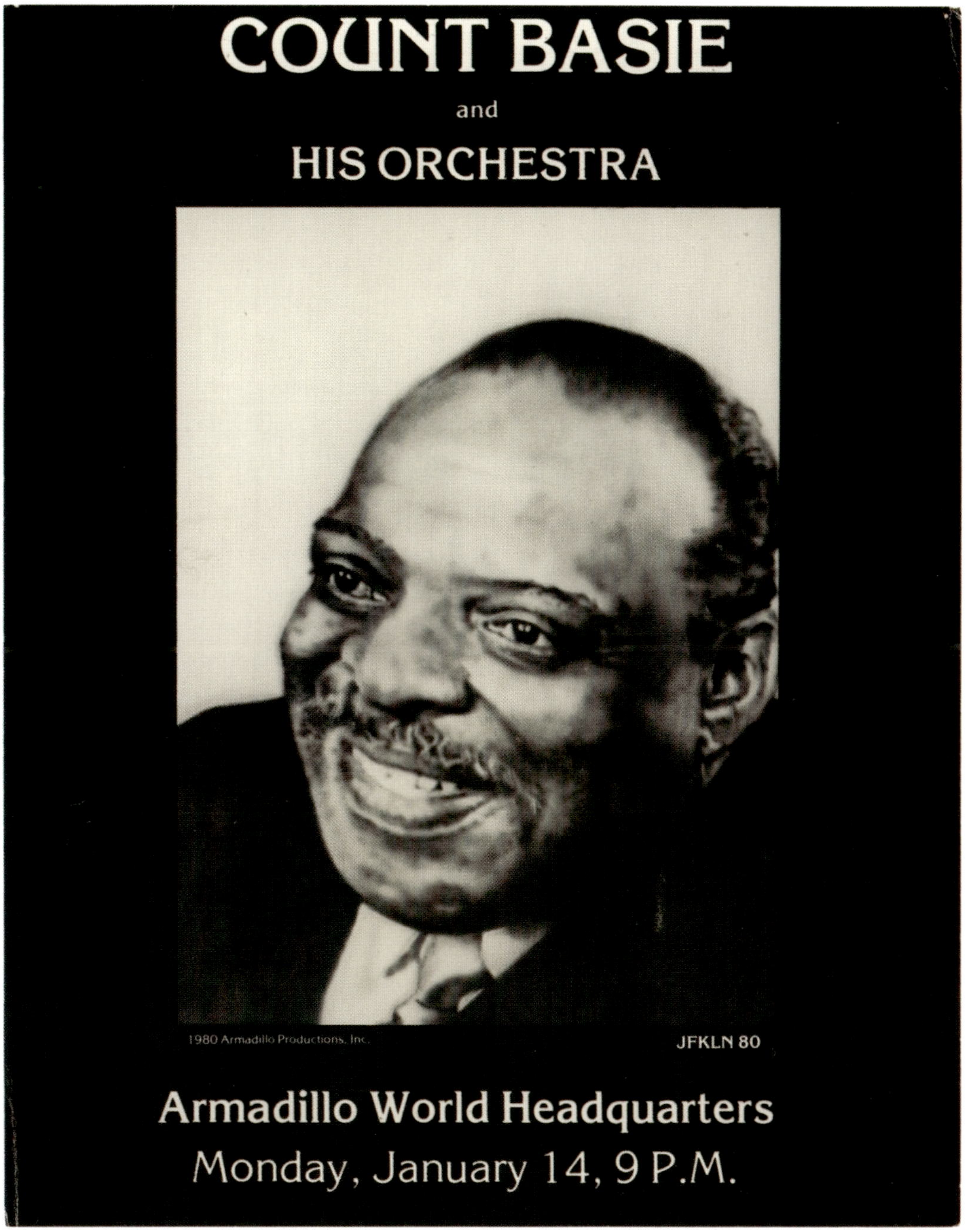

29 JIM FRANKLIN. Bukka White & Juke Boy Bonner. Ritz Theatre. November 13–16, 1974. 17" × 11".

In addition to the bold portrait of Bukka White, Franklin's poster offers a glimpse into the burgeoning blues music community in Austin in the mid-1970s. The poster advertises a benefit for Mance Lipscomb, a fixture at Kenneth Threadgill's North Lamar outpost in the 1960s, as well as a screening for the Les Blank film about the Navasota guitarist's life and music.

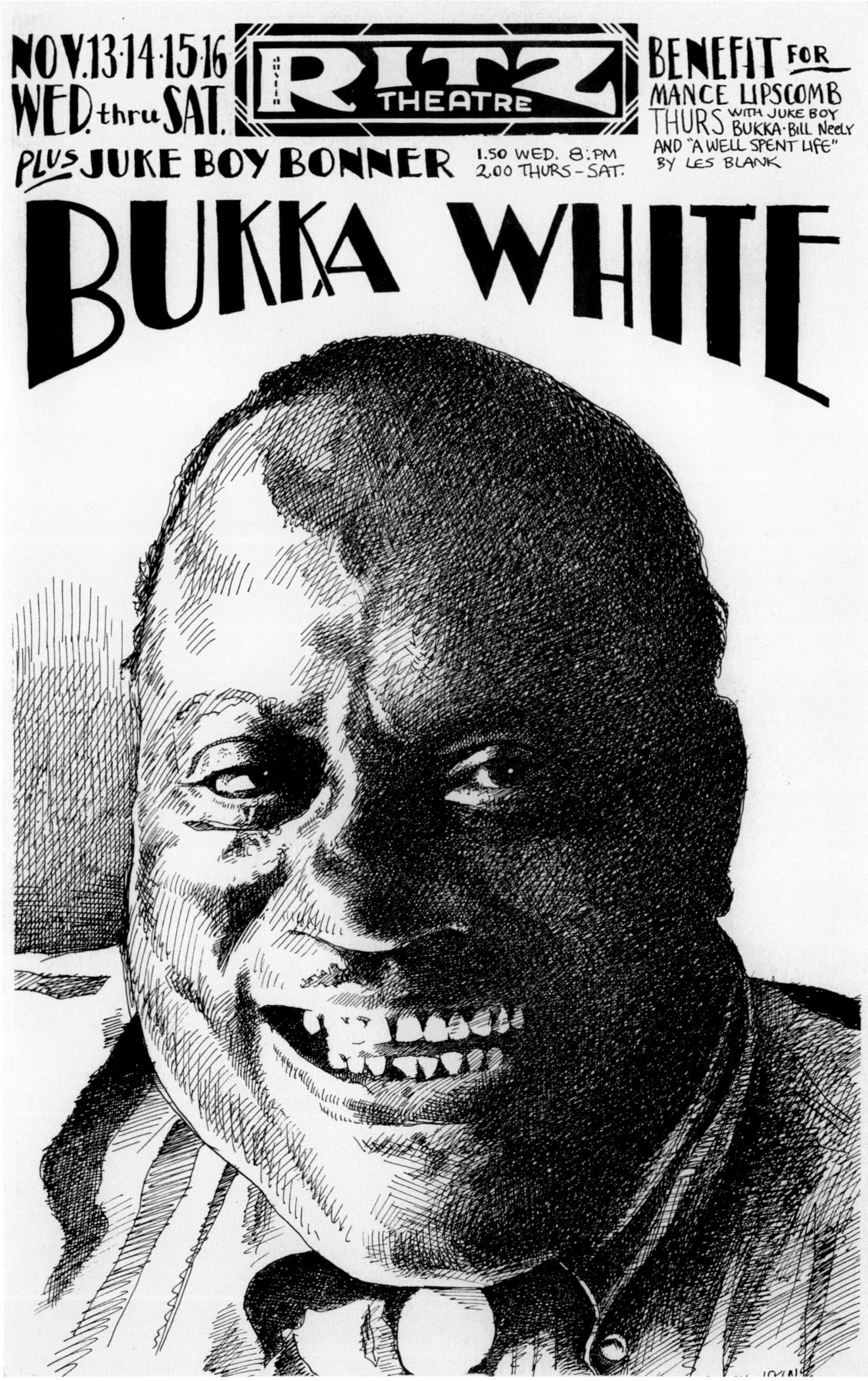

30 JIM FRANKLIN. Bo Diddley & Storm. Ritz Theatre. November 8, 1974. 17" × 11". © Jim Franklin.

Franklin, who took over the Ritz Theatre in 1974, says that it was a dream come true to book Bo Diddley at his own venue.

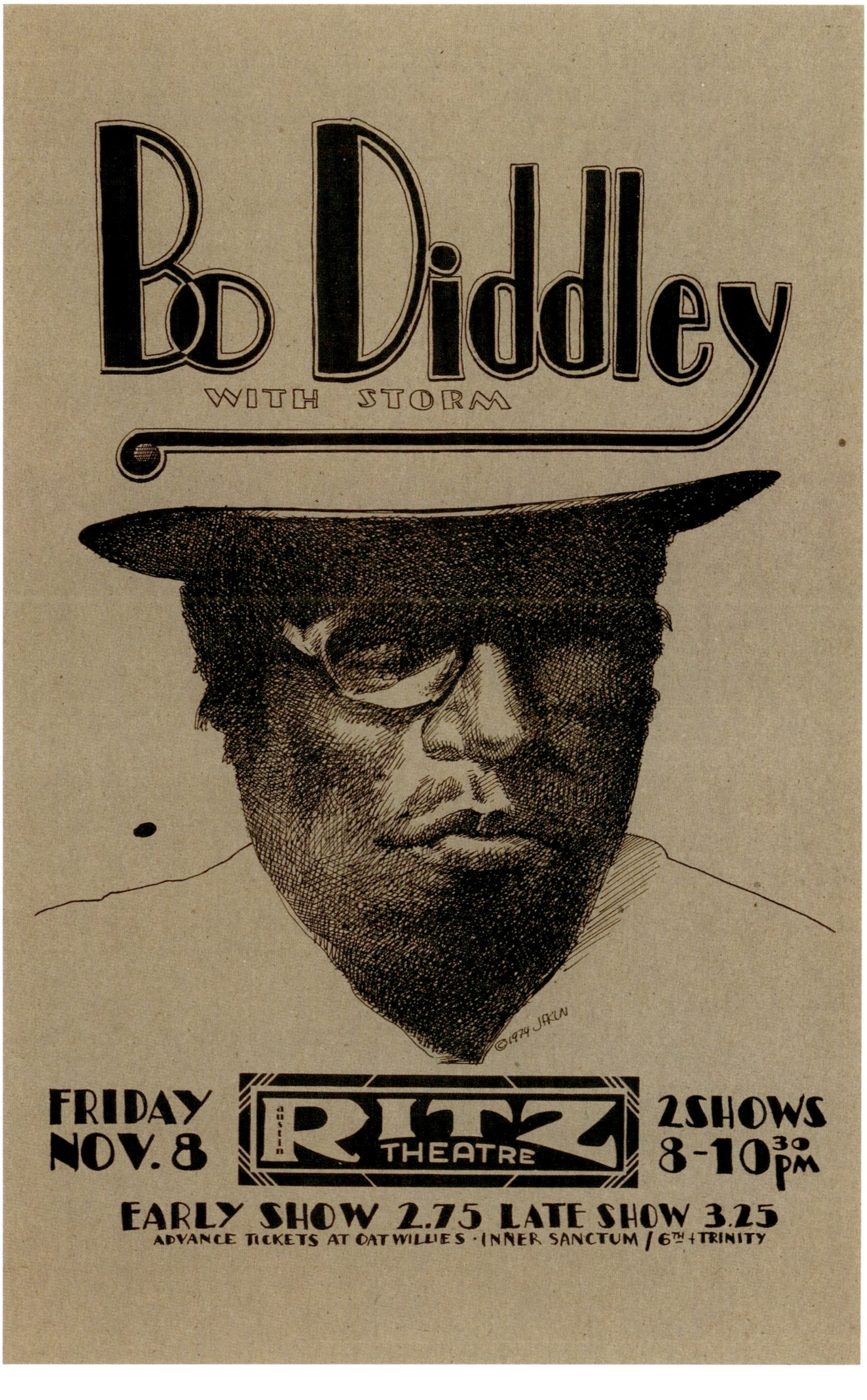

31 UNKNOWN ARTIST. B. B. King. Antone's. July 4, 1976. 17" × 11".

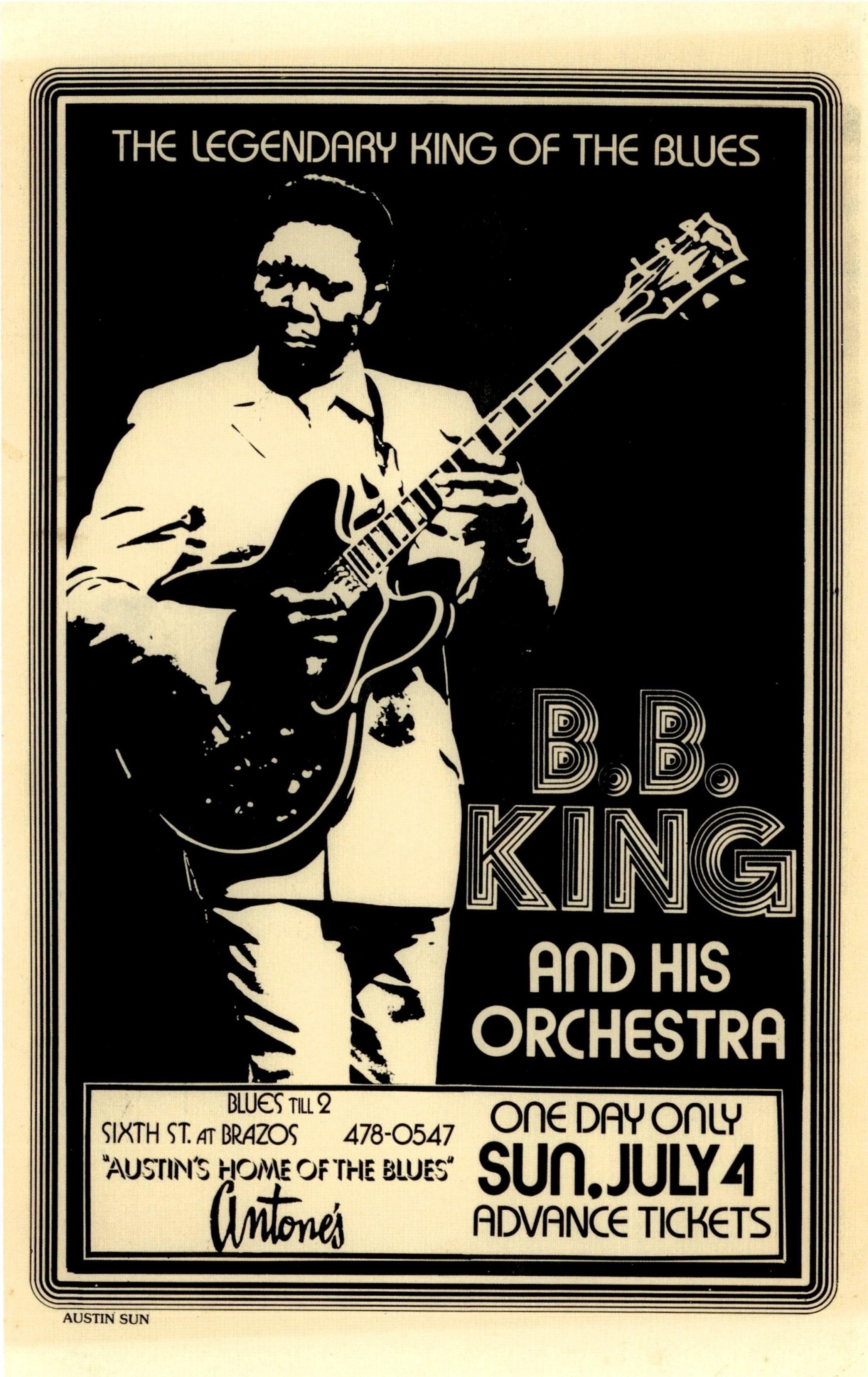

32 DANNY GARRETT. B. B. King. Antone's. Year unknown. 17" × 11". © Danny Garrett.

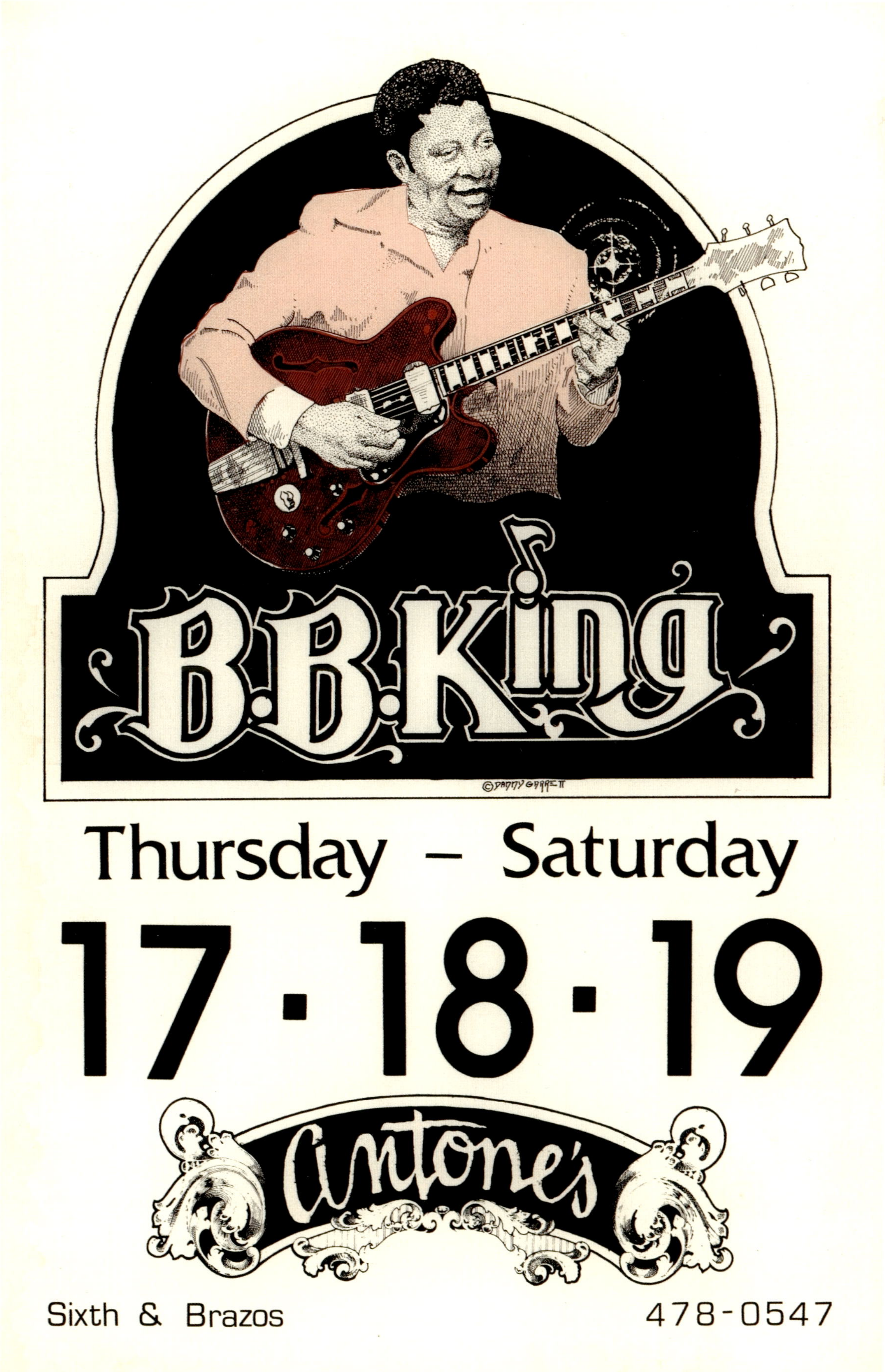

33 DANNY GARRETT. Muddy Waters. Antone's. April 18–22, 1978. 17" × 11". © Danny Garrett.

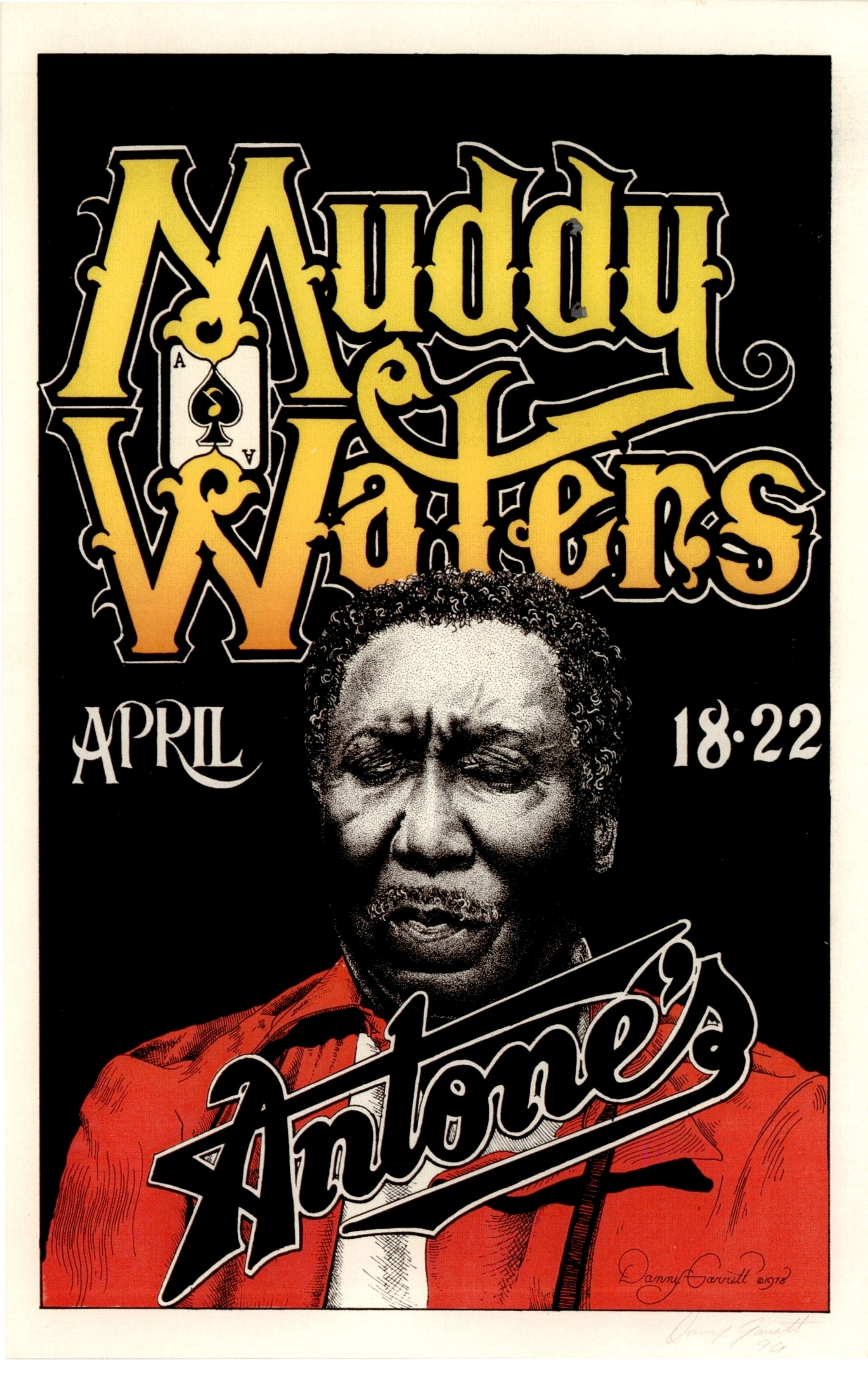

34 DANNY GARRETT. Muddy Waters. Antone's. June 20 & 21, 1980. 17" × 11". © Danny Garrett.

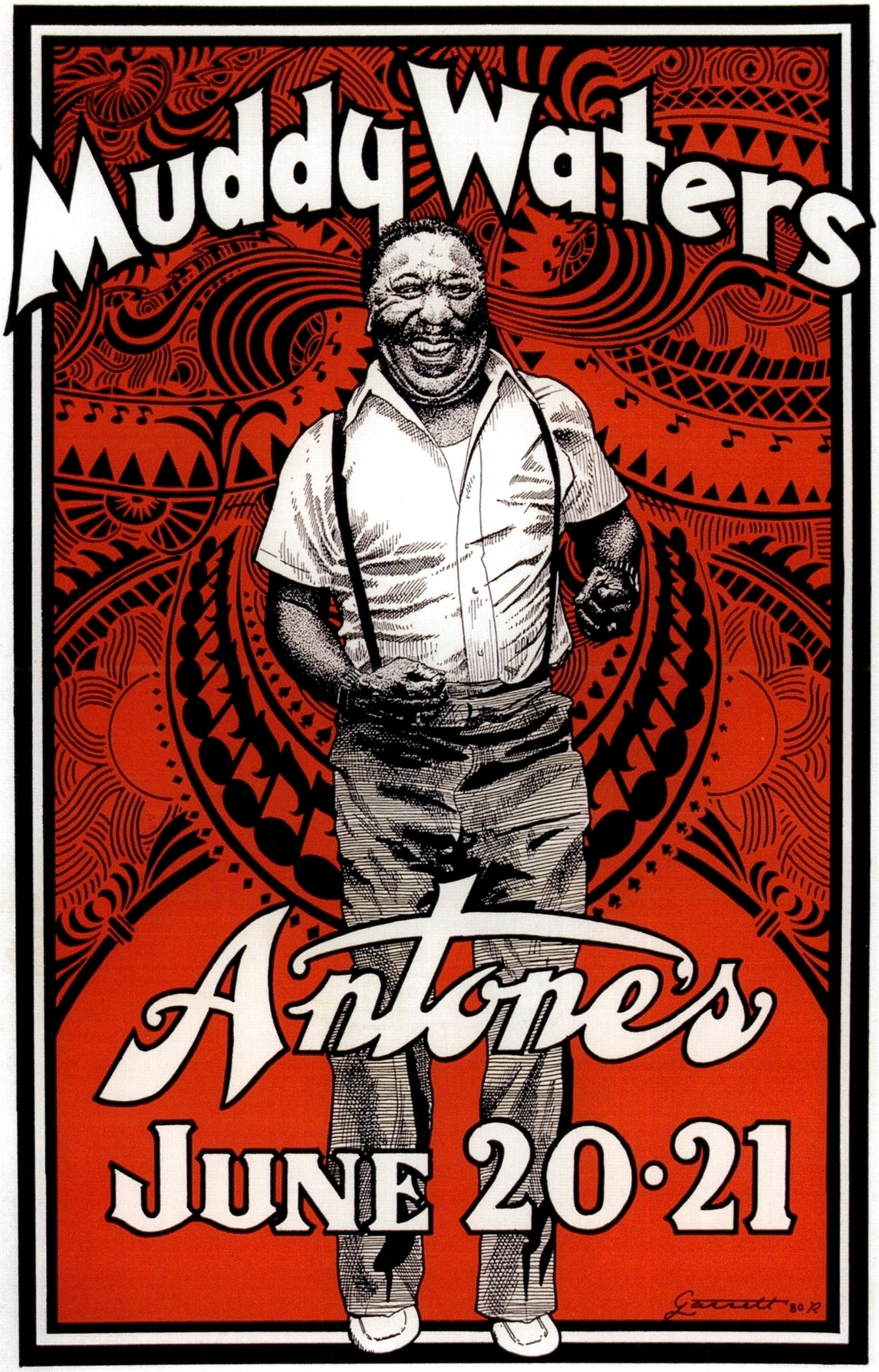

35 UNKNOWN ARTIST. Fats Domino. Antone's. August 16–18, 1978. 17" × 11".

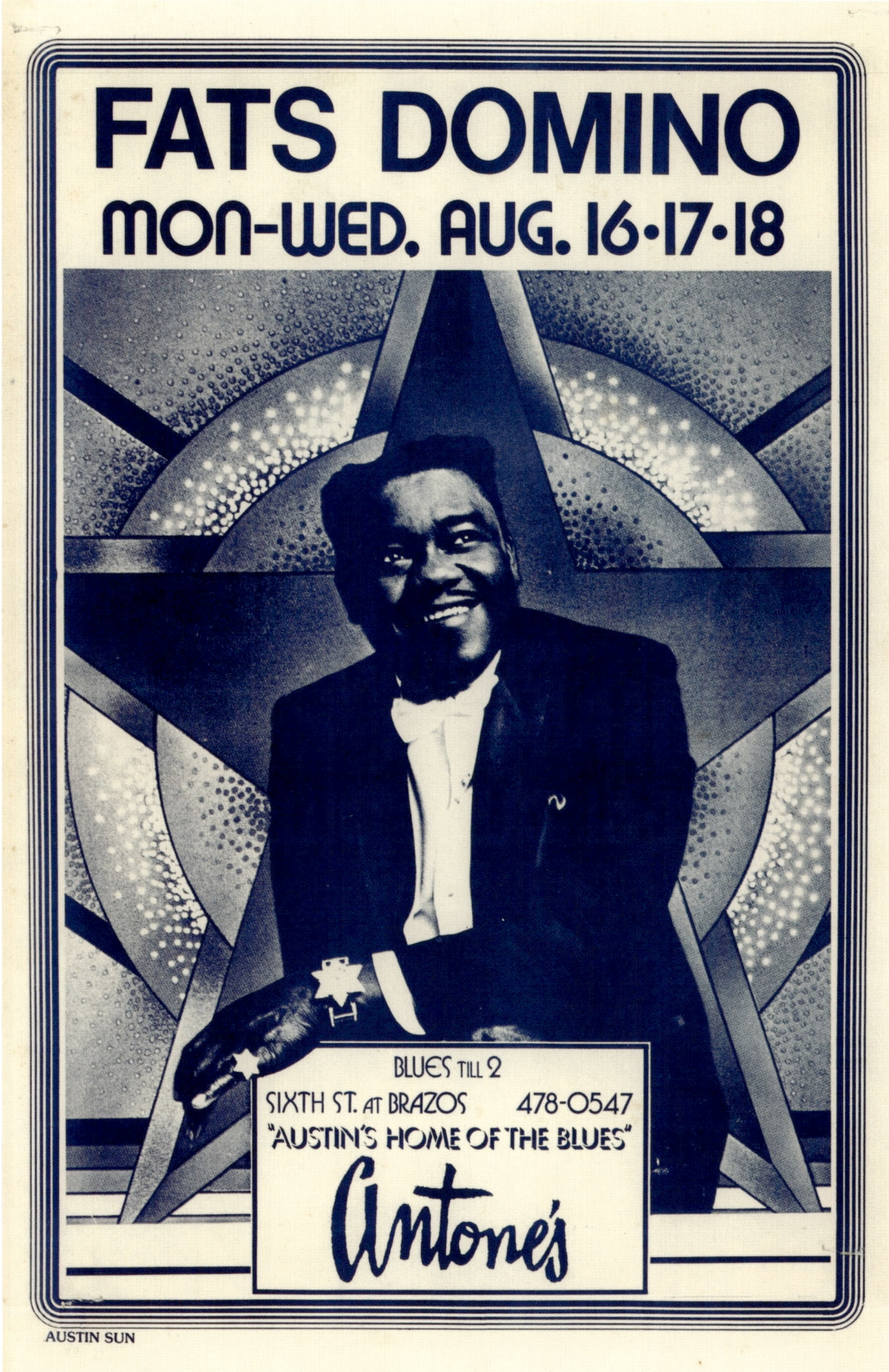

36 DANNY GARRETT. Clifton Chenier. Antone's. September 26–30, 1978. 17" × 11". © Danny Garrett.

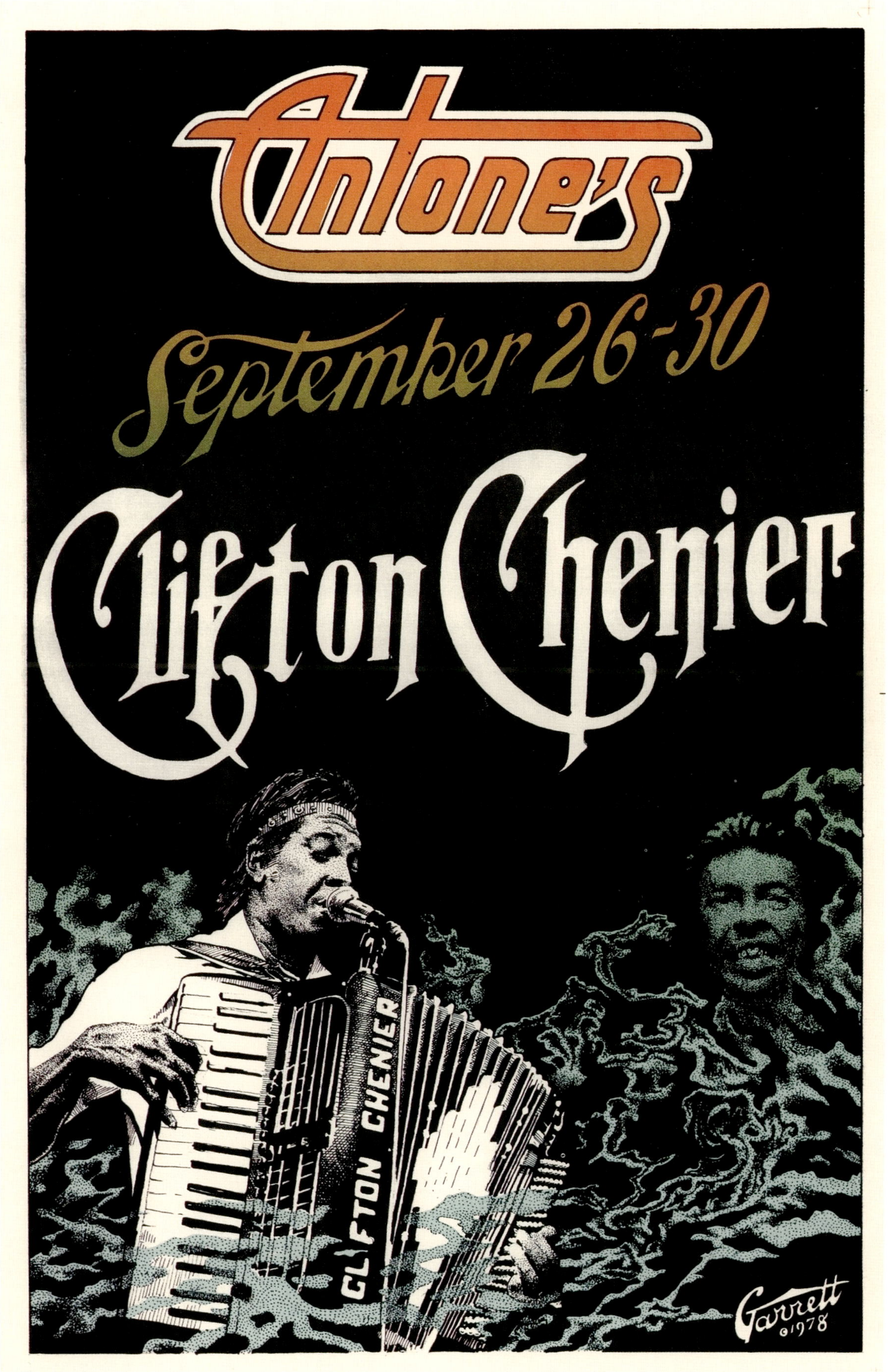

37 KERRY AWN. Soap Creek Saloon calendar. March 1978. 17" × 11". © Kerry Awn.

Kerry Awn's Soap Creek Saloon posters helped establish the club's visual aesthetic and advertised performances for several years. Based on a photograph by Ken Hoge, the portrait captures thc young Stevie Ray Vaughan with his band of Austin blues regulars.

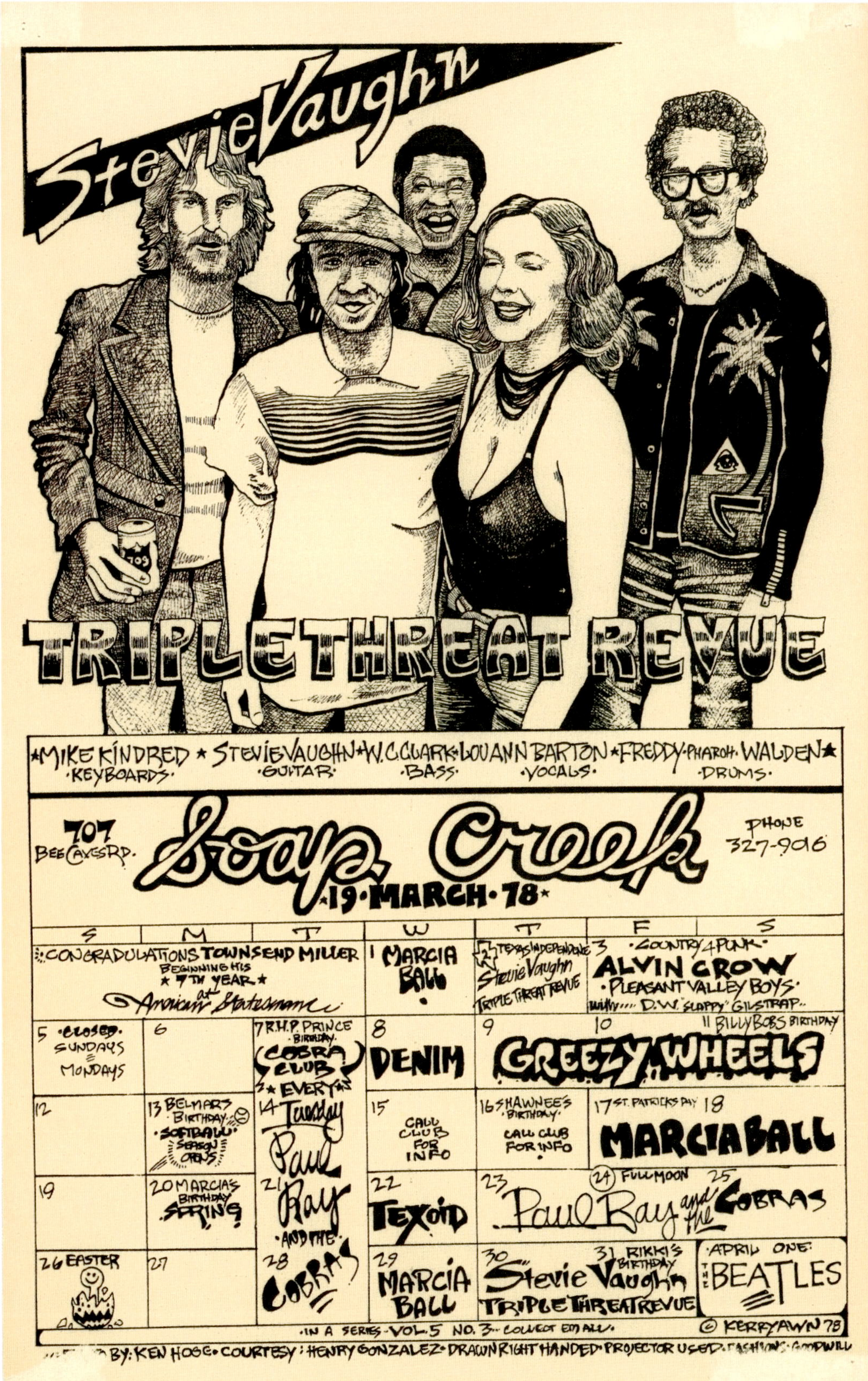

38 DANNY GARRETT. Stevie Ray Vaughan & Double Trouble. Antone's. October 1 & 2, 1982. 11" × 17". © Danny Garrett.

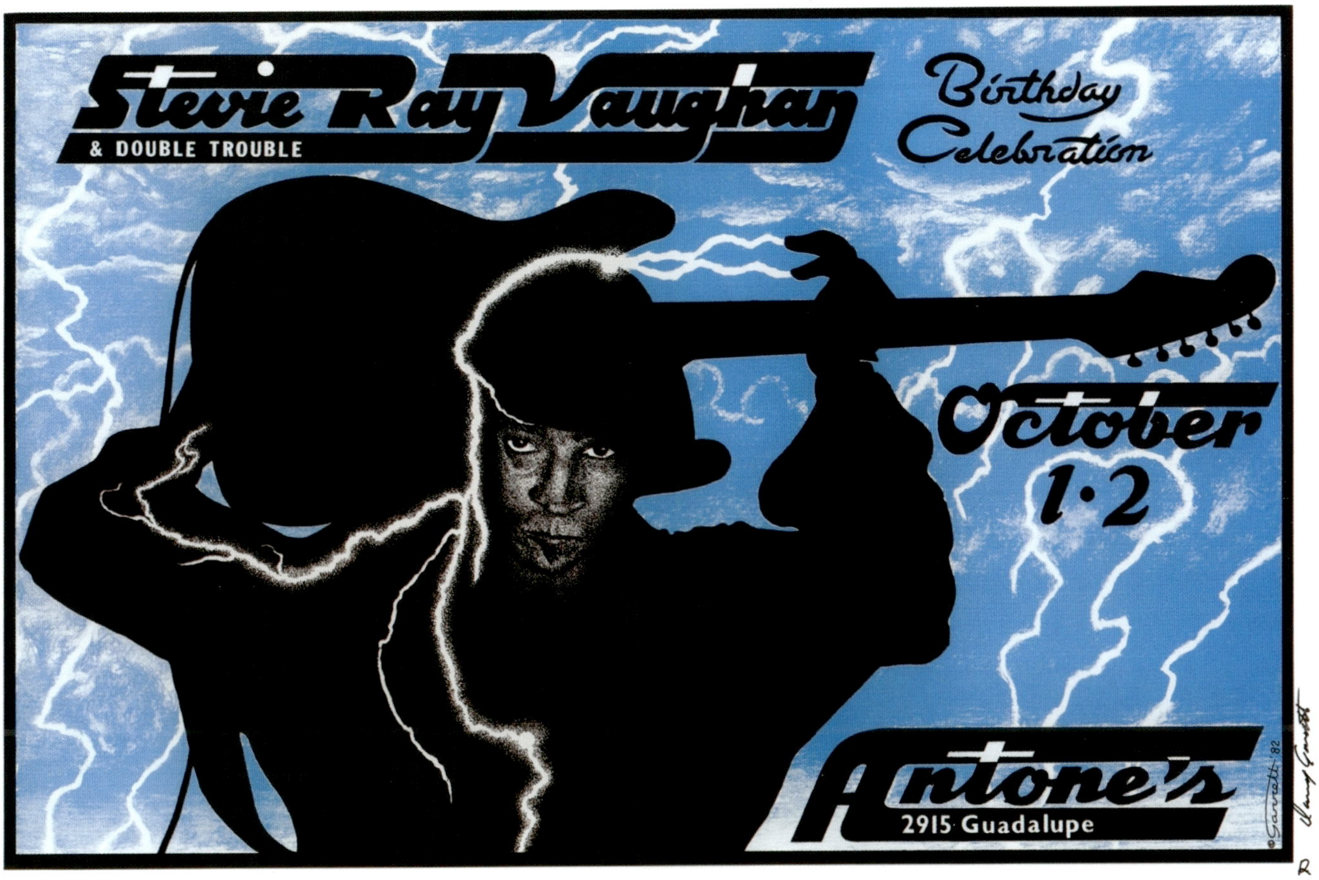

39 DANNY GARRETT. The Fabulous Thunderbirds. Antone's. April 18, 1980. 17" × 11". © Danny Garrett.

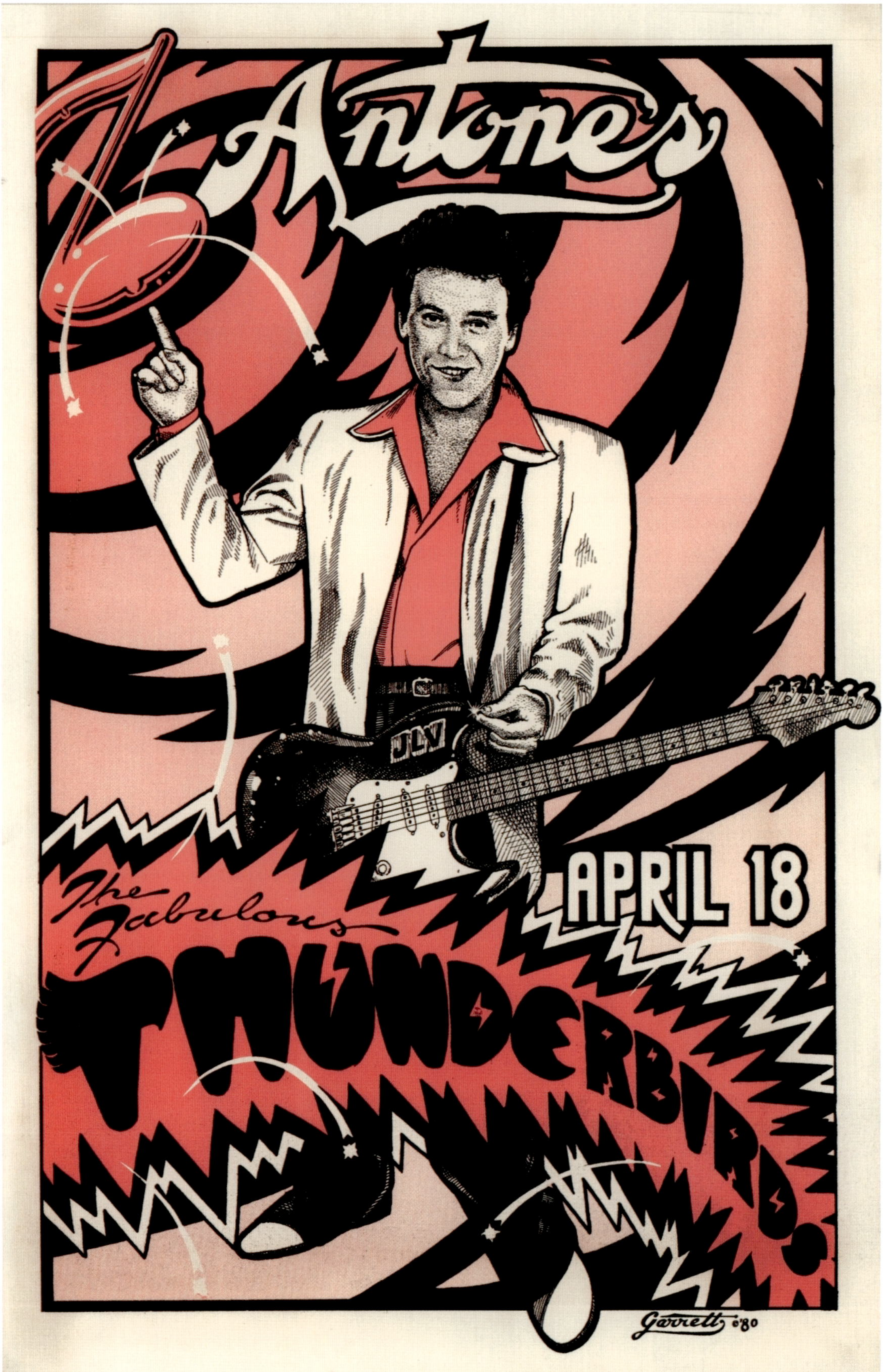

40 MICAEL PRIEST. Johnny Winter & Dragon. Armadillo World Headquarters. November 18 & 19, 1978. 17" × 11". © Micael Priest.

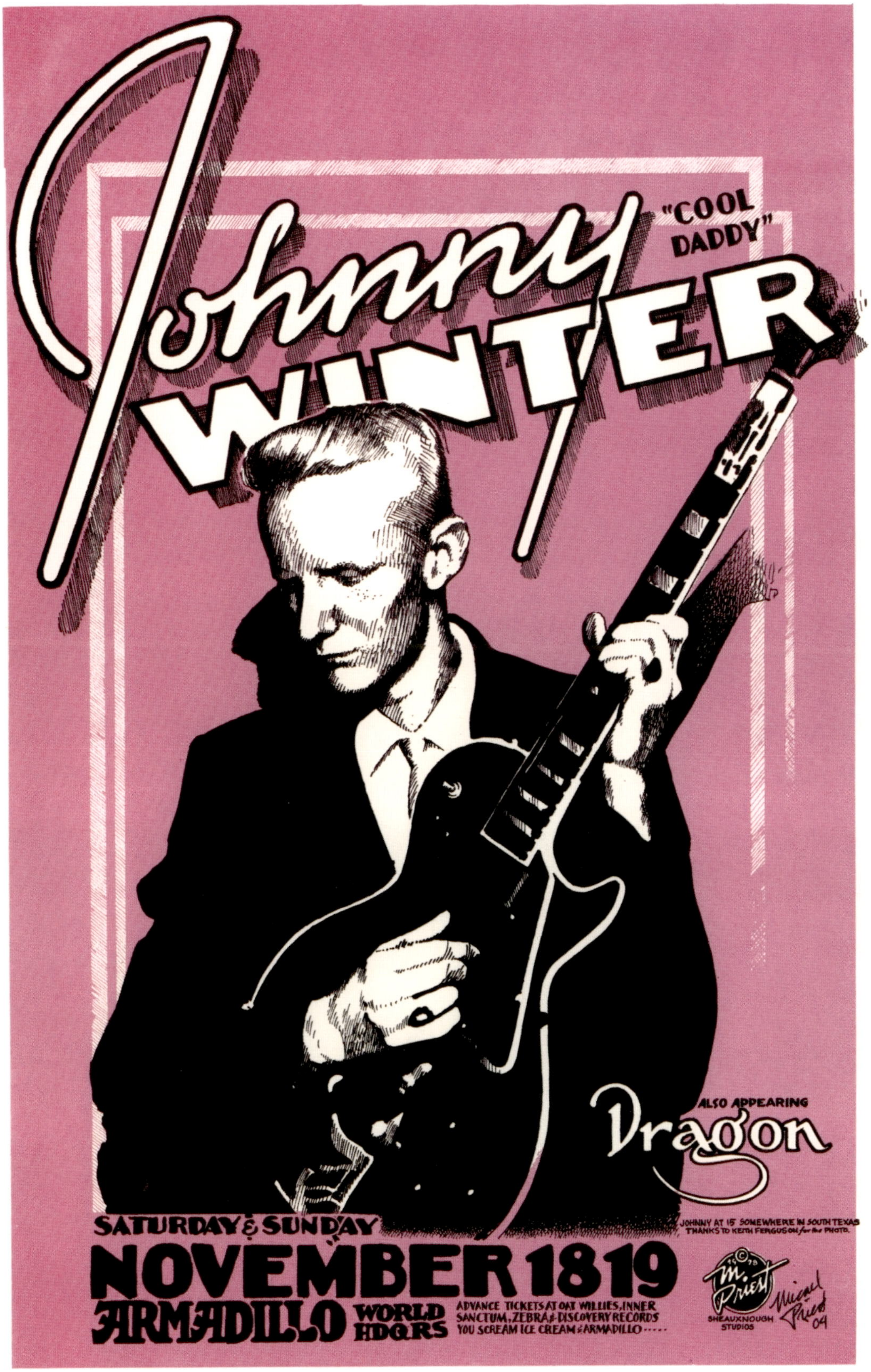

REIMAGINING TEXAS

As the city's rock-and-roll epicenter moved from the Vulcan Gas Company to the Armadillo World Headquarters, Austin poster art continued to move into innovative territories. A new and distinctly Texan approach began to emerge. Jim Franklin explains, "Here was this surrealist state, y'know, with all this exaggeration as part of the official imagery. The biggest this and the biggest that. Then there was the Jackalope and the giant fish strapped to a horse. All this brags of Texas. I took that all to be surreal. You don't have to go to Paris and copy Salvador Dali; you just stay in Texas and look around." Yet Franklin and his colleagues didn't simply rely on Texas clichés and images of Texana; they subverted these images and provided them with new meanings and contexts that illuminated the musical and artistic environment in Austin. The influence of psychedelia remained, but the grand spectacle of Texas skies, nature, and culture offered a vast body of new motifs to explore in poster art.

The shifts in poster styles reflected shifts in the musical landscape. As hippies and honky-tonkers began to merge their musical styles, Austin audiences responded kindly. The city continued to become a center for radical underground activity, and a well-known Texas mammal became a symbol for Austin's cosmic and countercultural milieu: the armadillo. Though he wasn't the first underground Texas artist to draw an armadillo, Jim Franklin is by far the most notable employer of this nocturnal connoisseur of worms in poster art. Franklin notes that the armadillo is "a mystical animal" that is "a perfect mascot for the hipsters." Perhaps Franklin's first meeting with the animal was a pivotal event in his life as an artist. Franklin describes a Gulf Coast hunting trip with his father in which a startled armadillo ran between the young artist's legs. The armadillo would figure prominently in Franklin's work not as a cartoon character but as a purveyor of "alternatives to the established ways of debauchery." The image that launched the armadillo phenomenon is found in a handbill for a love-in "bust benefit" at the Wooldridge Square Park bandstand, located just across from the Austin city jail, for some local scenesters who had been jailed on drug possession charges. Rather than try to visually represent the bands booked for the benefit—an arduous task considering the bill included New Atlantis, Lavender Hill Express, Georgetown Medical Band, and Eternal Life Corporation—Franklin chose an image to represent the audience: an armadillo smoking a joint.

Austin poster artists honored the beauty of the Texas landscape and its human and animal inhabitants while emphasizing the struggles and strife of life in the Lone Star State. In addition to the armadillo, other Texan and western motifs appear prominently in the work of Austin poster artists of the period. Cowboys, horses, rattlesnakes, and ramshackle stagecoaches are given a surreal treatment. The state's long and lonesome highways and the vehicles that traverse them are ever present, and the musical and spiritual advisers of the Texas underground stand proudly. The ropers and dopers were united by such acts as Willie Nelson, Doug Sahm, Freda and the Firedogs, the Flatlanders, Asleep at the Wheel, and others, and Austin poster artists captured the confluence of Texas cowboy and underground culture in their work.

41 JIM FRANKLIN. New Atlantis, Lavender Hill Express, Texas Pacific, Eternal Life Corporation, & Georgetown Medical Band. Wooldridge Park. September 29, 1968. 6" × 7". © Jim Franklin.

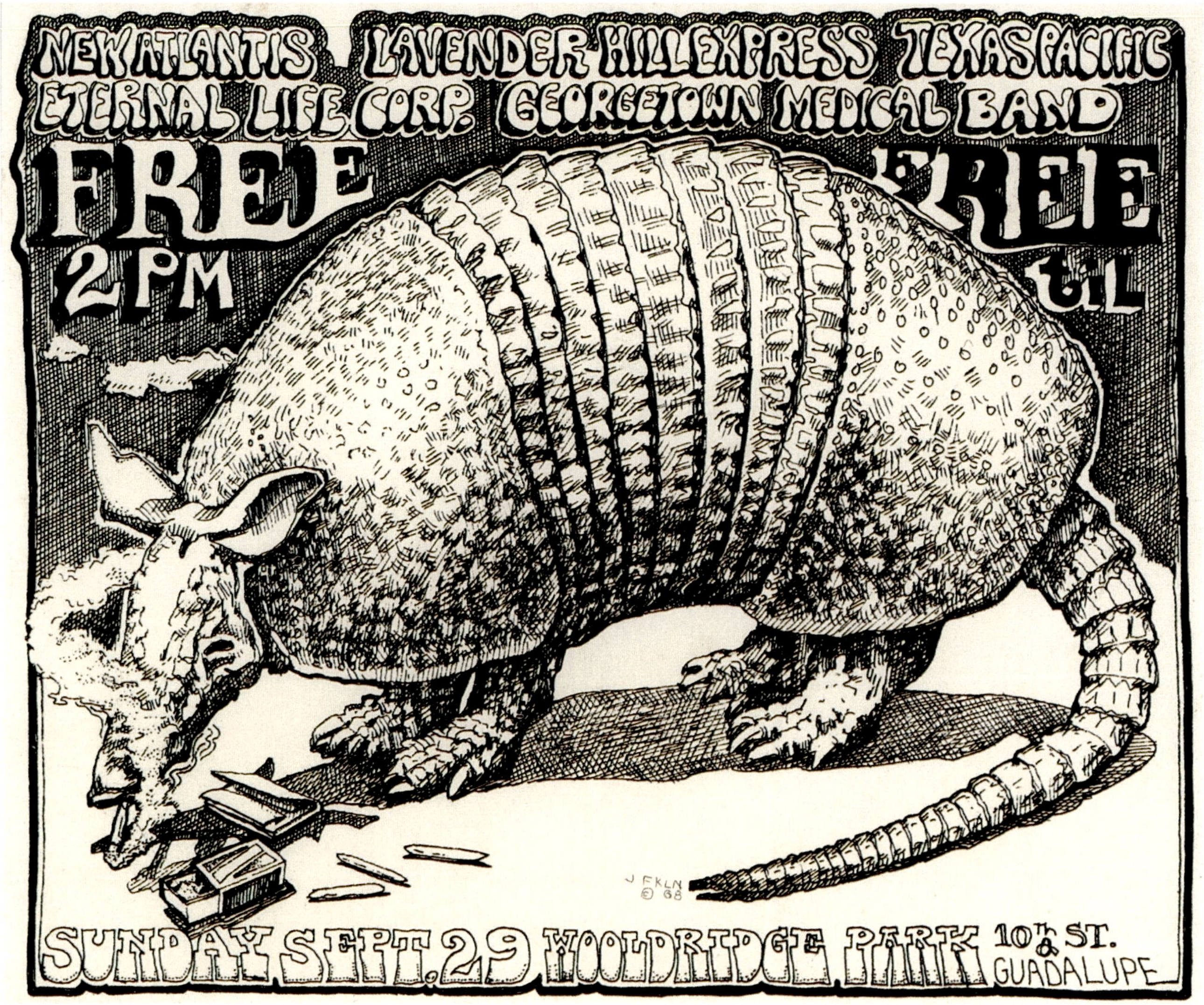

42 JIM FRANKLIN. Shiva's Headband, Hub City Movers, & Whistler. Armadillo World Headquarters. August 7 & 8, 1970. 11" × 17". © Jim Franklin.

Shiva's Headband and company would help usher in a decade of music at the grand opening of the Armadillo World Headquarters.

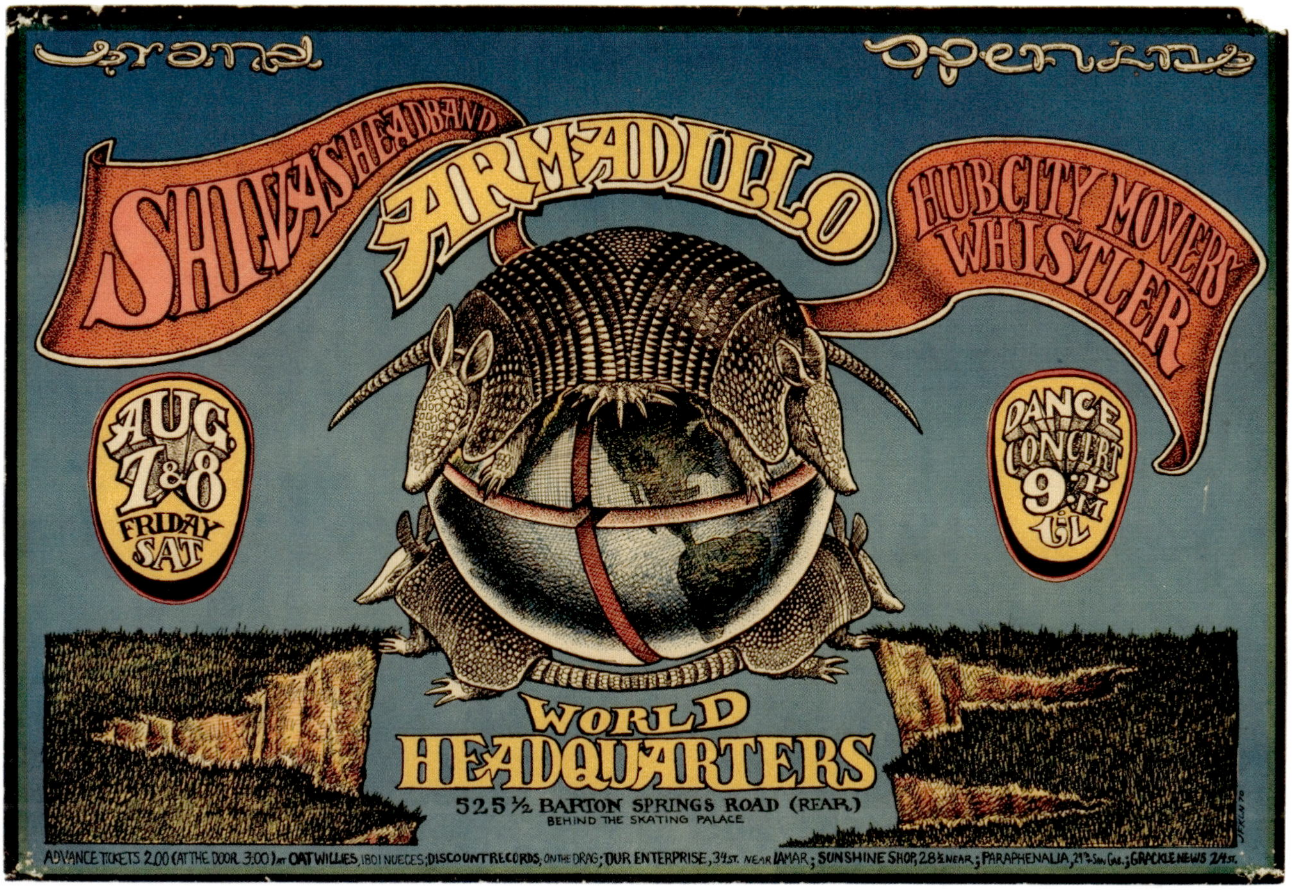

43 JIM FRANKLIN. Ramon, Ramon and the Four Daddyos, Crowbar, Onion Creek, Sweatarts, Lavender Hill Express, Fat Emma, & Amerikong. Fiesta Gardens Park. September 21, 1969. 9" × 8.5". © Jim Franklin.

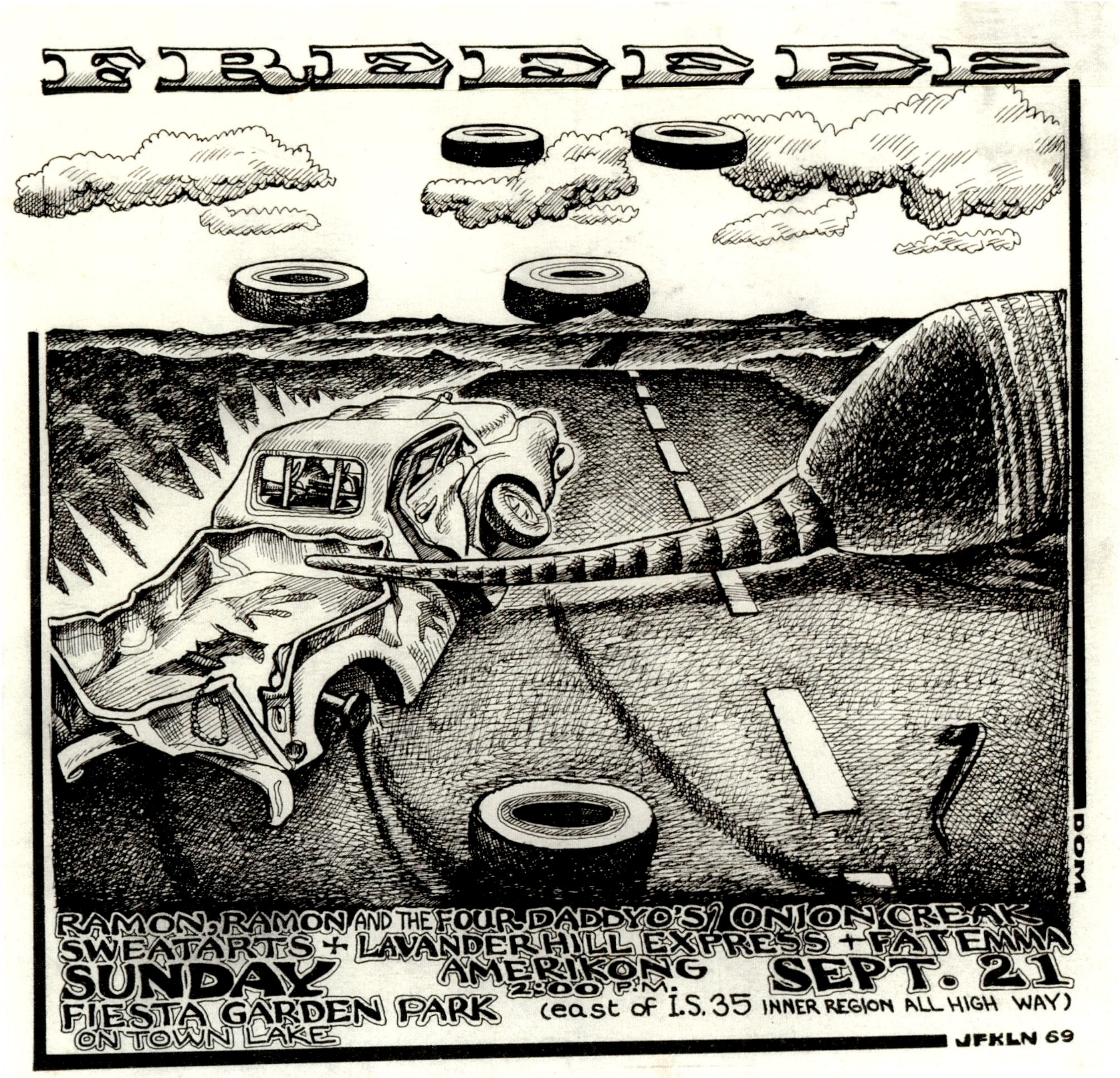

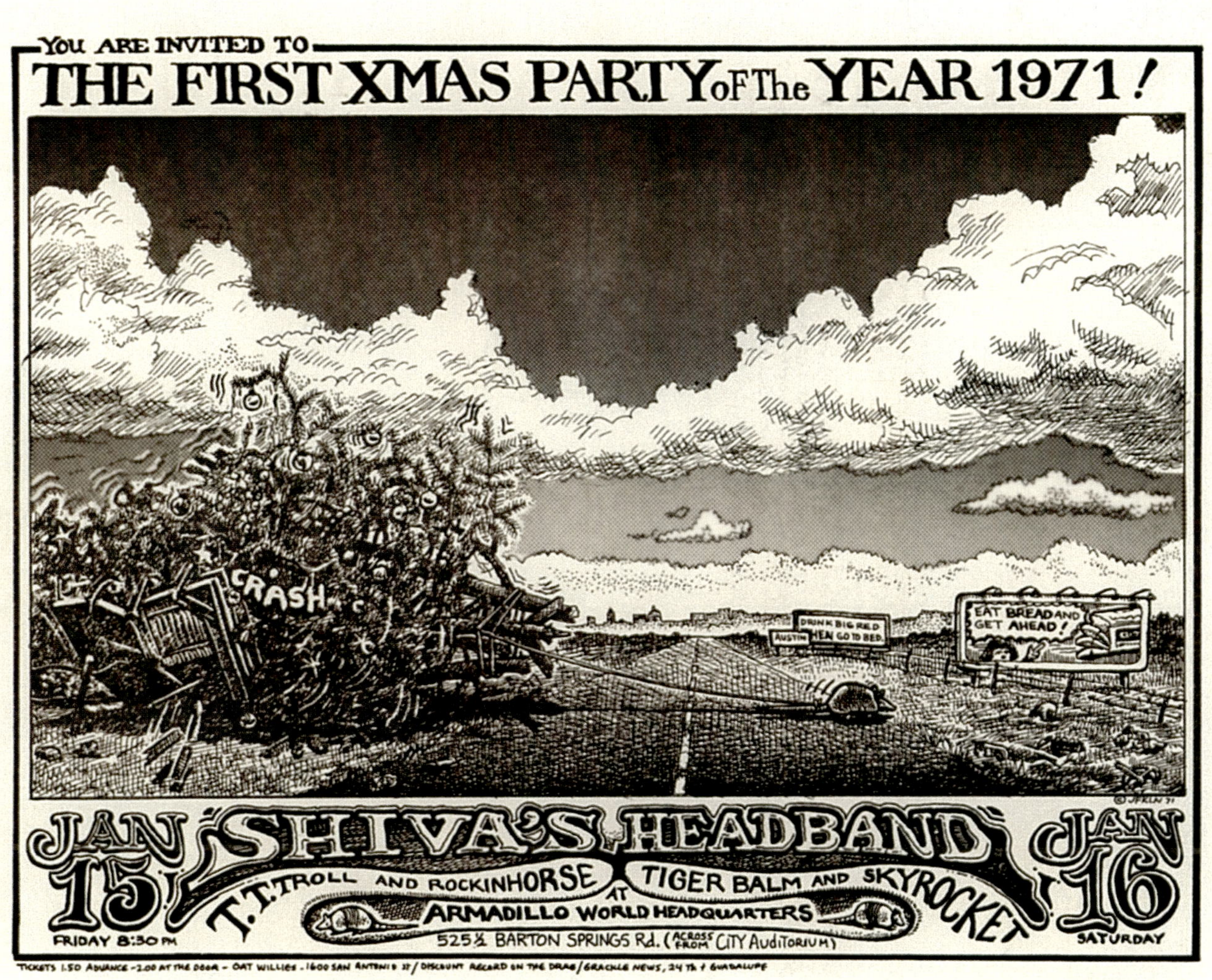

44 JIM FRANKLIN. Shiva's Headband, T. T. Troll, Rockinhorse, Tiger Balm, & Skyrocket. Armadillo World Headquarters. January 15 & 16, 1971. 8.5" × 11". © Jim Franklin.

45 MICAEL PRIEST. New Riders of the Purple Sage & Jon Emery. Armadillo World Headquarters. June 14, 1978. 17" × 11". © Micael Priest.

Priest references Lee Marvin's character Kid Shelleen, the drunken gunfighter from the comic western *Cat Ballou*. Priest's horse and gunfighter toke joints, and the saddle is outfitted with a small tray for cocaine.

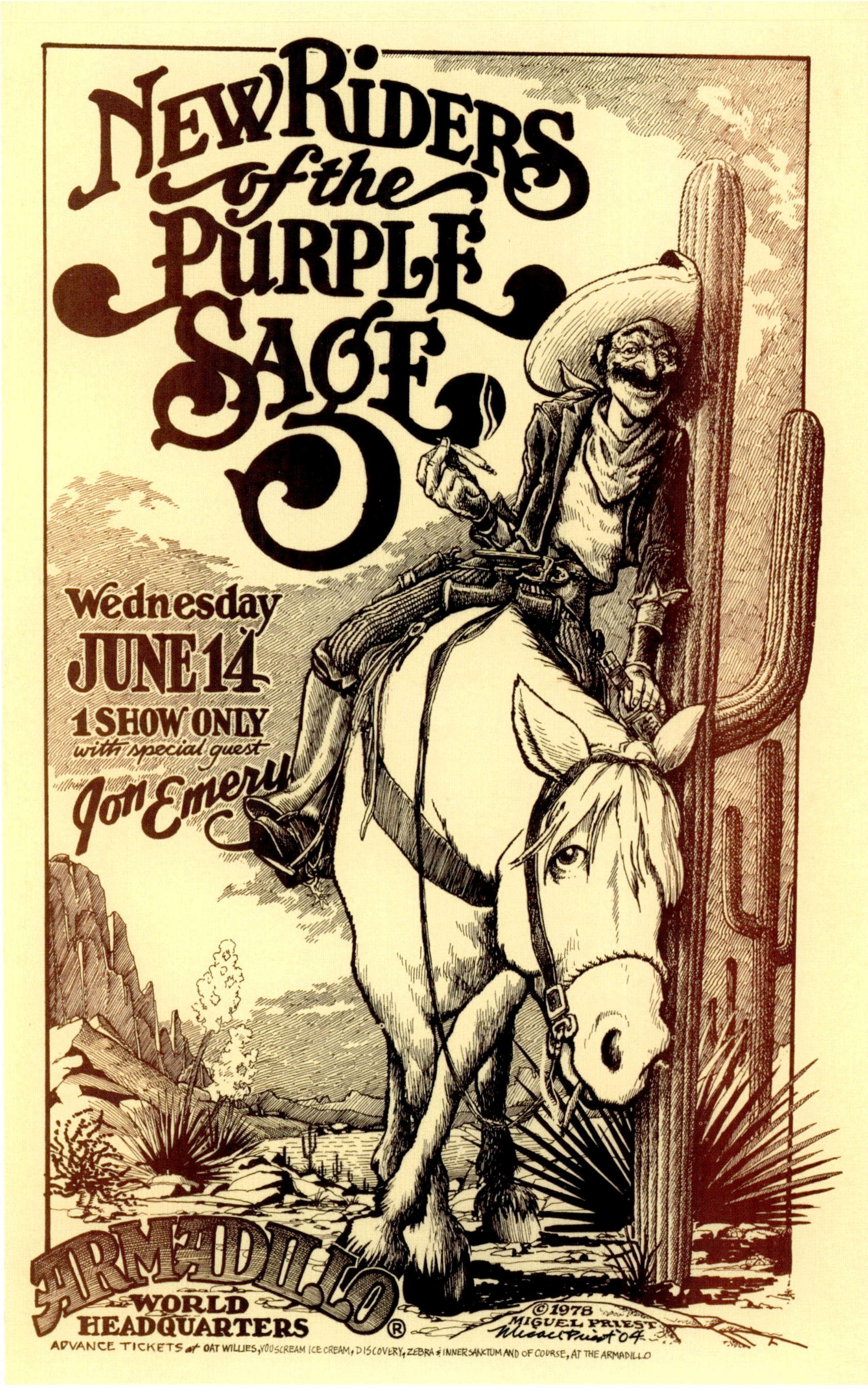

46 KEN FEATHERSTON. The Marshall Tucker Band. Armadillo World Headquarters. June 30, 1974. 17" × 11". © Ken Featherston.

This poster would provide the Marshall Tucker Band with the image for their *Searchin' for a Rainbow* album cover.

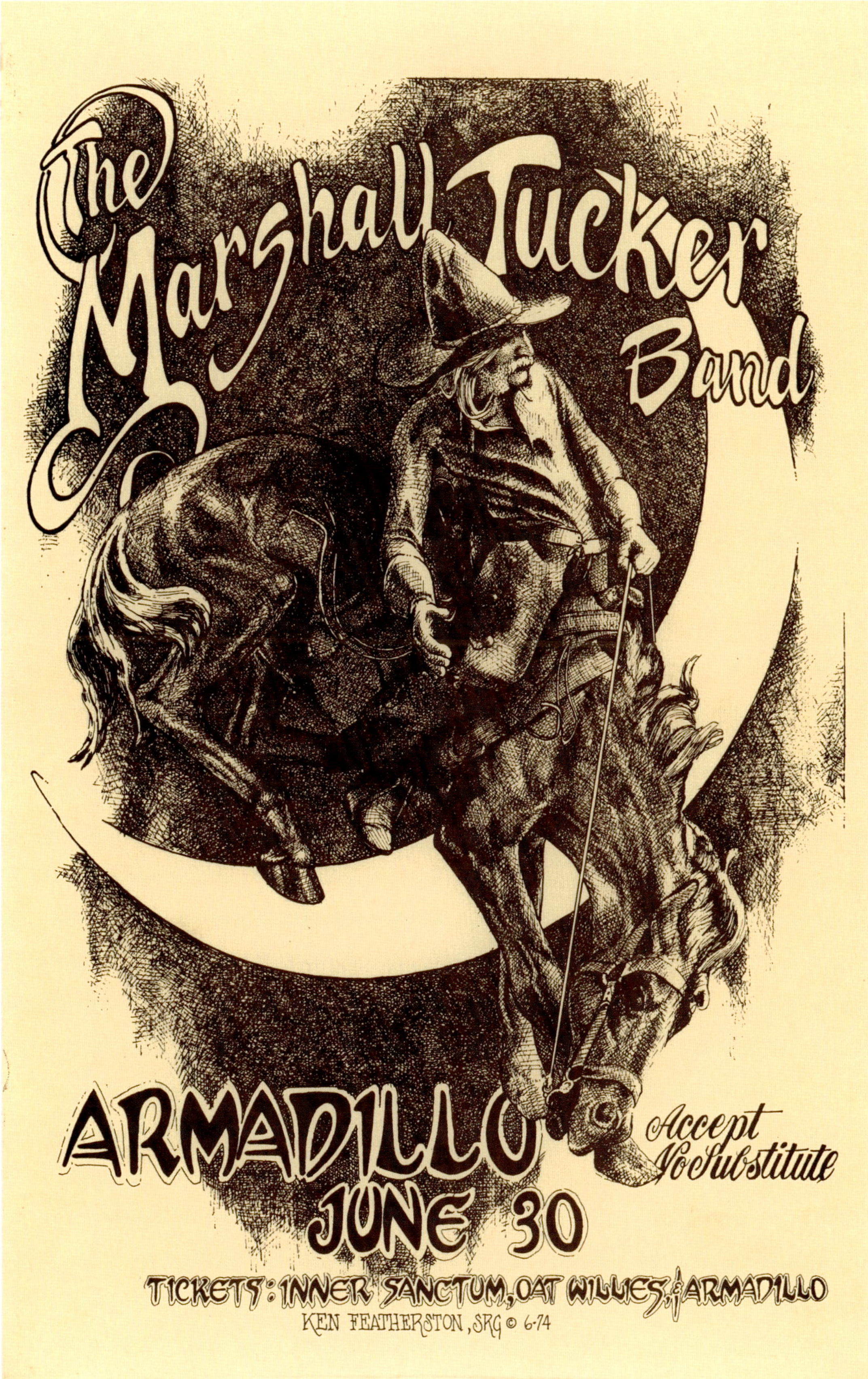

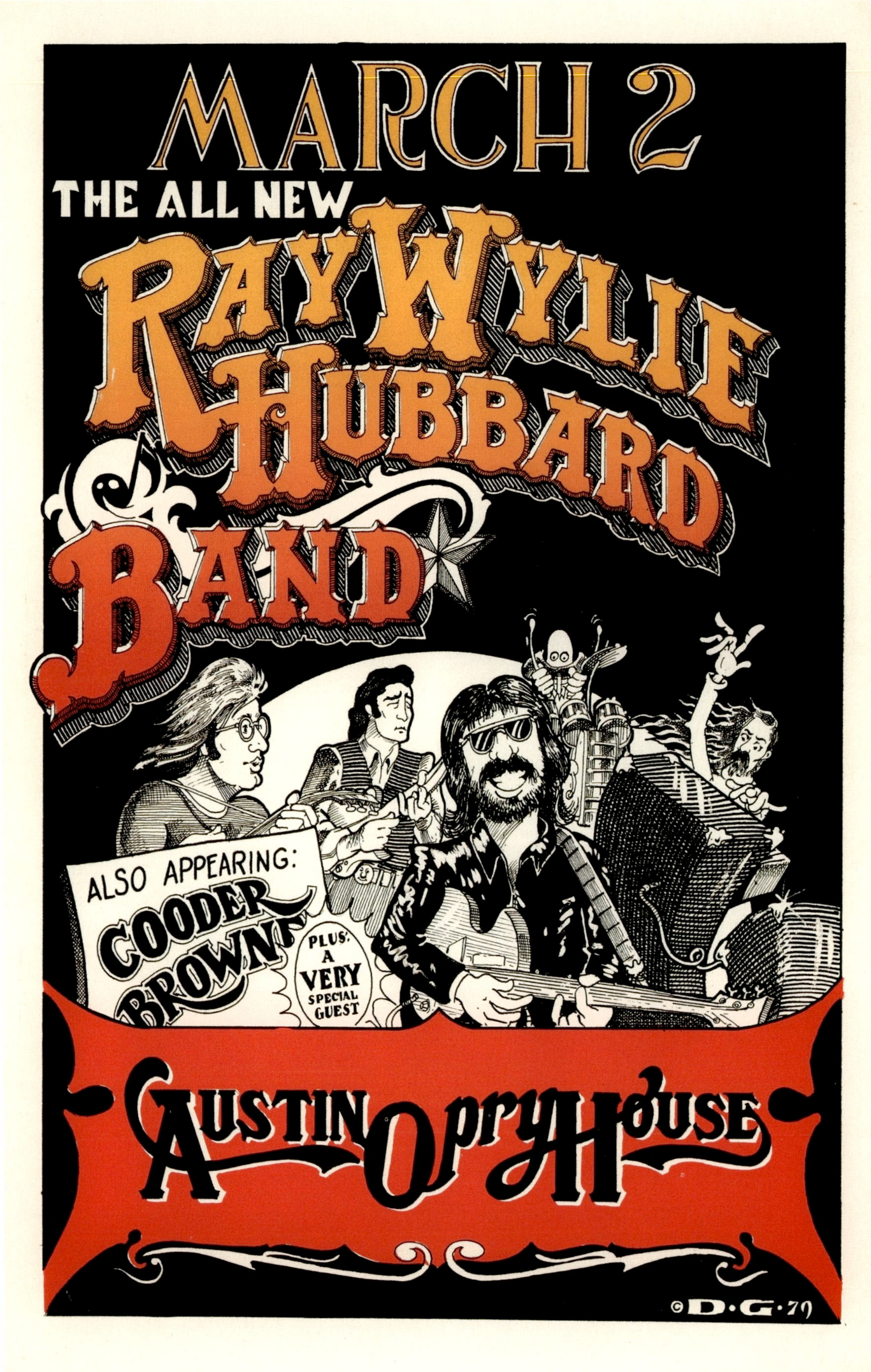

47 DANNY GARRETT. The All New Ray Wylie Hubbard Band & Cooder Browne. Austin Opry House. March 2, 1979. 17.5" × 11.5". © Danny Garrett.

48 DANNY GARRETT. The Lost Gonzo Band. Armadillo World Headquarters. February 7, 1980. 17" × 11". © Danny Garrett.

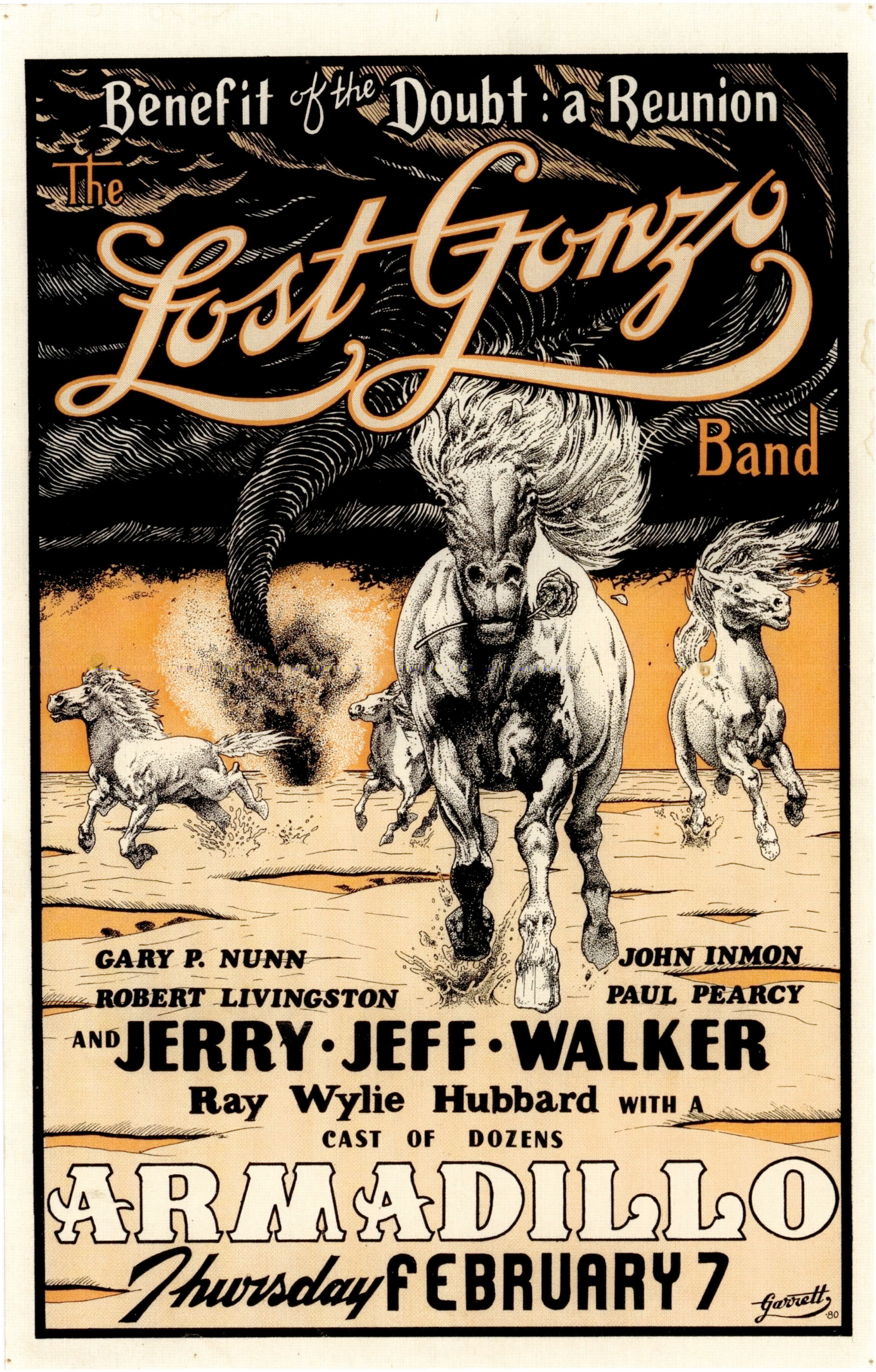

49 MICAEL PRIEST. Freda and the Firedogs. American Legion Hall, Smithville. April 14, 1973. 17" × 11". © Micael Priest.

Bobby Earl Smith, who started Freda and the Firedogs along with Marcia Ball, explains this "stock concert poster" that would be used to promote numerous gigs: "I'd ask Micael to letter each gig and then I'd take the new lettering to the printer and run off a hundred or so and put them up all around town. I told Micael that I wanted an identifiable logo so that once someone saw the poster, he or she would know immediately that it advertised a Freda and the Firedogs gig. I remember telling Priest that I wanted a logo that someone could recognize from the other side of the street."

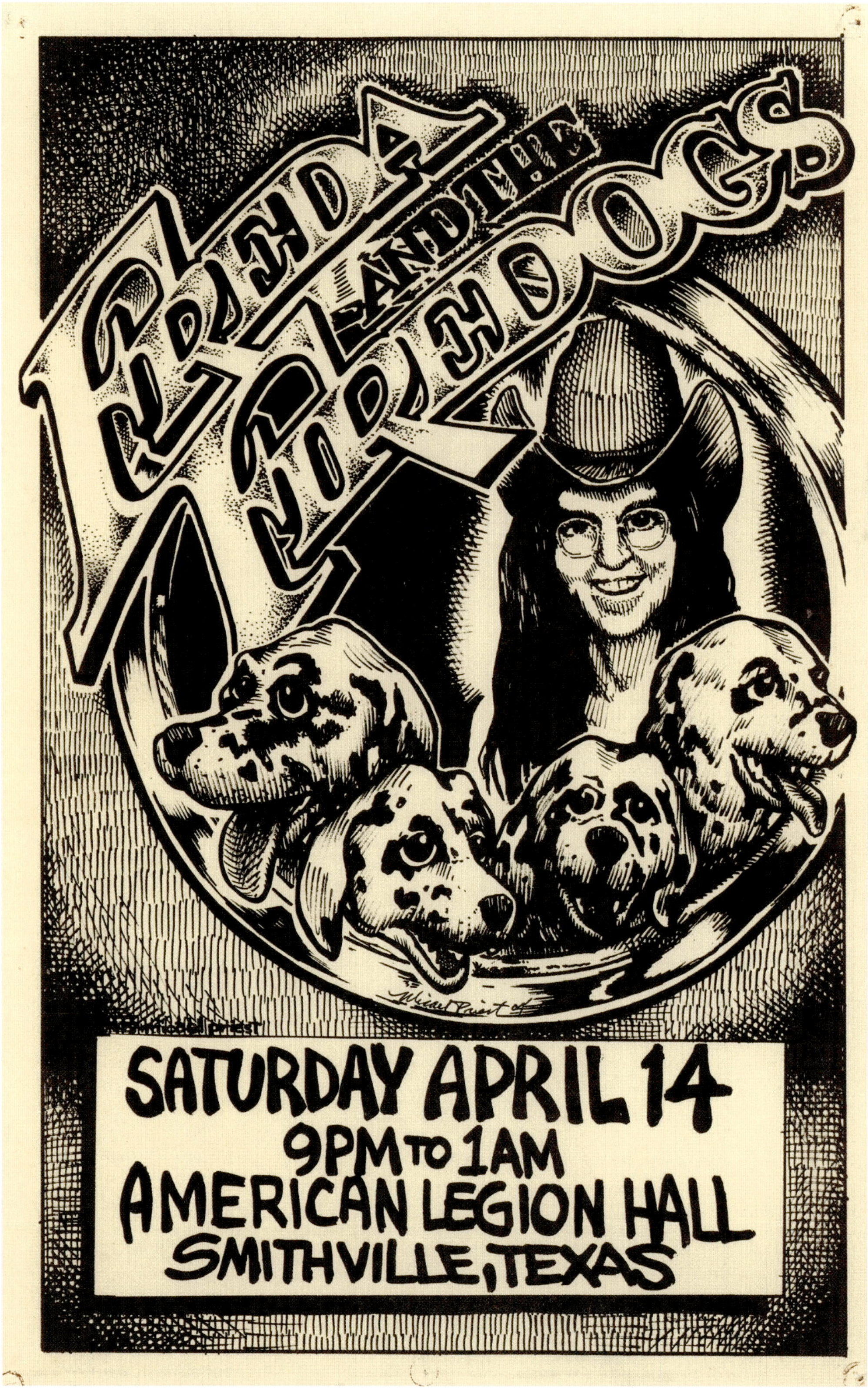

50 MICAEL PRIEST. "Genuine Texas Swing" with members of the Texas Playboys & Alvin Crow and the Pleasant Valley Boys. Broken Spoke. September 17, 1975. 13.5" × 11". © Micael Priest.

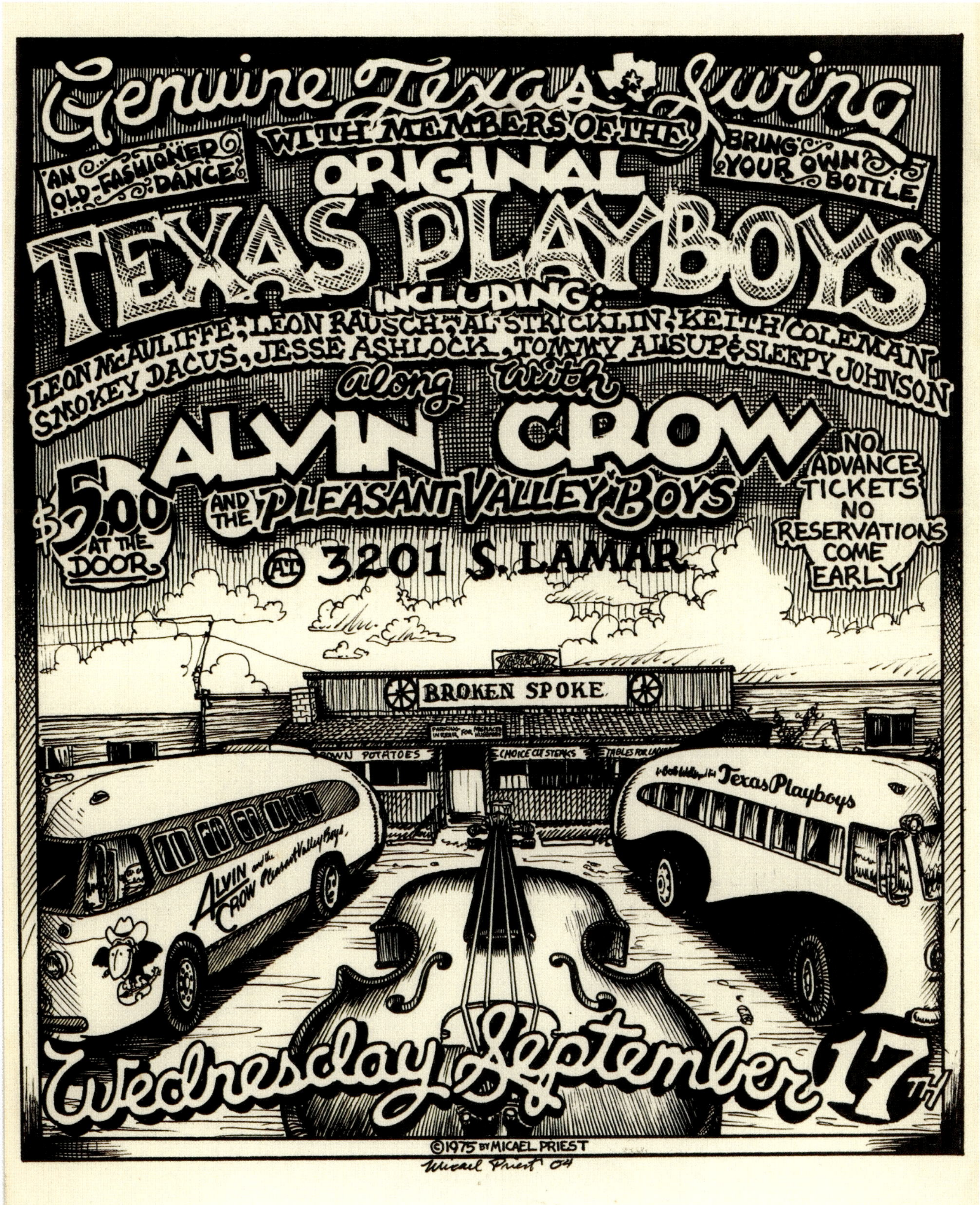

51 MICAEL PRIEST. Willie Nelson & Greezy Wheels. Armadillo World Headquarters. August 12, 1972. 17" × 11". © Micael Priest

Priest's sad cowboy drowns his sorrows to the tune of "Hello Walls," a classic Willie composition that Faron Young took to the top of the country charts in 1961. The poster advertises Willie's first Armadillo World Headquarters performance.

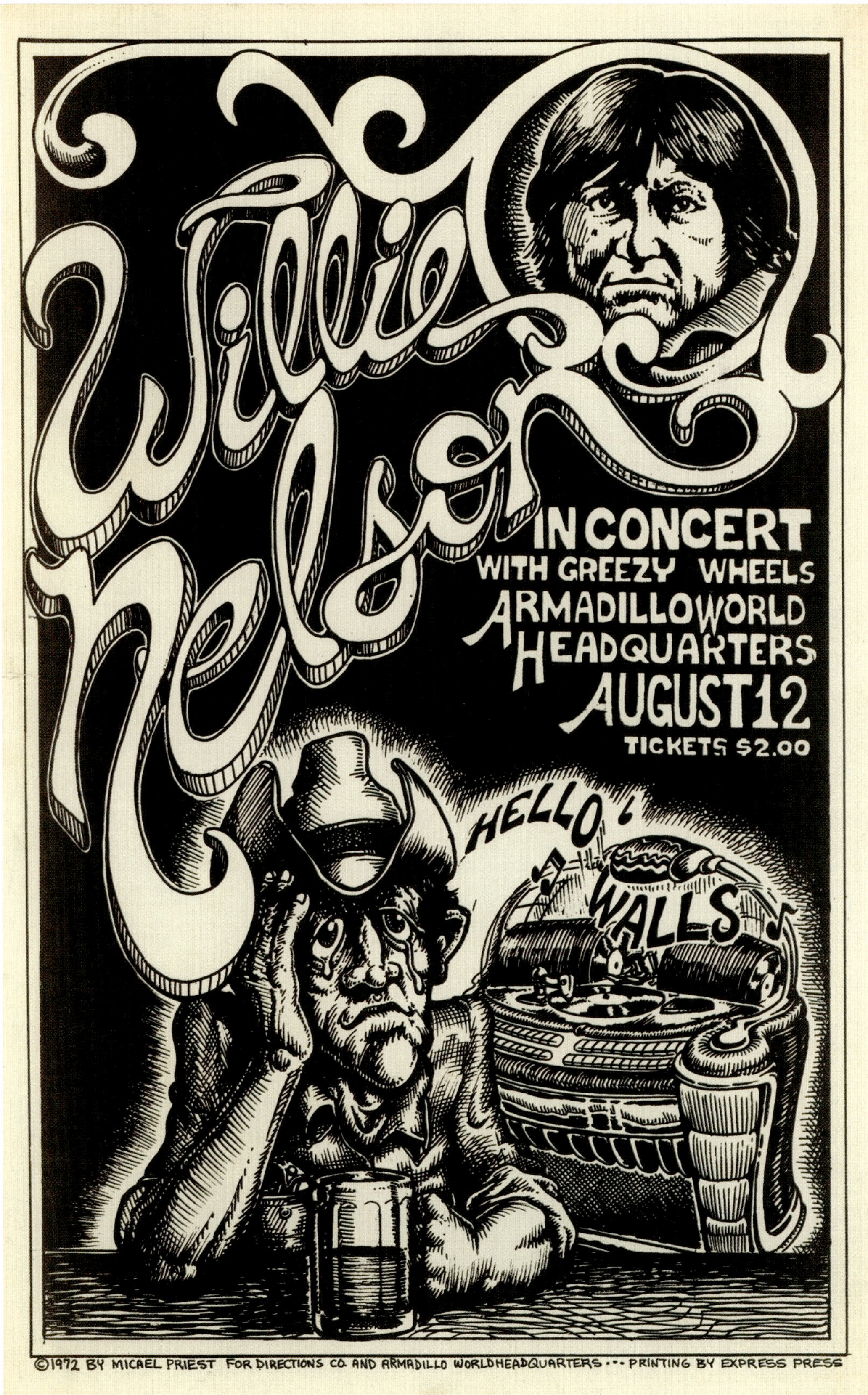

52 JIM FRANKLIN. Willie Nelson's 4th of July Picnic. Dripping Springs. July 4, 1973. 17" × 11". © Jim Franklin.

Willie's first 4th of July Picnic, an annual event that has continued for forty years, featured a who's who of early seventies country music.

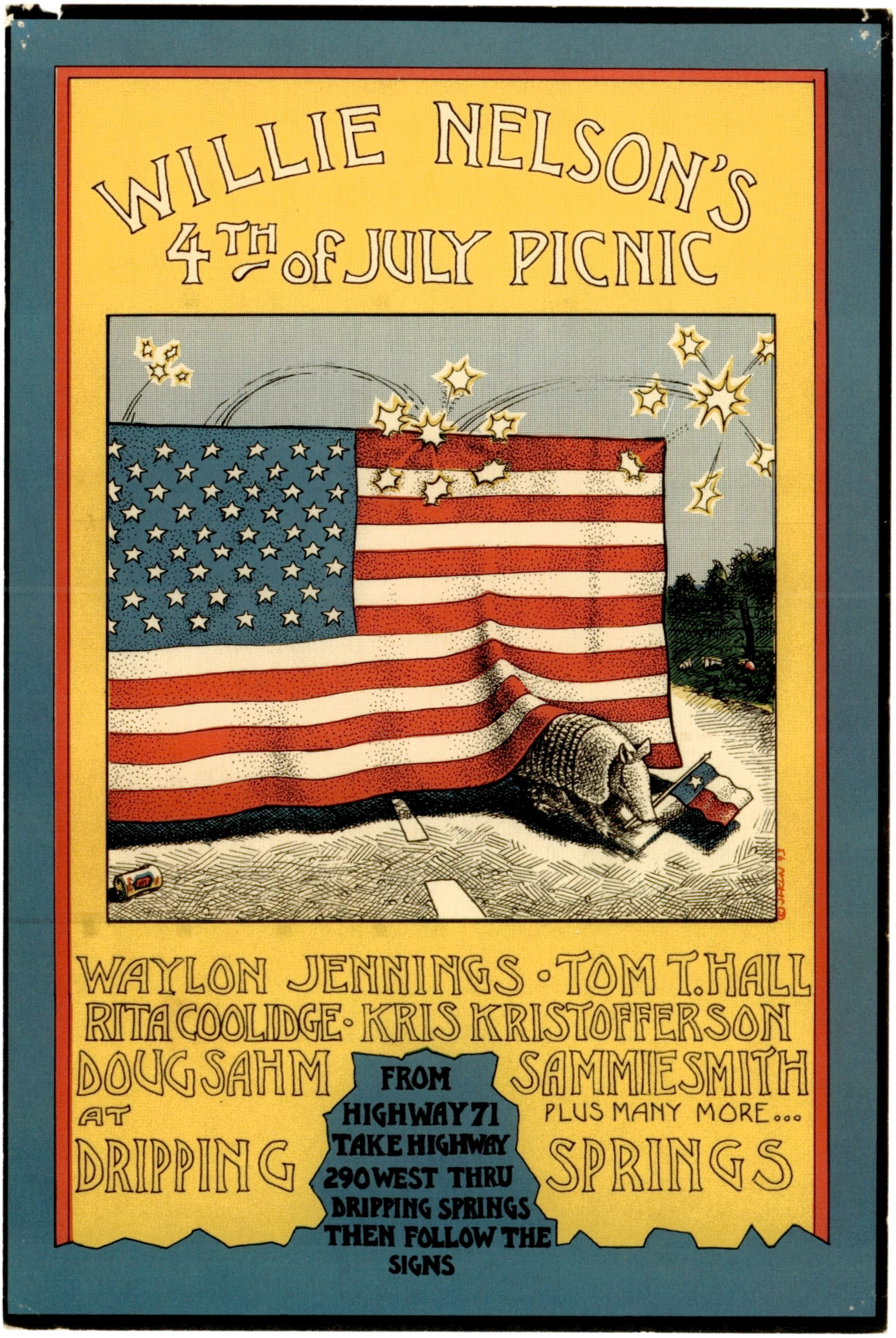

53 MICAEL PRIEST. Willie Nelson & Michael Murphey. Armadillo World Headquarters. September 15 & 16, 1972. 16.25" × 10.5". © Micael Priest.

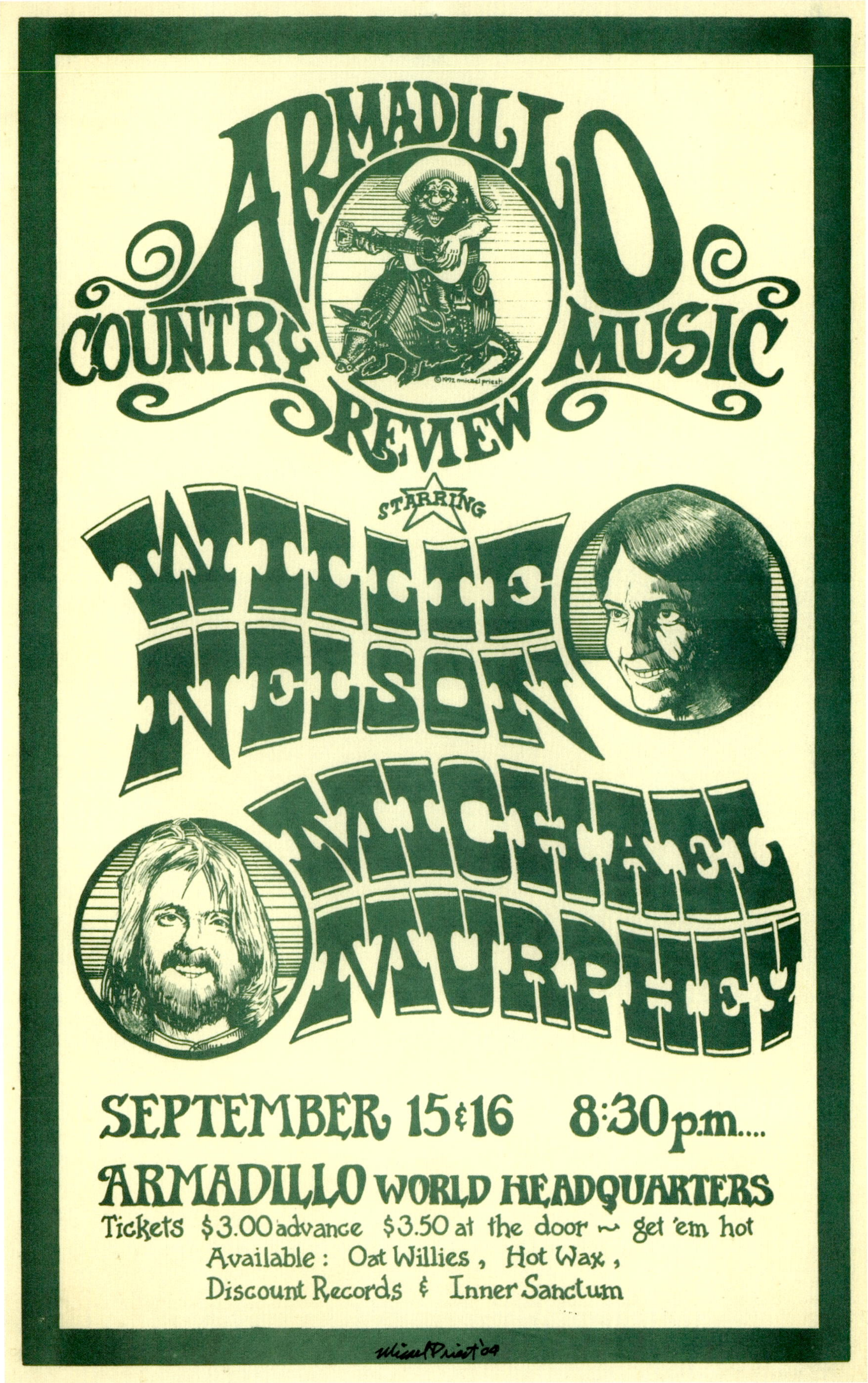

54 JIM FRANKLIN. Willie Nelson & Doak Snead. Ritz Theatre. November 11, 1974. 17" × 11". © Jim Franklin.

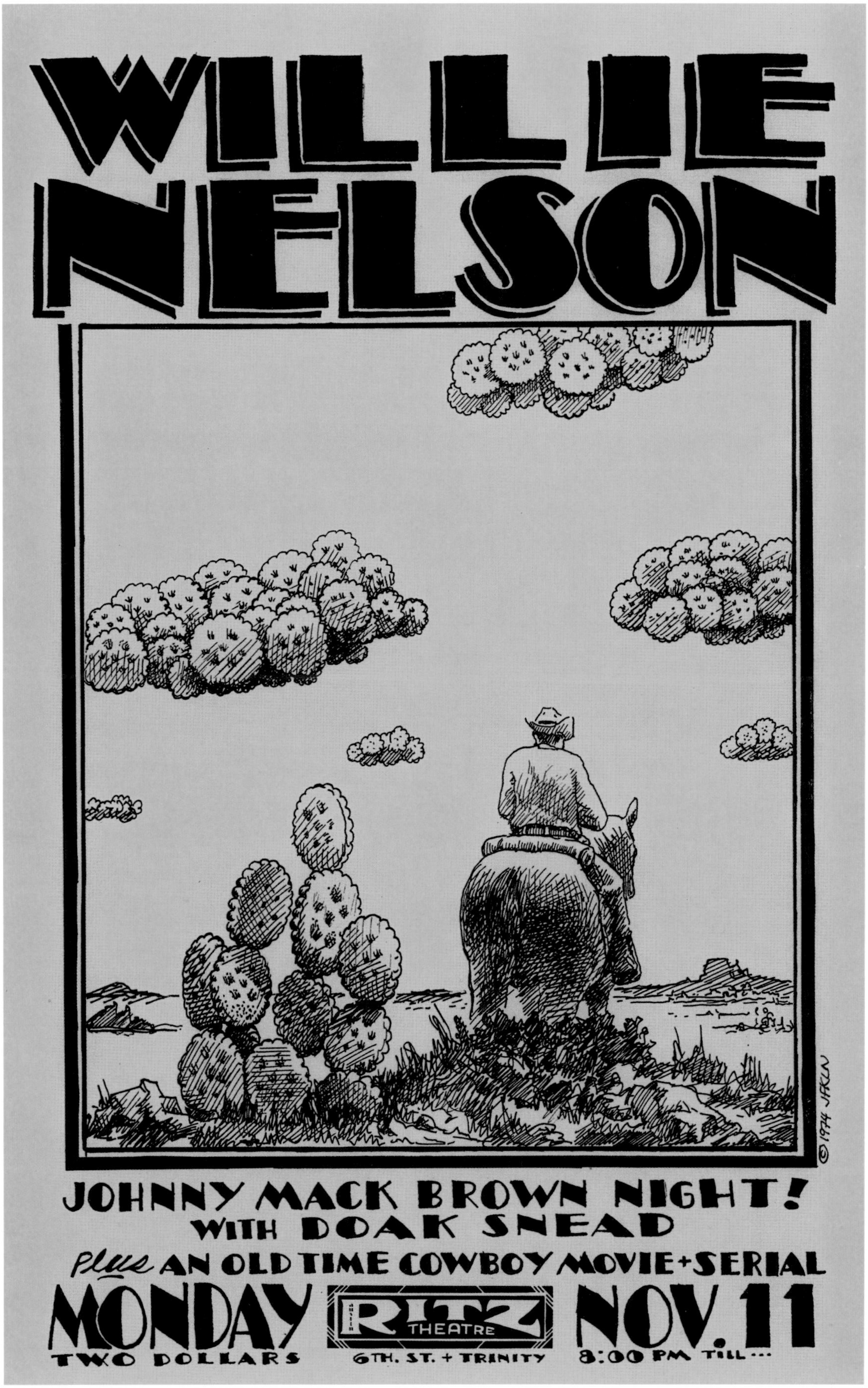

55 DANNY GARRETT. Willie Nelson's 4th of July Picnic. Austin Opry House. July 3 & 4, 1978. 17.5" × 11.5". © Danny Garrett.

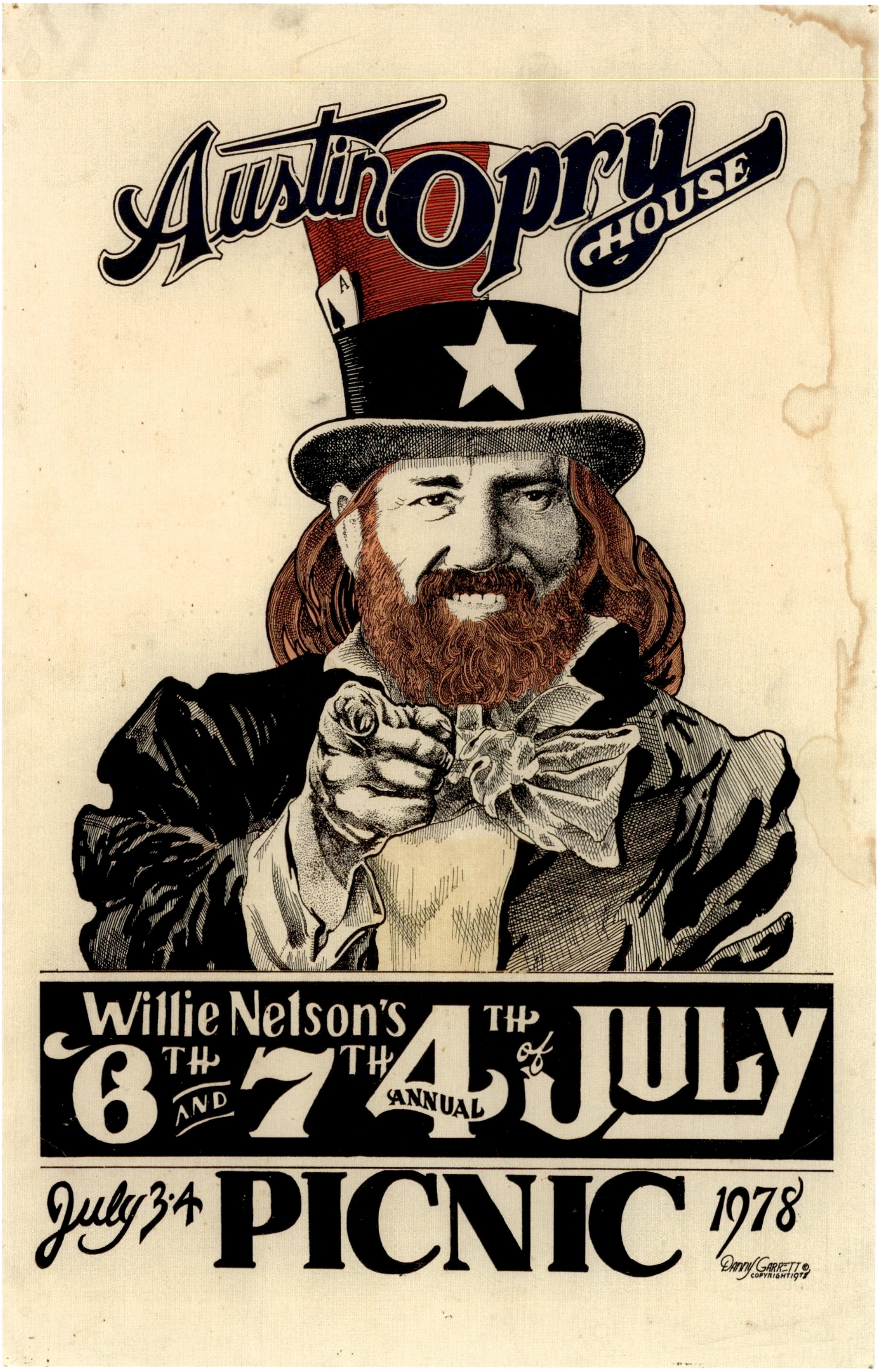

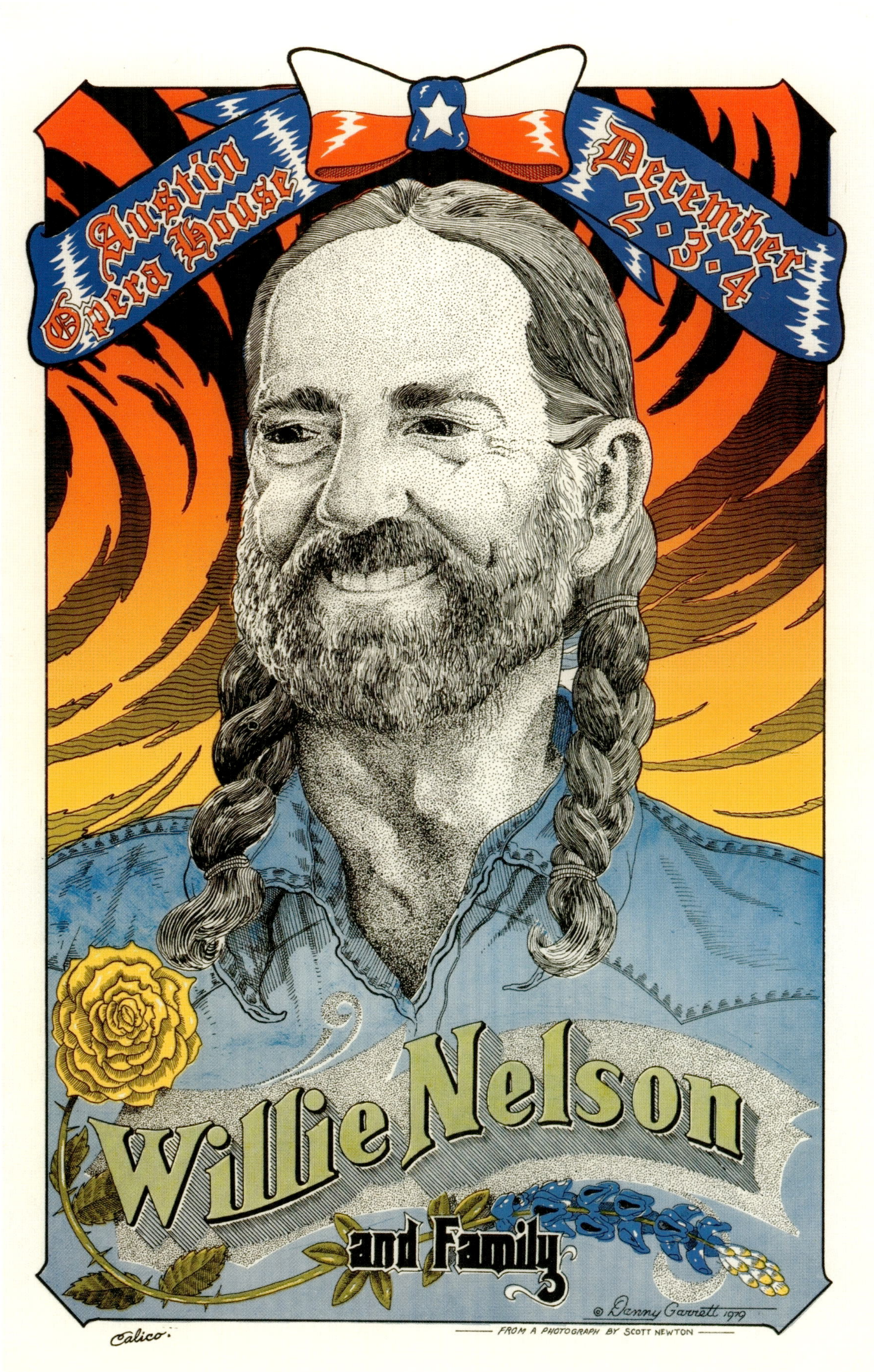

56 DANNY GARRETT. Willie Nelson. Austin Opera House. December 2–4, 1979. 17.5" × 11.5". © Danny Garrett.

57 KERRY AWN. Soap Creek Saloon calendar. Soap Creek Saloon. February 1974. 17" × 11". © Kerry Awn.

Kerry Awn's calendars became a staple of the Soap Creek Saloon aesthetic. Featured here is Awn's very first calendar for the venue.

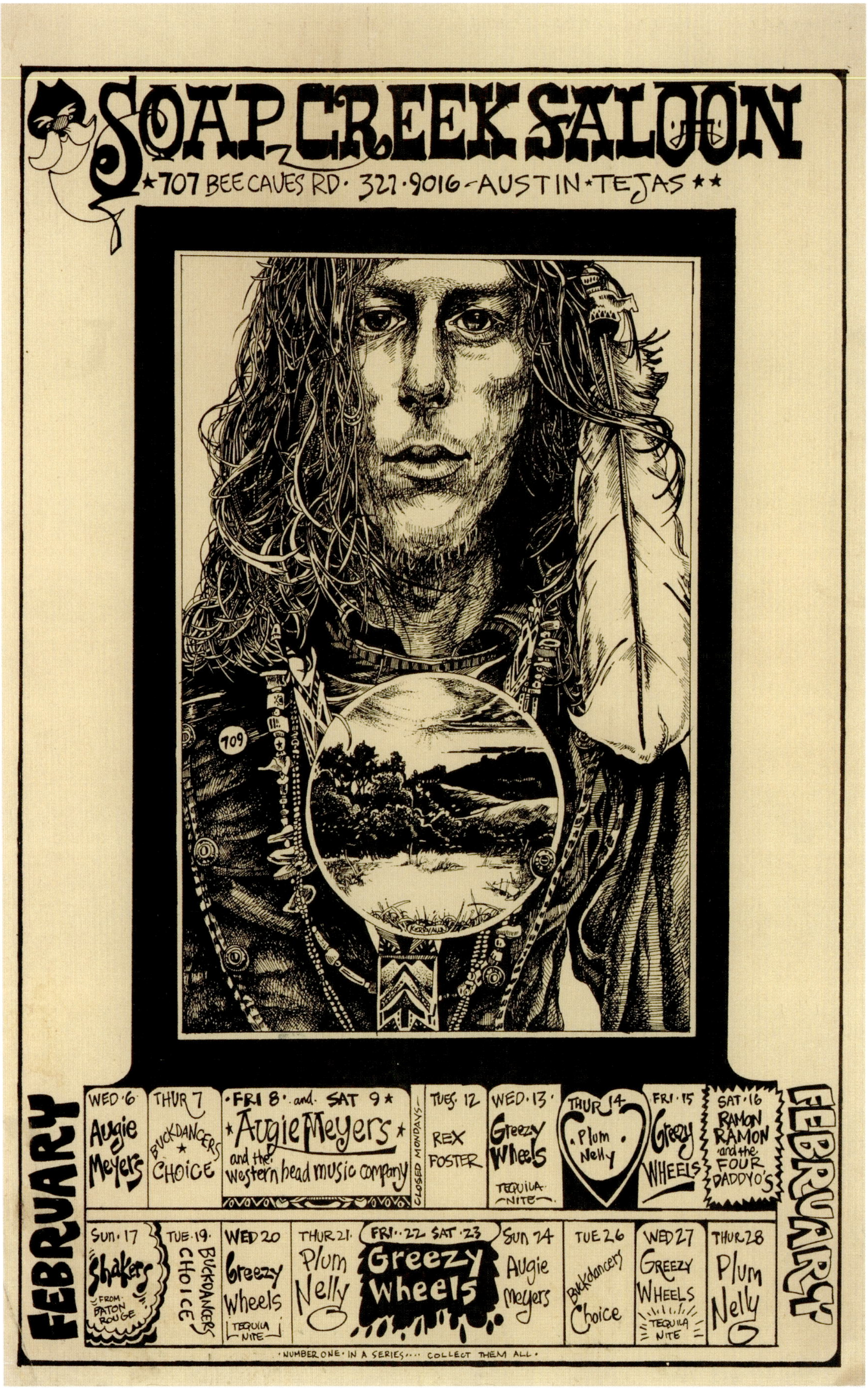

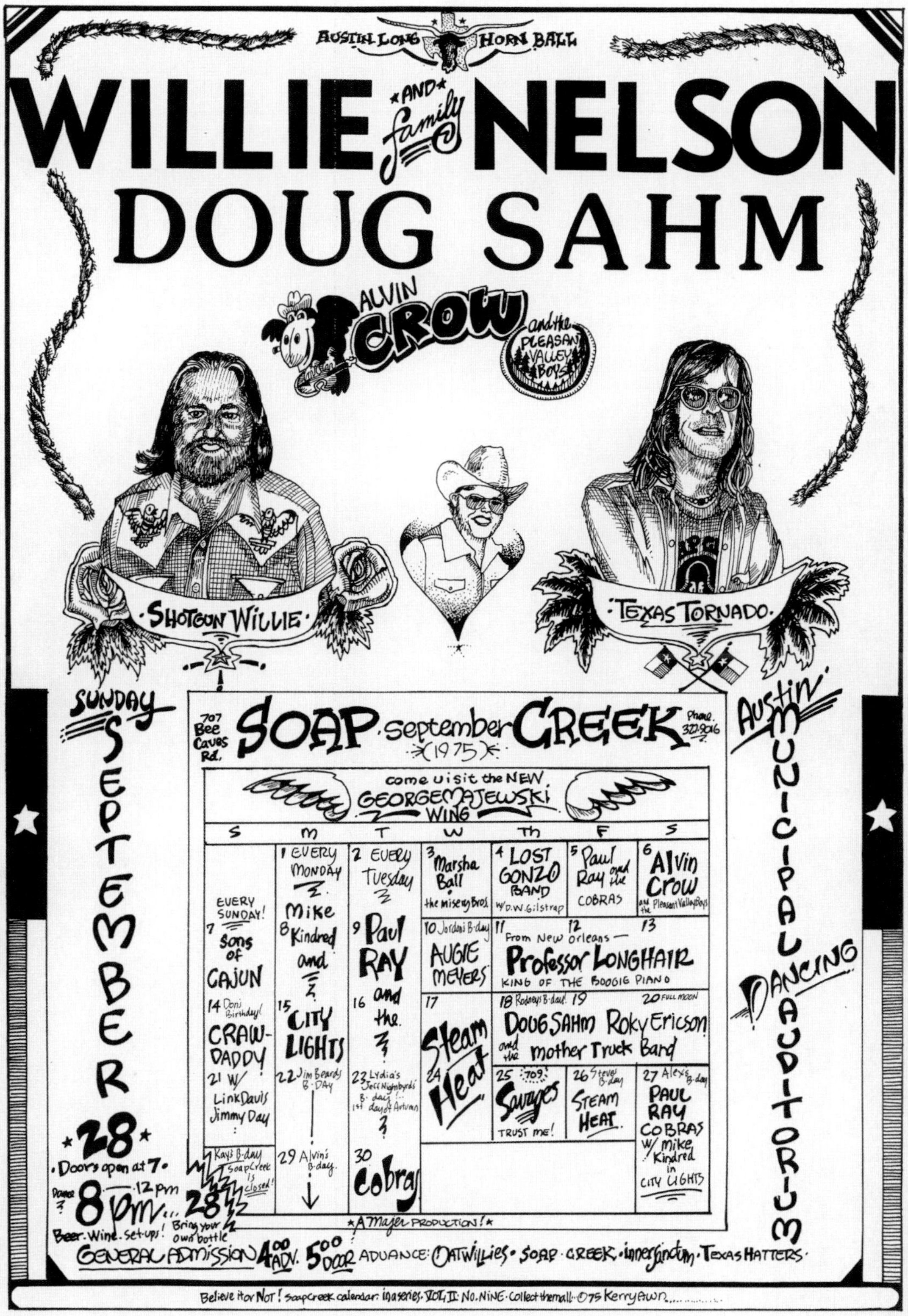

58 KERRY AWN. Soap Creek Saloon calendar: Willie Nelson, Doug Sahm, & Alvin Crow and the Pleasant Valley Boys. Soap Creek Saloon/Municipal Auditorium. September 1975. 17" × 11". © Kerry Awn.

59 KERRY AWN. Willie Nelson, Doug Sahm, & Alvin Crow and the Pleasant Valley Boys. Austin Municipal Auditorium. September 28, 1975. 17" × 11".

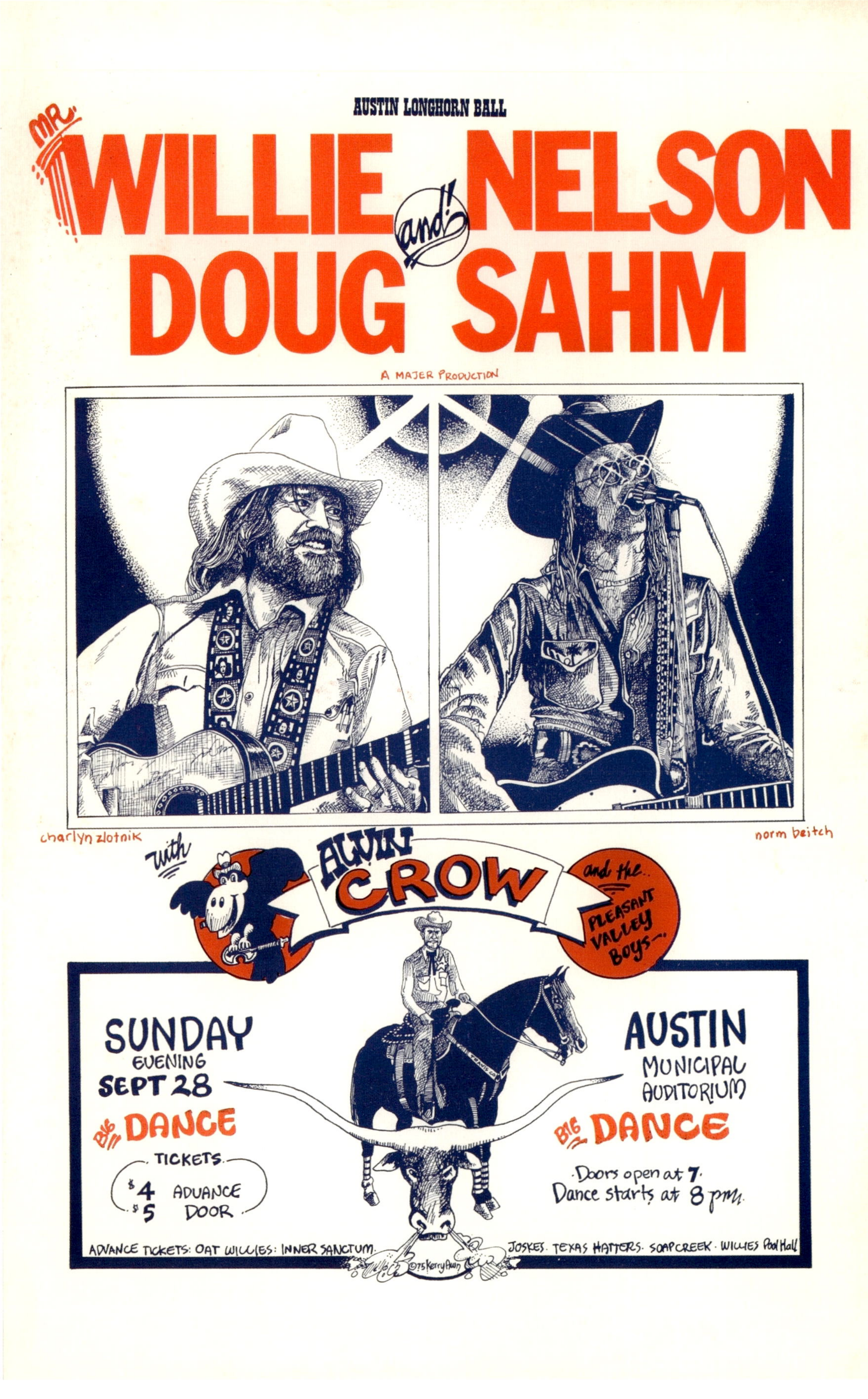

60 GUY JUKE. Rusty Wier & Steven Fromholz. Armadillo World Headquarters. August 4, 1976. 17.5" × 11.5". © Guy Juke.

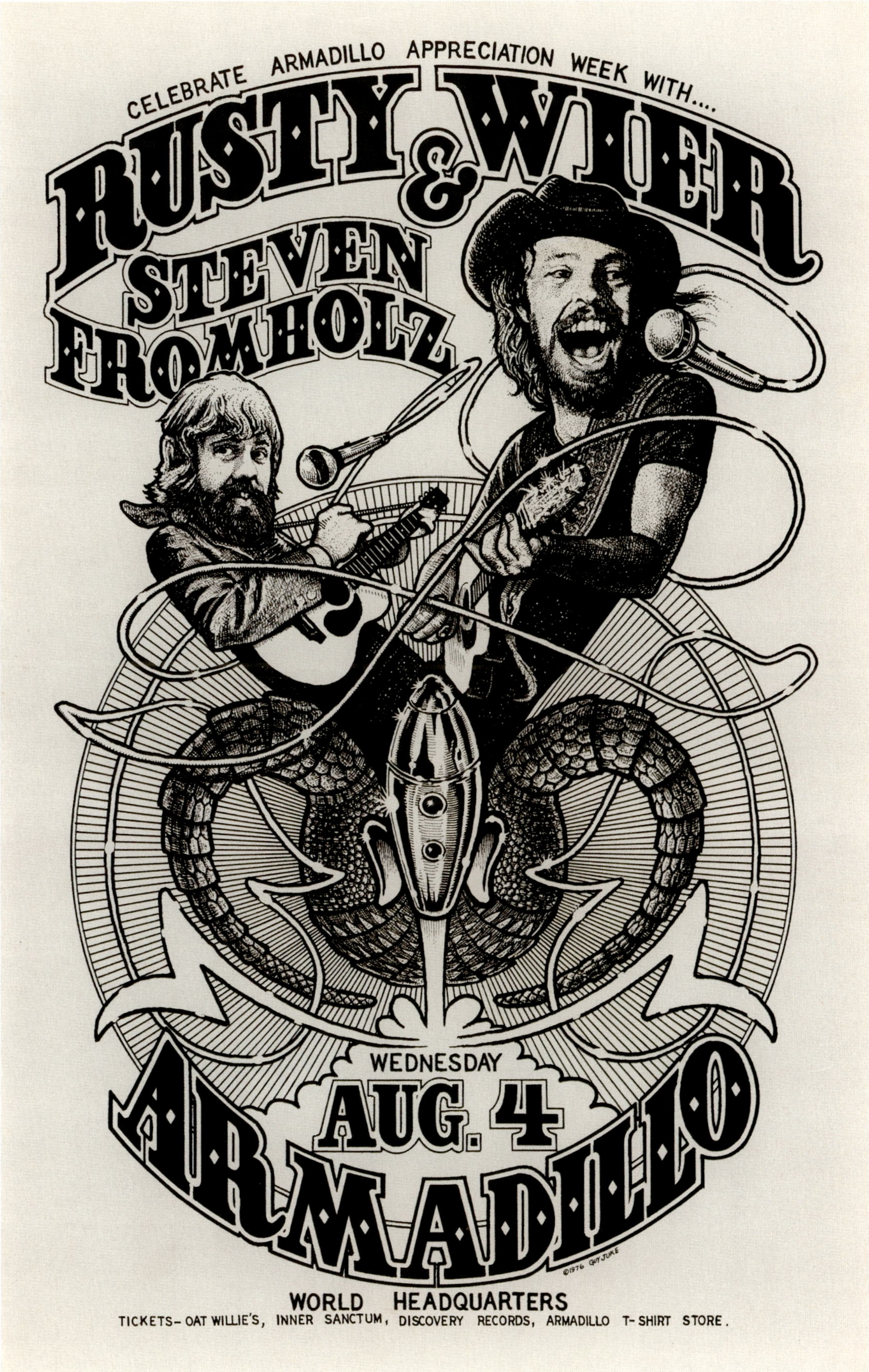

61 KEN FEATHERSTON. B. W. Stevenson & D. K. Little. Armadillo World Headquarters. May 18 & 19, 1973. 17" × 11". © Ken Featherston.

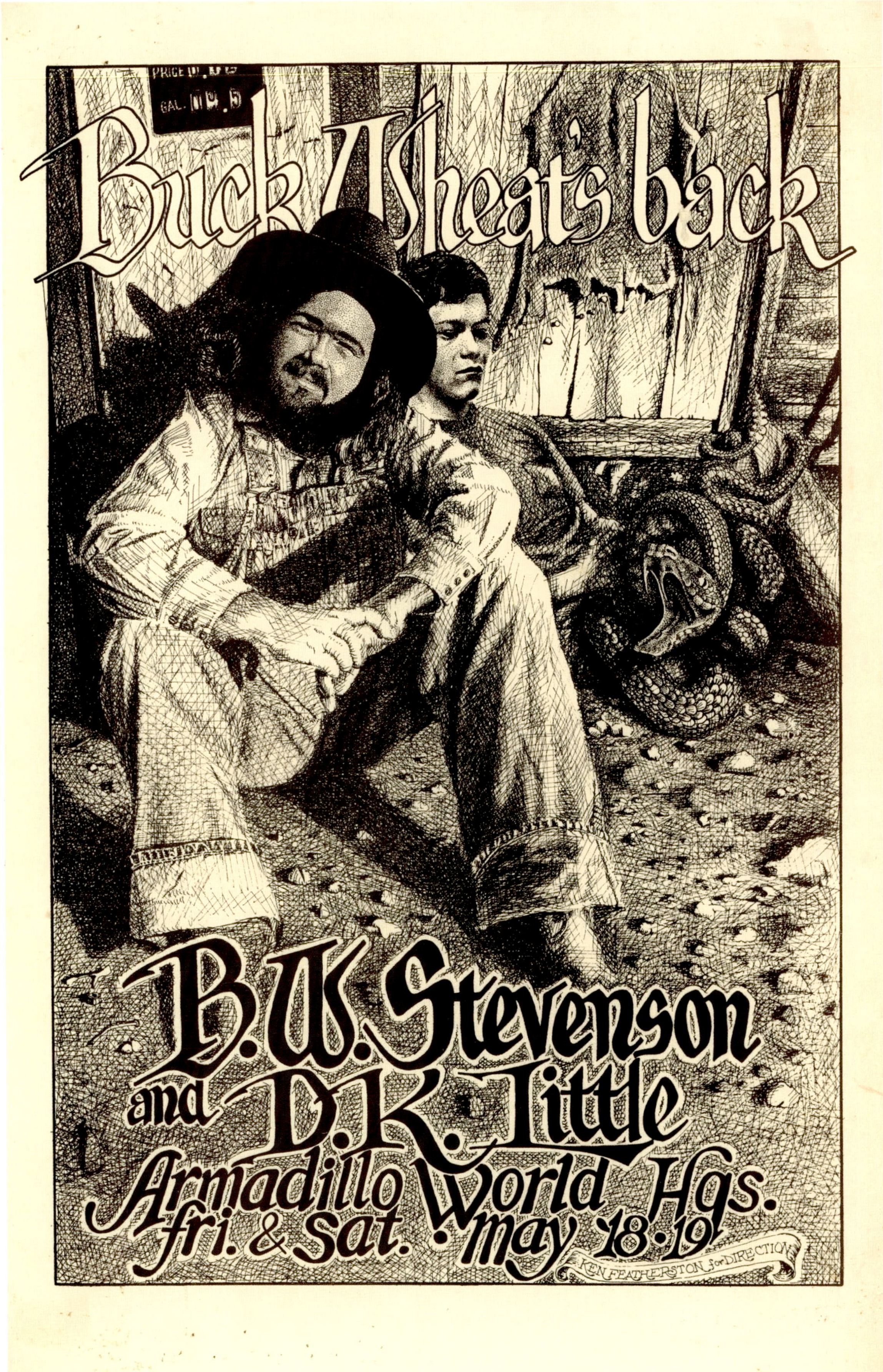

62 KEN FEATHERSTON. B. W. Stevenson & Kenneth Threadgill and the Velvet Cowpasture. Armadillo World Headquarters. February 9 & 10, 1973. 17" × 11". © Ken Featherston.

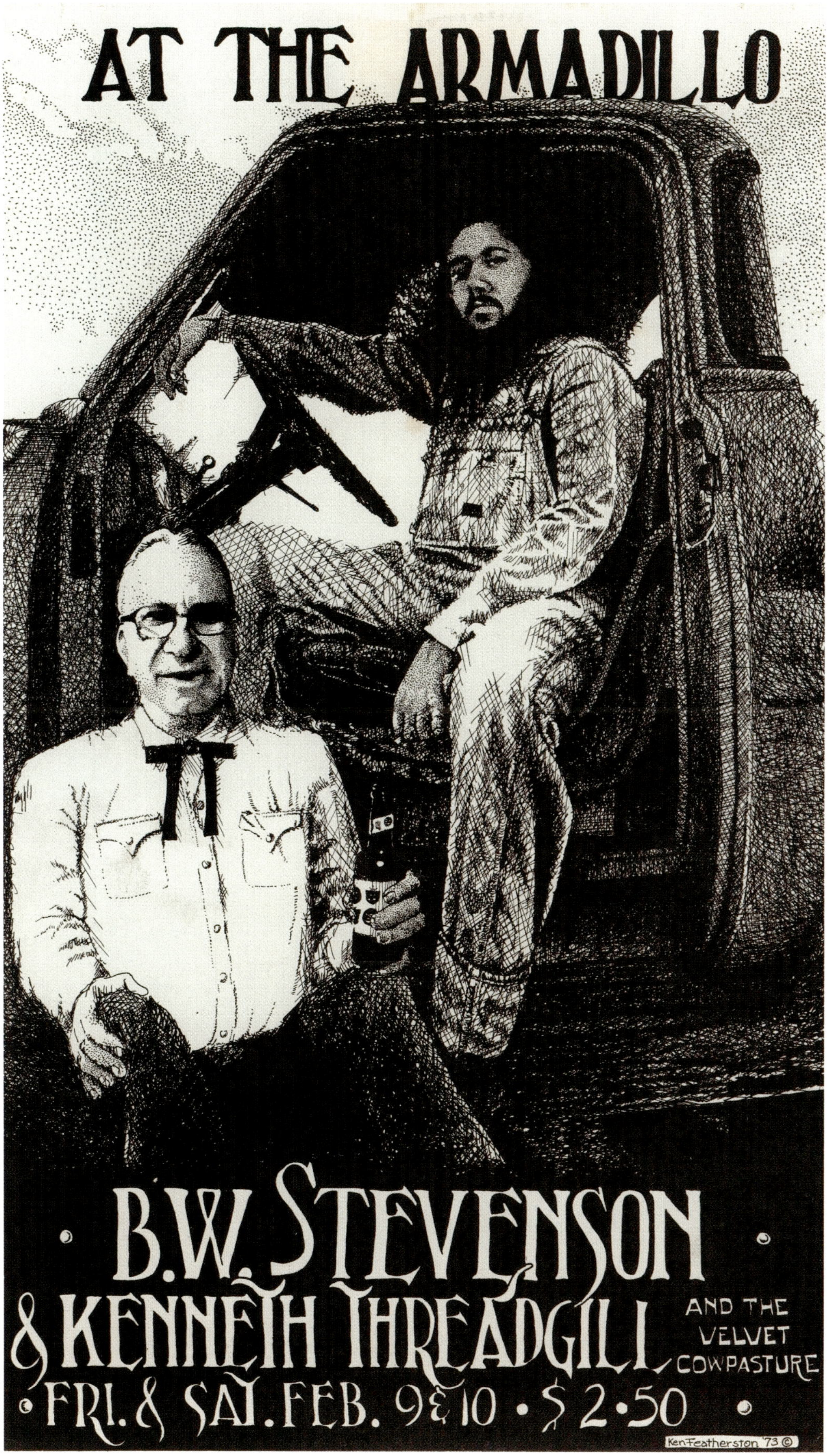

63 Top. GUY JUKE. Asleep at the Wheel & Linda Hargrove. Armadillo World Headquarters. June 27 & 28, 1975. 11" × 17". © Guy Juke.

64 Bottom. MICAEL PRIEST. Freddie Fender & Doug Sahm. Armadillo World Headquarters. August 16 & 17, 1975. 11" × 17". © Micael Priest.

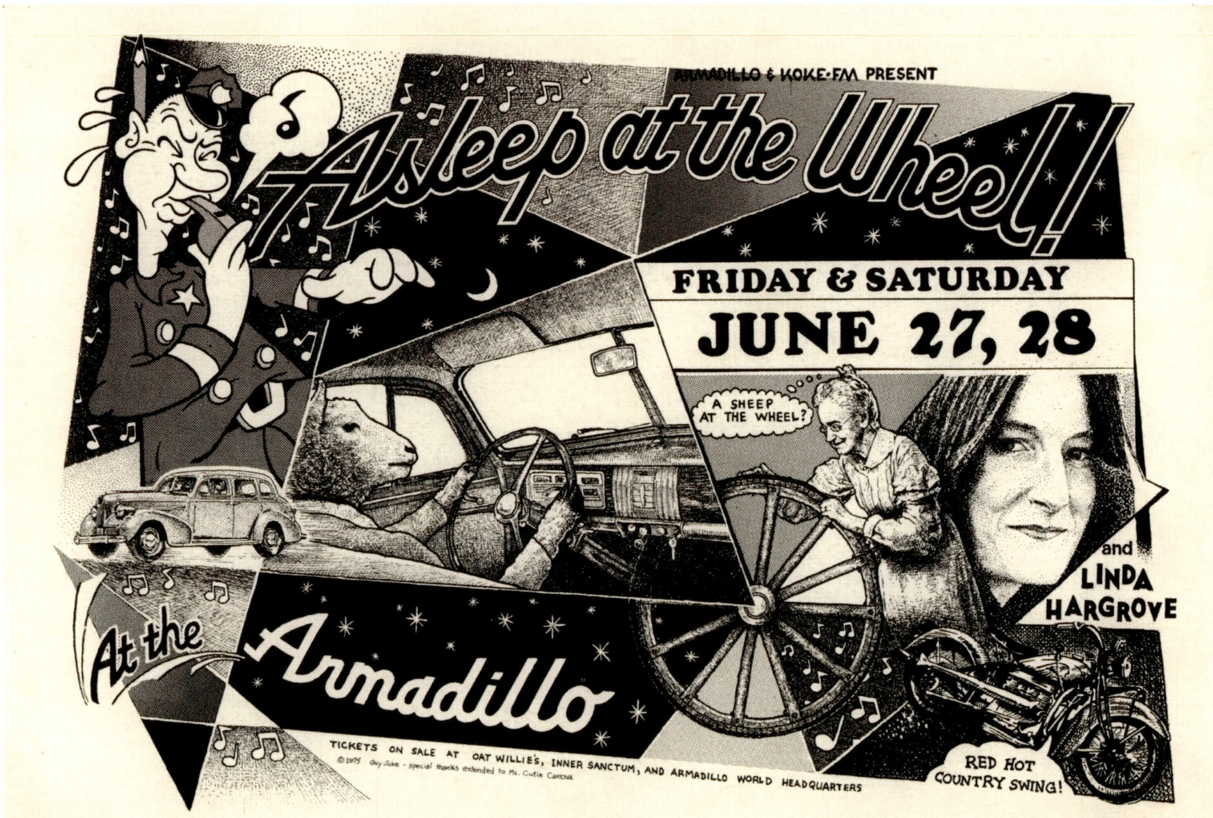

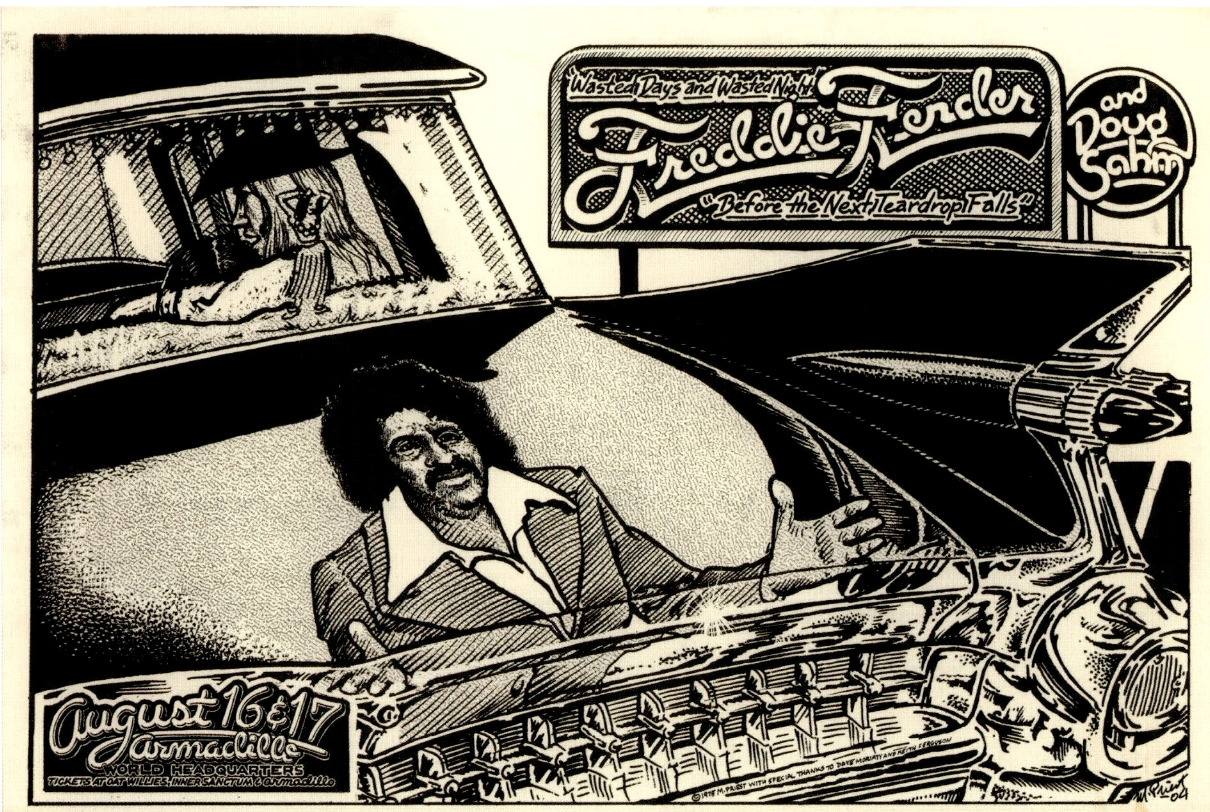

65 HENRY GONZALEZ. Ruben Ramos and the Mexican Revolution. March 30, 1977. Steve Jordan & El Molino. April 1, 1977. Armadillo World Headquarters. 11" × 17". © Henry Gonzalez.

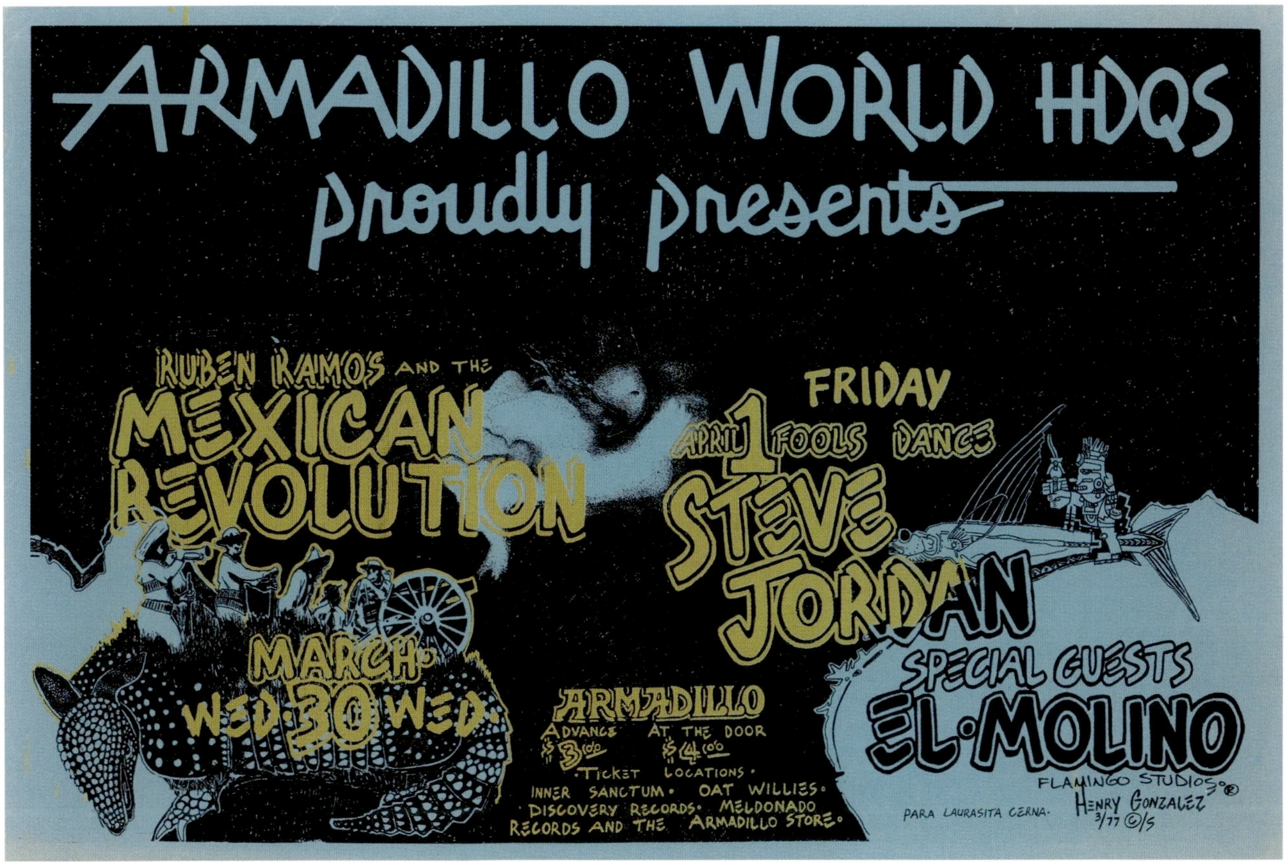

66 KERRY AWN. The Sons of Uranium Savage versus The Marsh Mongrels. Ritz Theatre. December 12, 1974. 25" × 18". © Kerry Awn.

Awn's Sons of Uranium Savage made their stage debut in this battle of the bands that also featured the Marsh Mongrels, a Beaumont-area rhythm-and-blues and swamp-pop group that included Clifford Antone on bass.

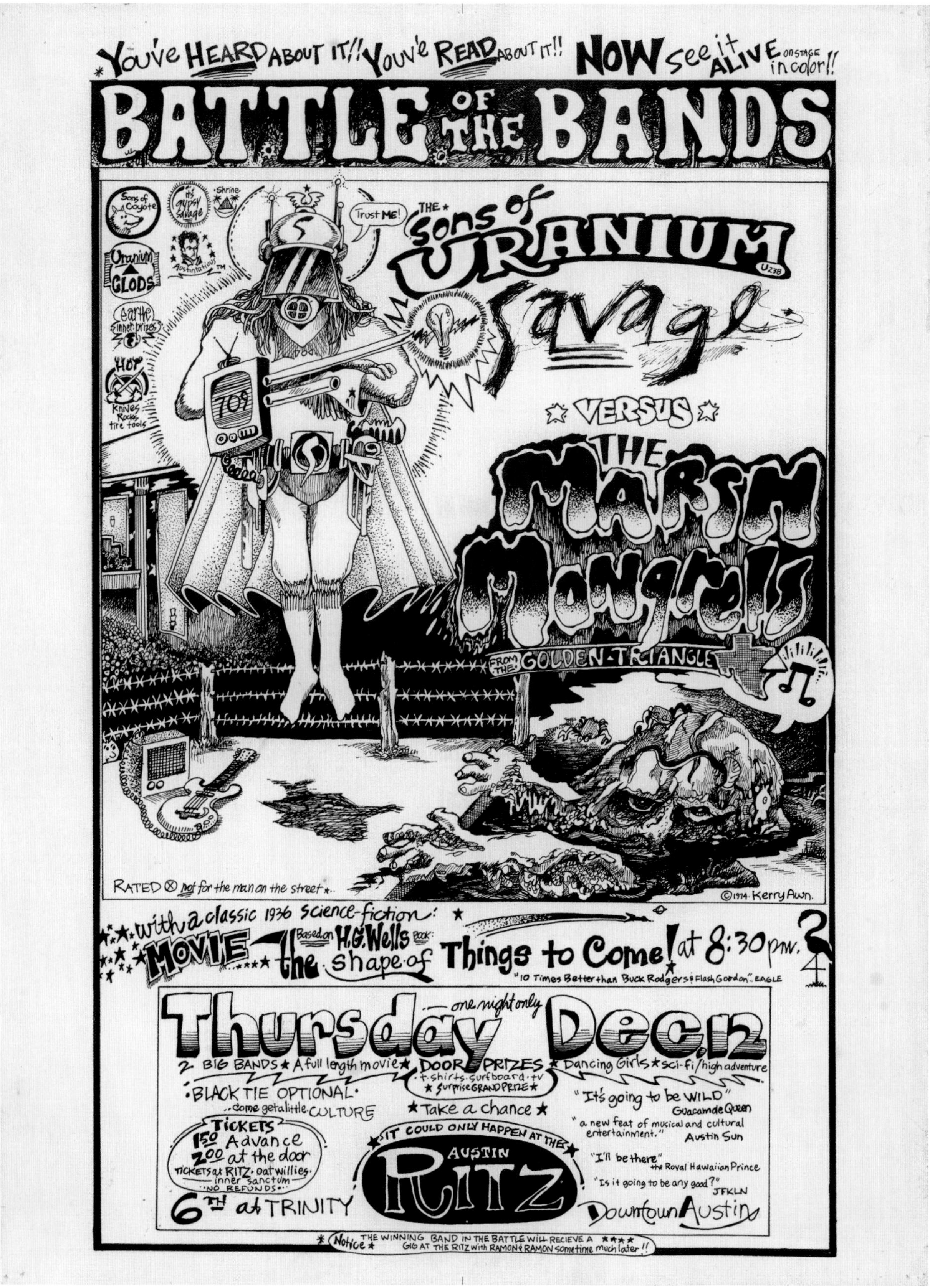

67 KERRY AWN. Greezy Wheels & Uranium Savages. Armadillo World Headquarters. March 19, 1976. 17" × 11". © Kerry Awn.

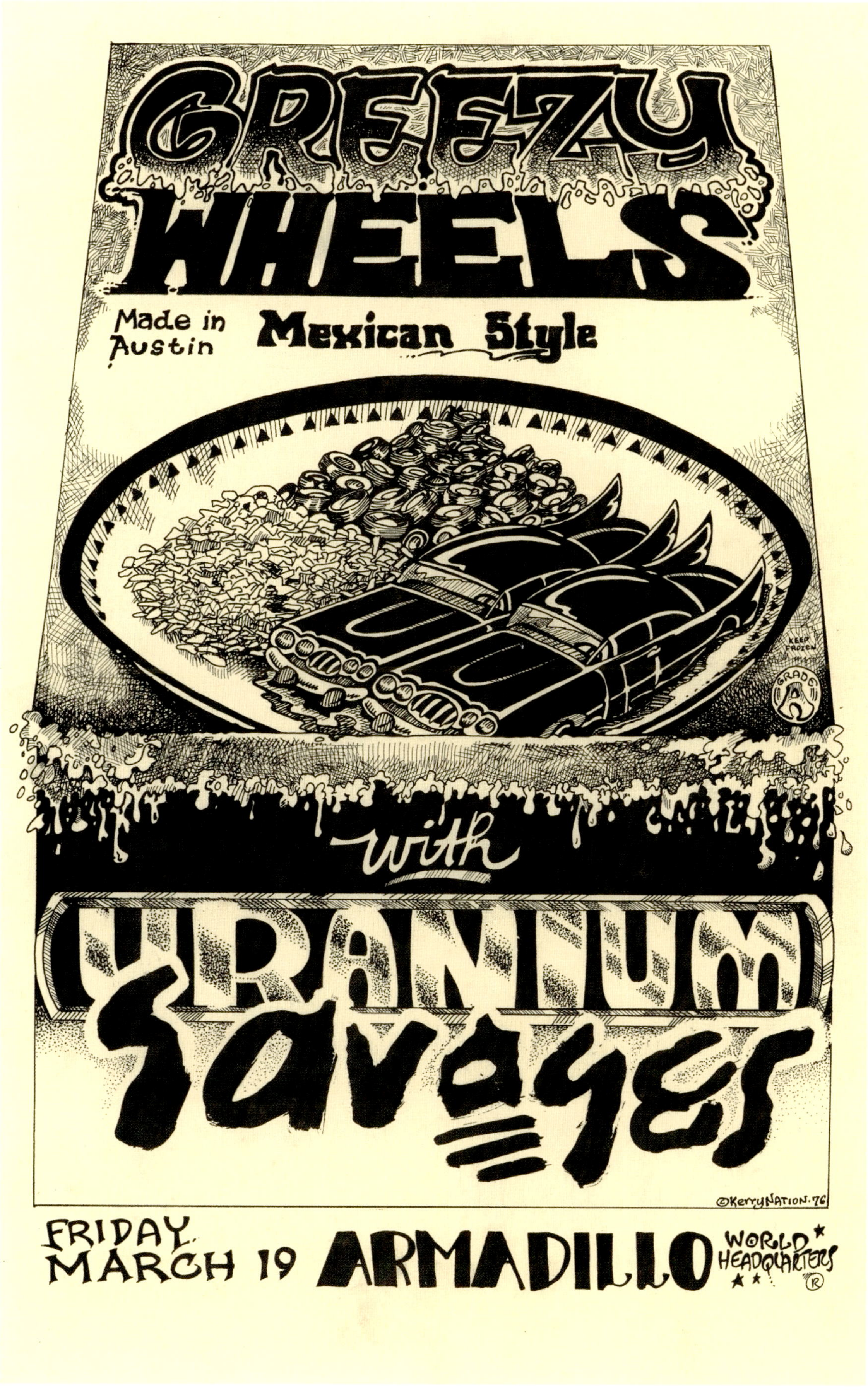

68 DANNY GARRETT. Asleep at the Wheel & Greezy Wheels. Armadillo World Headquarters. December 31, 1975. 17" × 11". © Danny Garrett.

Garrett, whose work often features hidden symbols that he describes as "Easter eggs," alludes to *The Urantia Book*, a collection of theses by unknown authors first published in 1955 that expounds on philosophy, science, and religion.

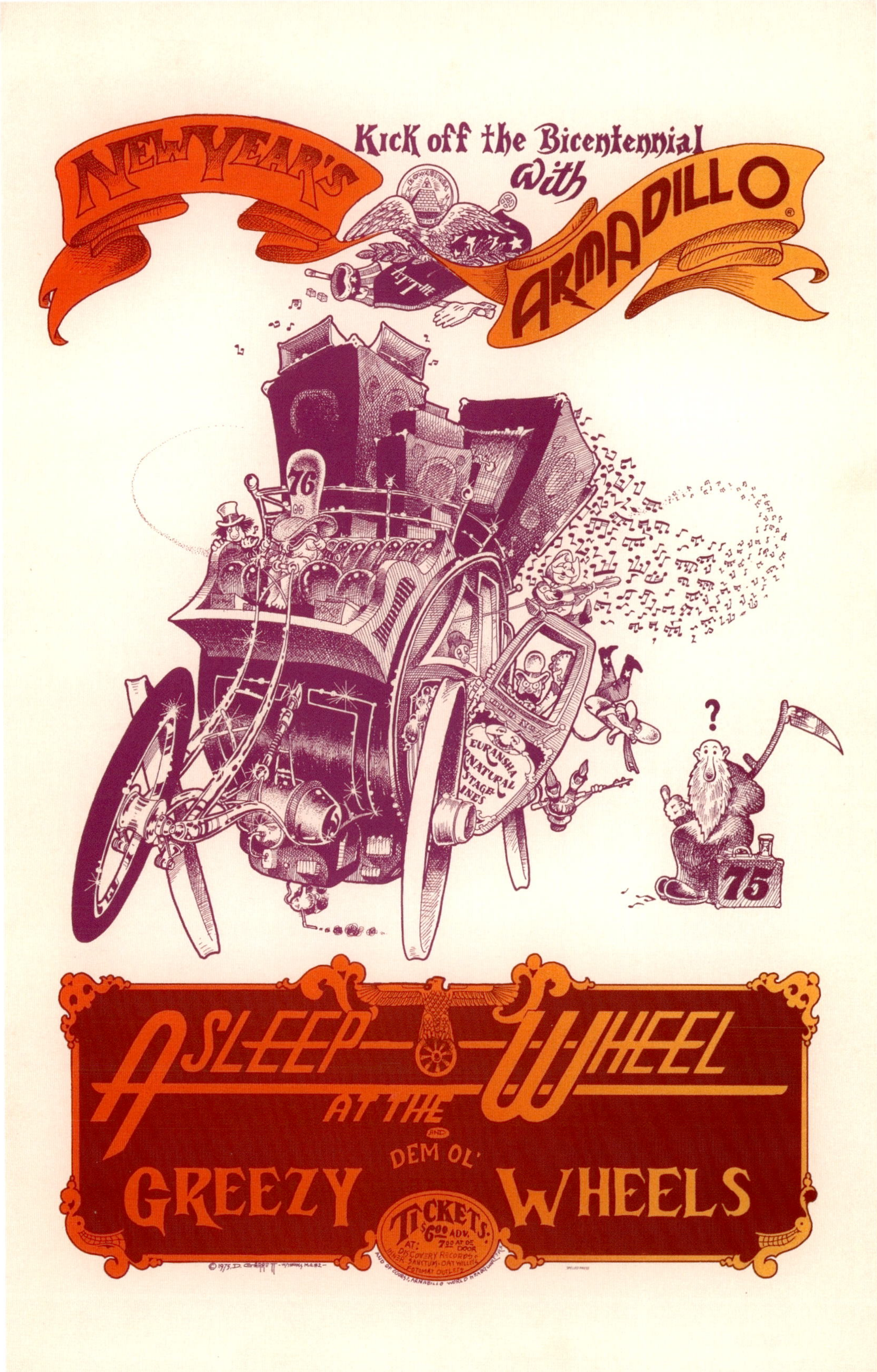

69 DANNY GARRETT. Asleep at the Wheel. Antone's. March 1, 1980. 17.5" × 11.5". © Danny Garrett.

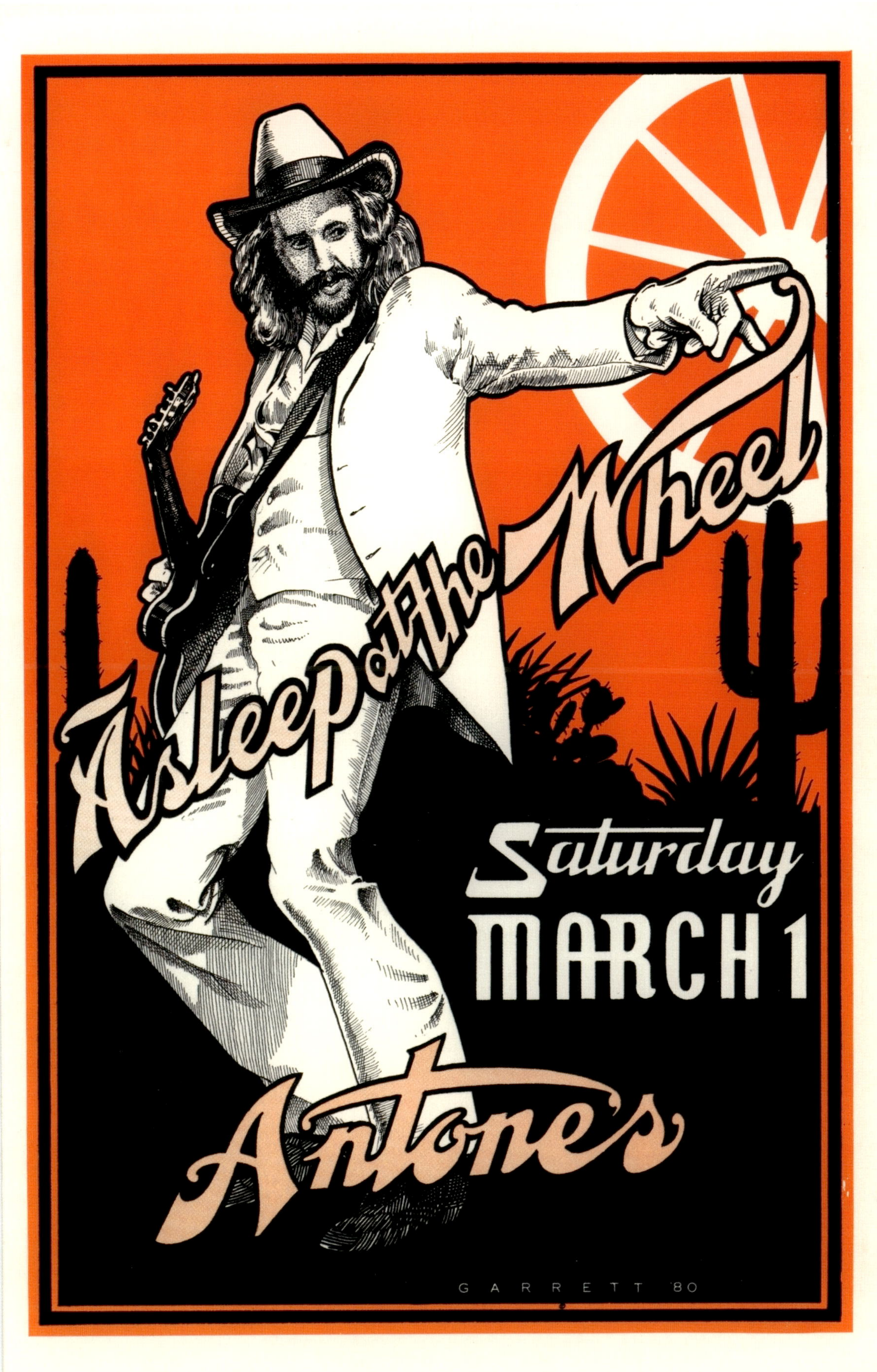

70 ED AIKEN. T. Gosney Thornton. Rome Inn/Split Rail. Year unknown. 17" × 11". © Ed Aiken.

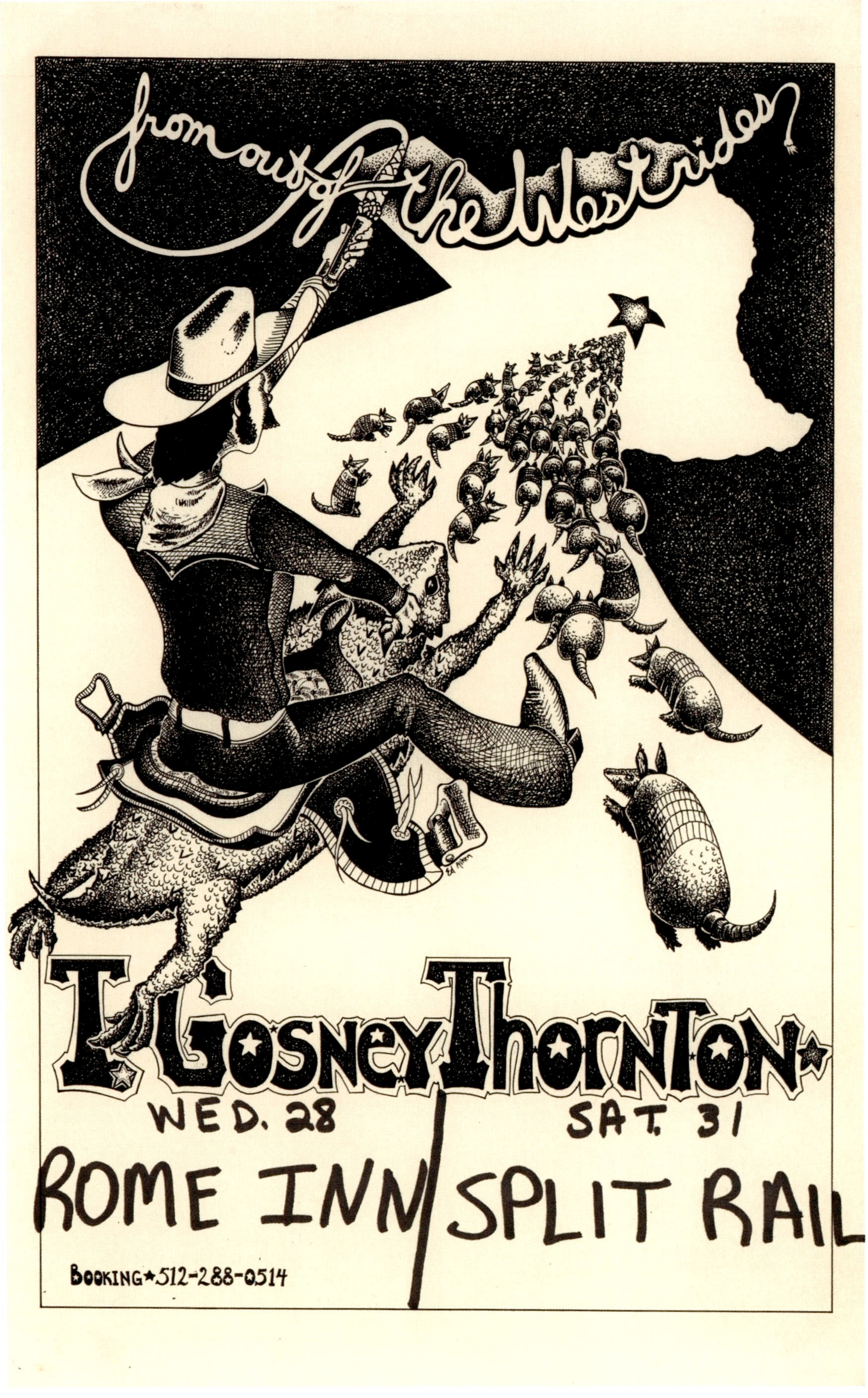

71 MICAEL PRIEST. Kinky Friedman and the Texas Jewboys. Armadillo World Headquarters. June 17 & 18, 1975. 17.5" × 11.5". © Micael Priest.

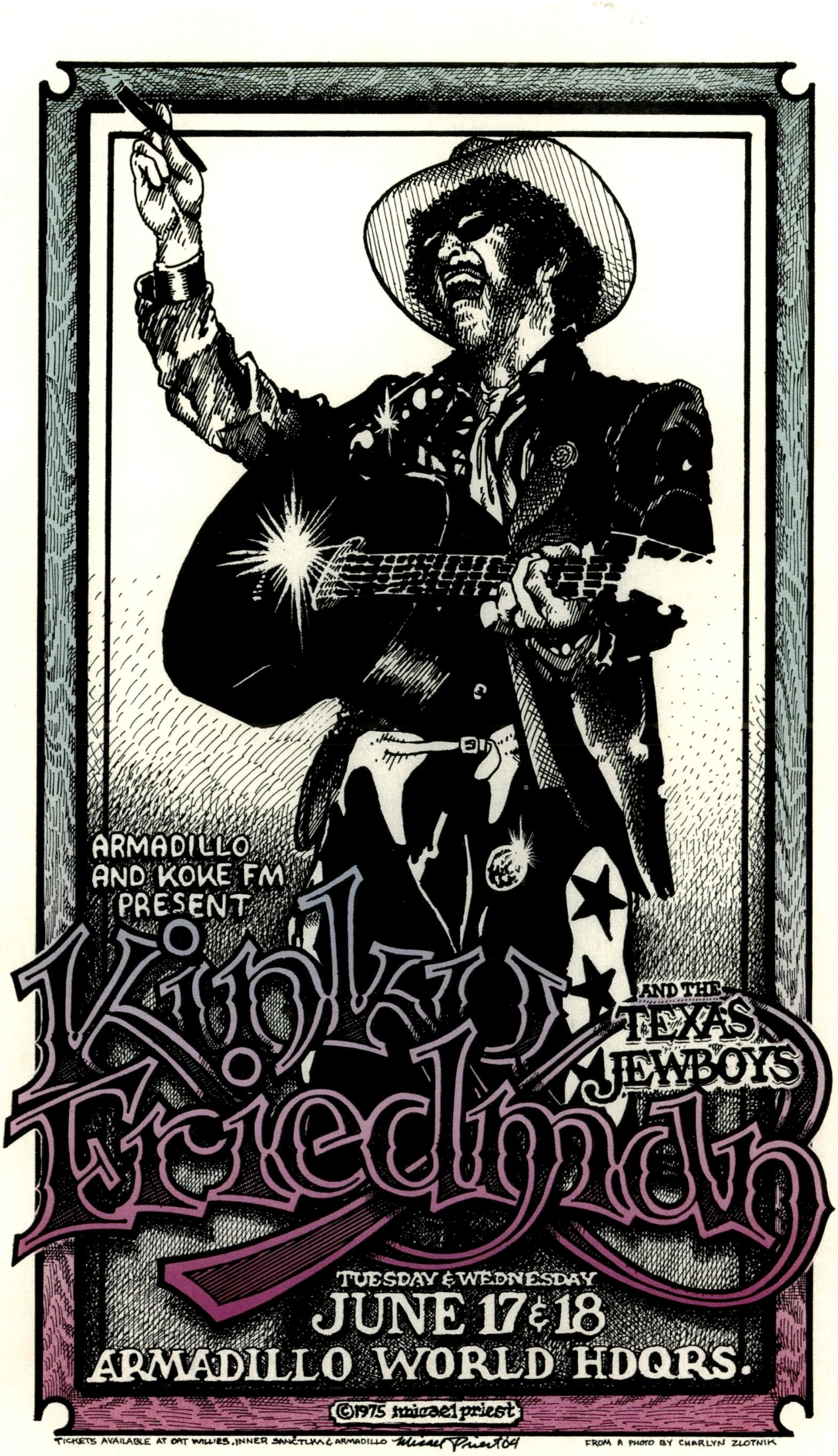

72 JIM FRANKLIN. Doug Sahm, Harry Anderson, & Uncle Uh-Uh and the Uh-Huh. Ritz Theatre. March 12, 1974. 17" × 11". © Jim Franklin.

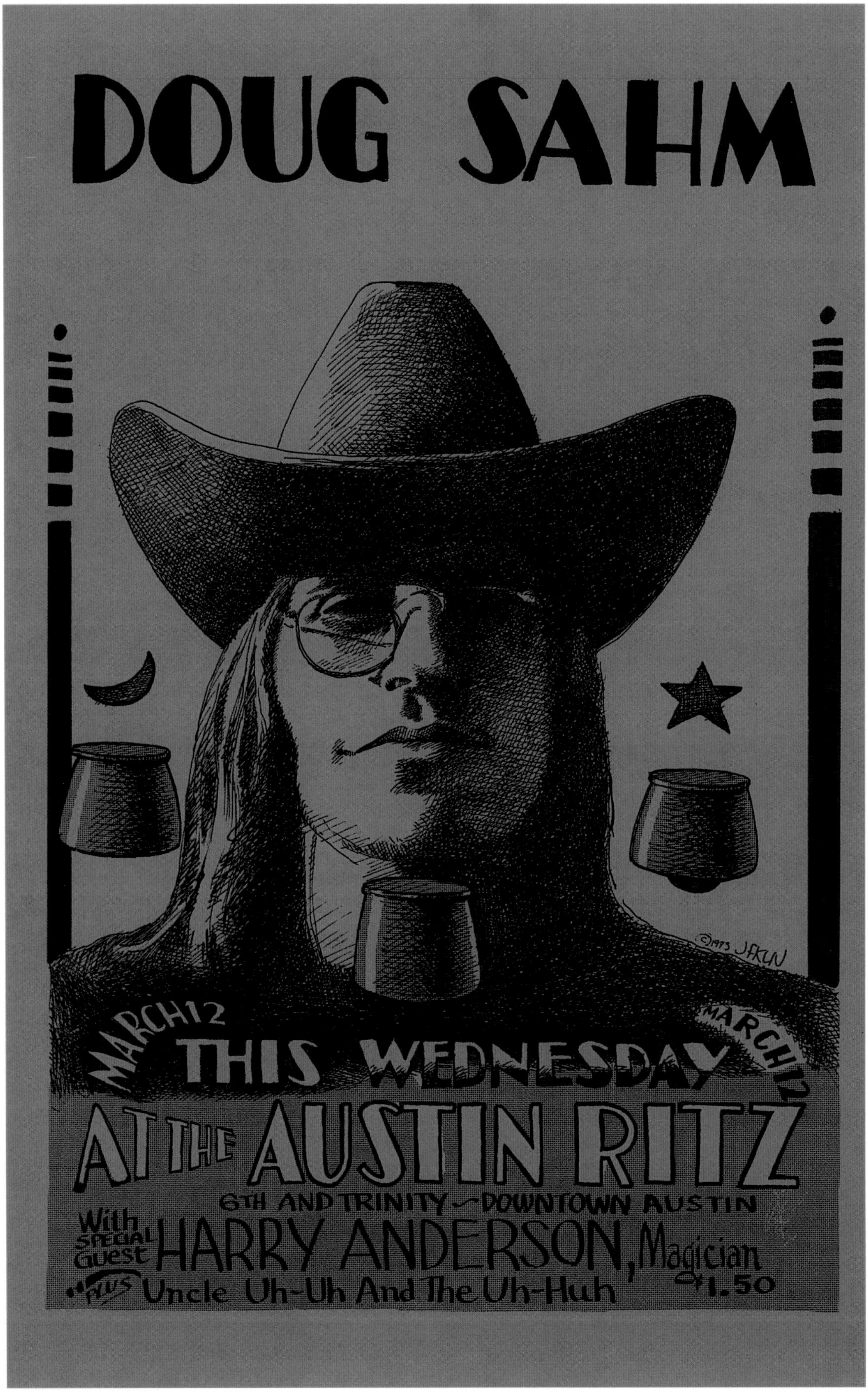

73 JAXON (JACK JACKSON). Sir Doug and the Texas Tornados. Tour poster featuring a stop at the Soap Creek Saloon. June & July 1976. 17" × 11". © Jaxon (Jack Jackson).

Jaxon was a major figure in the world of underground comix, both as an artist and, along with Gilbert Shelton, Fred Todd, and Dave Moriaty, a cofounder of Rip Off Press. His *God Nose* was one of the first underground comix.

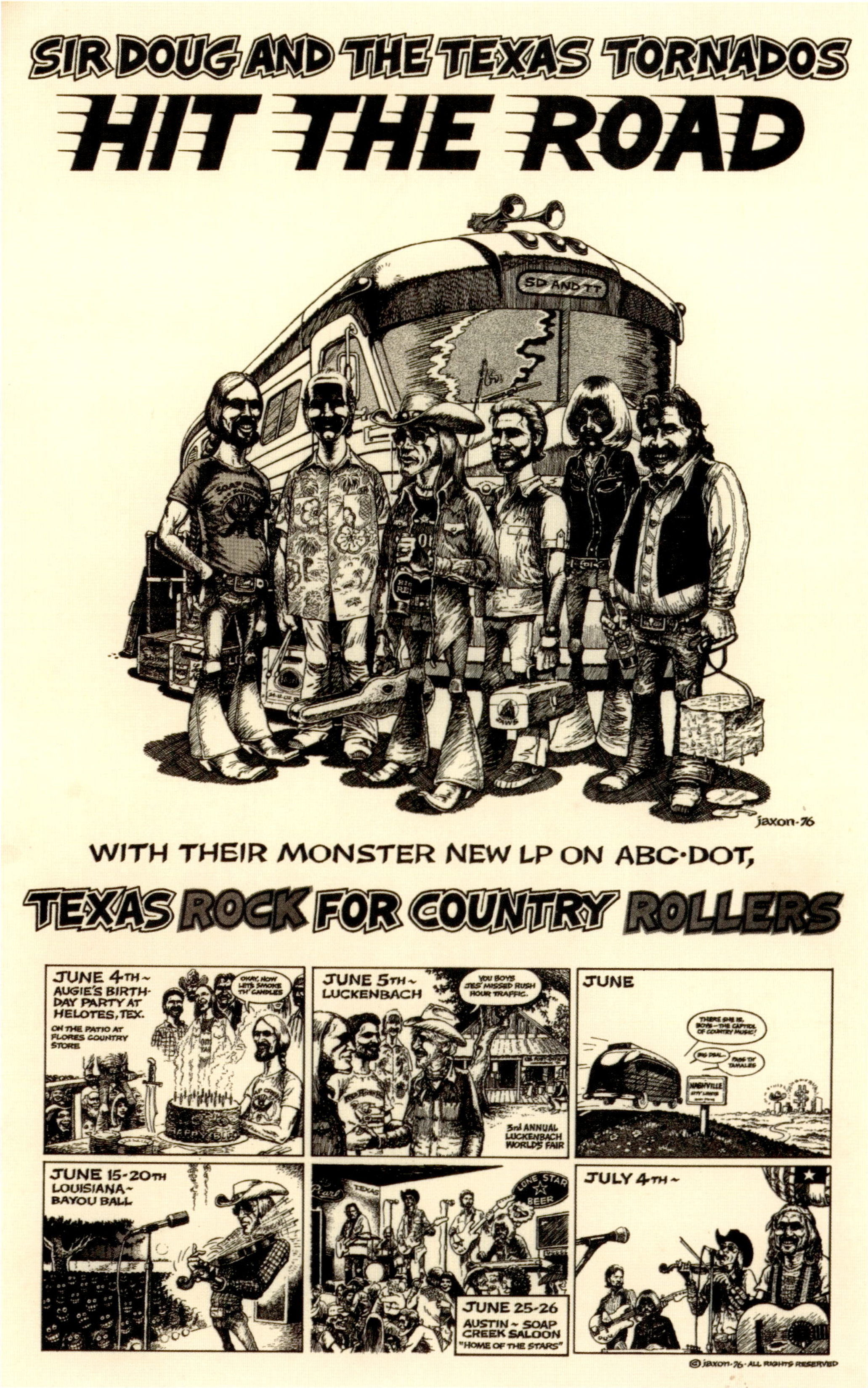

TRAVELING BANDS

Austin's emergence as a live music center in the late 1960s and early '70s led to a significant increase in the number of touring acts that would play the city's venues. The Vulcan Gas Company's progressive booking brought blues greats to Austin and three of the most innovative avant-garde rock-and-roll groups of the 1960s: Canned Heat, the Fugs, and the Velvet Underground. Only months after the Vulcan's demise, the Armadillo World Headquarters began its ten-year run of booking that broke down barriers between cliques, genres, and classes. The Armadillo welcomed West Coast innovators Captain Beefheart and Frank Zappa and burgeoning stars like Bruce Springsteen and Gram Parsons. As bookings increased, the demand for additional venues grew. The Austin Opry House hosted touring acts like Lou Reed, Tom Waits, and Warren Zevon. Austin promoters booked fine imports, too, like English purveyors of psychedelic folk the Incredible String Band or blues rockers Savoy Brown, as well as international stars like sitarist Ravi Shankar. Austin stages featured touring acts that pleased the hippies, freaks, punks, and rock and rollers. The word was out that Austin audiences were energetic, hospitable, and fond of powerful strains of marijuana. As booking in Austin became more diverse and adventurous, so too did Austin poster art.

The poster touted the spectacle of live music and the potential of a touring act with a visual narrative that a newspaper or radio advertisement simply lacked. Poster art gave music fans a glimpse into the world of sound that a Captain Beefheart or a Little Feat would bring to Austin. While clearly functioning as commercial art, poster art could also begin to tell the story of a touring act that was new to Austin stages, and there were certainly stories to tell and mysteries to unlock. Who was this Captain Beefheart who was coming to play at the Armadillo World Headquarters, and what did Jim Franklin's symmetrical beasts and flourishing rose in the concert poster mean to the music? Did Franklin offer potential audience members a clue into the vast and confusing world of Beefheart's desert-fried brand of electric blues and avant-rock? In any case, the concert poster created a sense of mystery and urgency around a traveling band, and it sold the music, the event, and a lifestyle.

74 JIM FRANKLIN. Captain Beefheart and the Magic Band & Ry Cooder. Armadillo World Headquarters. February 20 & 21, 1972. 7.5" × 10.25". © Jim Franklin.

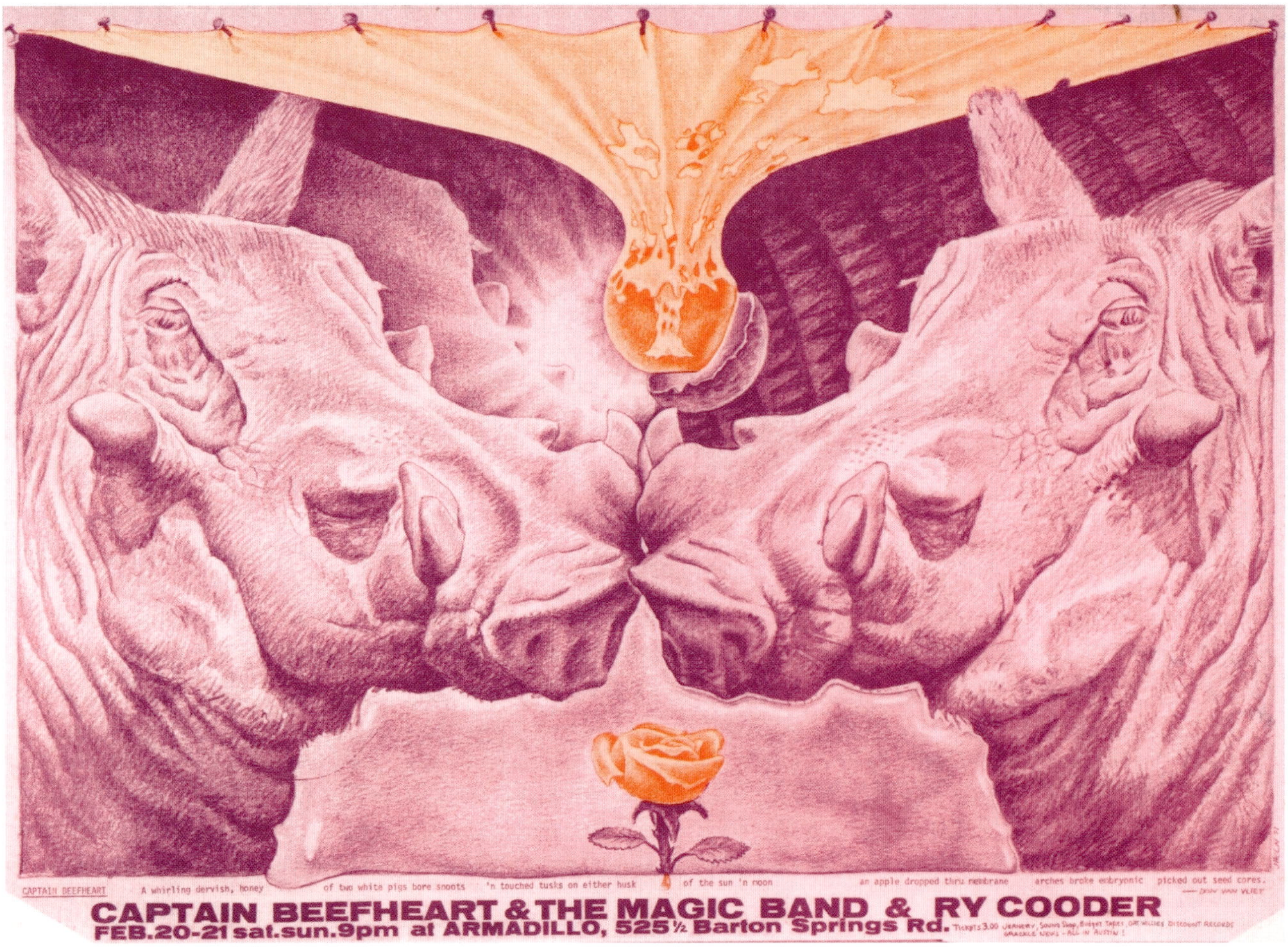

75 JIM FRANKLIN. Frank Zappa. Armadillo World Headquarters. March 10, 1973. 20.75" × 15.5". © Jim Franklin.

Franklin parodies the images he discovered in industrial manuals and catalogs, sources of inspiration that he often found in alleys behind his various studios near Sixth and Trinity Streets in downtown Austin.

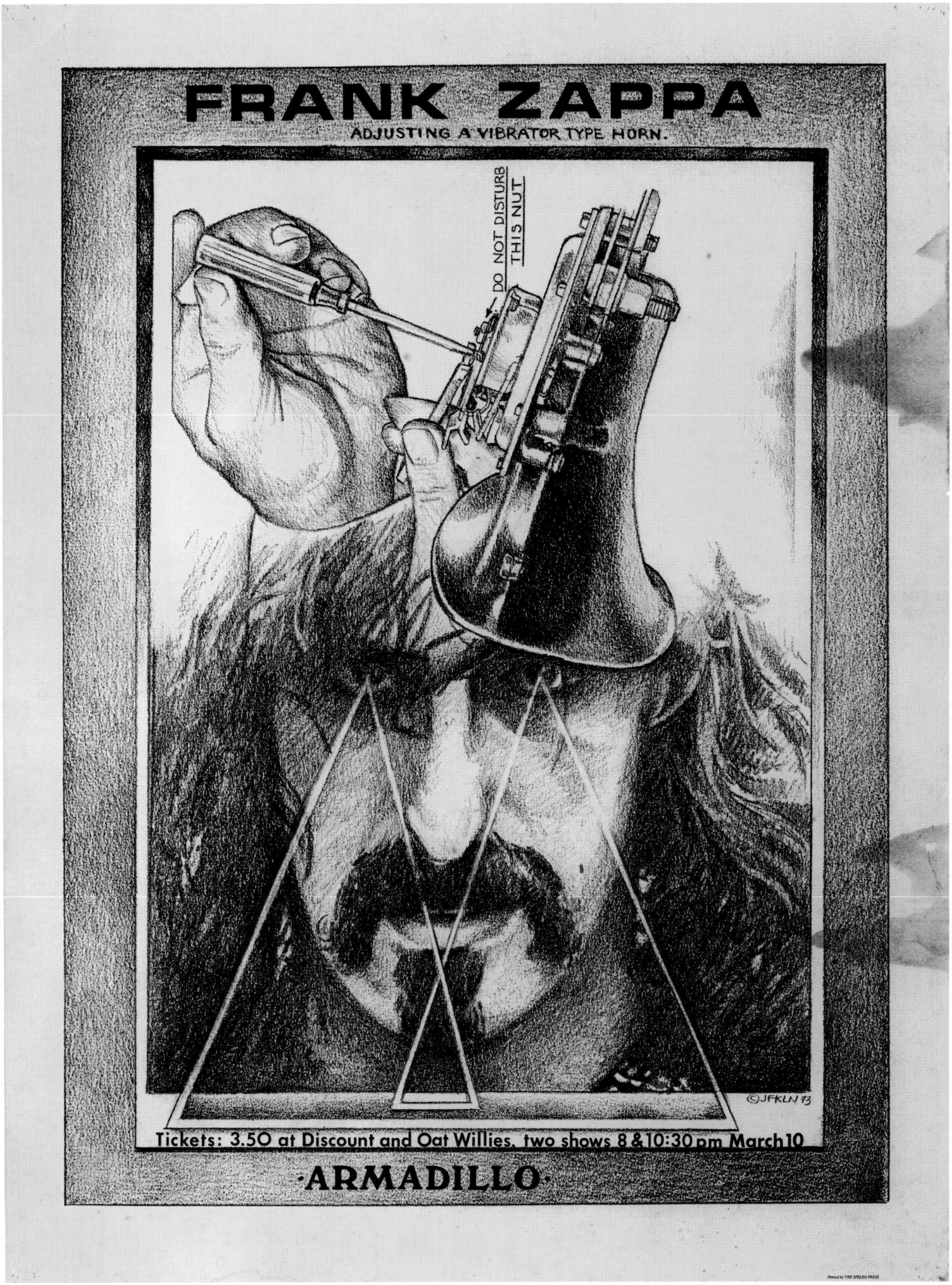

76 GUY JUKE & MICAEL PRIEST. Frank Zappa and the Mothers of Invention & Martin Mull. Armadillo World Headquarters. October 26 & 27, 1973. 17" × 11".

Priest notes that many of his posters feature portraits that recall "wanted" posters. Because rock and roll is a form of outlaw art and music, Priest suggests that the "wanted" poster is an appropriate means of advertising its performance.

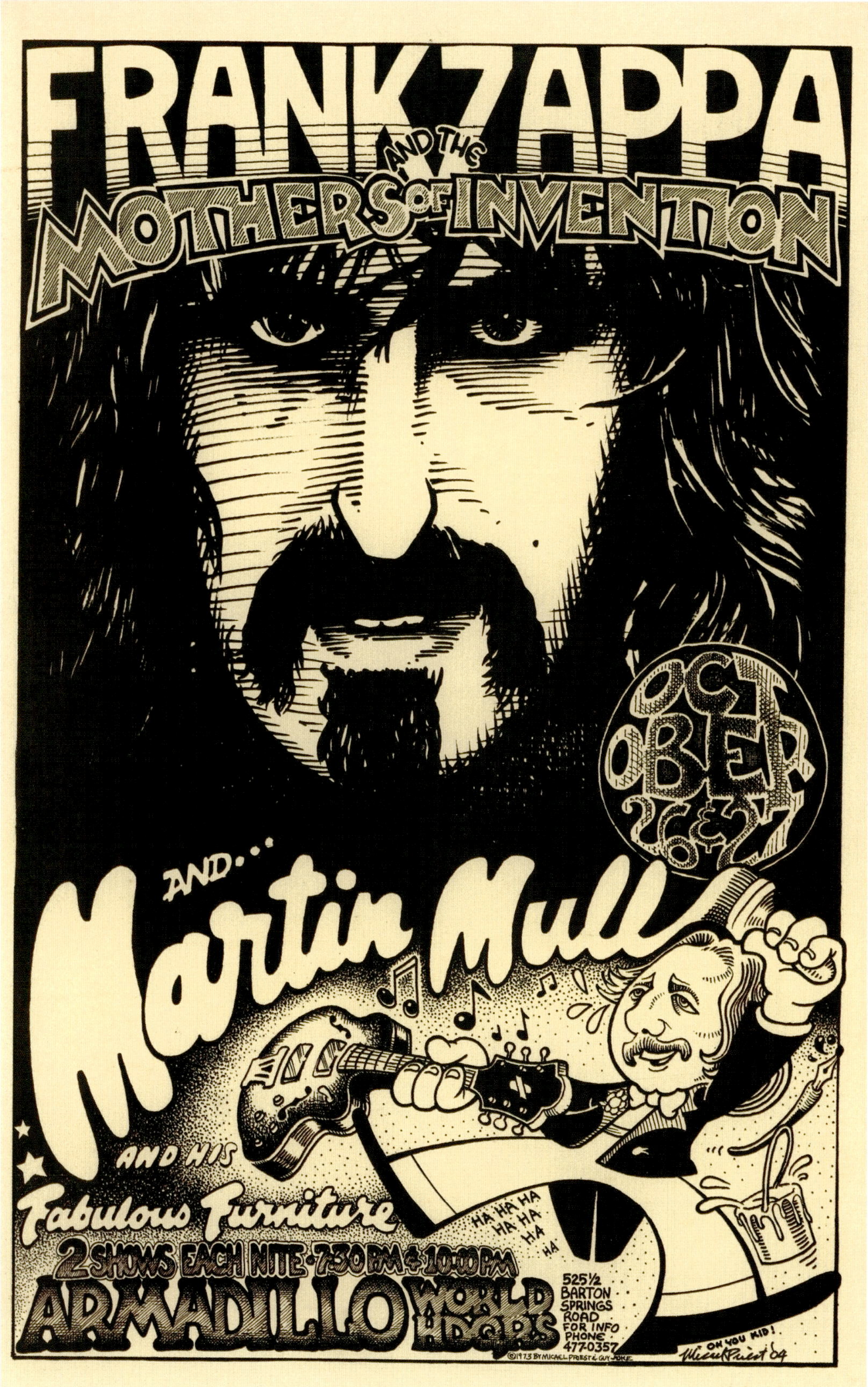

77 GUY JUKE. Frank Zappa and the Mothers. Armadillo World Headquarters. May 20 & 21, 1975. 17.75" × 11.75". © Guy Juke.

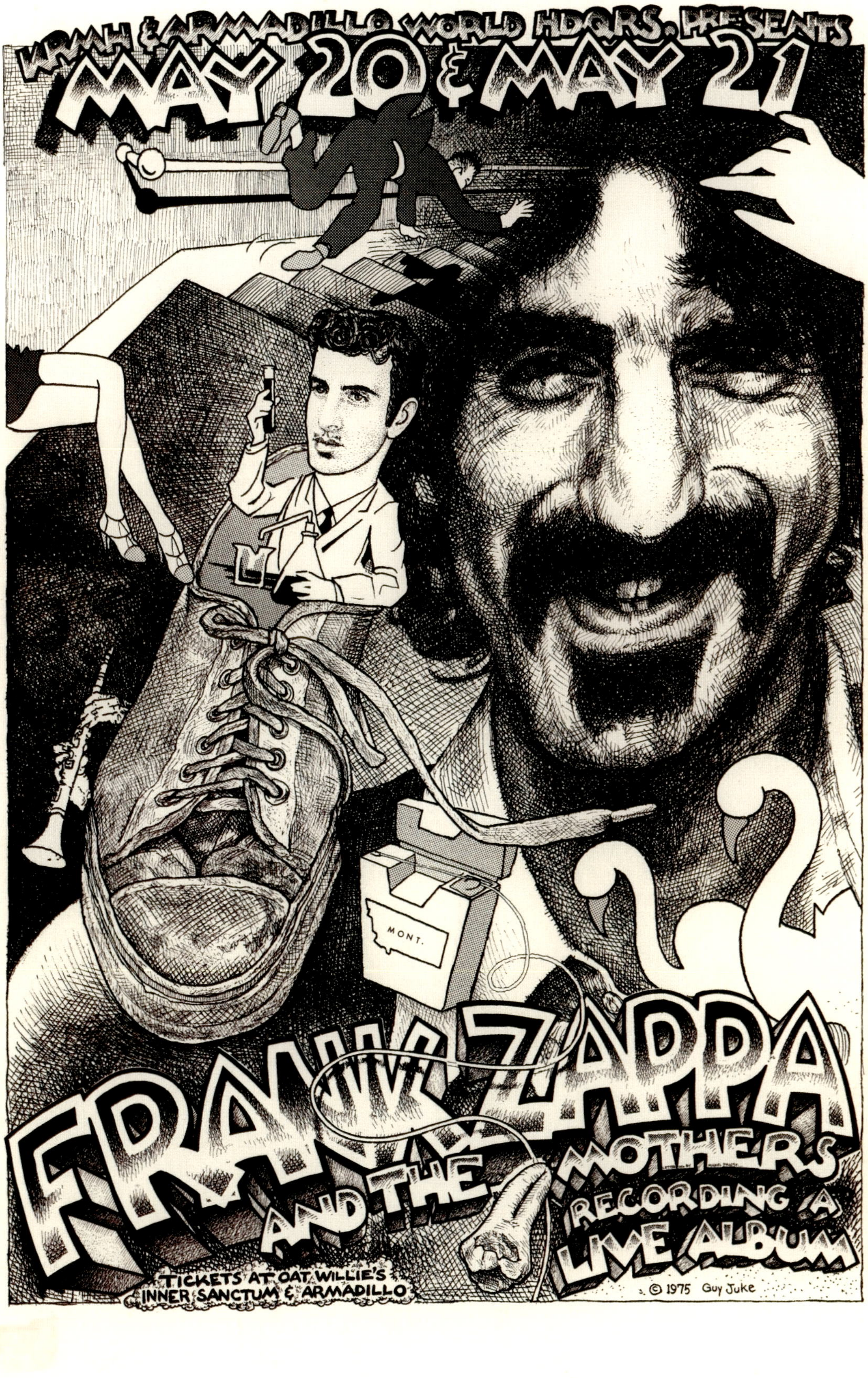

78 JOSE CARLOS CAMPOS. Savoy Brown. Armadillo World Headquarters. August 3, 1976. 17.5" × 11.5". © Jose Carlos Campos.

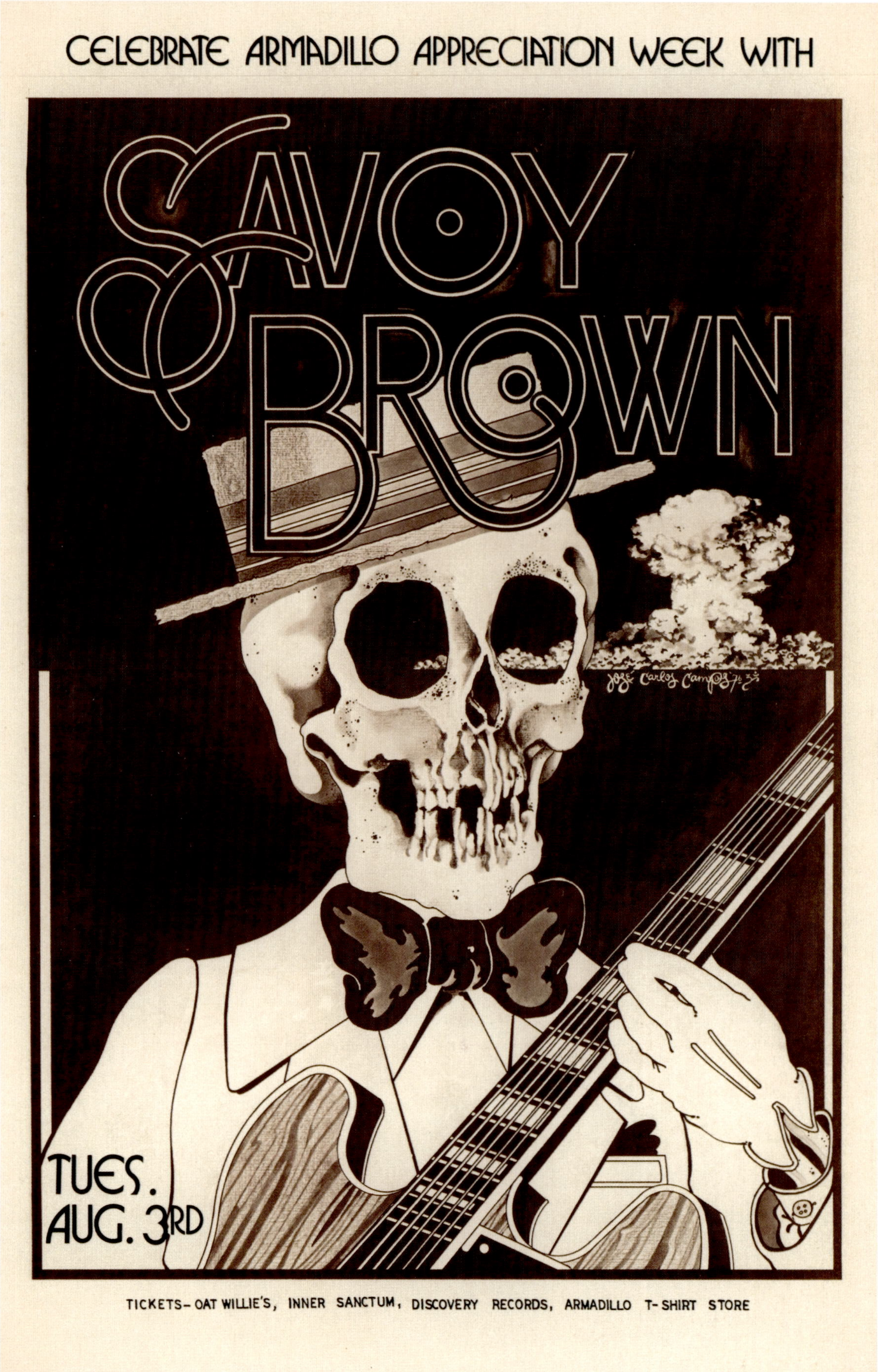

79 KEN FEATHERSTON. The Mahavishnu Orchestra. Armadillo World Headquarters. April 5 & 6, 1973. 17.5" × 11.5". © Ken Featherston.

Featherston riffs on the style of Czech artist Alphonse Mucha, the most notable purveyor of turn-of-the-century art nouveau.

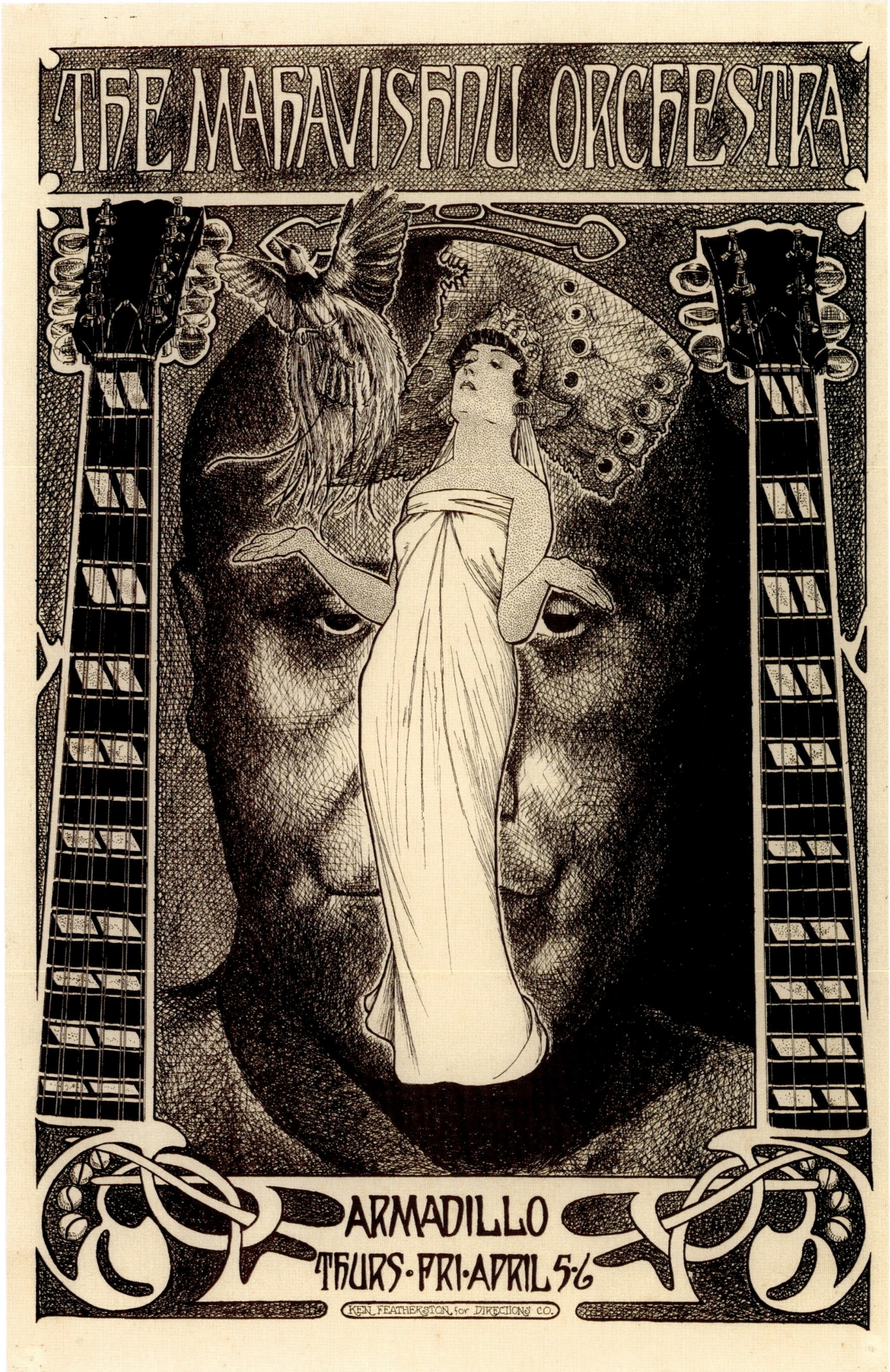

80 KEN FEATHERSTON. Gram Parsons. Armadillo World Headquarters. February 21, 1973. 17" × 11". © Ken Featherston.

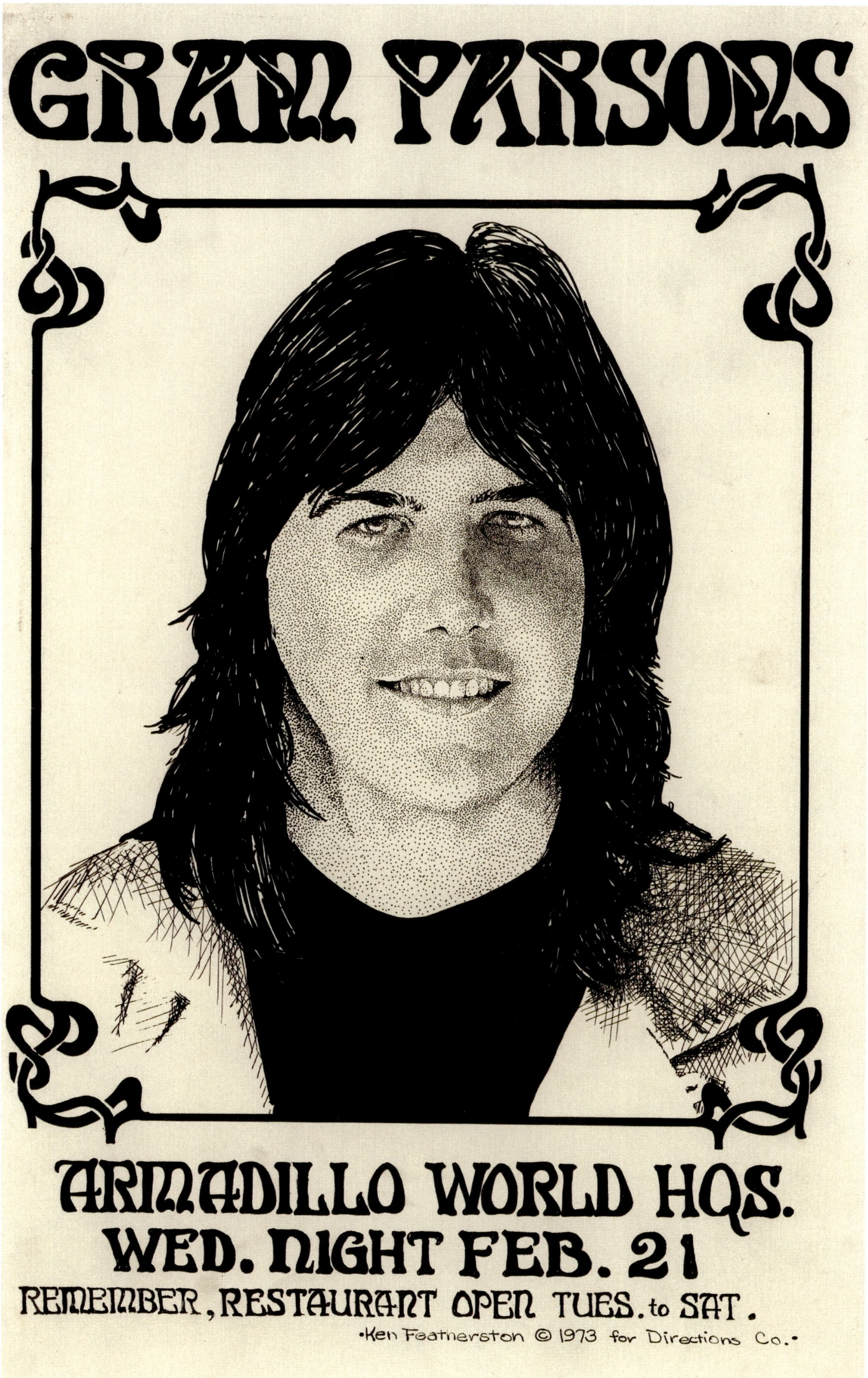

81 JIM FRANKLIN & MICAEL PRIEST. The Flying Burrito Brothers & Greezy Wheels. Armadillo World Headquarters. February 28–March 2, 1975. 17" × 11". © Jim Franklin & Micael Priest.

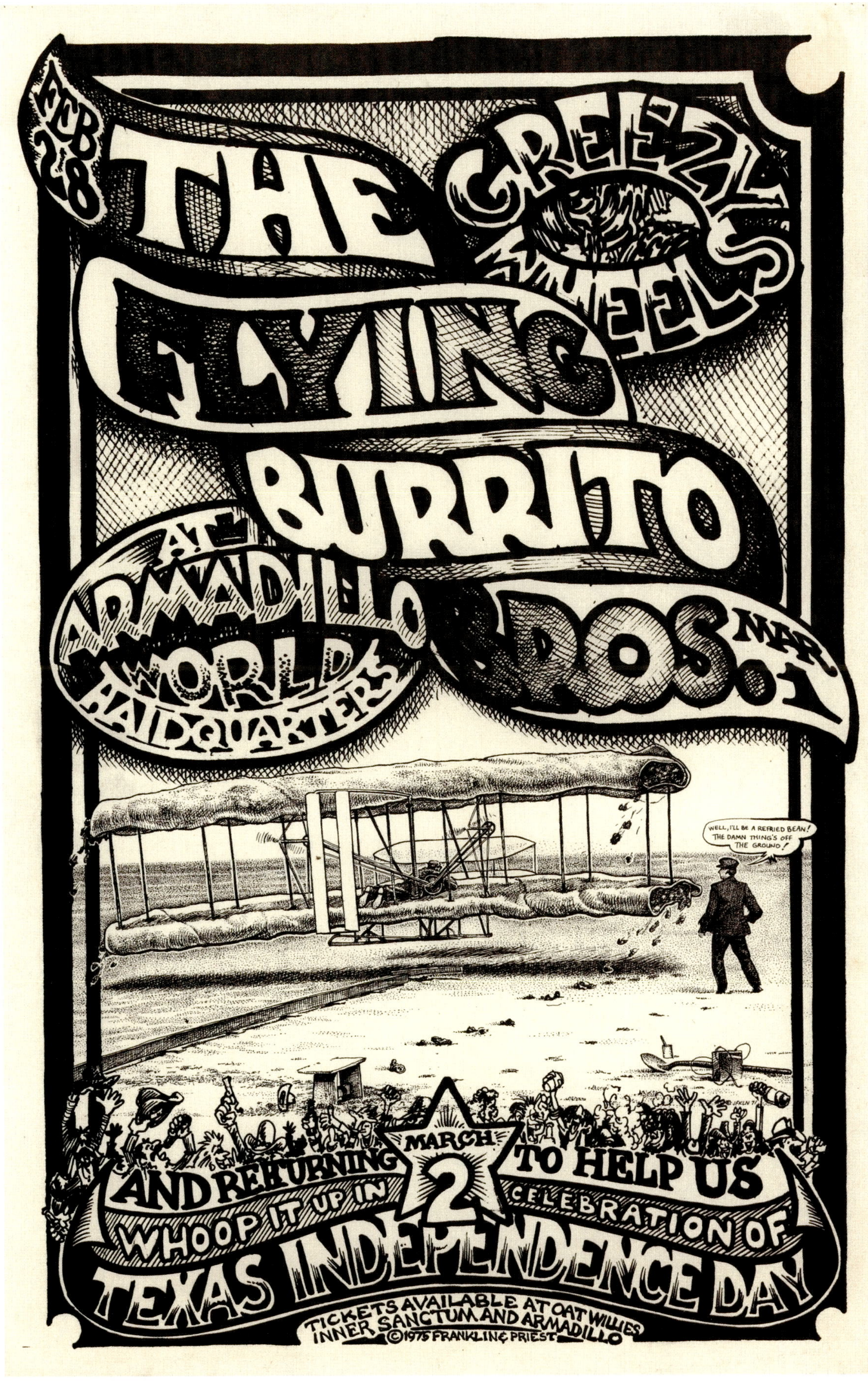

82 MICAEL PRIEST. Bobby Bare with Freda and the Firedogs & David Allen Coe. Austin Opry House. May 31 & June 1, 1974. 17" × 11". © Micael Priest.

Freda and the Firedogs backed Bobby Bare for these concerts. Bobby Earl Smith explains why Bare was surprised upon his arrival in Austin: "He showed up about an hour before the show was slated to start. The Firedogs were standing around backstage wondering where Bobby Bare was when we heard a knock at the door on the loading dock. We raised the sliding door, and there stood Bare all decked out in a cool Nashville-style white suit. He took one look at our Firedogs hippie Austin duds and smiled and said, 'Shit, I told my wife to pack some jeans.'"

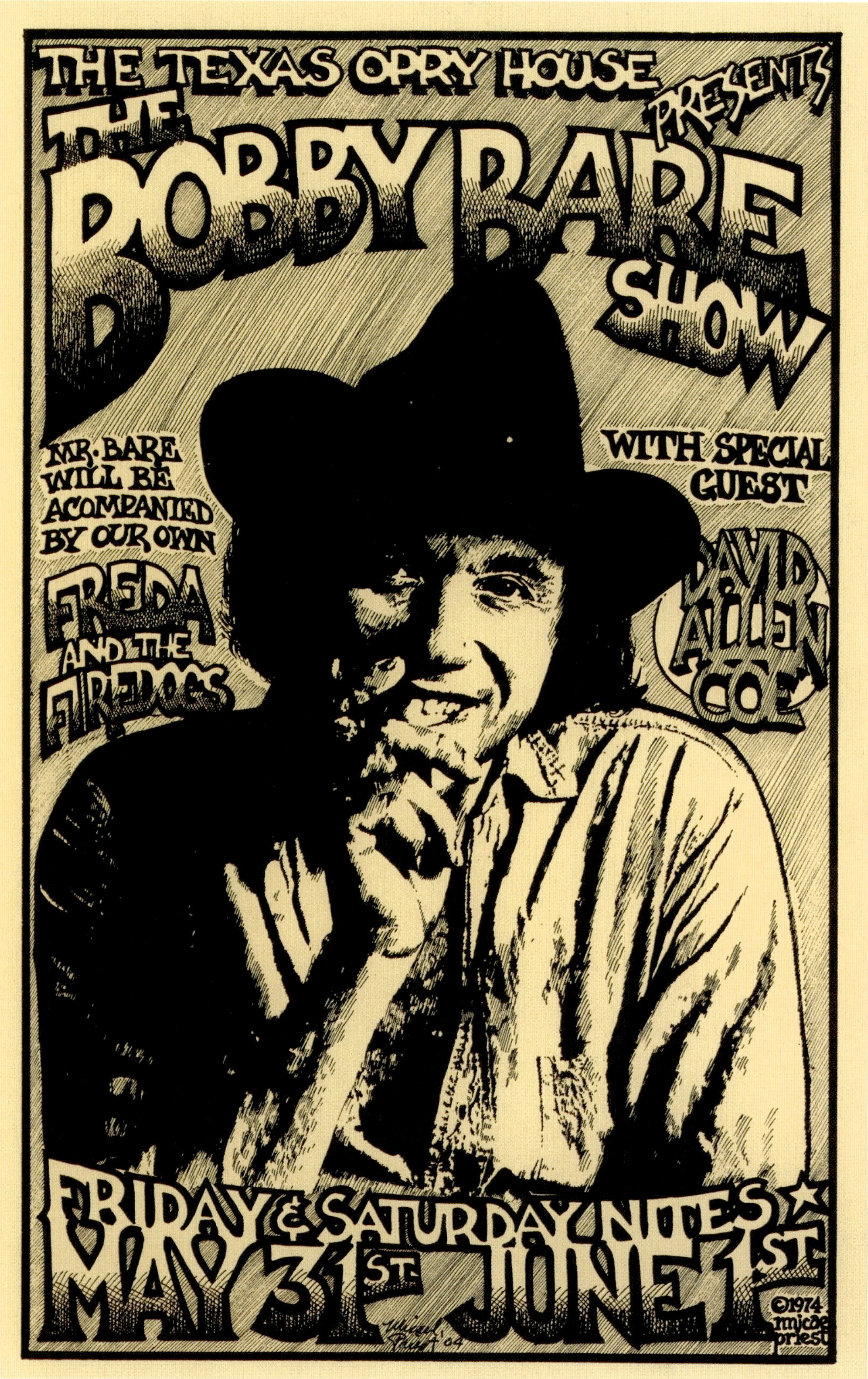

83 GUY JUKE. Country Gazette & Uncle Walt's Band. Armadillo World Headquarters. November 17, 1978. 17.5" × 11.5". © Guy Juke.

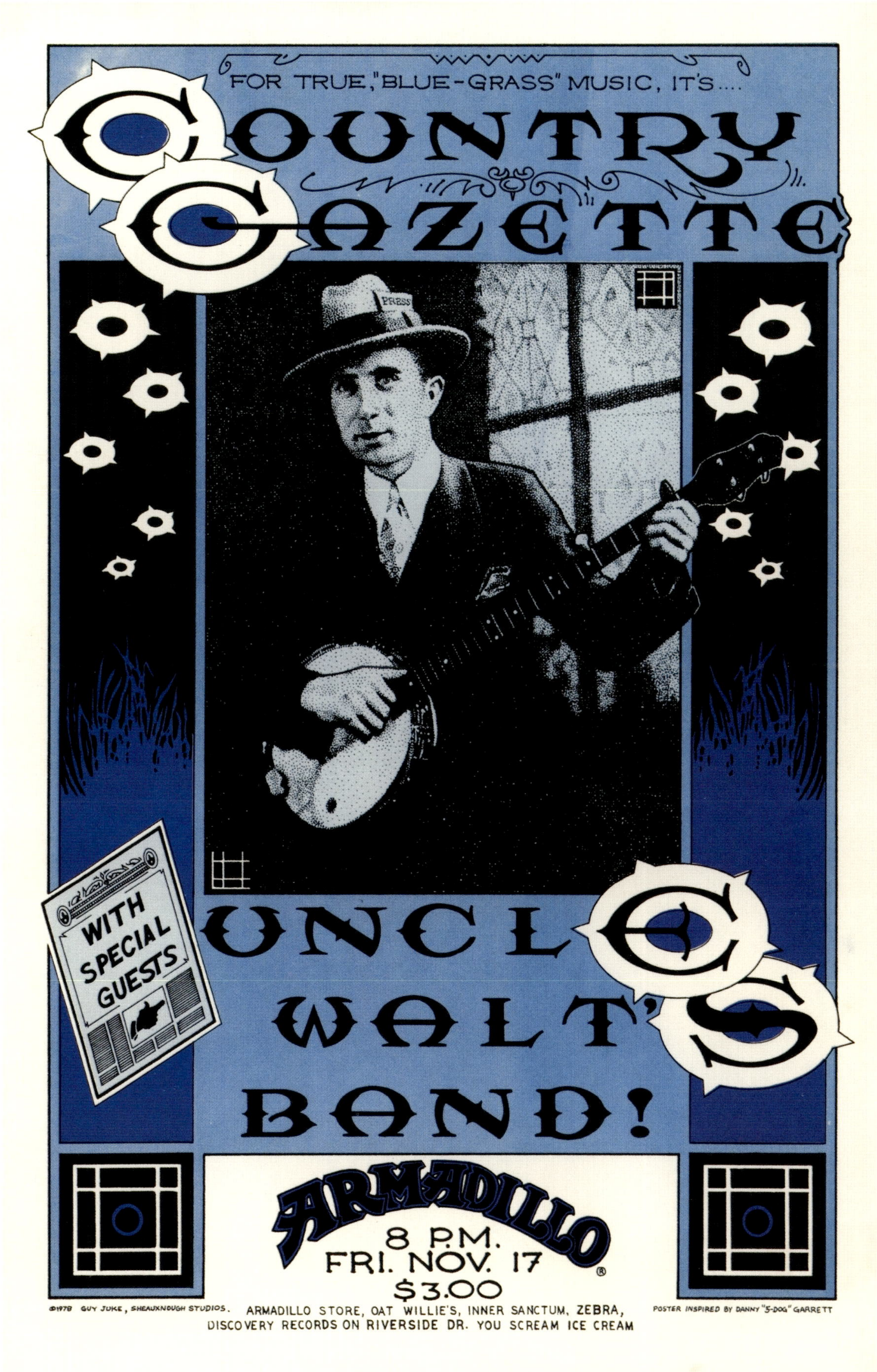

84 JIM FRANKLIN. The Incredible String Band & Shiva's Headband. Armadillo World Headquarters. November 20 & 21, 1970. 10.5" × 7". © Jim Franklin.

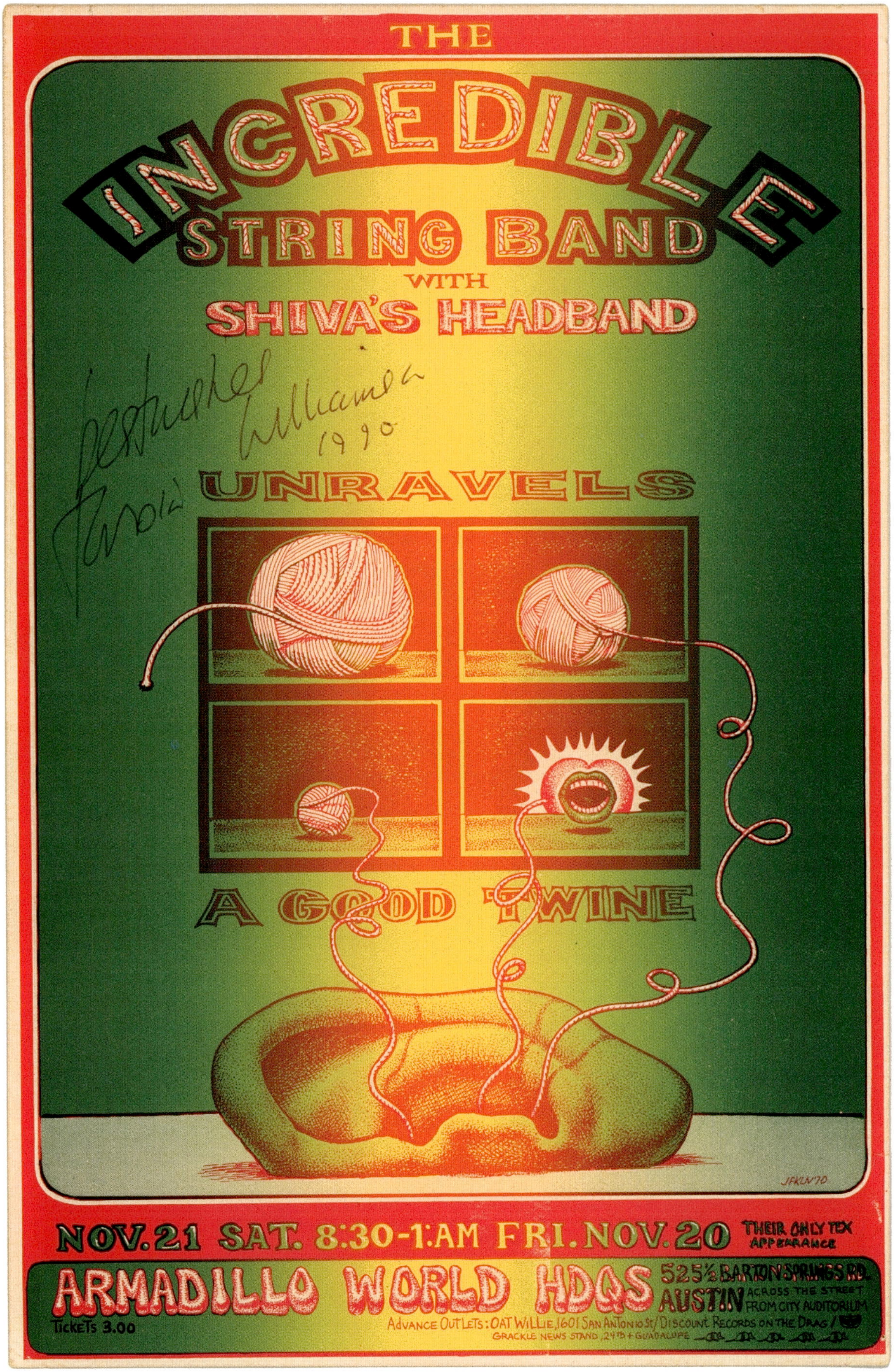

85 JIM HARTER. Earl Scruggs Revue & Rat Creek. Armadillo World Headquarters. November 5 & 6, 1971. 11.25" × 17.25". © Jim Harter.

Harter has worked successfully with the collage medium throughout his career. The photograph of the 1932 Ford was taken by the artist at the age of twelve when he was on a family vacation. Harter notes that a major influence on his collage work was Wilfried Satty, a German artist who became a key figure in the San Francisco art scene.

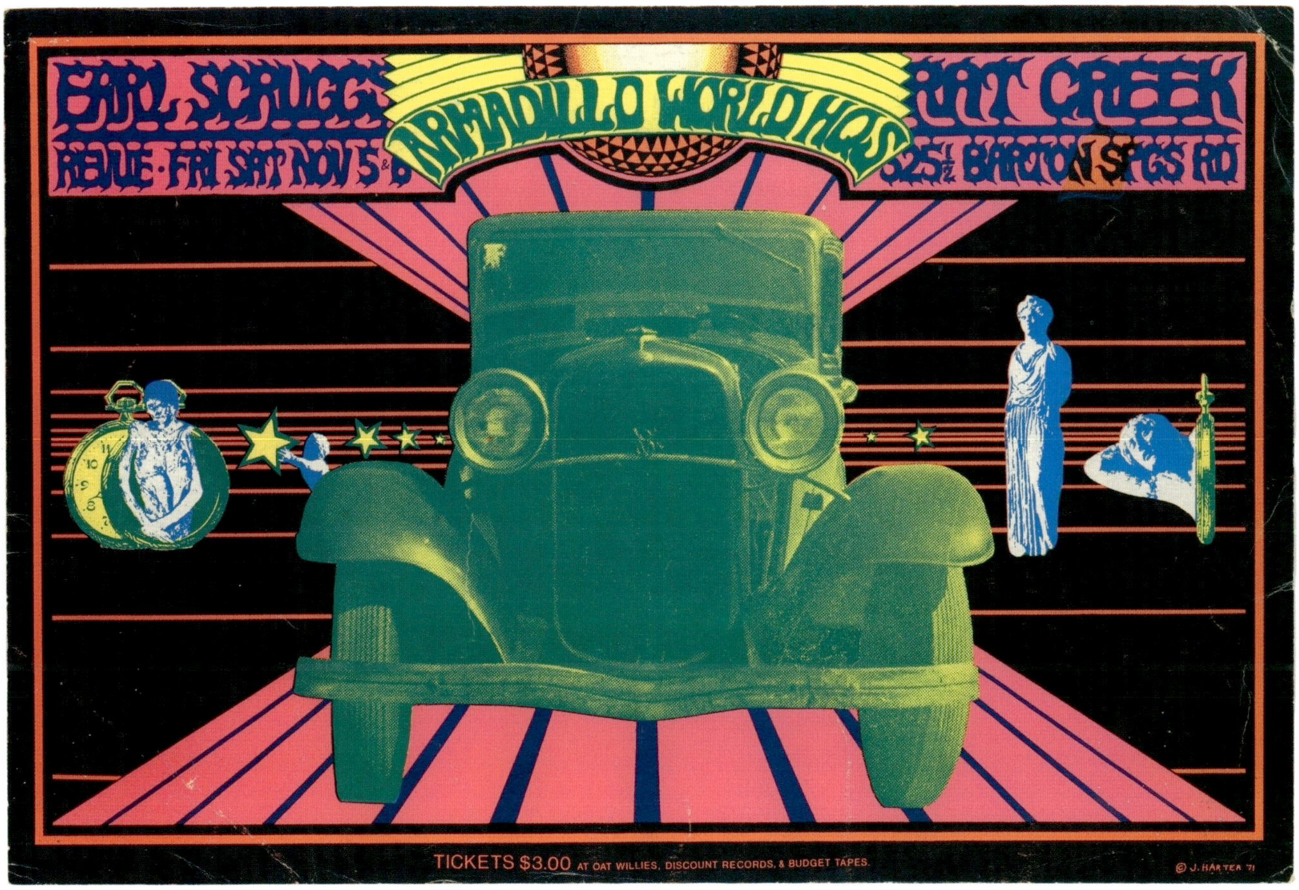

86 JIM FRANKLIN. Ravi Shankar. Armadillo World Headquarters. May 1, 1971. 6.5" × 10". © Jim Franklin.

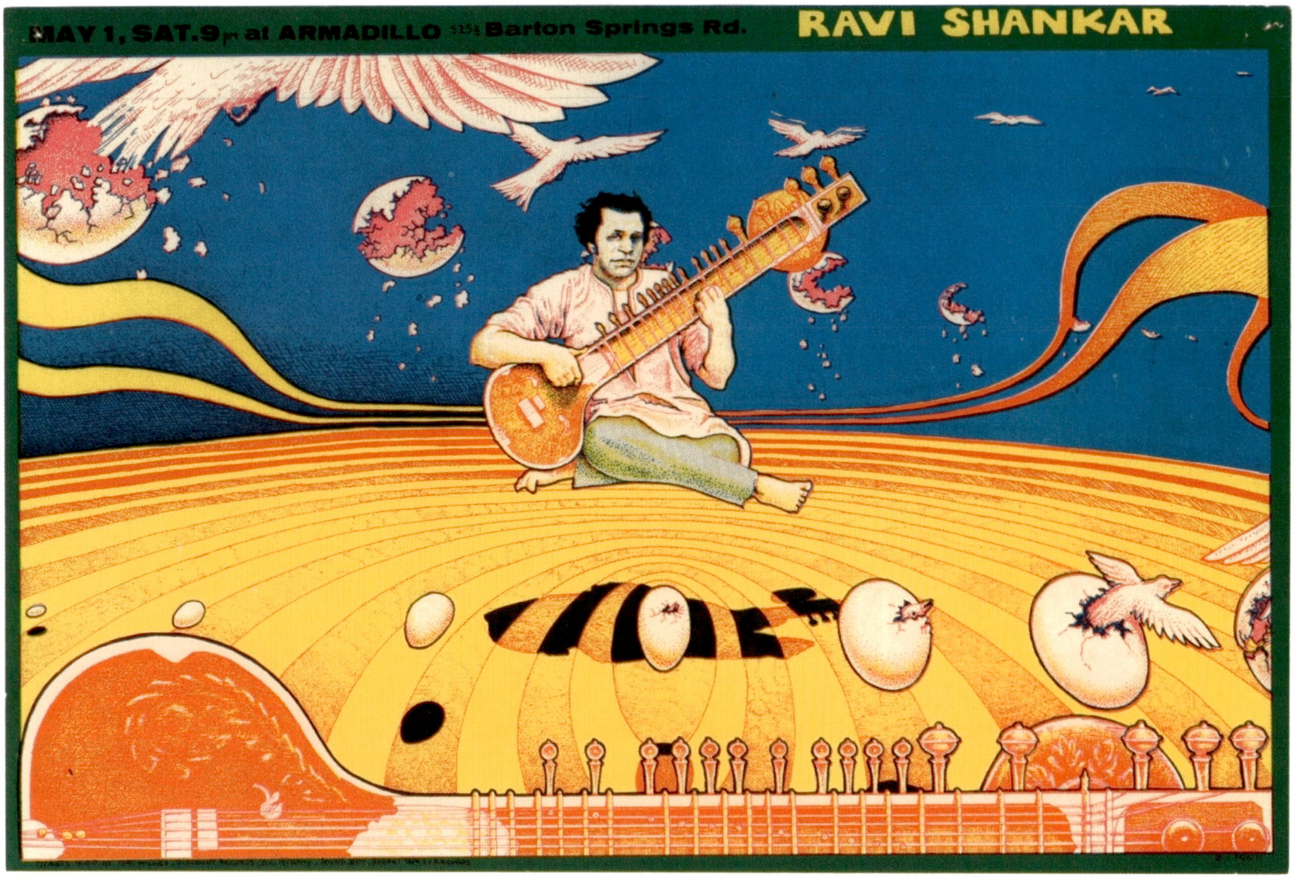

87 JIM FRANKLIN. Leo Kottke & Greezy Wheels. Armadillo World Headquarters. July 23 & 24, 1971. 10.25" × 7". © Jim Franklin.

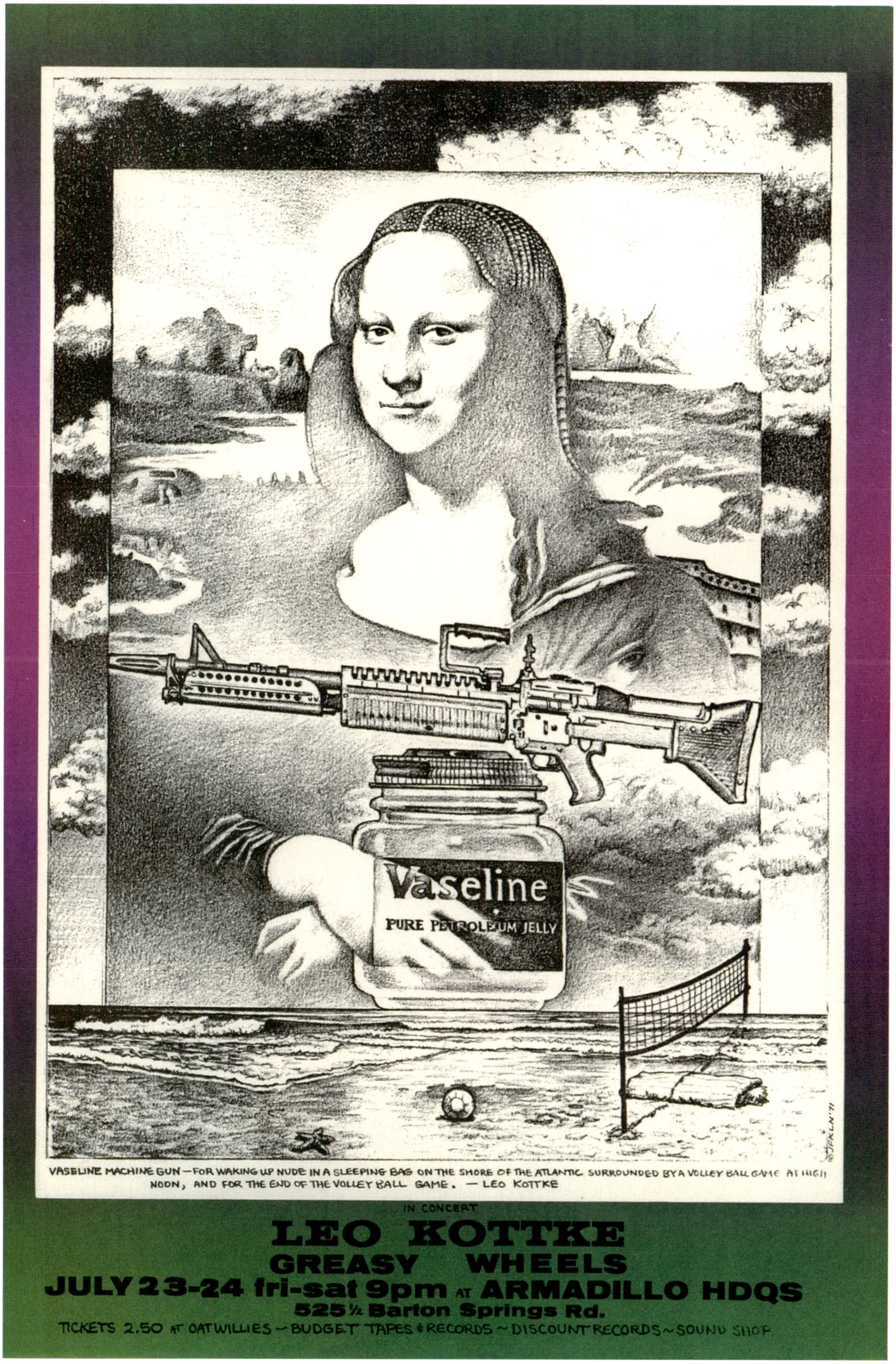

88 SAM YEATES. Bob Seger & Ruby Starr. Armadillo World Headquarters. December 17, 1976. 21.5" × 16". © Sam Yeates.

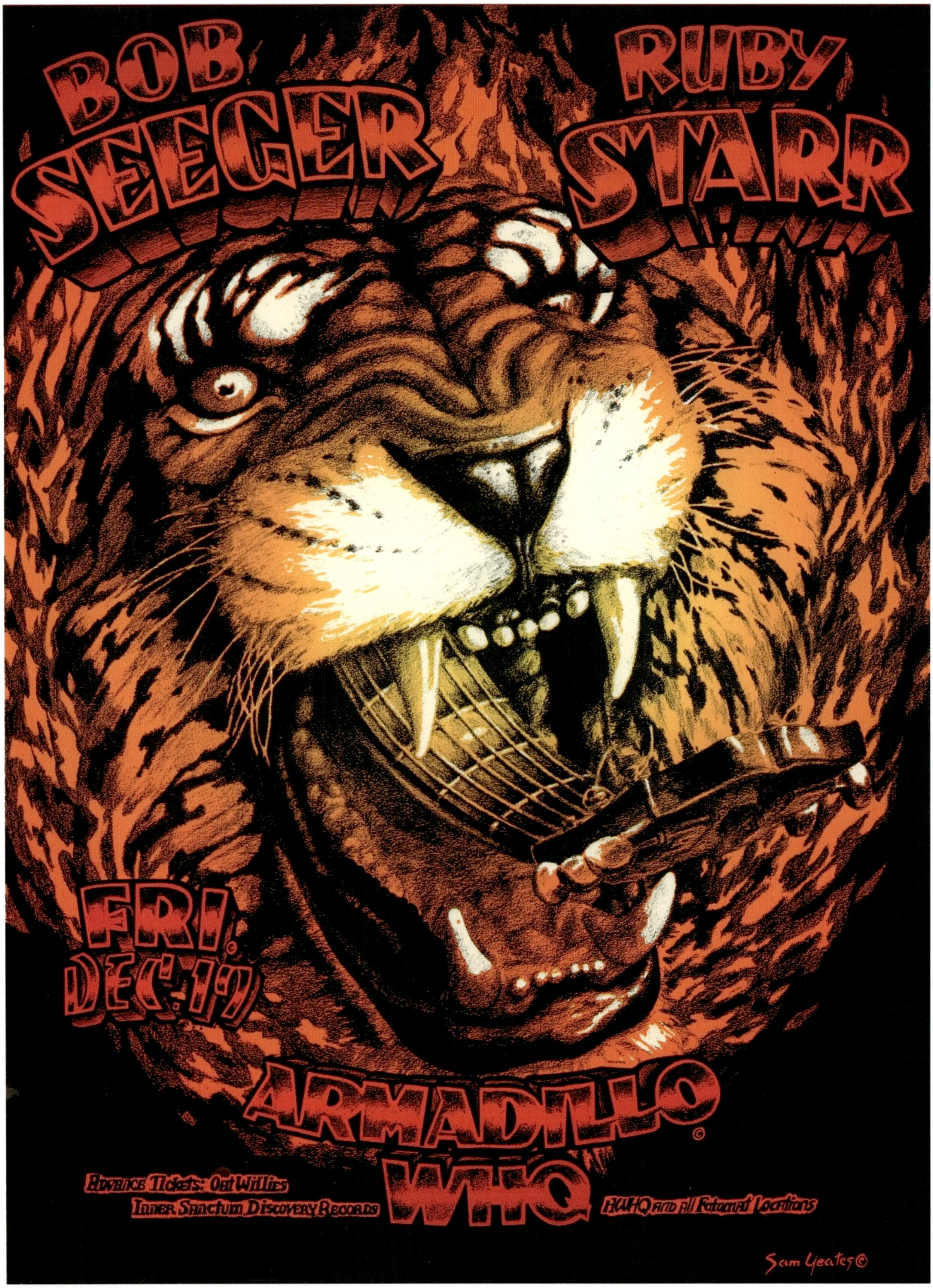

89 JIM FRANKLIN. Bruce Springsteen. Armadillo World Headquarters. March 15 & 16, 1974. 17.5" × 11.5". © Jim Franklin.

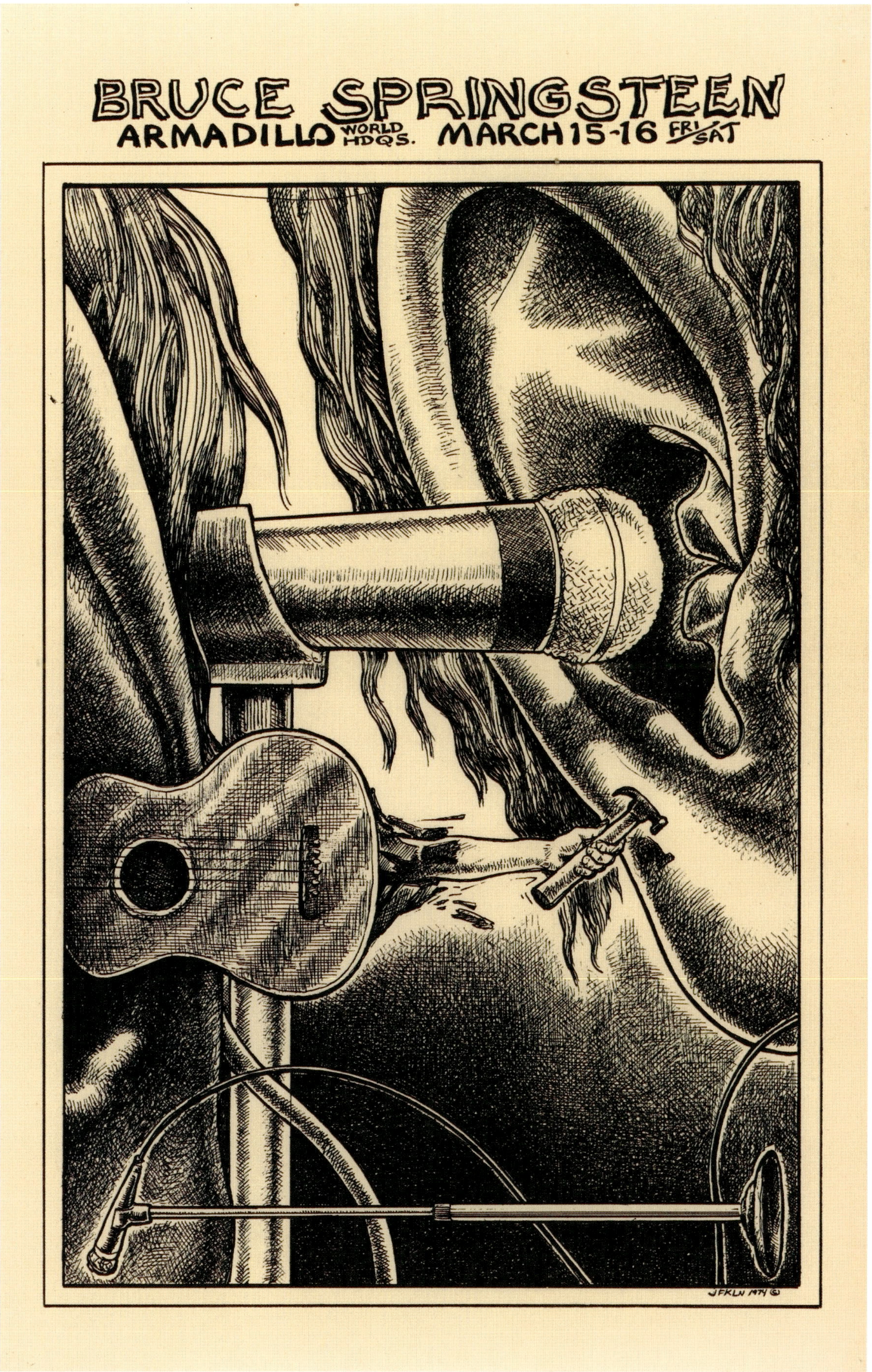

90 JIM FRANKLIN. Taj Mahal & Lightnin' Hopkins. October 22, 1971. Lightnin' Hopkins & Greezy Wheels. October 23, 1971. Armadillo World Headquarters. 17.5" × 11.5". © Jim Franklin.

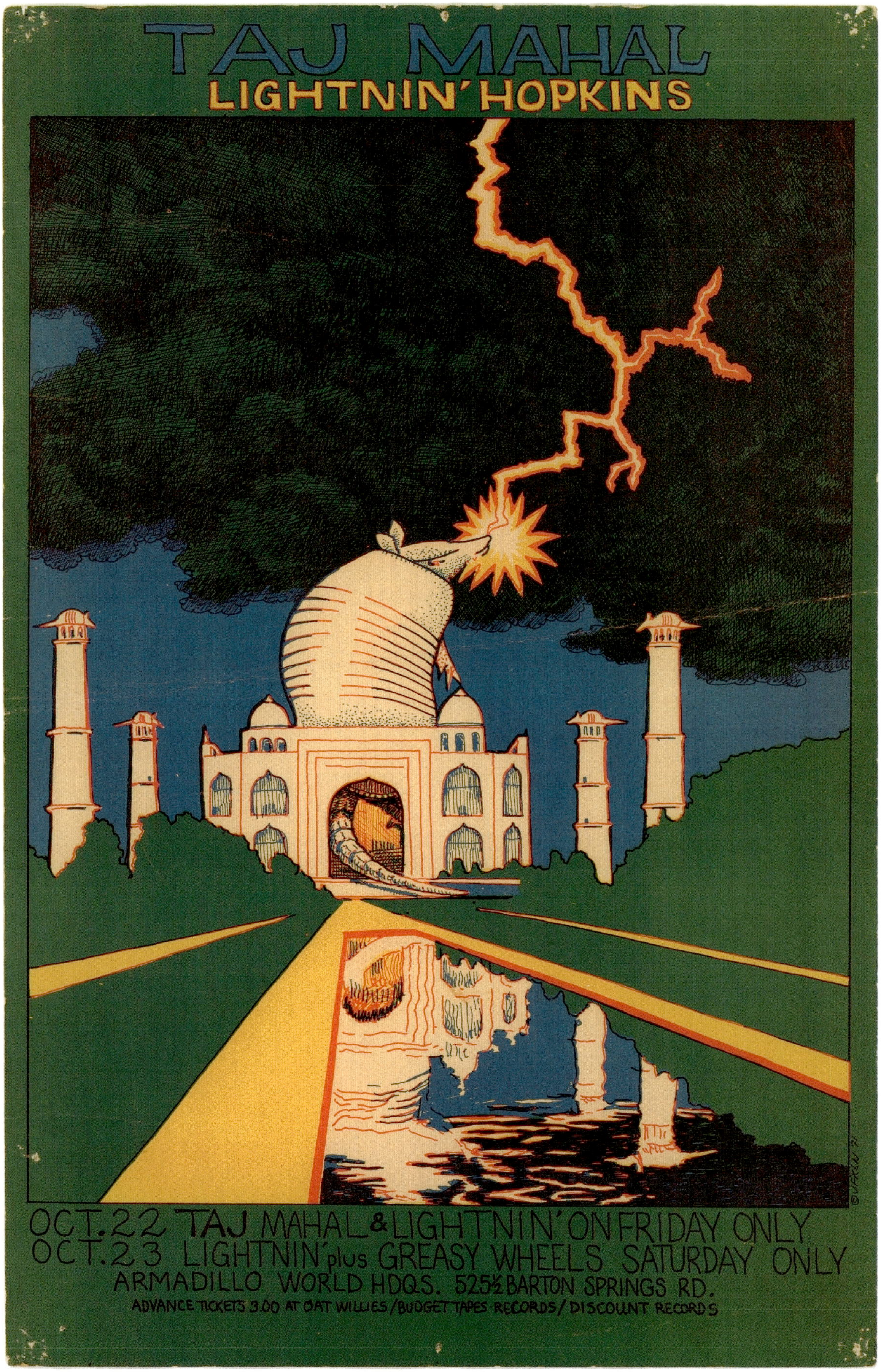

91 MICAEL PRIEST. Grateful Dead. Manor Downs. October 12, 1977. 17.5" × 11.5". © Micael Priest.

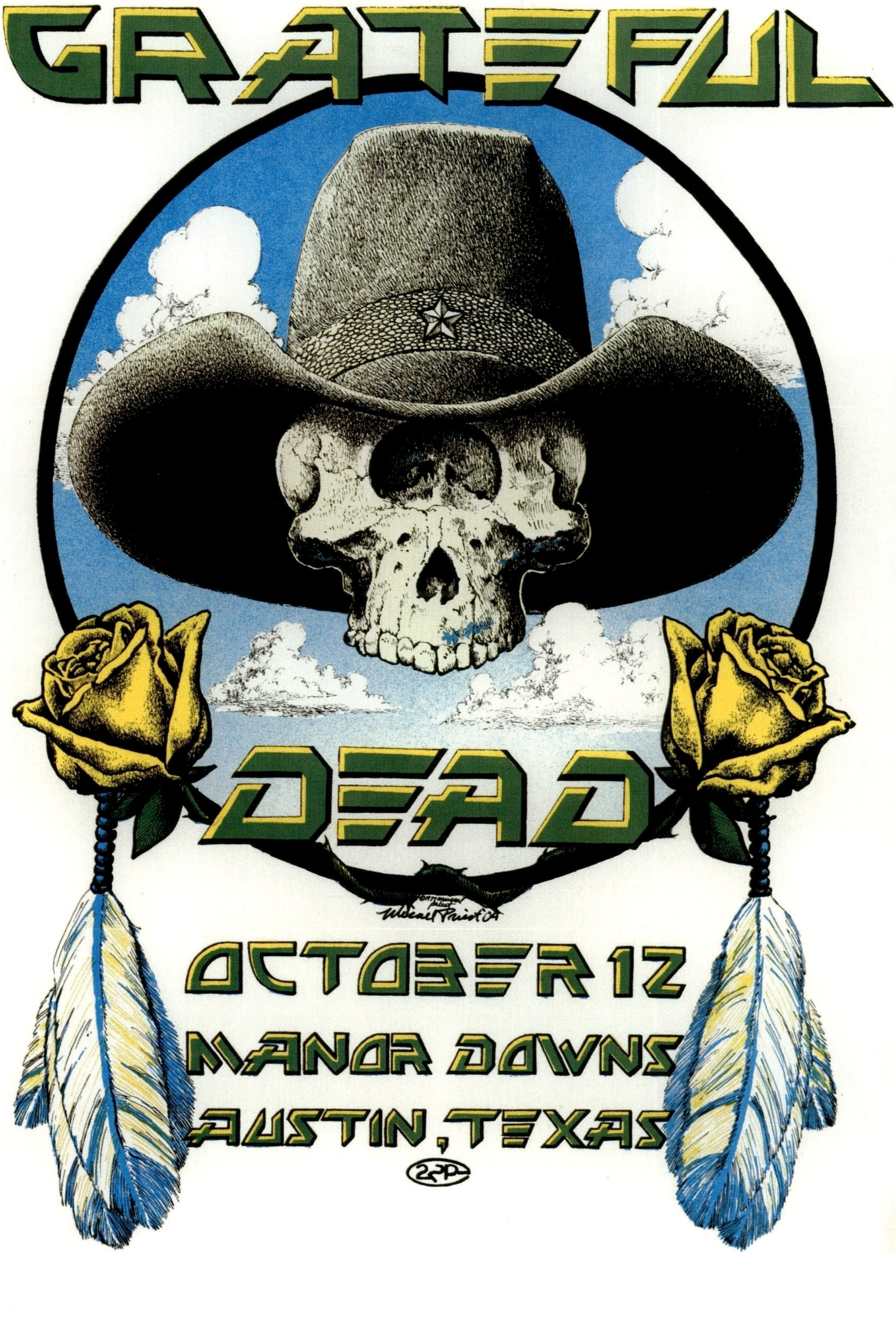

92 BILL NARUM. Holy Modal Rounders & Les Clamtones. Armadillo World Headquarters. March 5, 1977. 10.5" × 6.5". © Bill Narum.

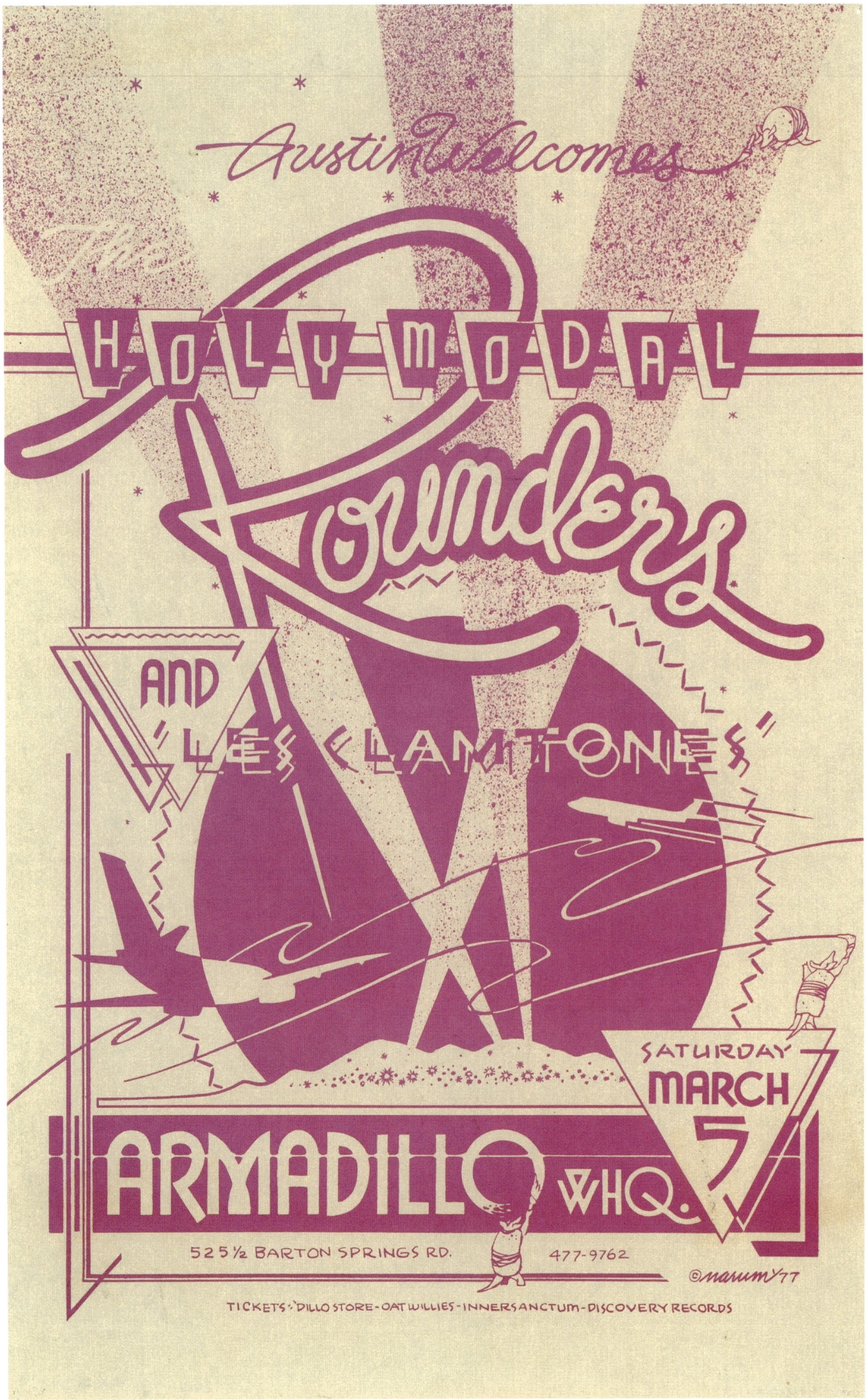

93 BILL NARUM. Taj Mahal & Navasota. Music Hall, Houston. October 21, 1971. 23" × 15.25". © Bill Narum.

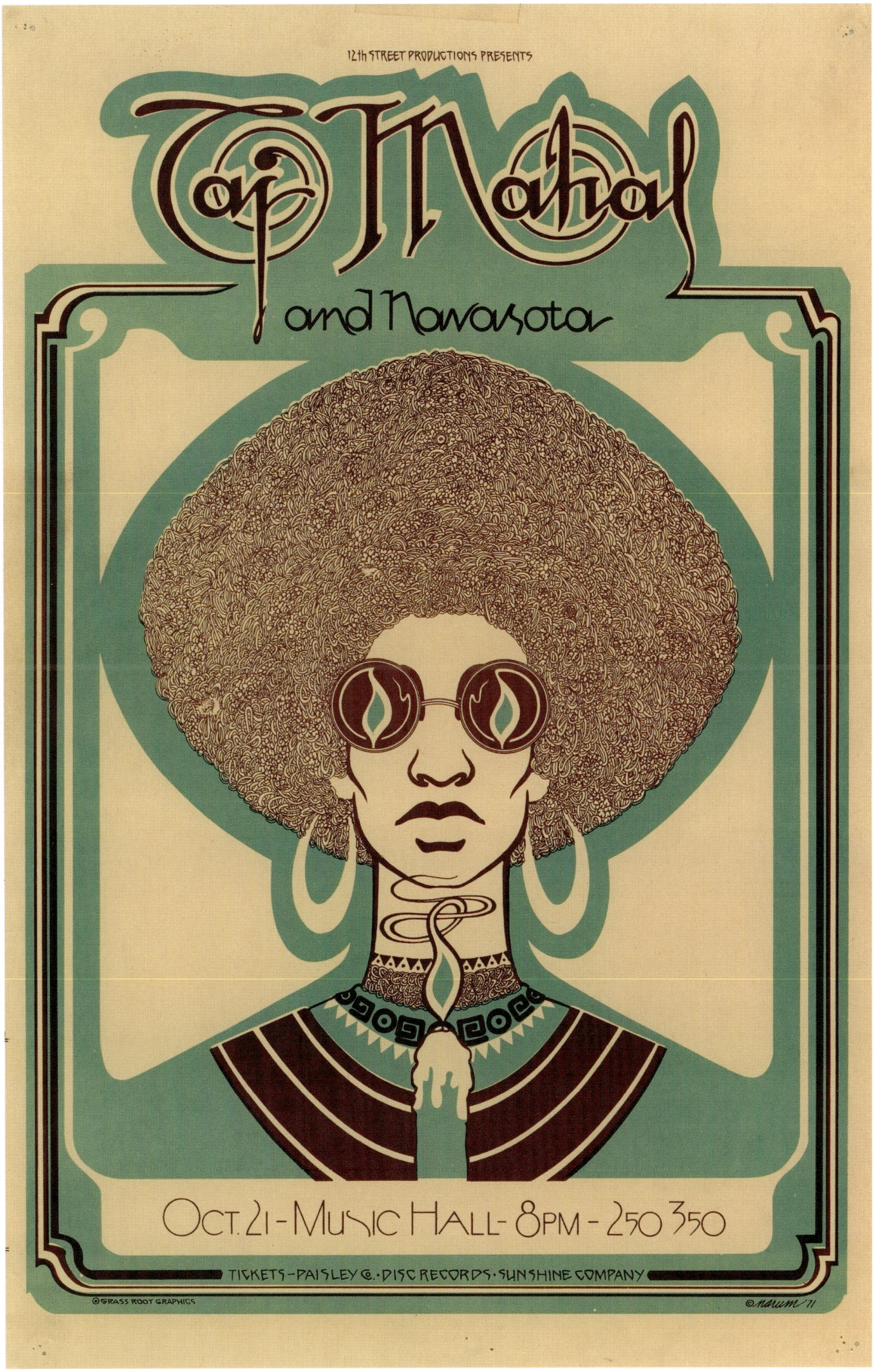

94 MICAEL PRIEST. The Pointer Sisters. Armadillo World Headquarters. November 9, 1975. 21.25" × 13.75". © Micael Priest.

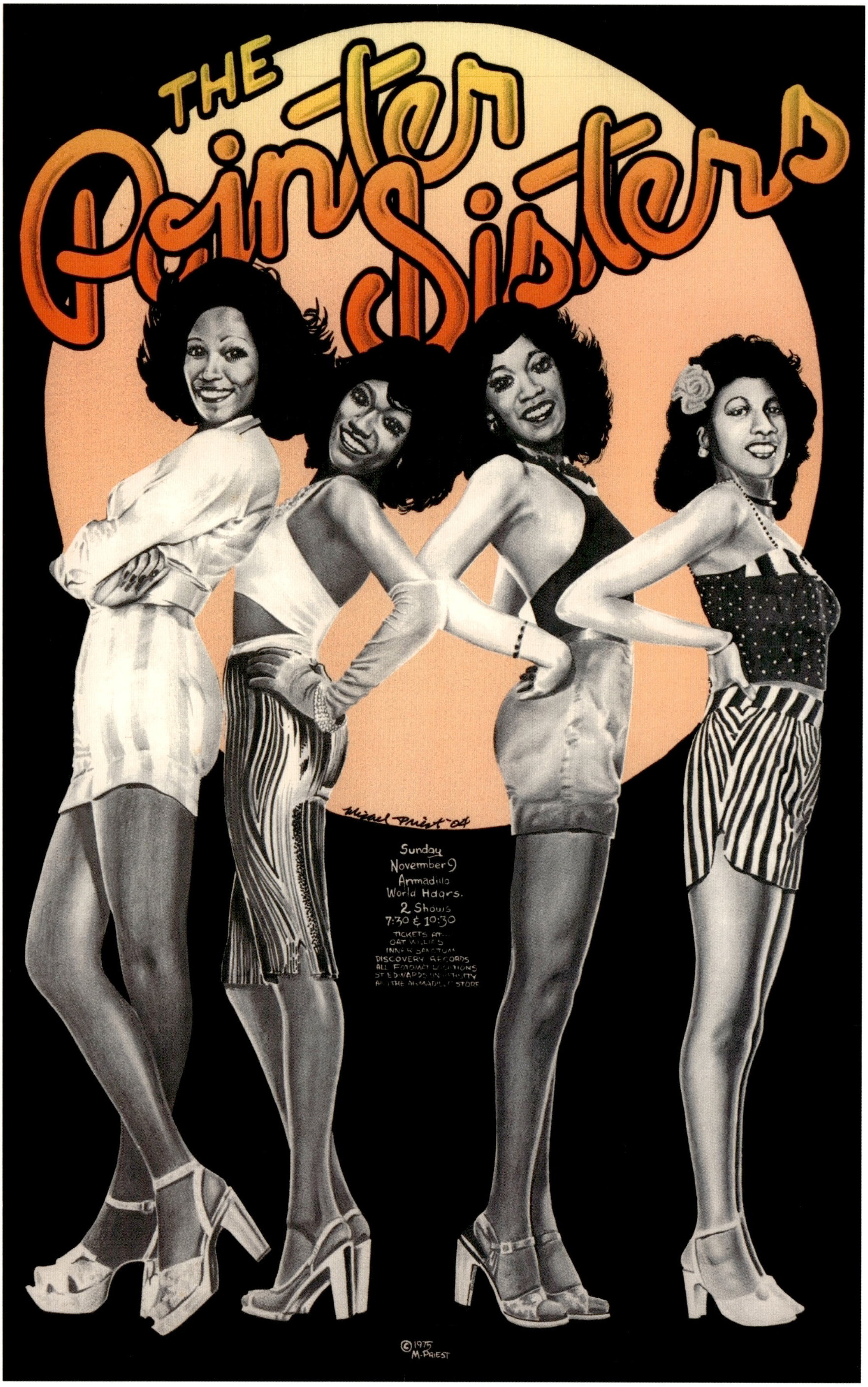

95 DALE WILKINS. J. J. Cale & Paul Craft. Austin Opry House. February 24, 1978. 17.5" × 11.5". © Dale Wilkins.

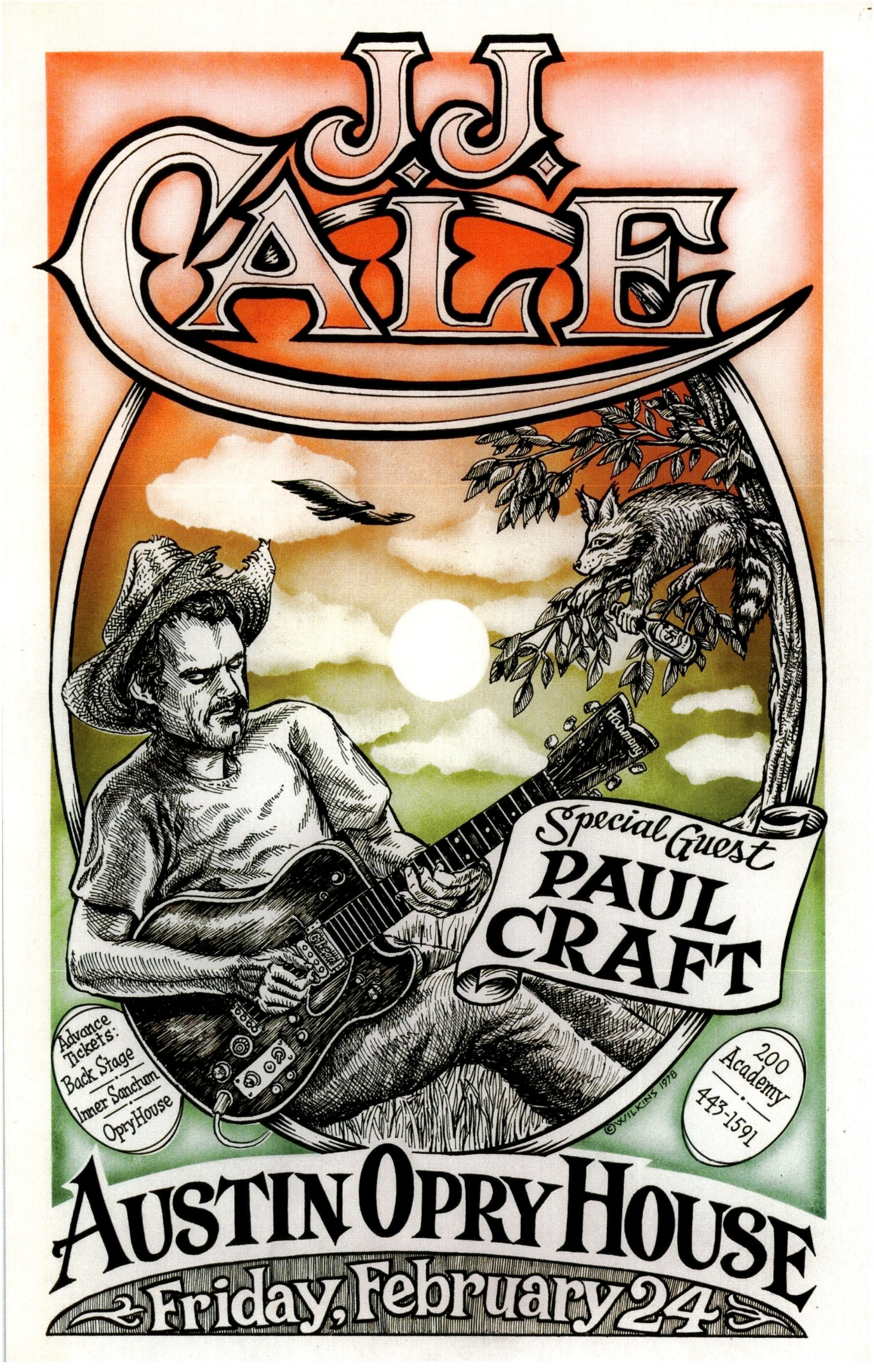

96 DANNY GARRETT. Bonnie Raitt & Muddy Waters. Austin Opry House. November 26, 1977. 17.5" × 11.5". © Danny Garrett.

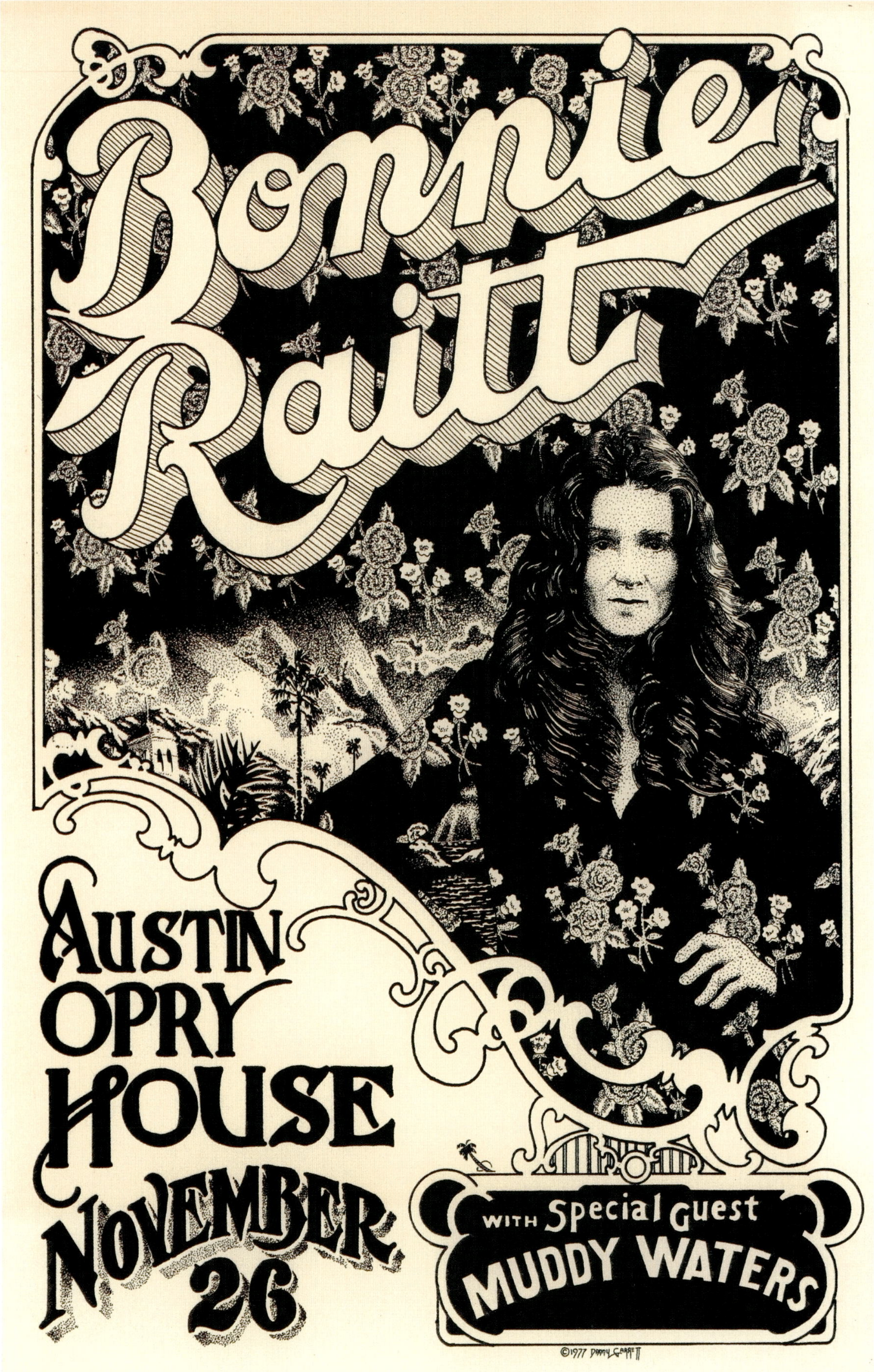

97 PAULINE WALSH JACOBSON. Tom Waits & Jonnie Barnett. Austin Opry House. November 12, 1977. 17" × 11". © Pauline Walsh Jacobson

Jacobson offers a take on the album art for Waits' debut release, *Closing Time.*

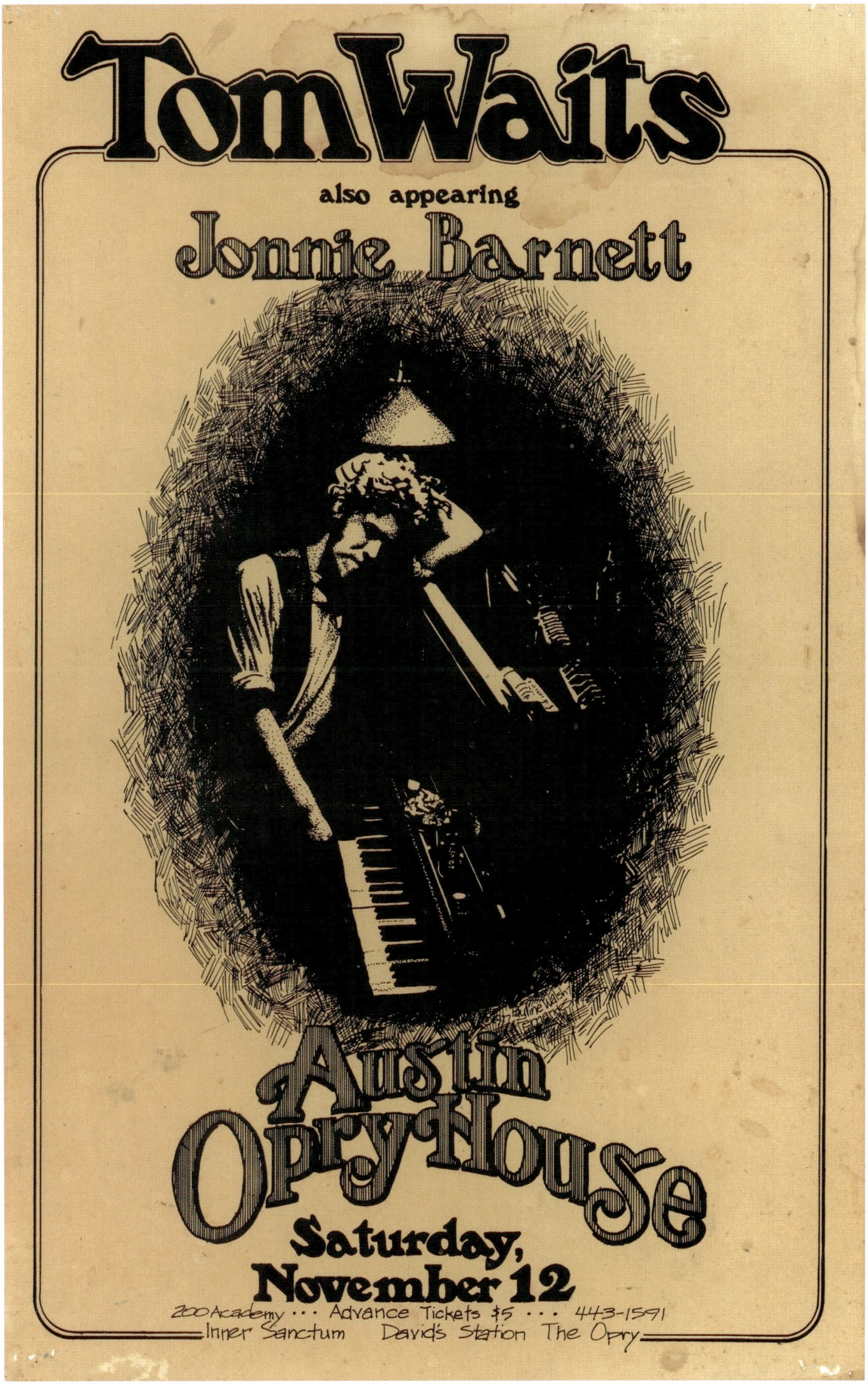

98 KEN FEATHERSTON. Dr. John & Greezy Wheels. Armadillo World Headquarters. April 15, 1974. 17" × 11". © Ken Featherston.

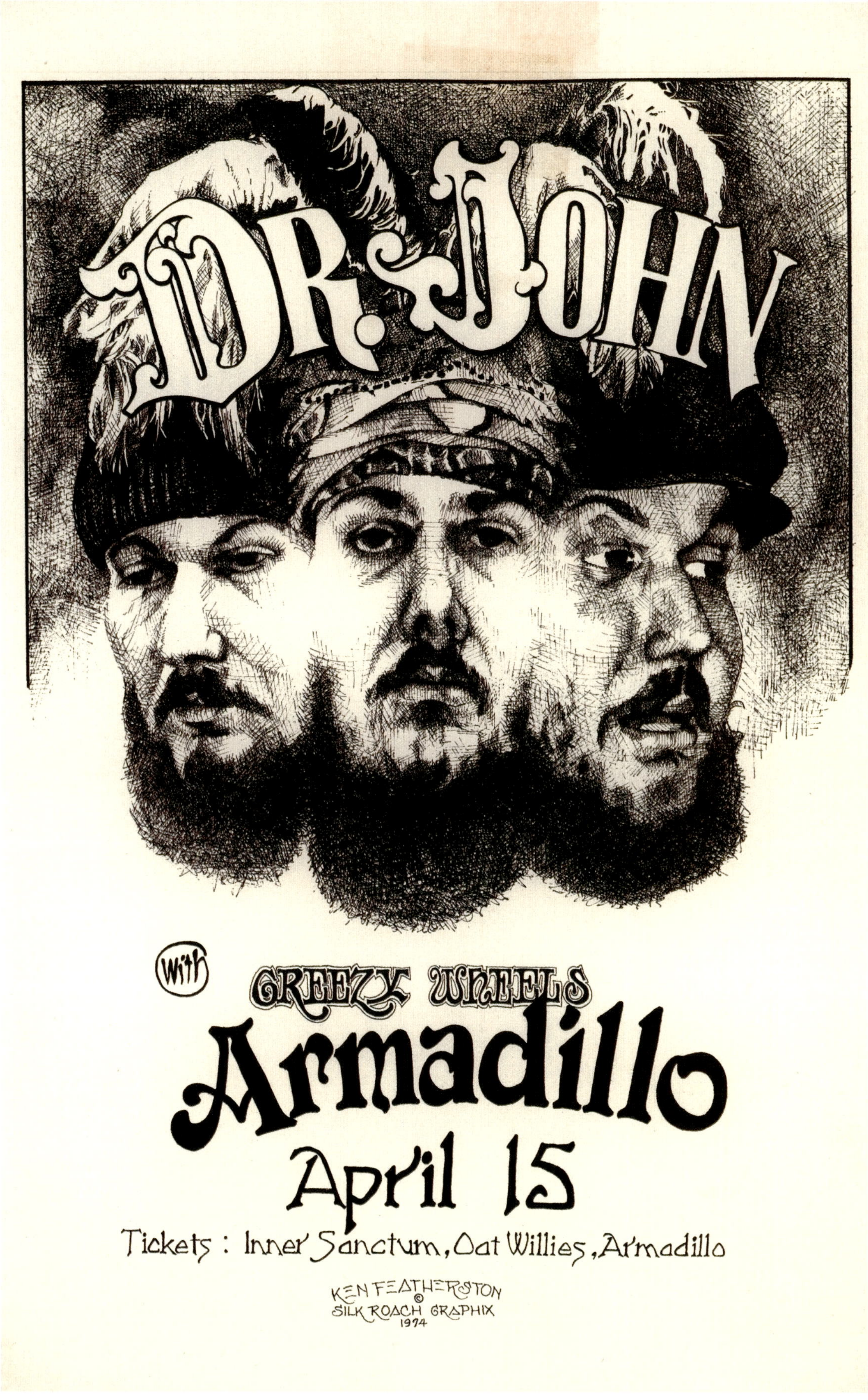

99 MICAEL PRIEST. Little Feat. Armadillo World Headquarters. February 8 & 9, 1974. 17.75" × 11.5". © Micael Priest.

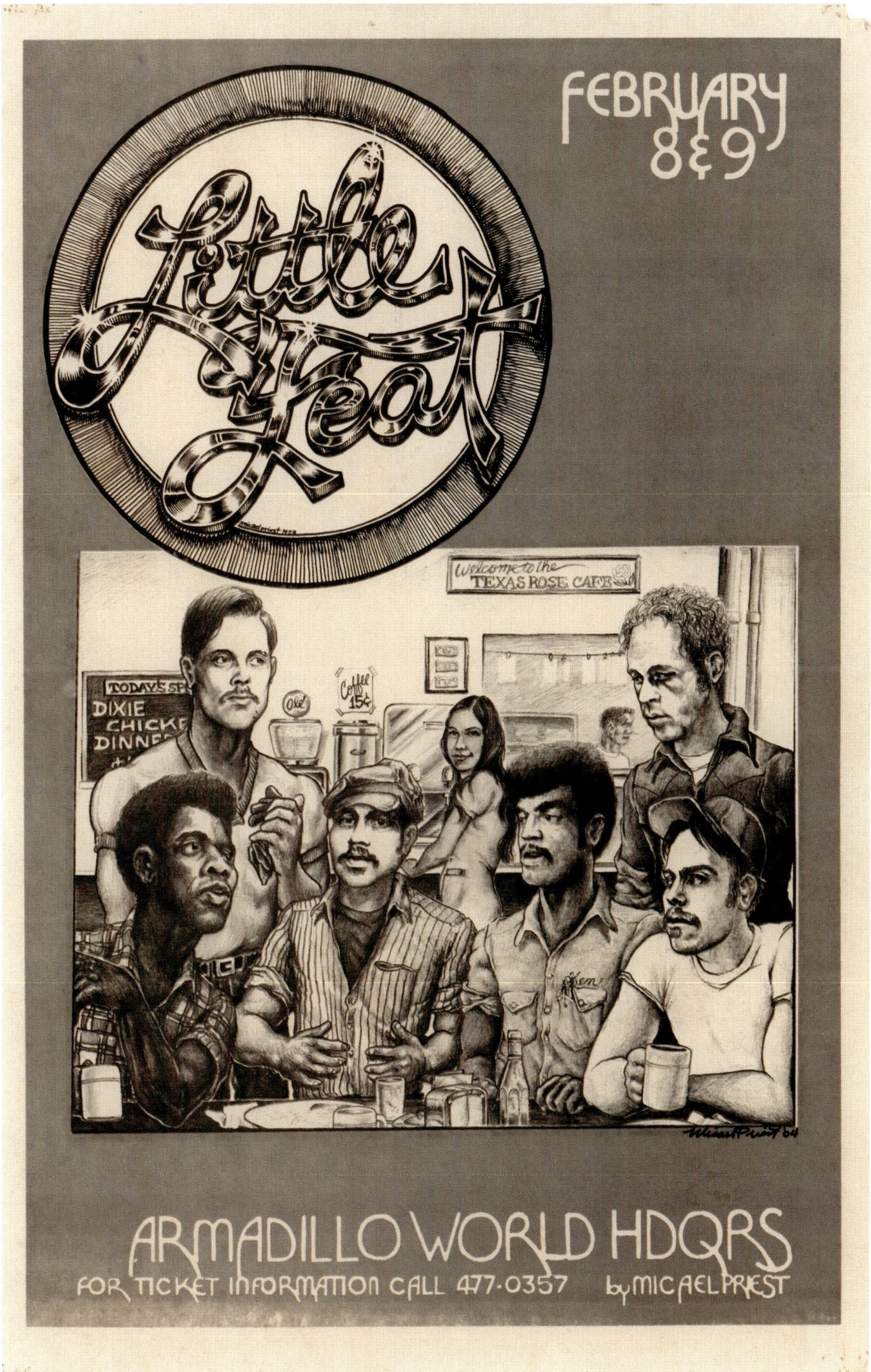

100 DANNY GARRETT. Warren Zevon. Austin Opry House. June 2, 1978. 17.5" × 11.5". © Danny Garrett.

Garrett references Zevon's "Roland the Headless Thompson Gunner" and "Werewolves of London."

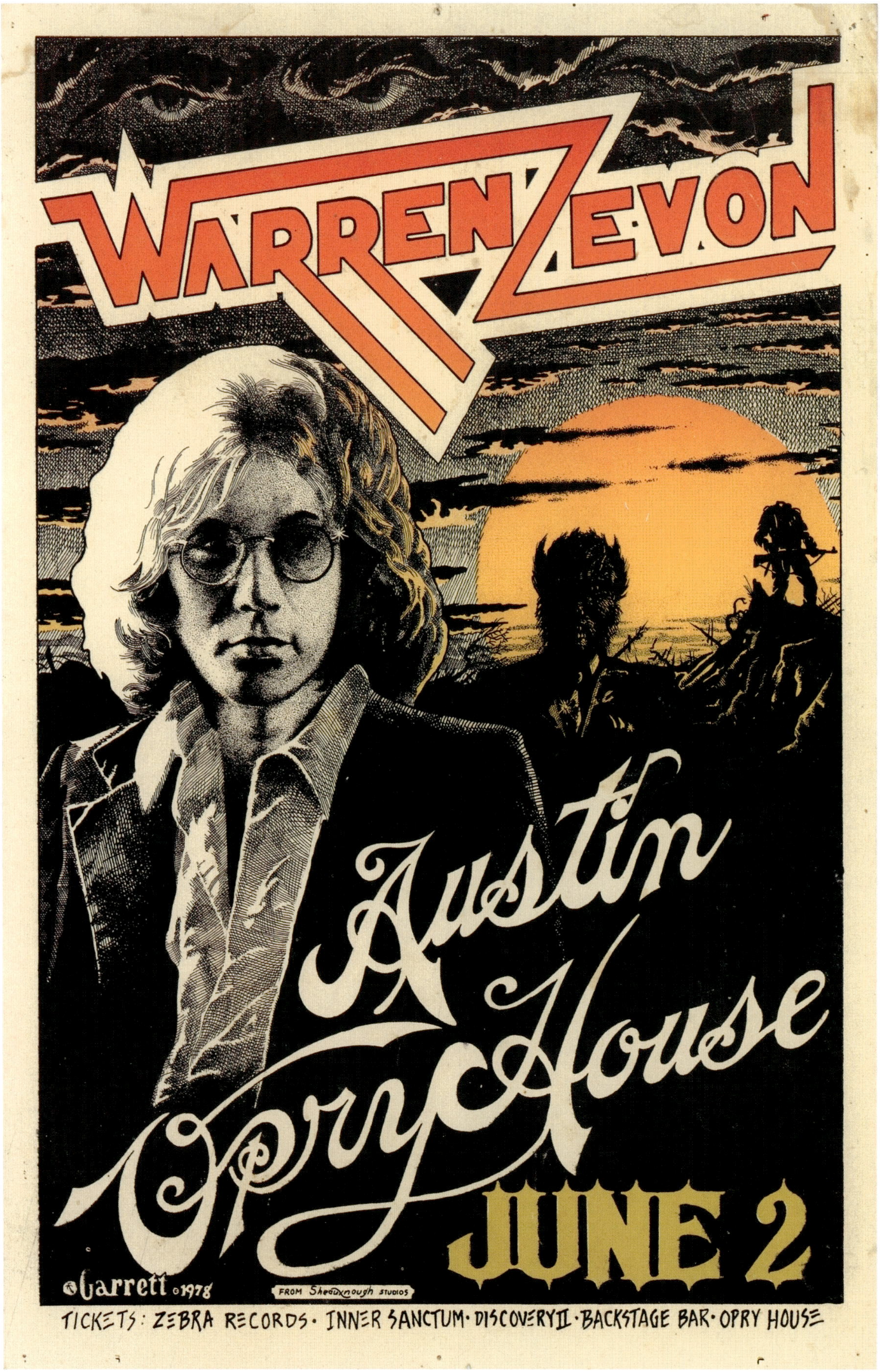

101 DANNY GARRETT. Lou Reed & Ian Dury. Austin Opry House. April 9, 1978. 17.5" × 11.75".

Garrett reinterprets Reed's *Street Hassle* album cover.

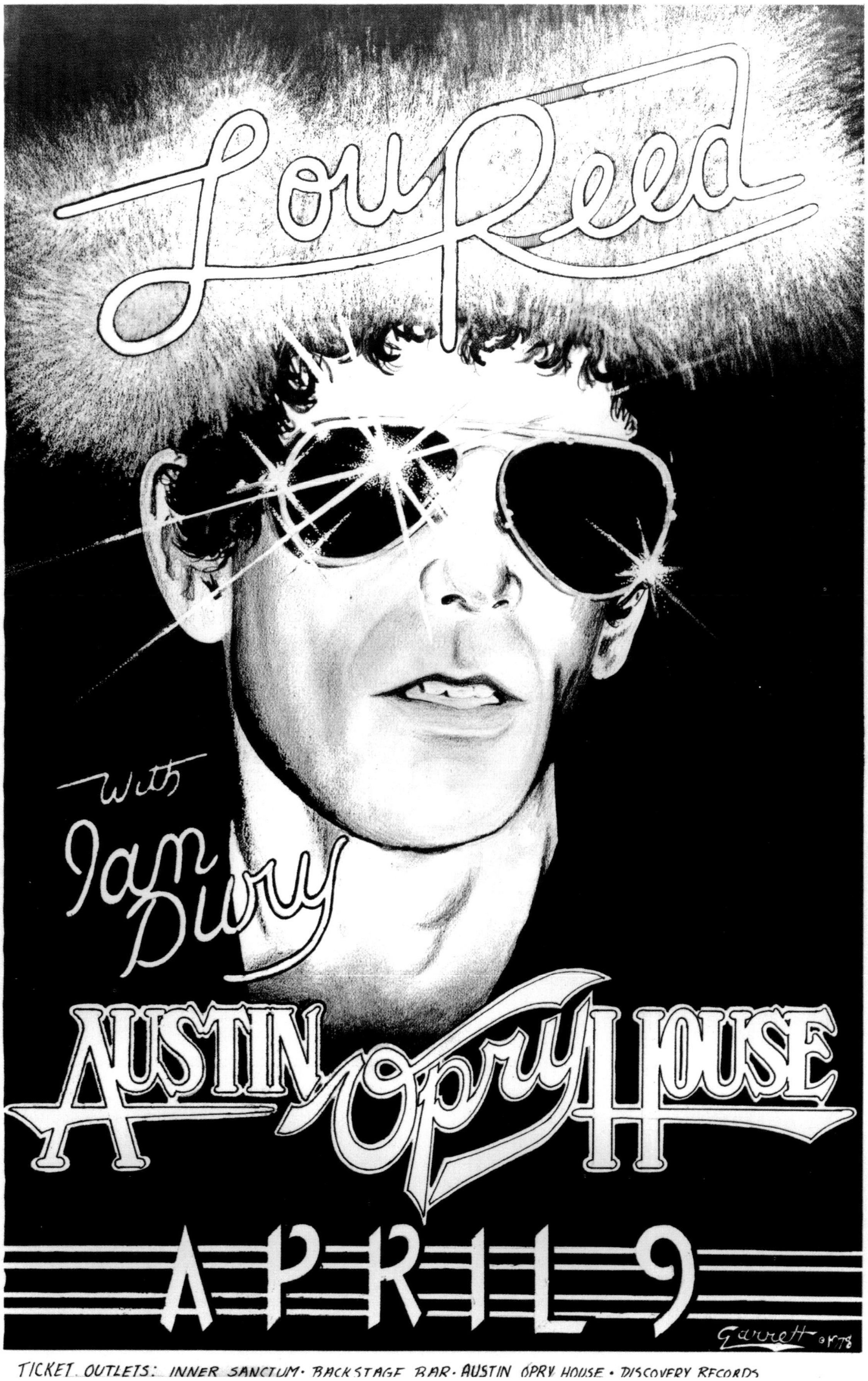

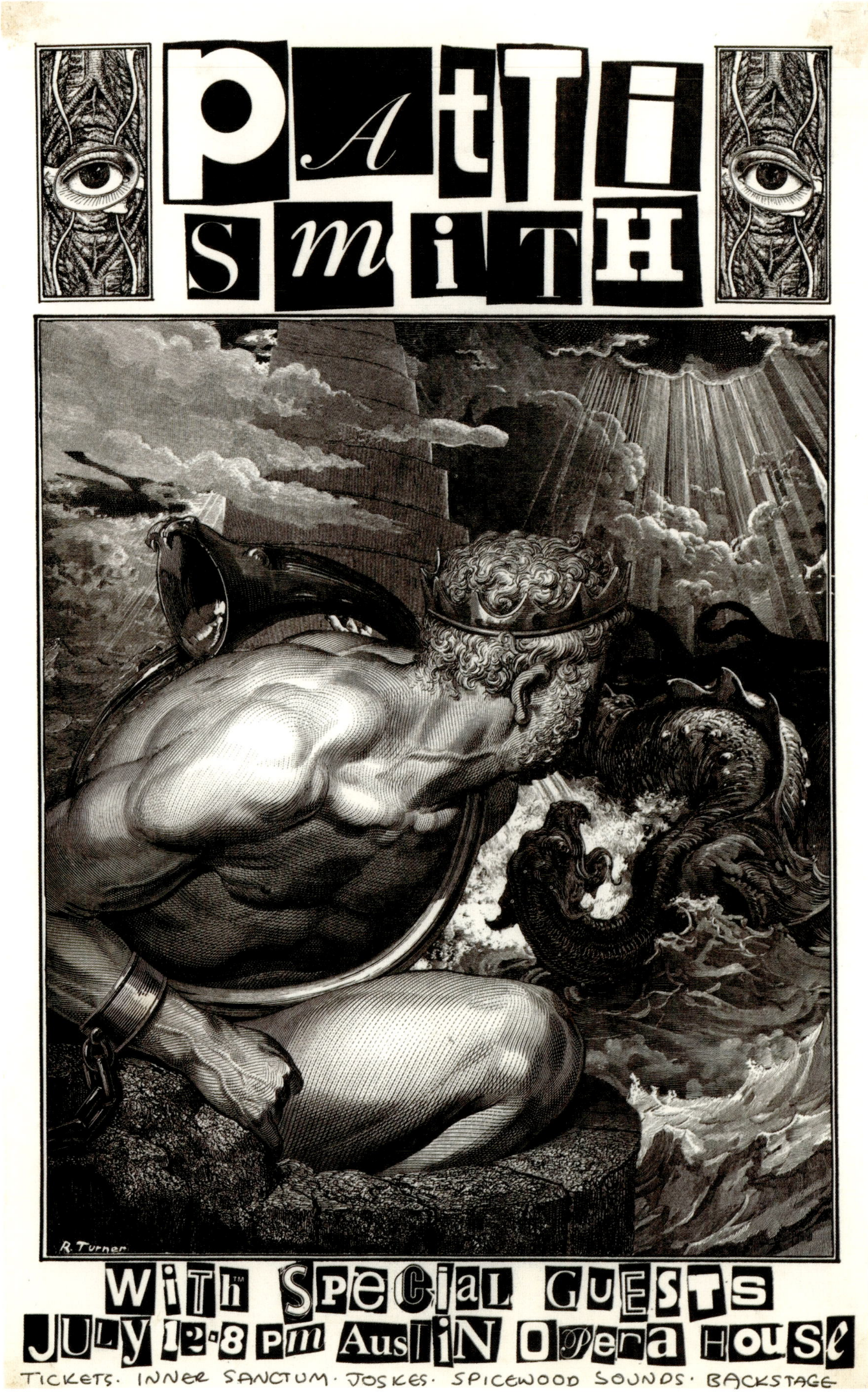

102 RICK TURNER. Patti Smith. Austin Opera House. July 12, 1978. 17" × 11". © Rick Turner.

PUNK &
THE NEW
WAVES

Austin cultivated its own unique brands of punk rock and other new waves of rock and roll in the late 1970s and early '80s, and with these developments came a refigured and confrontational visual aesthetic. Punk-era posters and handbills relied on traits and techniques that were not particularly new to rock-and-roll art: collage, comic-book aesthetics, and striking images of sexuality and radical lifestyles. Yet by the late 1970s Austin produced a roll call of young artists whose work captured the sensibilities of this revitalized new music. NOXX (Michael Nott) and Rick Turner produced posters and handbills for Raul's, a Tejano bar across the street from the University of Texas that became the center of Austin's first wave of punk. Following the demise of Raul's, Club Foot emerged as a larger downtown outpost for local and touring acts, and Jagmo (Nels Jacobson) began his career as a poster artist by producing flyers and handbills for the new club. These new figures on the art scene would produce enormous bodies of work. Musicians like Tim Kerr, Chris Gates, and Randy "Biscuit" Turner of the Big Boys, as well as Davy Jones of the Next, Cam King of the Explosives, and Jesse Sublett of the Skunks, designed posters and flyers. Fans, too, produced art for bands, and many of these pieces are unattributed.

Punk fanzines influenced the visual aesthetic of the new music. Austin produced a vital fanzine in *Sluggo!*, a revolutionary publication headed by Nick West that served as an impetus for underground media and guerrilla art in Austin. In addition to zine publication, the *Sluggo!* crew printed posters and handbills on their vintage press and inspired a slew of Austinites to publish their documents on the new music and pursue remarkable new visual forms.

Austin poster artists had always worked with limited budgets, and the artists who promoted punk gigs effectively navigated their way through economic constraints. The photocopied handbill, often black and white and always cheap to produce, became a primary medium for promoting bills at clubs like Raul's, Duke's Royal Coach Inn, the Continental Club, and Club Foot.

While the new wave of artists reigned in the arena of punk promotion, established figures of the poster scene adapted to the new aesthetics. Guy Juke's "cubist bebop" style, a term coined by Micael Priest to describe the artistic shift that Juke initiated in the late 1970s, figured prominently in his posters for Devo and the Dicks. It was Priest, a driving force behind the Armadillo Art Squad, who created the poster for one of the first major punk concerts in Austin, the Ramones at the Armadillo World Headquarters in 1977.

Austin produced one of the more unique scenes in the early days of punk, and its visual artists promoted and documented the music with an arresting body of work.

103 MICAEL PRIEST. The Ramones & Aalon. Armadillo World Headquarters. July 14, 1977. 17.5" × 11.5". © Micael Priest.

Priest explains that he wanted the lettering of the poster to look like "raw steaks with the little rind of fat." He also cites *Famous Monsters of Filmland* magazine as an inspiration for the lettering.

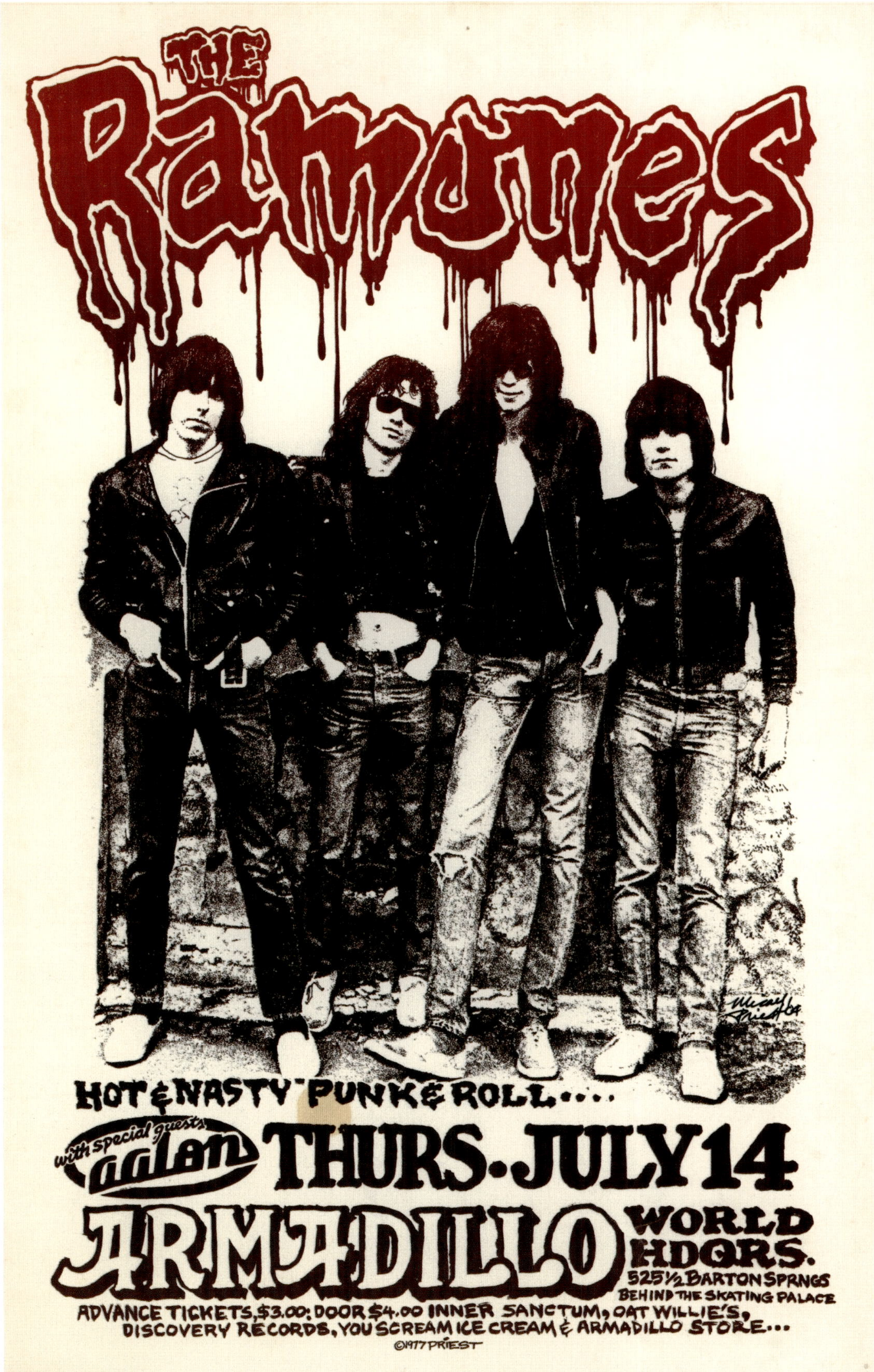

104 JESSE SUBLETT. The Violators & The Skunks. Raul's. February 23, 1978. 11" × 8.5". © Jesse Sublett.

Sublett, a founding member of the Skunks, Austin's early pioneering punk band, had been a cartoonist and writer before he stepped onto the rock-and-roll stage. This flyer advertises one of the first punk shows at Raul's, a key venue in Austin's burgeoning punk scene. The band members depicted in the flyer sport Iggy and the Stooges–inspired T-shirts. Sublett notes, "If you ended up at Raul's in 1978, it's about a 99% chance that you were a big fan of Iggy Pop."

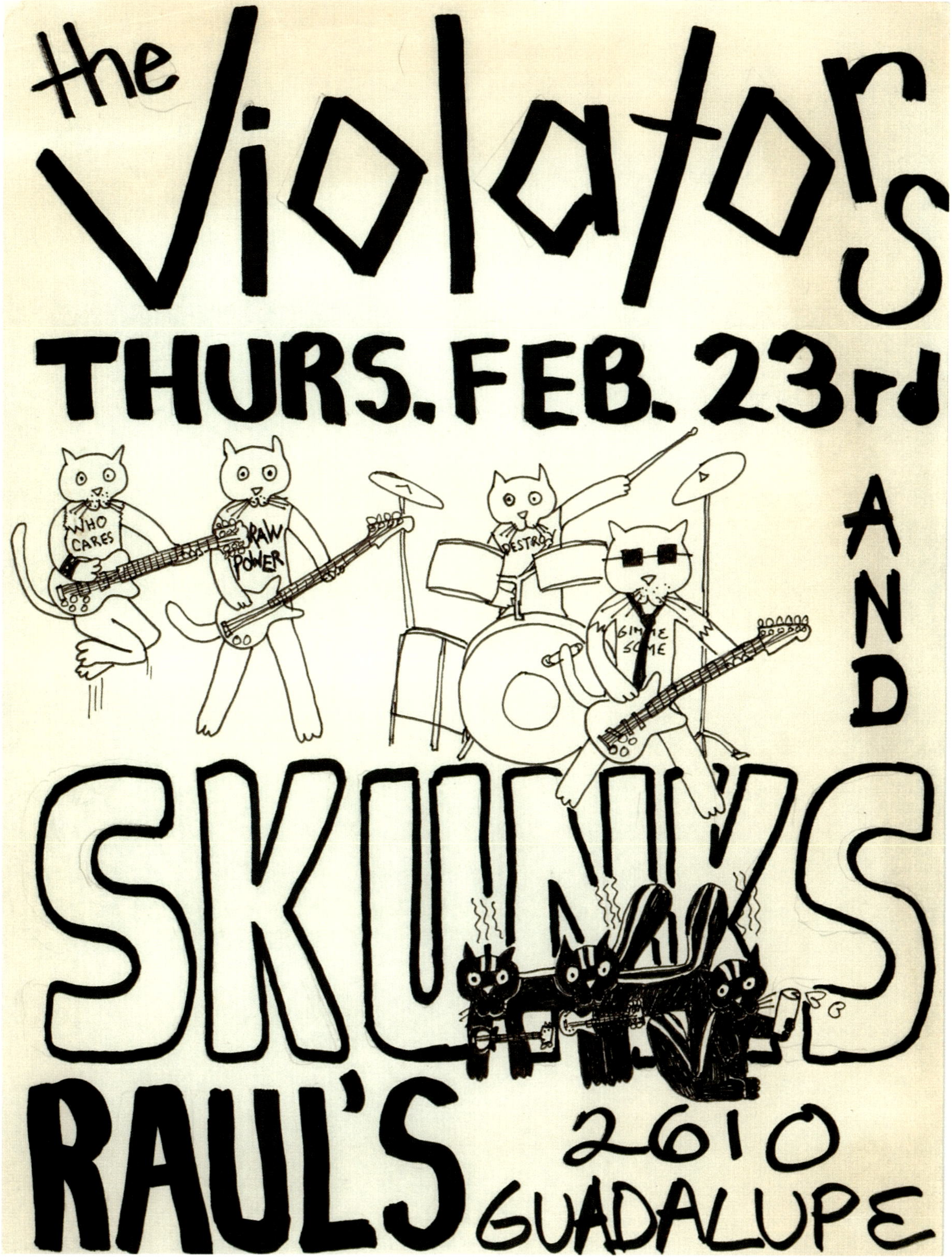

105 UNKNOWN ARTIST. Iggy Pop & Terminal Mind. Armadillo World Headquarters. March 29, 1980. 11" × 8.5".

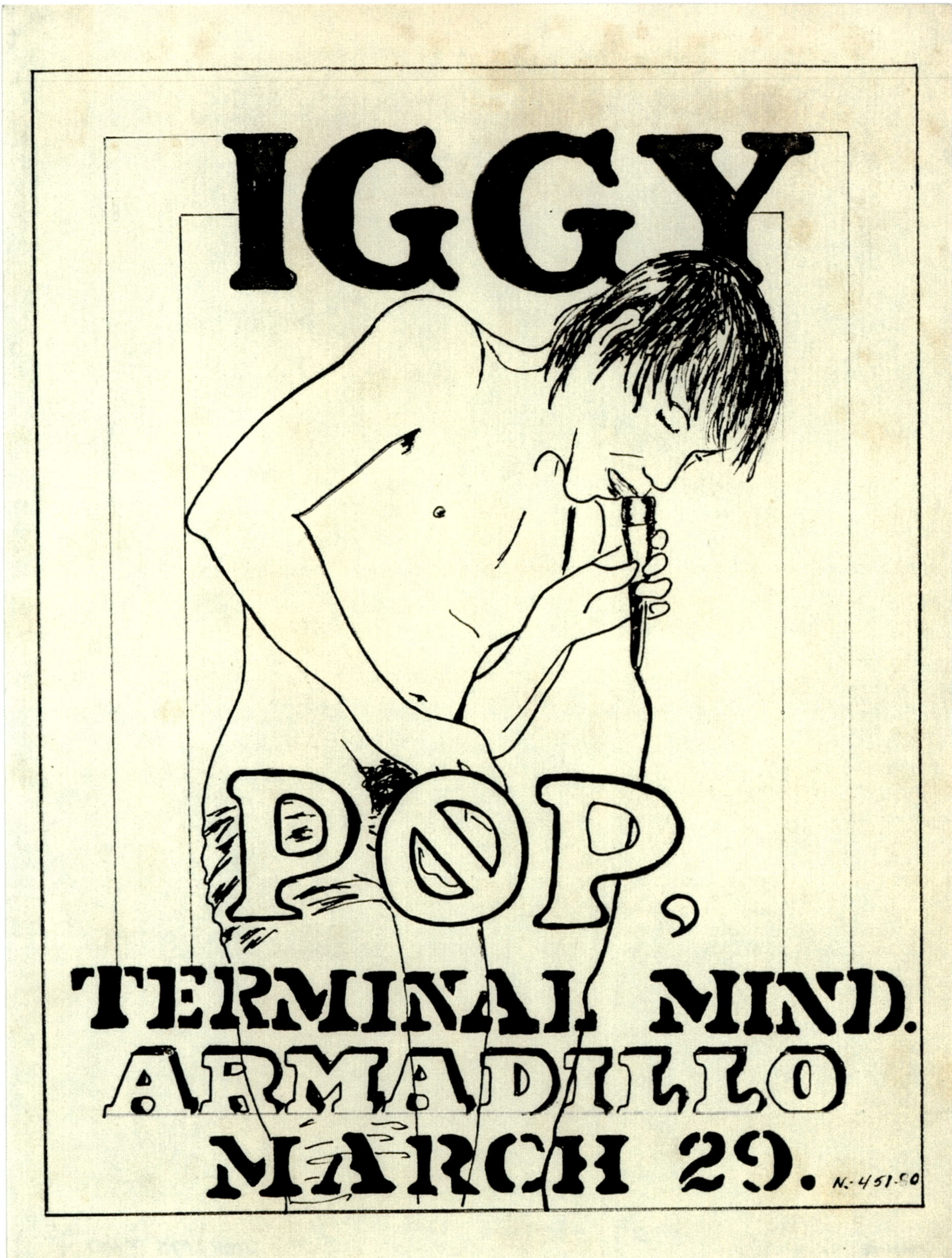

106 MICAEL PRIEST. Roky Erickson and Bleib Alien. Ritz Theatre. April 25 & 26, 1975. 14" × 8.5". © Micael Priest.

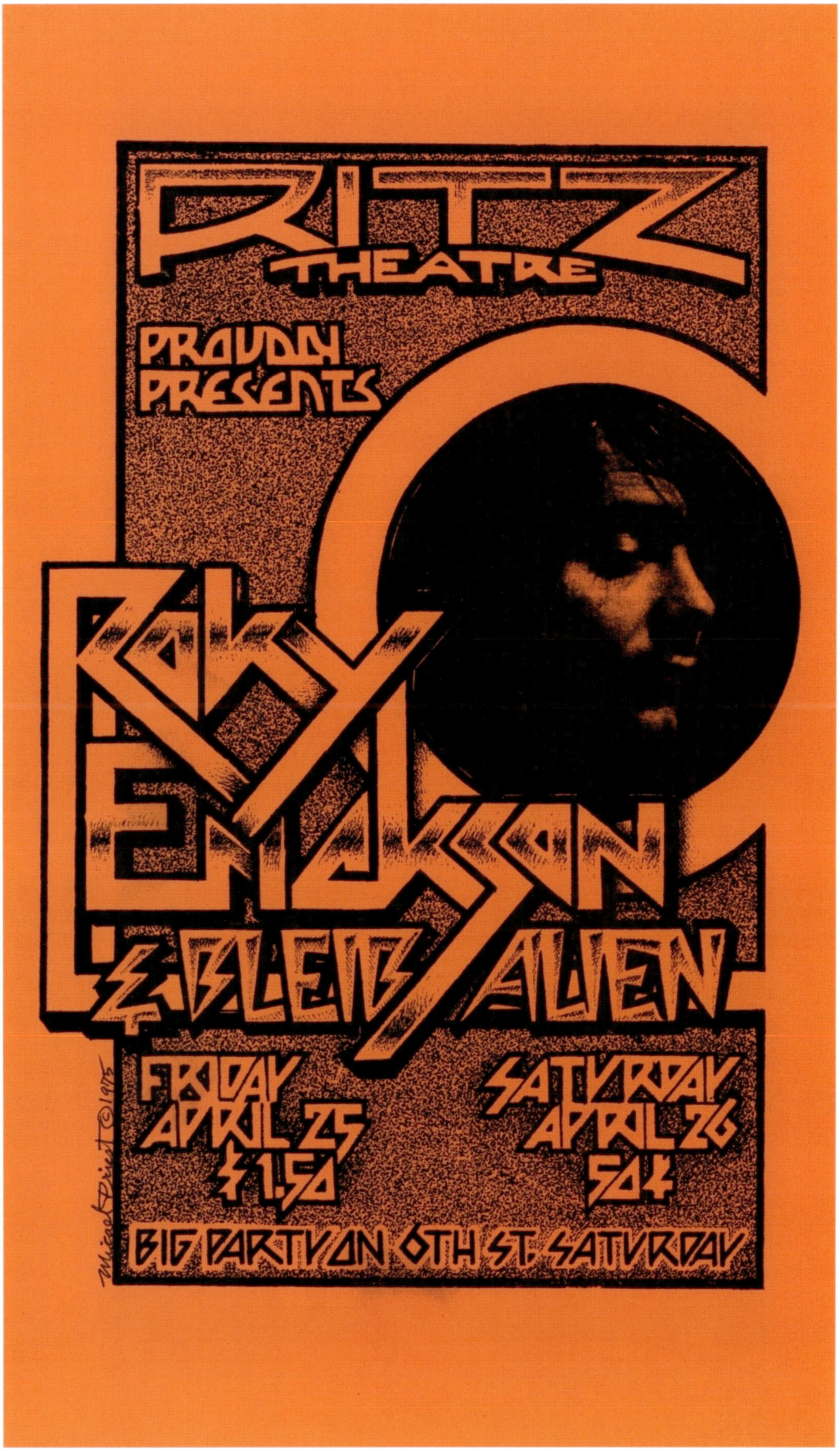

107 CAM KING. Roky Erickson and the Explosives. Steamboat. December 5, 1979. 17" × 11". © Cam King of Flathead Studios.

In addition to his work as guitarist for the Explosives, a power-pop act that moonlighted as one of Roky Erickson's great backing bands, Cam King produced posters and promotional material for his own Flathead Studios.

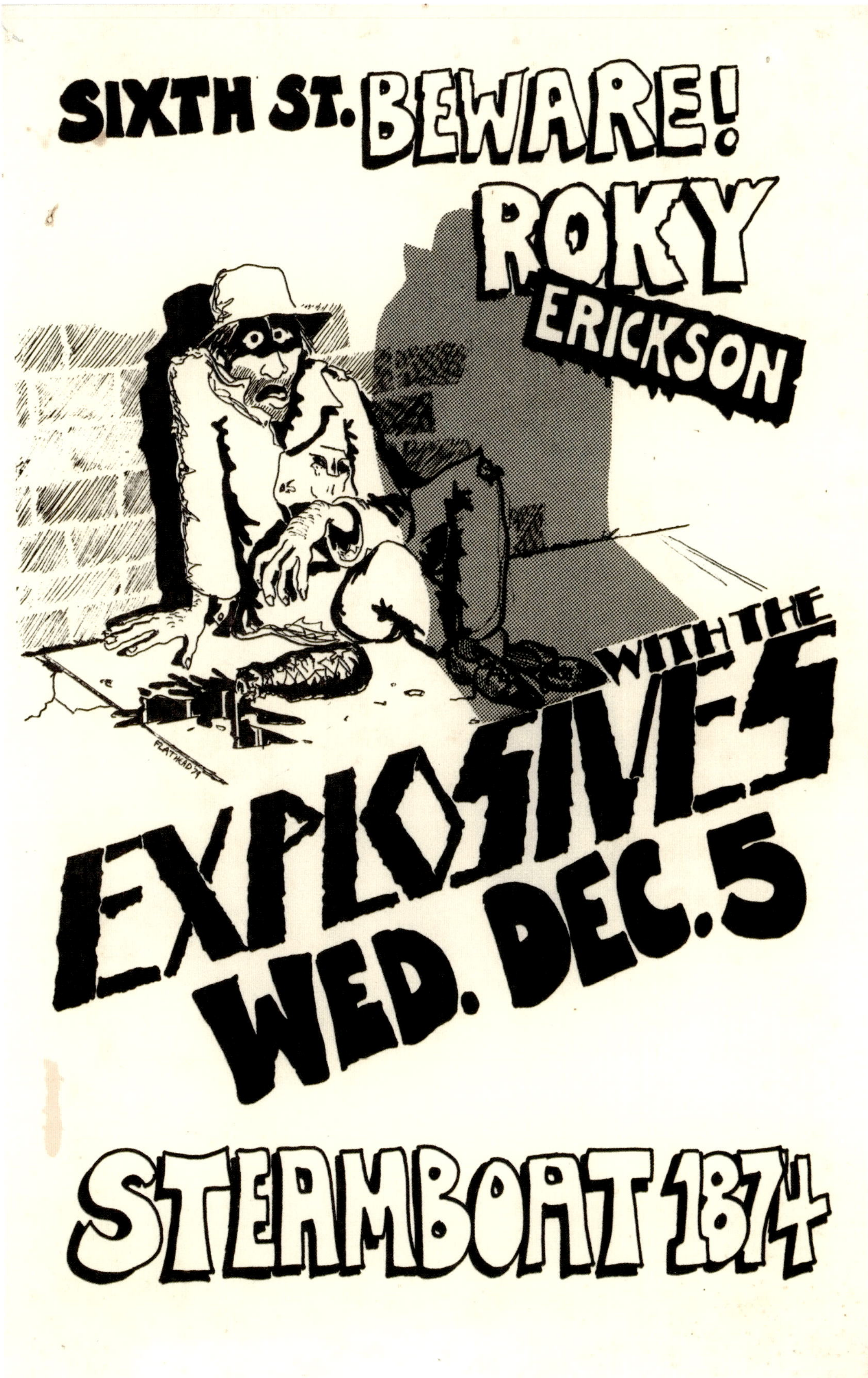

108 CAM KING. Roky Erickson and the Explosives & The Blame. Raul's. August 30, 1979. 17" × 11".

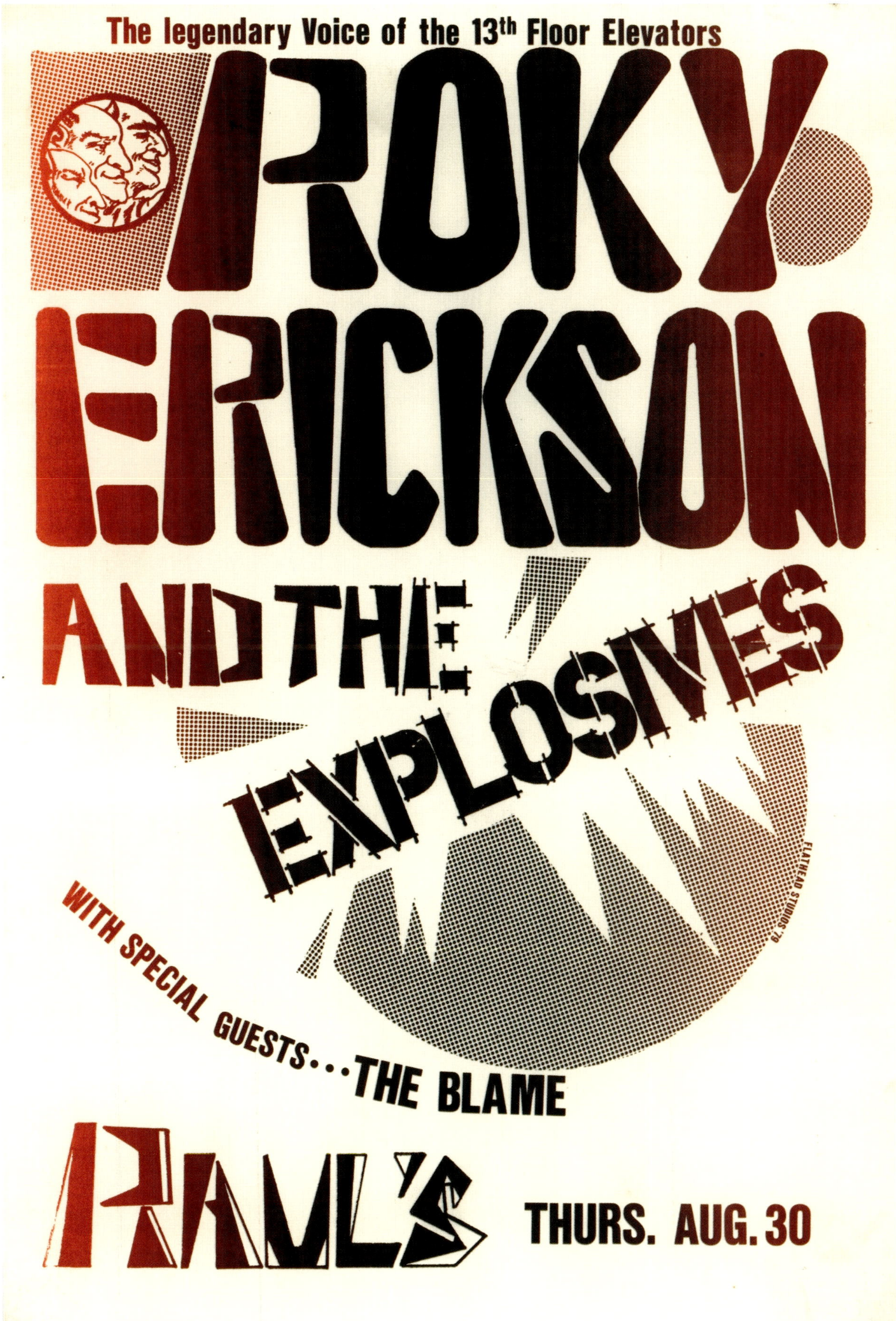

109 JOE NICK PATOSKI. Joe "King" Carrasco and Los Crowns, The Delinquents, & The Shades. Raul's. November 14, 1979. 11" × 8.5". © Joe Nick Patoski.

Patoski, a Texas music and popular-culture scholar and former manager of Carrasco, produced this notable example of a collage-based flyer, a medium that proved to be affordable and effective in the late 1970s and early 1980s.

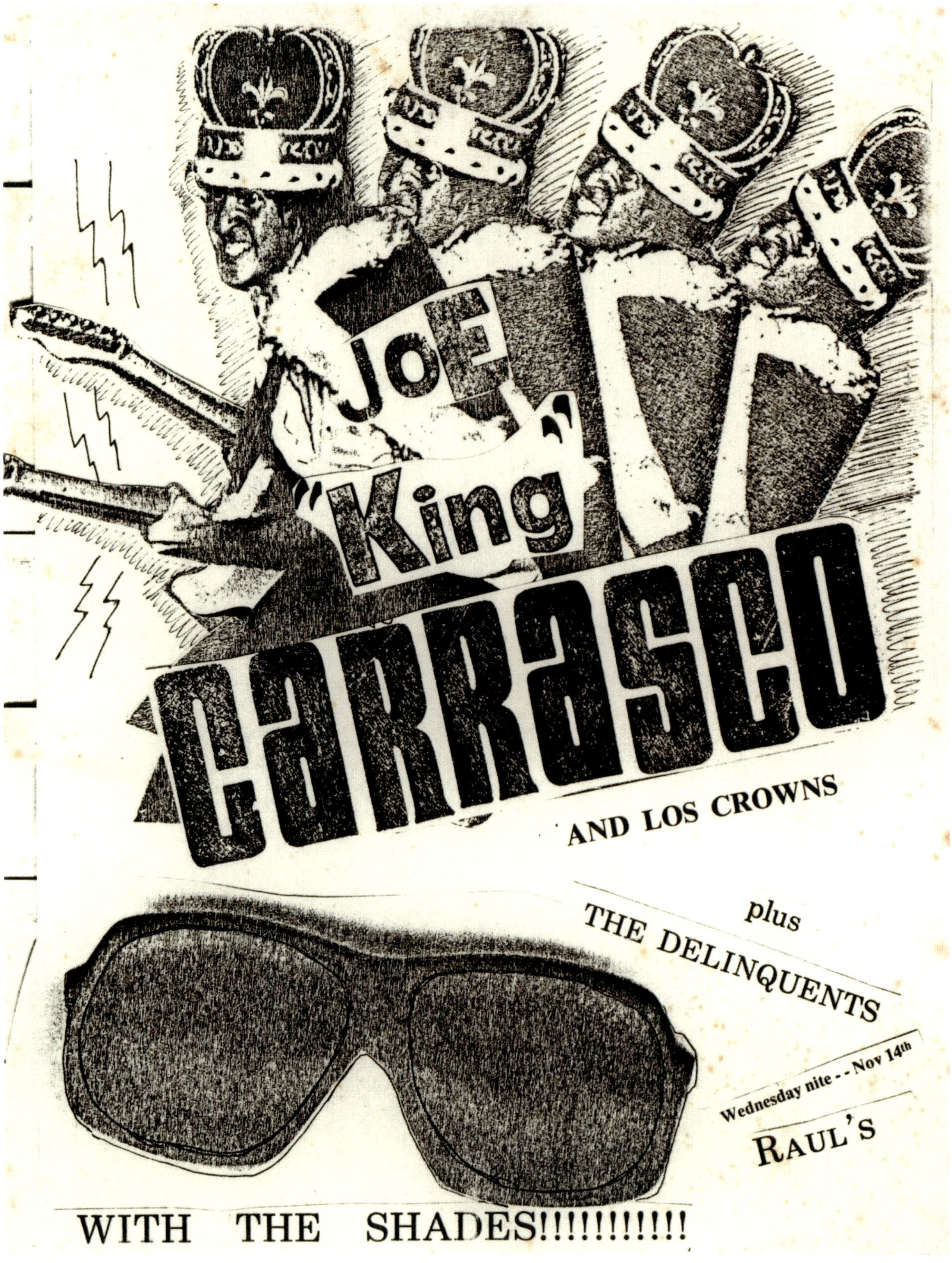

110 RANDY "BISCUIT" TURNER. The Judys, Big Boys, & Electric Tools. Raul's. January 16, 1981. 11" × 8.5". © Randy "Biscuit" Turner.

Randy "Biscuit" Turner, one of many punk musicians who also produced flyers and a wide array of visual art, fronted the Big Boys, one of punk rock's most groundbreaking and genre-defying bands. This flyer captures Biscuit's idea of punk, funk, and all-night fun. Known primarily for his work in the Big Boys, Biscuit also appeared with the Kerry Awn–led Uranium Savages before starting the Big Boys.

111 GUY JUKE. Dinettes, The Next, & The Dicks. Raul's. June 25 & 26, 1980. 14" × 8.5". © Guy Juke.

Guy Juke progressed with ease from one style to the next. This poster offers an example of what Micael Priest describes as Juke's "cubist bebop" phase.

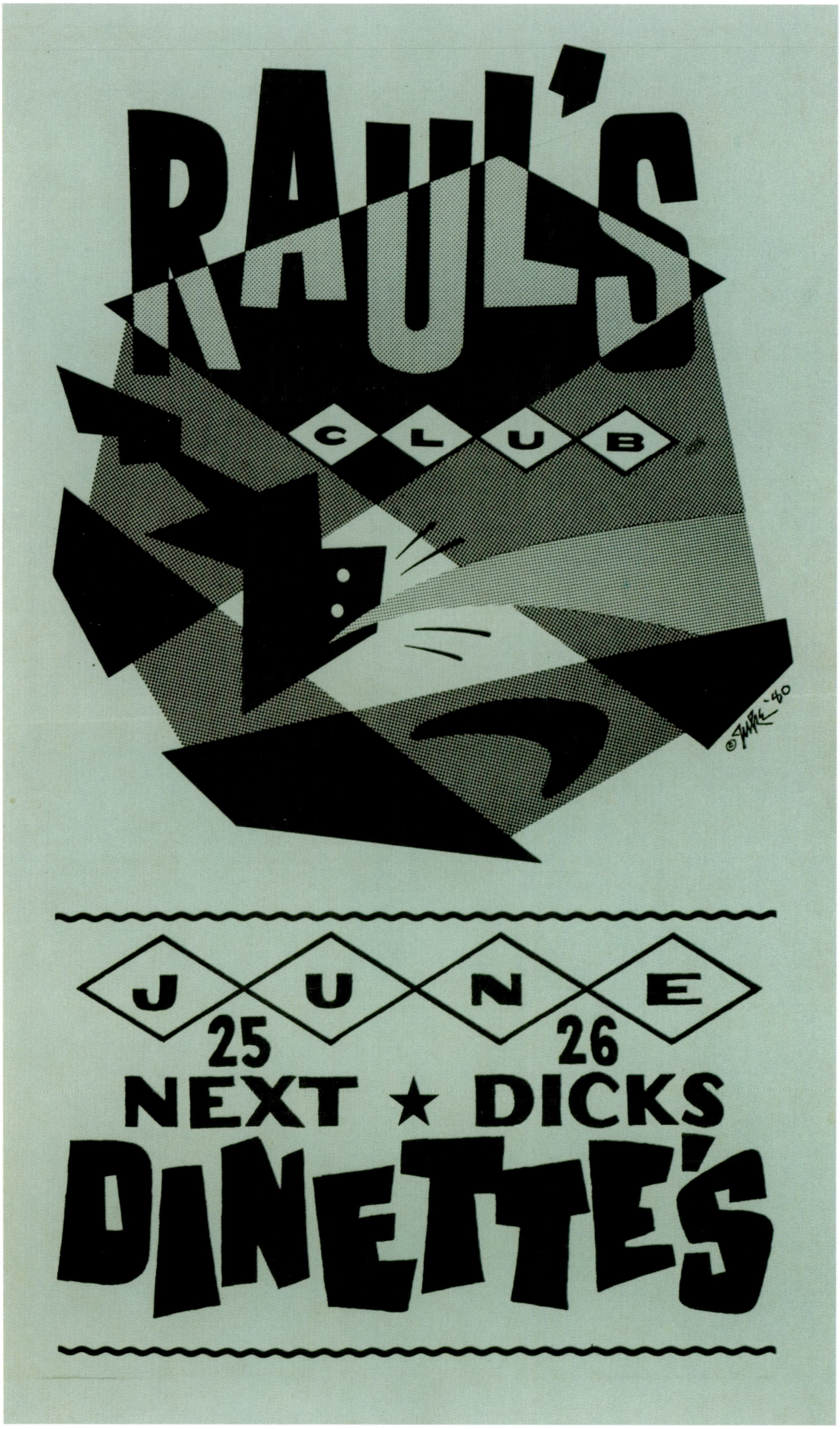

112 NOXX (MICHAEL NOTT). Big Boys & The Dicks. Raul's. September 19 & 20, 1980. 11" × 8.5".
© NOXX (Michael Nott).

NOXX was one of Austin's most prolific punk handbill and poster artists. This poster advertises the live recording sessions at Raul's that would result in the Dicks/Big Boys split live LP, a classic Austin punk record.

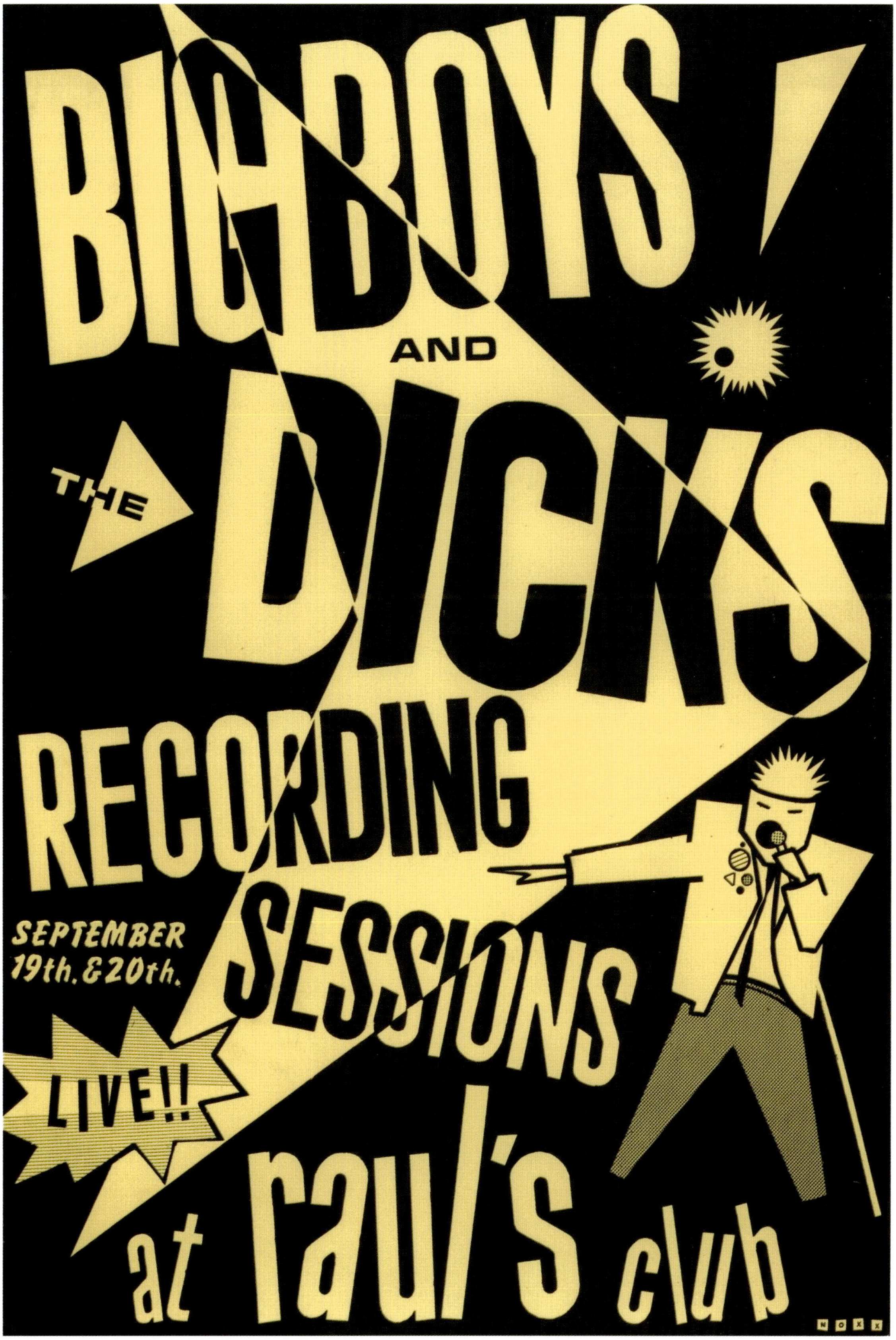

113 NOXX (MICHAEL NOTT). The Next & Inserts. Raul's. 1981. 15.5" × 10.75". © NOXX (Michael Nott).

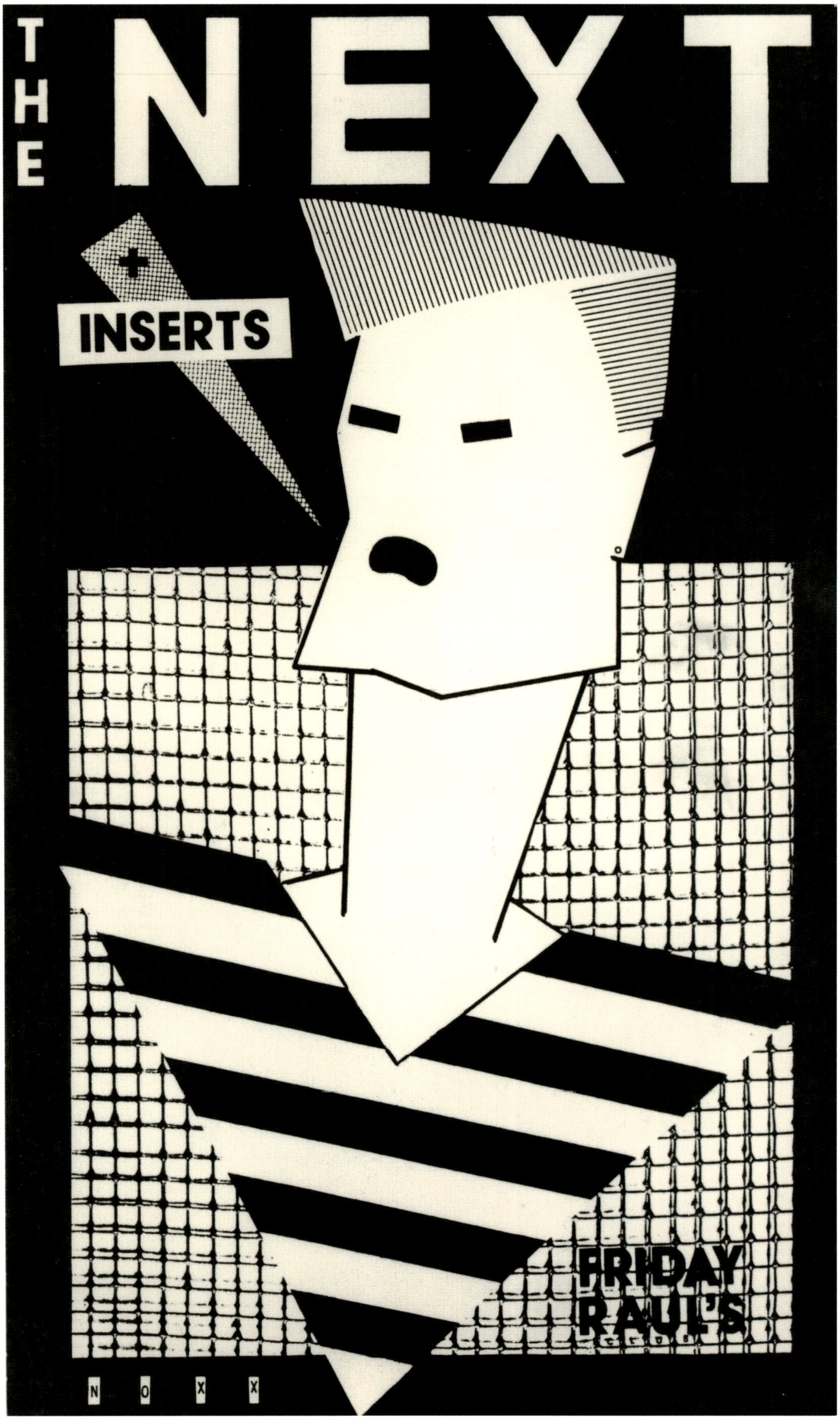

114 NOXX (MICHAEL NOTT). "Newave Extravaganza" with The Judys, STB, Big Boys, Delta, The Devices, & Aces 88. Texas Union. April 17, 1981. 17" × 10". © NOXX (Michael Nott).

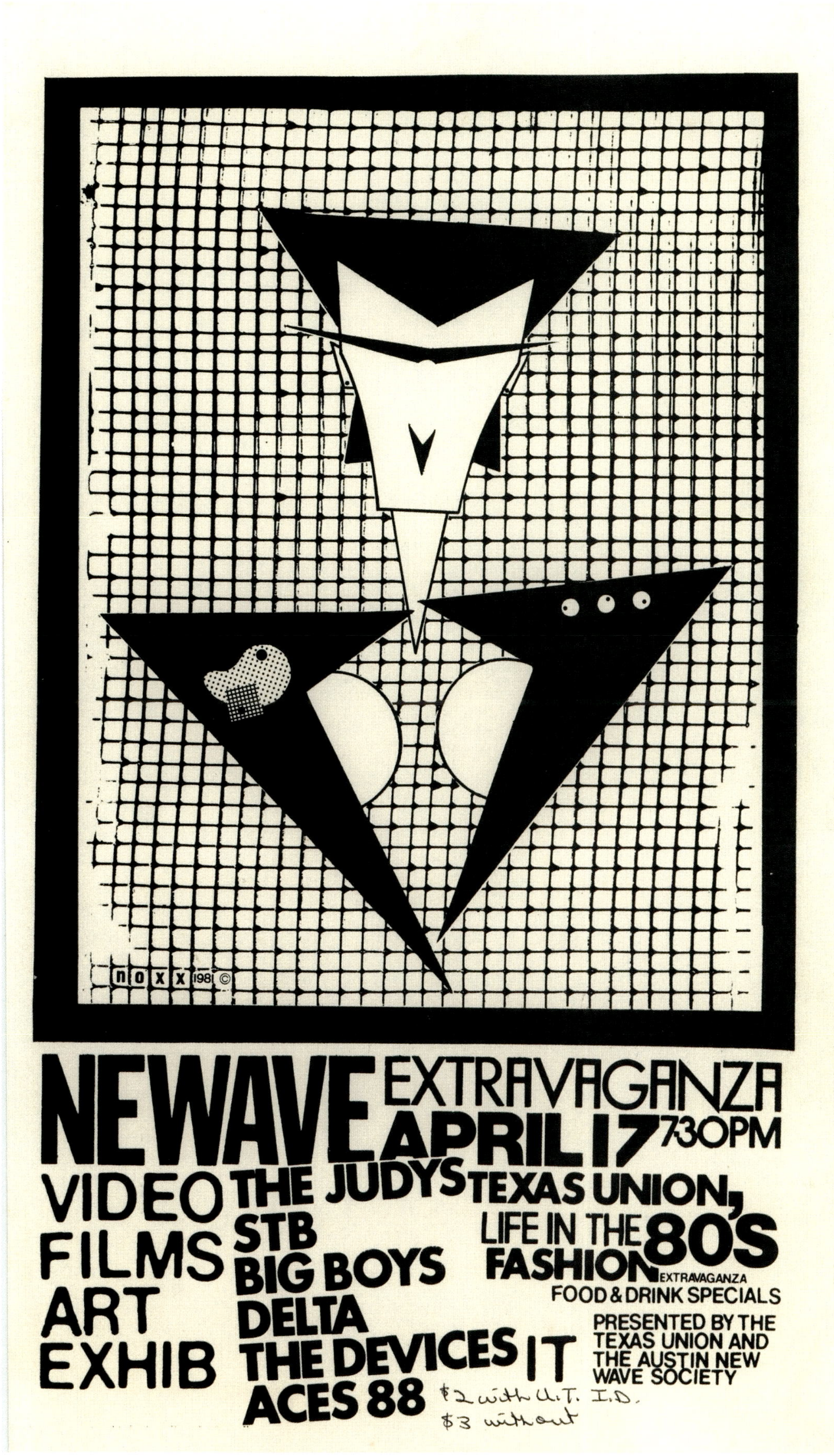

115 GUY JUKE. Devo. Armadillo World Headquarters. August 8, 1980. 17" × 11". © Guy Juke.

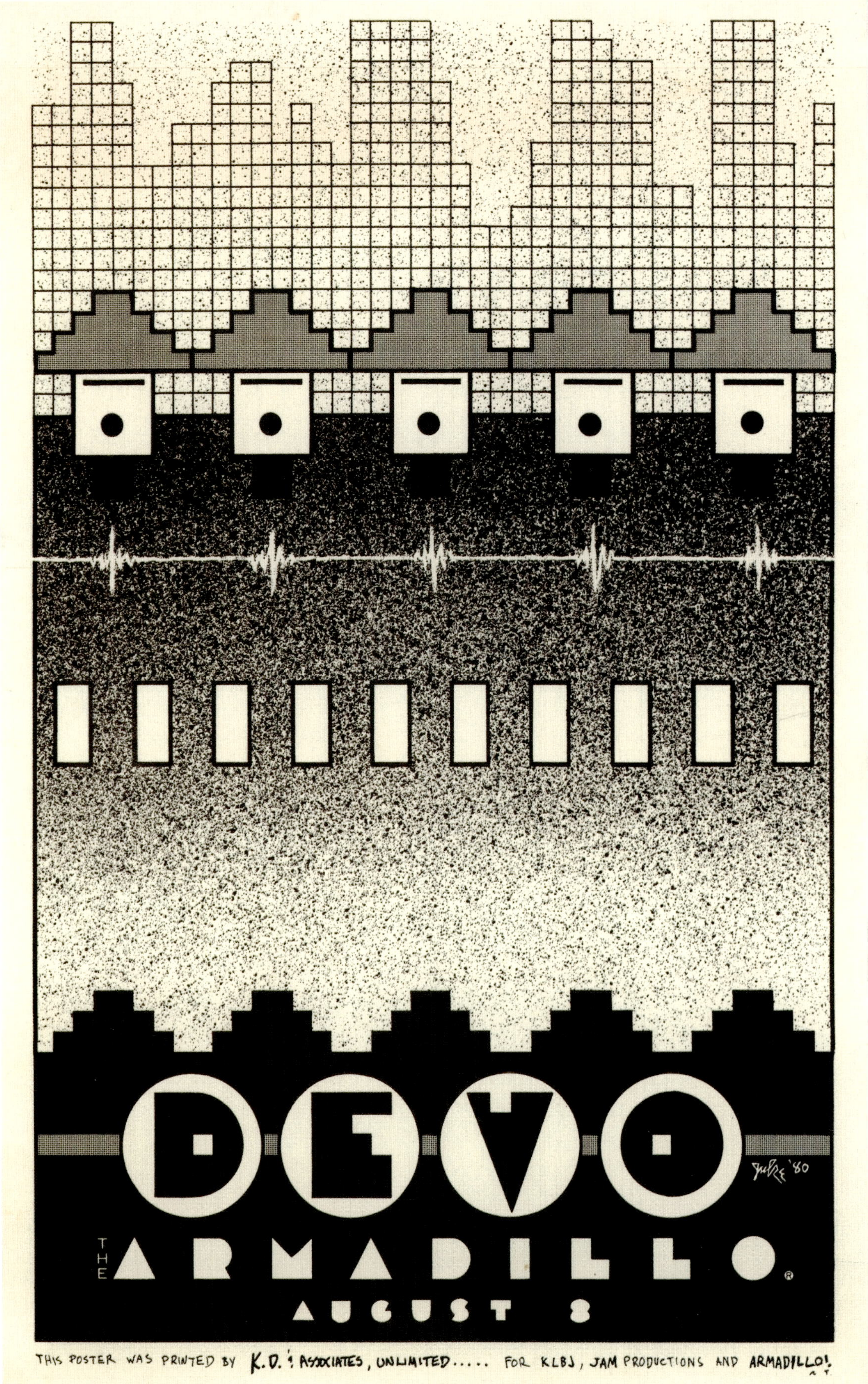

116 DAVY JONES. The Next & The Dicks. Continental Club. August 30, 1982. 11" × 8.5". © Davy Jones.

Davy Jones, a veteran Austin guitarist who has played with the Next, the Dicks, and the Hickoids, among other bands, offers the Dicks singer Gary Floyd in place of John Travolta in this parody of the Bee Gee's *Saturday Night Fever.*

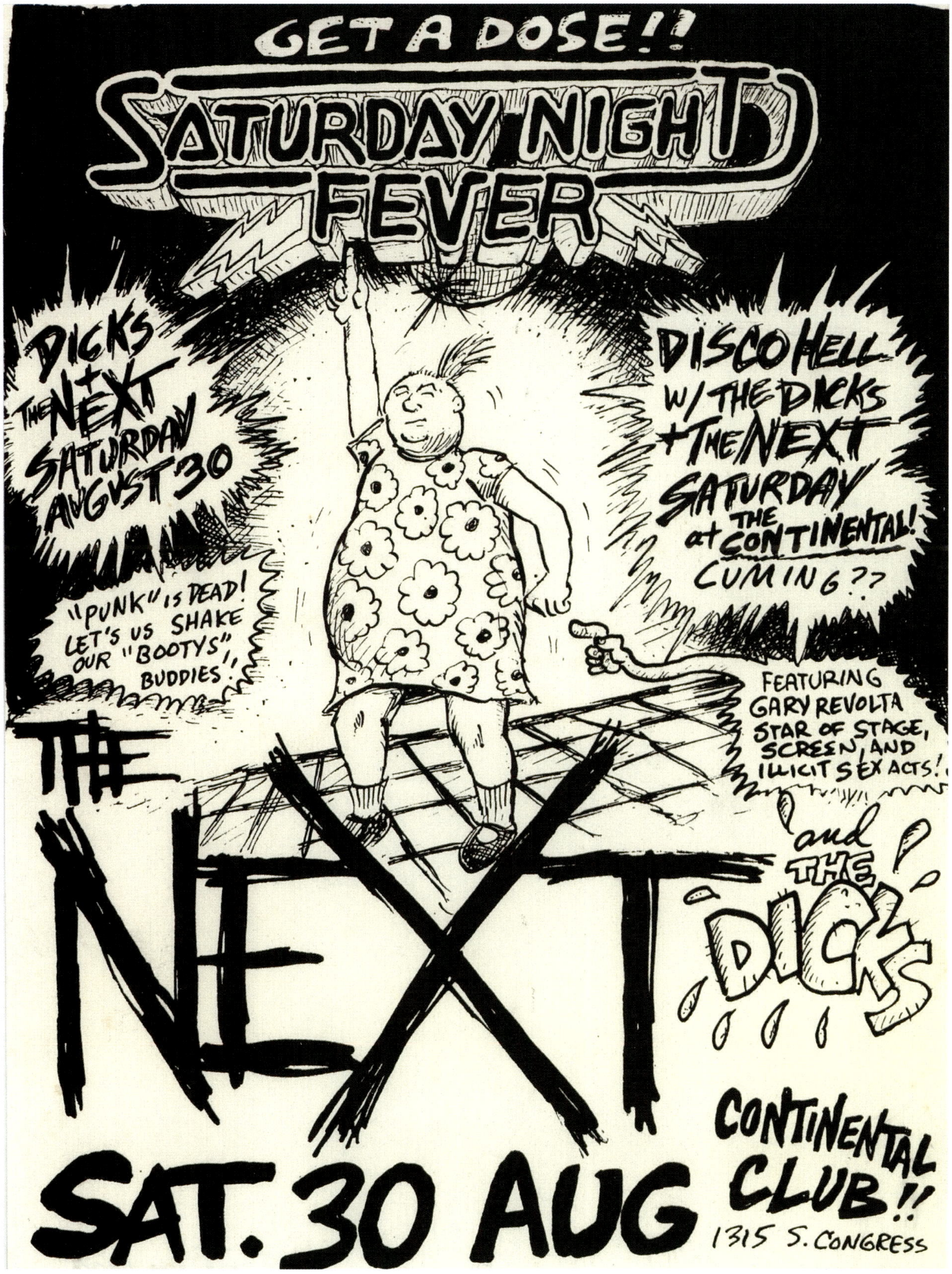

117 RIC CRUZ. Austin Strangler & The Electric Tools. Duke's Royal Coach Inn. August 27, 1980. 8.5" × 11". © Ric Cruz.

Duke's Royal Coach Inn was at 316 Congress Avenue, the same building that once housed the Vulcan Gas Company. Duke's was a short-lived venue that hosted a slew of Austin's early punk bands.

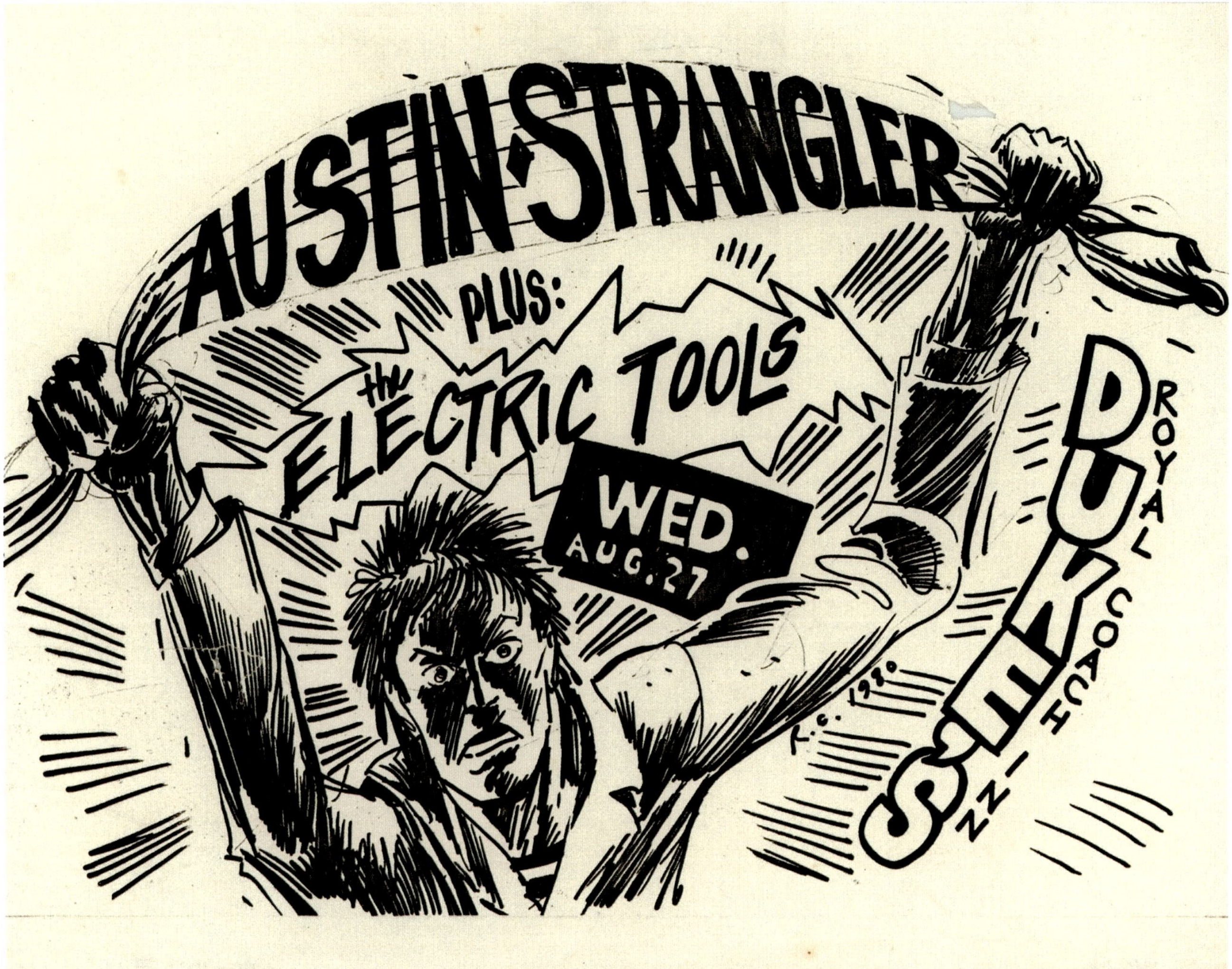

118 RANDY "BISCUIT" TURNER. Big Boys & Inserts. Raul's. September 11, 1980. 8.5" × 11". © Randy "Biscuit" Turner.

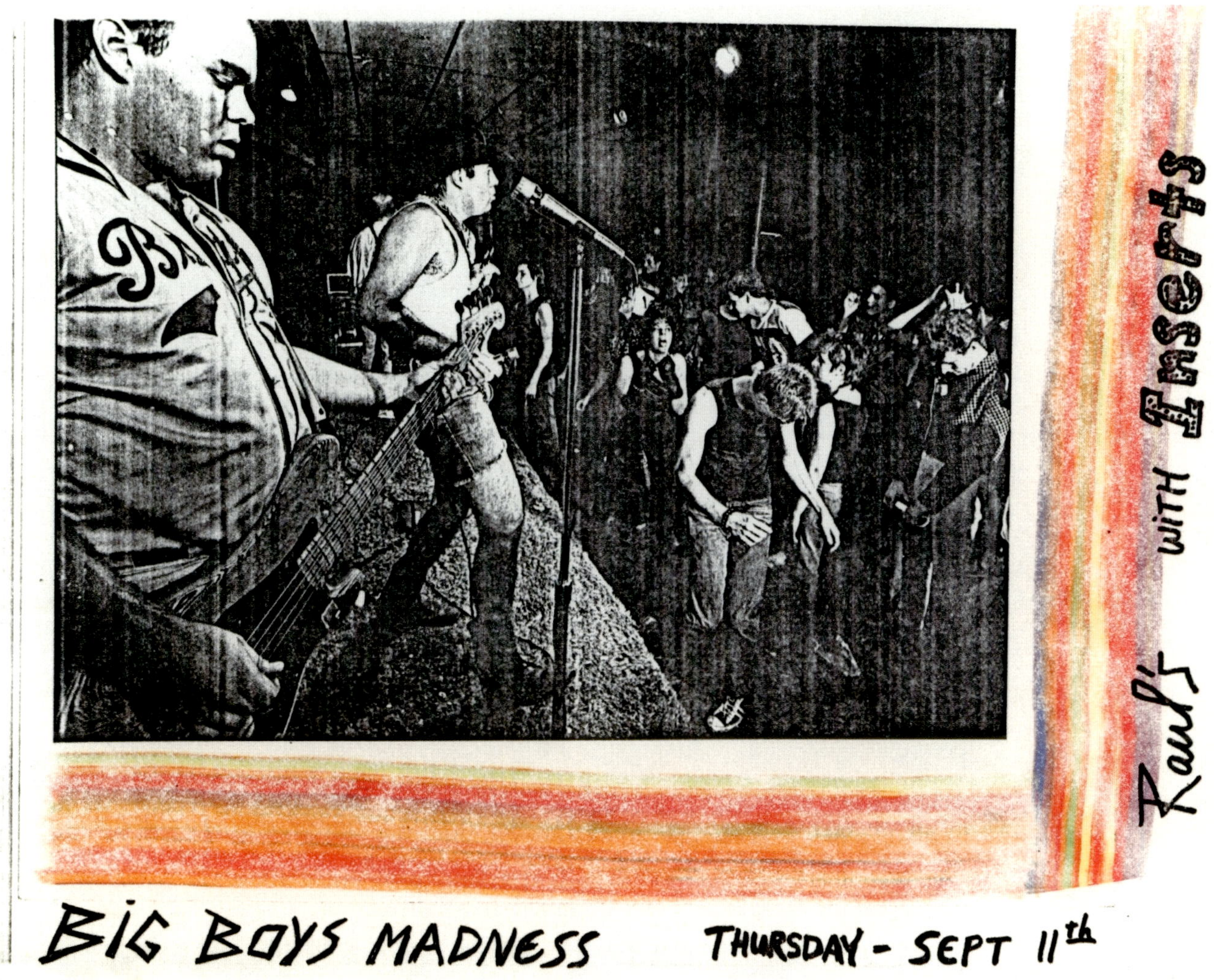

119 JAGMO (NELS JACOBSON). David Johansen. Club Foot. July 4, 1982. 11" × 8.5". © Jagmo (Nels Jacobson).

Jacobson became one of Austin's most notable poster artists of the 1980s. His entrée into the world of rock-and-roll art began when he worked at Club Foot, a larger downtown venue that filled the void when Raul's shut its doors.

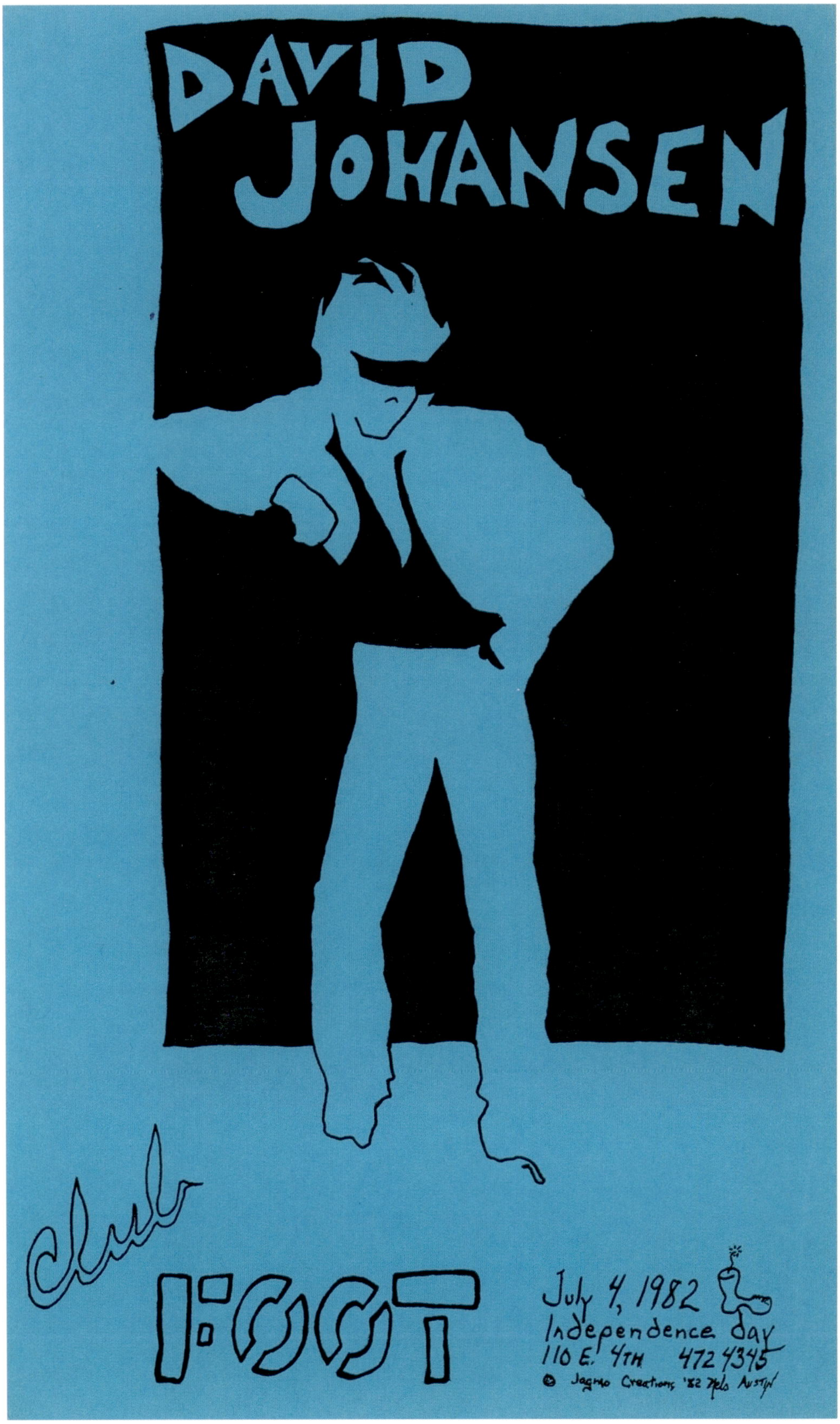

120 JAGMO (NELS JACOBSON). Translator. Club Foot. September 19, 1982. 11" × 8.5".

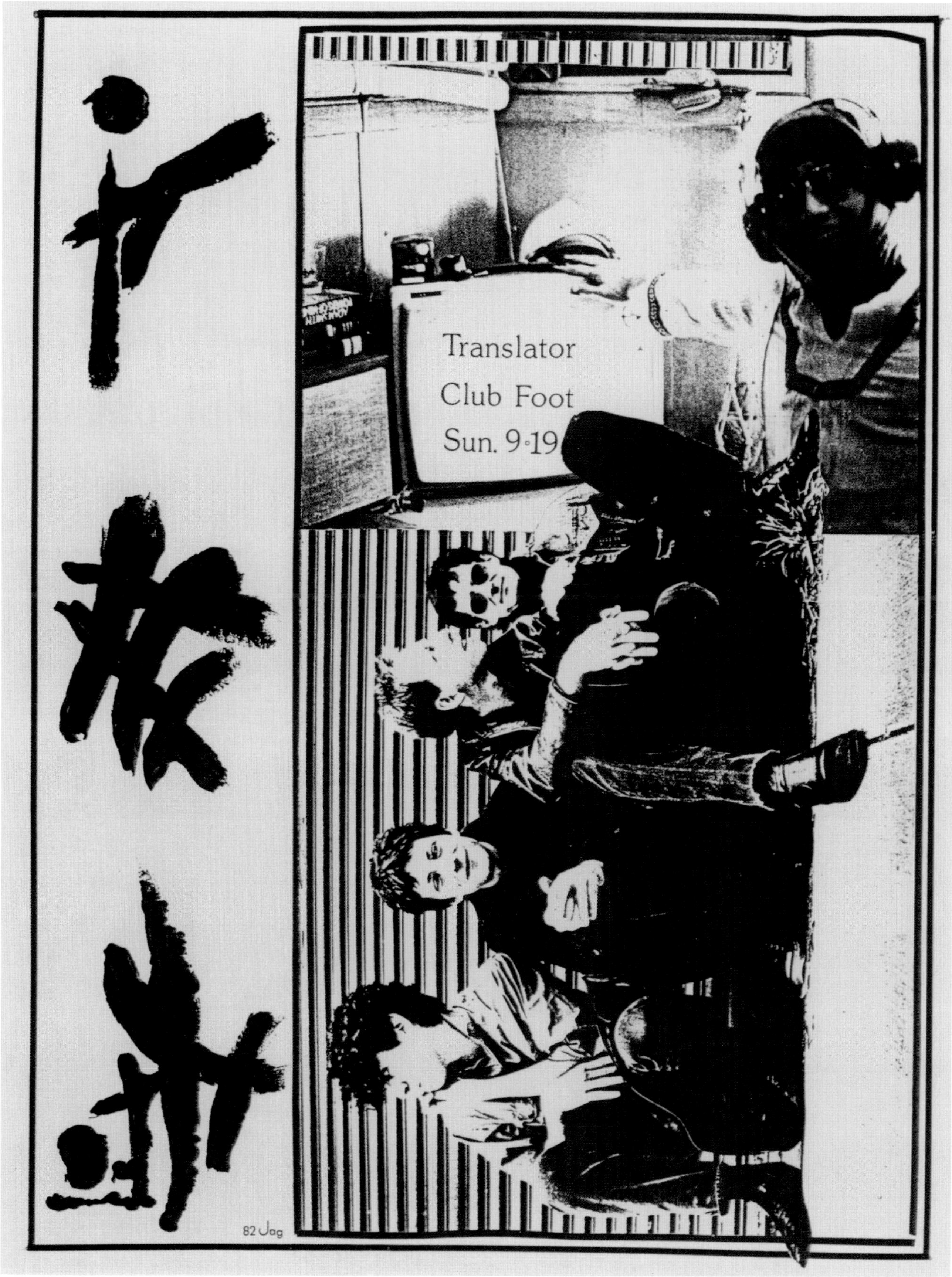

121 UNKNOWN ARTIST. Maya. November 25–30. Year unknown. 11" × 8.5".

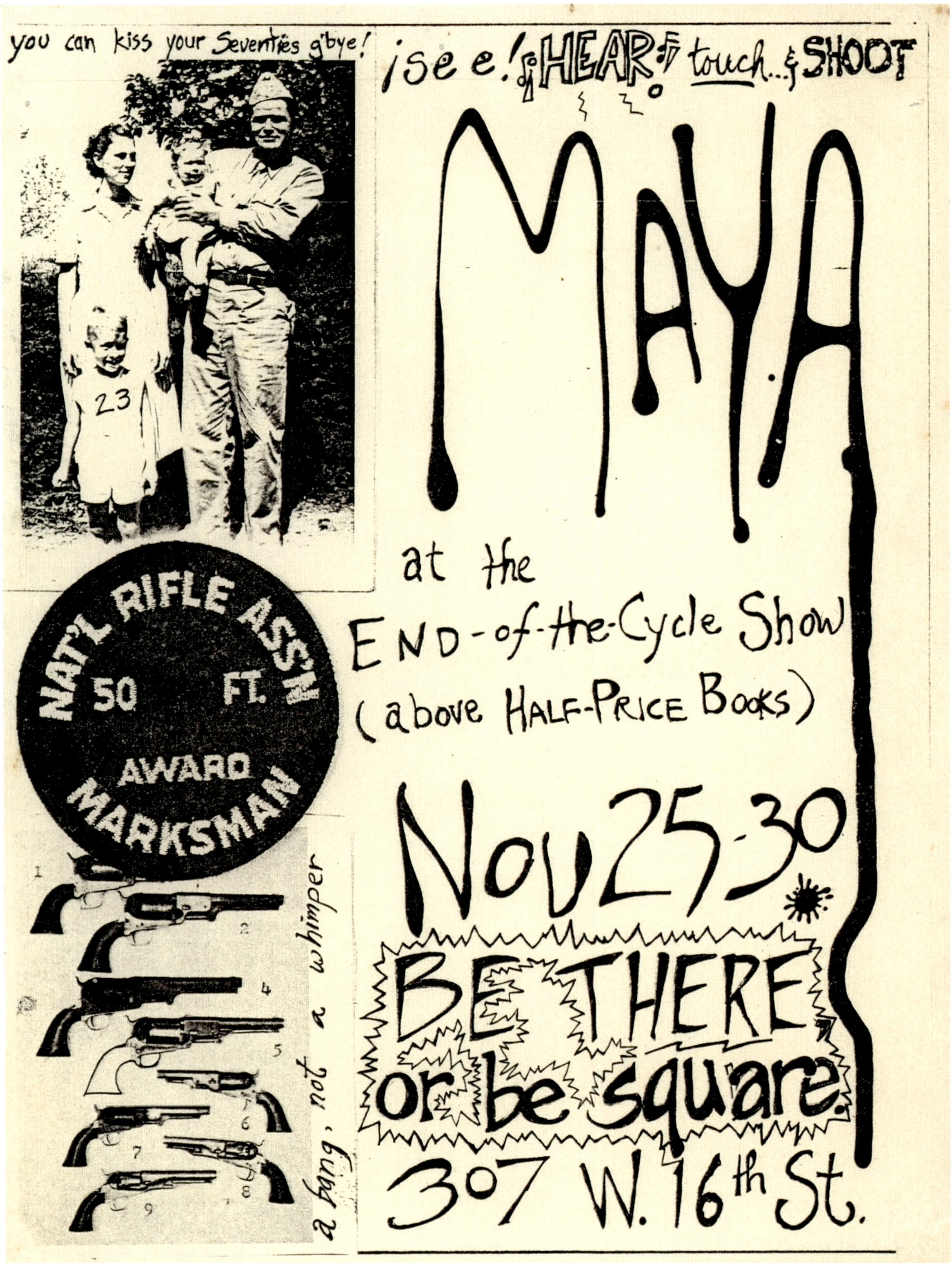

122 UNKNOWN ARTIST. Perverted Popes. Raul's. Undated. 11" × 8.5".

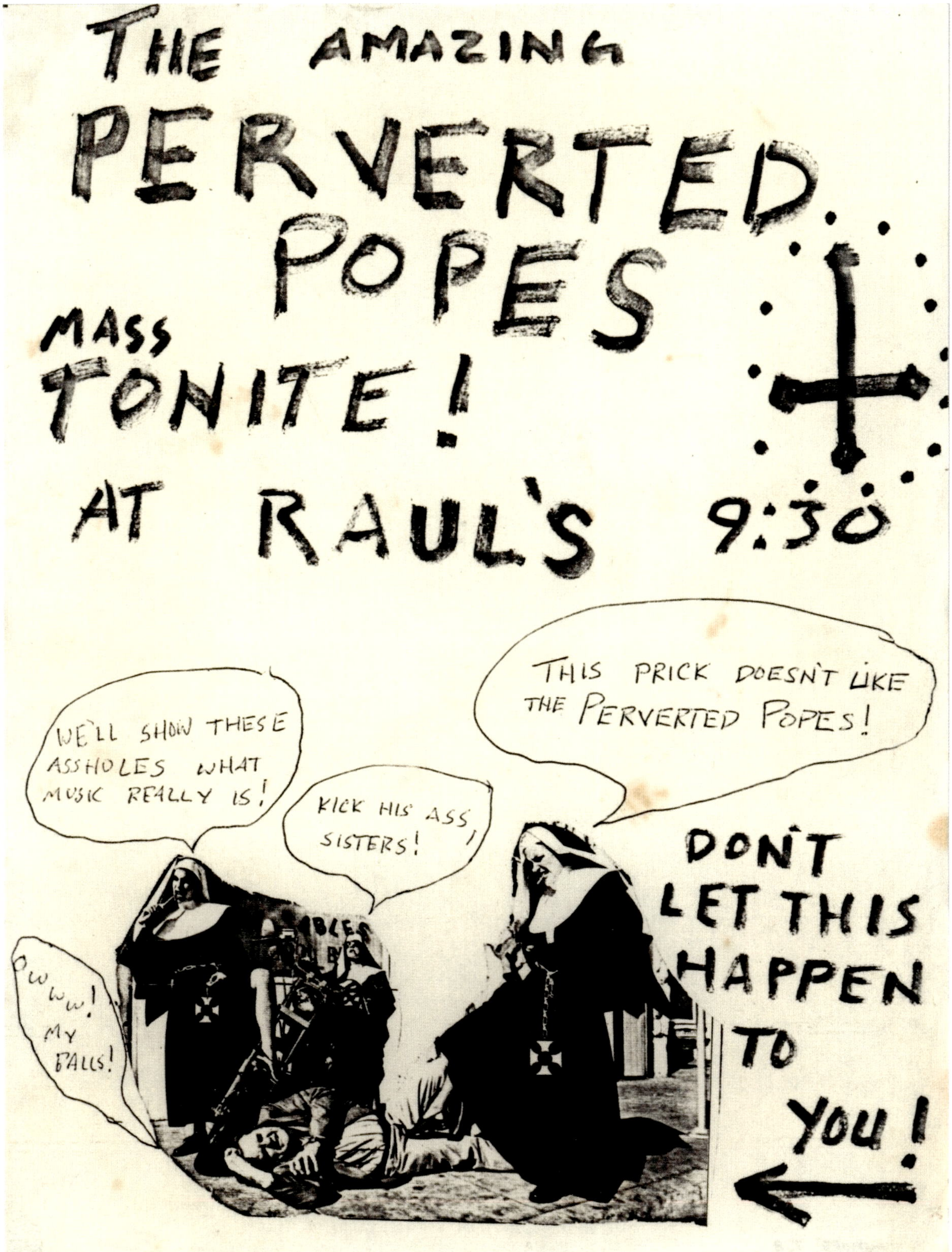

LIST OF POSTERS

1. Gilbert Shelton & Tony Bell. Conqueroo & The Swiss Movement. Vulcan Gas Company, November 10 & 11, 1967.
2. Gilbert Shelton. The Golden Dawn & The Thingies. Vulcan Gas Company, November 24 & 25, 1967.
3. Tony Bell. Lightnin' Hopkins & Conqueroo. Vulcan Gas Company, December 1 & 2, 1967.
4. Gilbert Shelton. The 13th Floor Elevators, The Swiss Movement, The South Canadian Overflow, & Shiva's Headband. Vulcan Gas Company, December 8–10, 1967.
5. Gilbert Shelton. Conqueroo & The Afro Caravan. December 22 & 23, 1967. Conqueroo & The Golden Dawn. December 29, 1967. Shiva's Headband & The Golden Dawn. December 30, 1967. Shiva's Headband & Conqueroo. December 31, 1967. Vulcan Gas Company
6. Gilbert Shelton. Shiva's Headband & Rubaiyat. April 12 & 13, 1968. Conqueroo & Sleepy John Estes. April 19 & 20, 1968. Vulcan Gas Company.
7. Gilbert Shelton. Conqueroo & Shiva's Headband. May 10, 1968. Canned Heat, Conqueroo & Shiva's Headband. May 11, 1968. Vulcan Gas Company.
8. Gilbert Shelton & Jim Franklin. Conqueroo & Bubble Puppy. Vulcan Gas Company, May 31 & June 1, 1968.
9. Jim Franklin. Shiva's Headband, Conqueroo, & Rubaiyat. February 16 & 17, 1968. Lightnin' Hopkins & Conqueroo. February 26 & 27, 1968. Vulcan Gas Company.
10. Jim Franklin. Shiva's Headband & Bubble Puppy. Vulcan Gas Company, December 6 & 7, 1968.
11. Jim Franklin. Ramon Ramon and the Four Daddyos, Water Brothers, Texas Rangers, & Crowbar. Vulcan Gas Company, October 10 & 11, 1969.
12. Jim Franklin. New Atlantis. August 12, 1969. Ramon, Ramon, Ramon. & Jomo. August 13, 1969. Mother Earth & Shiva's Headband. August 15 & 16, 1969. Vulcan Gas Company,
13. Jim Franklin. Fugs & Shiva's Headband. Vulcan Gas Company, February 21 & 22, 1969.
14. Jim Franklin. The Velvet Underground, Ramon Ramon and the Four Daddyos, Crowbar, & Water Brothers. Vulcan Gas Company, October 23–25, 1969.
15. Jim Harter & Jim Franklin. Shiva's Headband & Onion Creek. Vulcan Gas Company, July 4 & 5, 1969.
16. Jim Harter. New Moan Hey, Onion Creek, & Shiva's Headband. Vulcan Gas Company, July 18 & 19, 1969.
17. John Shelton. Shiva's Headband & Sunnyland Special. Vulcan Gas Company, April 11 & 12, 1969.
18. John Shelton. Johnny Winter, African Descent, & Hub City Movers. Vulcan Gas Company, March 10 & 11, 1970.
19. Jim Franklin. Mance Lipscomb & Conqueroo. Vulcan Gas Company, January 19 & 20, 1968.
20. Unknown artist. Sun Ra. Armadillo World Headquarters, November 8, 1978.
21. Jim Franklin. Big Joe Williams & Sky Blues. Vulcan Gas Company, September 27 & 28, 1968.
22. Jim Franklin. Big Joe Williams & New Atlantis. Vulcan Gas Company, January 17 & 18, 1969.
23. Jim Franklin. Freddie King backed by Storm & Wildfire. October 2 & 3, 1970. Mance Lipscomb, Ginger Valley, & Storm. October 9 & 10, 1970. Armadillo World Headquarters.
24. Jim Franklin. Sonny Terry & Brownie McGhee. Armadillo World Headquarters, January 16–20, 1973.
25. Micael Priest. Freddie King. Armadillo World Headquarters, March 15–17, 1973.
26. Sam Yeates. Freddie King & John Hammond. Armadillo World Headquarters, October 31, 1976.
27. Micael Priest. Mose Allison & Alex Moore. Armadillo World Headquarters, June 15, 1974.
28. Jim Franklin. Count Basie and His Orchestra. Armadillo World Headquarters, January 14, 1980.
29. Jim Franklin. Bukka White & Juke Boy Bonner. Ritz Theatre, November 13–16, 1974.

30. Jim Franklin. Bo Diddley & Storm. Ritz Theatre, November 8, 1974.

31. Unknown artist. B. B. King. Antone's, July 4, 1976.

32. Danny Garrett. B. B. King. Antone's, year unknown.

33. Danny Garrett. Muddy Waters. Antone's, April 18–22, 1978.

34. Danny Garrett. Muddy Waters. Antone's, June 20 & 21, 1980.

35. Unknown artist. Fats Domino. Antone's, August 16–18, 1978.

36. Danny Garrett. Clifton Chenier. Antone's, September 26–30, 1978.

37. Kerry Awn. Soap Creek Saloon calendar, March 1978.

38. Danny Garrett. Stevie Ray Vaughan & Double Trouble. Antone's, October 1 & 2, 1982.

39. Danny Garrett. The Fabulous Thunderbirds. Antone's, April 18, 1986.

40. Micael Priest. Johnny Winter & Dragon. Armadillo World Headquarters, November 18 & 19, 1978.

41. Jim Franklin. New Atlantis, Lavender Hill Express, Texas Pacific, Eternal Life Corporation, & Georgetown Medical Band. Wooldridge Park, September 29, 1968.

42. Jim Franklin. Shiva's Headband, Hub City Movers, & Whistler. Armadillo World Headquarters, August 7 & 8, 1970.

43. Jim Franklin. Ramon Ramon and the Four Daddyos, Crowbar, Onion Creek, Sweatarts, Lavender Hill Express, Fat Emma, & Amerikong. Fiesta Gardens Park, September 21, 1969.

44. Jim Franklin. Shiva's Headband, T. T. Troll, Rockinhorse, Tiger Balm, & Skyrocket. Armadillo World Headquarters, January 15 & 16, 1971.

45. Micael Priest. New Riders of the Purple Sage & Jon Emery. Armadillo World Headquarters, June 14, 1978.

46. Ken Featherston. The Marshall Tucker Band. Armadillo World Headquarters, June 30, 1974.

47. Danny Garrett. The All New Ray Wylie Hubbard Band & Cooder Browne. Austin Opry House, March 2, 1979.

48. Danny Garrett. The Lost Gonzo Band. Armadillo World Headquarters, February 7, 1980.

49. Micael Priest. Freda and the Firedogs. American Legion Hall, Smithville, April 14, 1973.

50. Micael Priest. "Genuine Texas Swing" with members of the Texas Playboys & Alvin Crow and the Pleasant Valley Boys. Broken Spoke, September 17, 1975.

51. Micael Priest. Willie Nelson & Greezy Wheels. Armadillo World Headquarters, August 12, 1972.

52. Jim Franklin. Willie Nelson's 4th of July Picnic. Dripping Springs, July 4, 1973.

53. Micael Priest. Willie Nelson & Michael Murphey. Armadillo World Headquarters, September 15 & 16, 1972.

54. Jim Franklin. Willie Nelson & Doak Snead. Ritz Theatre, November 11, 1974.

55. Danny Garrett. Willie Nelson's 4th of July Picnic. Austin Opry House, July 3 & 4, 1978.

56. Danny Garrett. Willie Nelson. Austin Opera House, December 2–4, 1979.

57. Kerry Awn. Soap Creek Saloon calendar. Soap Creek Saloon, February 1974.

58. Kerry Awn. Soap Creek Saloon calendar: Willie Nelson, Doug Sahm, & Alvin Crow and the Pleasant Valley Boys. Soap Creek Saloon/Municipal Auditorium, September 1975.

59. Kerry Awn. Willie Nelson, Doug Sahm, & Alvin Crow and the Pleasant Valley Boys. Austin Municipal Auditorium, September 28, 1975.

60. Guy Juke. Rusty Wier & Steven Fromholz. Armadillo World Headquarters, August 4, 1976.

61. Ken Featherston. B. W. Stevenson & D. K. Little. Armadillo World Headquarters, May 18 & 19, 1973.

62. Ken Featherston. B. W. Stevenson & Kenneth Threadgill and the Velvet Cowpasture. Armadillo World Headquarters, February 9 & 10, 1973.

63. Guy Juke. Asleep at the Wheel & Linda Hargrove. Armadillo World Headquarters, June 27 & 28, 1975.

64. Micael Priest. Freddie Fender & Doug Sahm. Armadillo World Headquarters, August 16 & 17, 1975.

65. Henry Gonzalez. Ruben Ramos and the Mexican Revolution. March 30, 1977. Steve Jordan & El Molino. April 1, 1977. Armadillo World Headquarters.

66. Kerry Awn. The Sons of Uranium Savage versus The Marsh Mongrels. Ritz Theatre, December 12, 1974.

67. Kerry Awn. Greezy Wheels & Uranium Savages. Armadillo World Headquarters, March 19, 1976.

68. Danny Garrett. Asleep at the Wheel & Greezy Wheels. Armadillo World Headquarters, December 31, 1975.

69. Danny Garrett. Asleep at the Wheel. Antone's, March 1, 1980.

70. Ed Aiken. T. Gosney Thornton. Rome Inn/Split Rail, year unknown.

71. Micael Priest. Kinky Friedman and the Texas Jewboys. Armadillo World Headquarters, June 17 & 18, 1975.

72. Jim Franklin. Doug Sahm, Harry Anderson, & Uncle Uh-Uh and the Uh-Huh. Ritz Theatre, March 12, 1974.

73. Jaxon (Jack Jackson). Sir Doug and the Texas Tornados. Tour poster featuring a stop at the Soap Creek Saloon, June & July 1976.

74. Jim Franklin. Captain Beefheart and the Magic Band & Ry Cooder. Armadillo World Headquarters, February 20 & 21, 1972.

75. Jim Franklin. Frank Zappa. Armadillo World Headquarters, March 10, 1973.

76. Guy Juke & Micael Priest. Frank Zappa and the Mothers of Invention & Martin Mull. Armadillo World Headquarters, October 26 & 27, 1973.

77. Guy Juke. Frank Zappa and the Mothers. Armadillo World Headquarters, May 20 & 21, 1975.

78. Jose Carlos Campos. Savoy Brown. Armadillo World Headquarters, August 3, 1976.

79. Ken Featherston. The Mahavishnu Orchestra. Armadillo World Headquarters, April 5 & 6, 1973.

80. Ken Featherston. Gram Parsons. Armadillo World Headquarters, February 21, 1973.

81. Jim Franklin & Micael Priest. The Flying Burrito Brothers & Greezy Wheels. Armadillo World Headquarters, February 28–March 2, 1975.

82. Micael Priest. Bobby Bare with Freda and the Firedogs & David Allen Coe. Austin Opry House, May 31 & June 1, 1974.

83. Guy Juke. Country Gazette & Uncle Walt's Band. Armadillo World Headquarters, November 17, 1978.

84. Jim Franklin. The Incredible String Band & Shiva's Headband. Armadillo World Headquarters, November 20 & 21, 1970.

85. Jim Harter. Earl Scruggs Revue & Rat Creek. Armadillo World Headquarters, November 5 & 6, 1971.

86. Jim Franklin. Ravi Shankar. Armadillo World Headquarters, May 1, 1971.

87. Jim Franklin. Leo Kottke & Greezy Wheels. Armadillo World Headquarters, July 23 & 24, 1971.

88. Sam Yeates. Bob Seger & Ruby Starr. Armadillo World Headquarters, December 17, 1976.

89. Jim Franklin. Bruce Springsteen. Armadillo World Headquarters, March 15 & 16, 1974.

90. Jim Franklin. Taj Mahal & Lightnin' Hopkins. October 22, 1971. Lightnin' Hopkins & Greezy Wheels. October 23, 1971. Armadillo World Headquarters.

91. Micael Priest. Grateful Dead. Manor Downs, October 12, 1977.

92. Bill Narum. Holy Modal Rounders & Les Clamtones. Armadillo World Headquarters, March 5, 1977.

93. Bill Narum. Taj Mahal & Navasota. Music Hall, Houston, October 21, 1971.

94. Micael Priest. The Pointer Sisters. Armadillo World Headquarters, November 9, 1975.

95. Dale Wilkins. J. J. Cale & Paul Craft. Austin Opry House, February 24, 1978.

96 Danny Garrett. Bonnie Raitt & Muddy Waters. Austin Opry House, November 26, 1977.

97. Pauline Walsh Jacobson. Tom Waits & Jonnie Barnett. Austin Opry House, November 12, 1977.

98. Ken Featherston. Dr. John & Greezy Wheels. Armadillo World Headquarters, April 15, 1974.

99. Micael Priest. Little Feat. Armadillo World Headquarters, February 8 & 9, 1974.

100. Danny Garrett. Warren Zevon. Austin Opry House, June 2, 1978.

101. Danny Garrett. Lou Reed & Ian Dury. Austin Opry House, April 9, 1978.

102. Rick Turner. Patti Smith. Austin Opera House, July 12, 1978.

103. Micael Priest. The Ramones & Aalon. Armadillo World Headquarters, July 14, 1977.

104. Jesse Sublett. The Violators & The Skunks. Raul's, February 23, 1978.

105. Unknown artist. Iggy Pop & Terminal Mind, Armadillo World Headquarters, March 29, 1980.

106. Micael Priest. Roky Erickson and Bleib Alien. Ritz Theatre, April 25 & 26, 1975.

107. Cam King. Roky Erickson and the Explosives. Steamboat, December 5, 1979.

108. Cam King. Roky Erickson and the Explosives & The Blame. Raul's, August 30, 1979.

109. Joe Nick Patoski. Joe "King" Carrasco and Los Crowns, The Delinquents, & The Shades. Raul's, November 14, 1979.

110. Randy "Biscuit" Turner. The Judys, Big Boys, & Electric Tools. Raul's, January 16, 1981.

111. Guy Juke. Dinettes, The Next, & The Dicks. Raul's, June 25 & 26, 1980.

112. NOXX (Michael Nott). Big Boys & The Dicks. Raul's, September 19 & 20, 1980.

113. NOXX (Michael Nott). The Next & Inserts. Raul's, 1981.

114. NOXX (Michael Nott). "Newave Extravaganza" with The Judys, STB, Big Boys, Delta, The Devices, & Aces 88. Texas Union, April 17, 1981.

115. Guy Juke. Devo. Armadillo World Headquarters, August 8, 1980.

116. Davy Jones. The Next & The Dicks. Continental Club, August 30, 1982.

117. Ric Cruz. Austin Strangler & The Electric Tools. Duke's Royal Coach Inn, August 27, 1980.

118. Randy "Biscuit" Turner. Big Boys & Inserts. Raul's, September 11, 1980.

119. Jagmo (Nels Jacobson). David Johansen. Club Foot, July 4, 1982.

120. Jagmo (Nels Jacobson). Translator. Club Foot, September 19, 1982.

121. Unknown artist. Maya, November 25–30, year unknown.

122. Unknown artist. Perverted Popes. Raul's, undated.

BIBLIOGRAPHY

Quotations from artists and musicians throughout the book come from numerous interviews conducted by Alan Schaefer, Katie Salzmann, Joe Nick Patoski, and Nels Jacobson.

"A By-No-Means-Comprehensive List of Austinite Comics Writers and Artists." *Austinchronicle.com*, 22 Dec. 2006.

Corcoran, Michael. "The Town Was Hoppin'." *Austin chronicle.com*, 30 Mar. 2012.

Faires, Robert. "Texas in Bold, Dark Strokes: Jack Jackson, 1941–2006." *Austinchronicle.com*, 16 June 2006.

Gastaut, Amélie, and Jean-Pierre Criqui. *Off the Wall: Psychedelic Rock Posters from San Francisco*. London: Thames and Hudson, 2005.

Grushkin, Paul D. *The Art of Rock*. New York: Artabras, 1987.

Hickey, Dennis. "The Complete Illustrated List of Vulcan Gas Company Posters and Handbills." 2005. Available at http://people.missouristate.edu/DennisHickey/vulcan.htm.

Jacobson, Nels. "Armadillos, Peccadillos, and the Maverick Posterists of Austin, Texas." In *Prints and Printmakers of Texas: Proceedings of the Twentieth Annual North American Print Conference*, ed. Ron Tyler. Austin: Texas State Historical Association, 1997.

——. "The Maverick Tradition: Postering in Austin, Texas." *Jagmo.com*, 2013.

Lieck, Ken. "Mine Eyes Have Seen the Glory: Thirty Years of Music History through the Lens of Burton Wilson." *Austinchronicle.com*, 18 May 2001.

Mellard, Jason. *Progressive Country: How the 1970s Transformed the Texan in Popular Culture*. Austin: University of Texas Press, 2013.

Moser, Margaret. "Bill Narum: We Call That Art." *Austin chronicle.com*, 20 Nov. 2009.

——. "Groover's Paradise: The Ballad of Soap Creek Saloon." *Austinchronicle.com*, 12 Oct. 2001.

——. "A Lot of Cojones and a Little Faith: The Art of Micael Priest." *Austinchronicle.com*, 6 Oct. 2006.

——. "Saw It on the X–Bill Narum: That Little Ol' Artist from Austin." *Austinchronicle.com*, 1 Apr. 2005.

——. "Tales behind the Posters." *Austinchronicle.com*, 6 Oct. 2006.

Moser, Margaret, Kerry Fitzgerald, Mack White, Guy Juke, and Mariann G. Wizard. "General Jackson." *Austinchronicle.com*, 11 Aug. 2006.

Patoski, Joe Nick. *Willie Nelson: An Epic Life*. New York: Back Bay Books, 2008.

Raines, Terry. *A Listing of the Music Graphics of Texas*. Austin: Raines Graphics, 1991.

Savlov, Marc. "Re-Re-Re-Re-Reopening Night." *Austin chronicle.com*, 2 Nov. 2007.

——. "Violators Will Be Punished." *Austinchronicle.com*, 12 Sept. 1997.

Shank, Barry. *The Rock 'n' Roll Scene in Austin, Texas*. Middletown, CT: Wesleyan University Press, 1994.

Simon, Cheryl L. "Vulcan Gas Company." *Handbook of Texas Online*, Texas State Historical Association, 2012.

Wheat, John. "Armadillo World Headquarters." *Handbook of Texas Online*, Texas State Historical Association, 2012.

ACKNOWLEDGMENTS

Katie Salzmann, curator of *Homegrown: Austin Music Posters 1967 to 1982*, for giving life to this project; Steve Davis; David Coleman; Casey Kittrell; Carla Ellard; Tom Wilmore; Linda Wilmore; Houston White; Nancy Coplin; Jody Fischer; Bobby Earl Smith; Nels Jacobson; Joe Nick Patoski; Eddie Wilson; Jon Marc Smith; Leea Mechling and the South Austin Popular Culture Center; Henry Gonzalez; John Wheat; Gloria Hill; Joel Minor; Anne Schroll; Troy Campbell; Mark Busby; Lisa Heston; Margo Boykin; Sam Jackson; Mikiel Featherston; Woody Roberts; Don Hyde; Nico D'Auterive; Gretchen Otto; Lindsay Starr; Cynthia Lindlof; Christine Gever; and all of the artists for their inspiration, and particularly the following for their generous support of this project: Kerry Awn, Jim Franklin, Danny Garrett, Michael Nott, Micael Priest, Gilbert Shelton, Jesse Sublett, and Sam Yeates.

The Southwestern Writers Collection Series originates from the Wittliff Collections, a repository of literature, film, music, and southwestern and Mexican photography established at Texas State University.